Political

Abolitionism

in Wisconsin,

1840–1861

Political Abolitionism in Wisconsin, 1840–1861

❧

Michael J. McManus

The Kent State University Press

KENT, OHIO, & LONDON

© 1998 by The Kent State University Press,
Kent, Ohio 44242
All rights reserved
Library of Congress Catalog Card Number 98-12683
ISBN 0-87338-601-9
Manufactured in the United States of America

04 03 02 01 00 99 98   5 4 3 2 1

Library of Congress Cataloging-in-Publication Data

McManus, Michael J., 1949–
Political abolitionism in Wisconsin, 1840–1861 / Michael J.
McManus.
p.   cm.
Includes bibliographical references and index.
ISBN 0-87338-601-9 (cloth) ∞
1. Wisconsin—Politics and government—1848–1950.   2. Antislavery
movements—Wisconsin—History—19th century.   3. Political parties—
Wisconsin—History—19th century.   I. Title.
F586.M33   1998
973.7'114'09775—dc21   98-12683

British Library Cataloging-in-Publication data are available.

To my mother,

Florence Ann McManus,

and my father,

James Raymond McManus,

with gratitude and love.

And to my siblings,

Susan, Kathy, Jane, and Brian

—we are family.

CONTENTS

PREFACE

IN MARCH 1860, eight months before Abraham Lincoln was elected sixteenth president of the United States, a Republican legislator from Wisconsin matter-of-factly wrote that his party fought the expansion of slavery because it was morally and politically wrong. He maintained further that once slavery was confined within its existing borders, in fulfillment of his party's primary antislavery pledge, it soon would shrivel and die. For that reason, he affirmed, Republican party principles were manifestly abolitionist.

The purpose of this study is to trace the meaning and history of political abolitionism in Wisconsin from territorial days to the outbreak of the Civil War. Employing Liberty party principles as a benchmark, it follows their progress as the state's Free Soilers and Republicans shaped those principles to their own needs in response to national and local events and the demands of majoritarian politics. Because supporters of all three antislavery parties held in common the belief that preventing slavery's expansion in due course would destroy it, the terms "abolitionist" and "antislavery" in this study generally mean the same thing. Newspaper and manuscript sources, used in conjunction with a statistical method of evaluating election returns, pinpoint the changes in the antislavery appeal and the voting groups that embraced it.

Wisconsin is an appropriate state in which to chart the course of antislavery politics. Along with neighboring Michigan, the Republican party achieved its first electoral success here owing to the determination of its leaders to push their antislavery agenda above all else and to the presence of large numbers of native New Yorkers and New Englanders unequivocally opposed to slavery. But other values and submission to the constitutional and legislative compromises relating to the South's "peculiar institution" effectively subordinated antislavery attitudes until the mid-1850s. Then, the press of national and local events merged with the growing conviction that proponents of slavery, in firm control of all branches of the federal government, stood ready to risk the nation's republican ideals and institutions to expand and perpetuate black bondage. This fusion of circumstance and belief ultimately created the conditions that led to the triumph of political abolitionism through the agency of the Republican party. And while the emphasis changed and the moral character of original political abolitionism lessened, what stands out most is the endurance of Liberty party principles as Free Soilers and their Republican successors adapted them.

Antislavery politics in Wisconsin also evinced at least two characteristics of particular interest. One relates to the subordination of Unionism to antislavery policies. From the earliest days of the Republic, the concept of a perpetual Union had vied for supremacy with states' rights doctrines. The situation in Wisconsin suggests that as sectional amity deteriorated in the twenty years prior to the outbreak of war, so too did the Unionism of those who embraced the politics of abolitionism. At the very least, loyalty to the Union was somewhat more conditional than traditional interpretations have indicated and surely was present in other Northern states to some degree. Indeed, uncritical Unionism, as much as anything else, distinguished Wisconsin's Democrats from Liberty men, Free Soilers, and most Republicans and checked the possibility that they would endorse a political party whose avowed object was the eventual destruction of slavery. It was the South's rejection of the legitimate outcome of the presidential election of 1860, Abraham Lincoln's steadfast adherence to the Union, and the outbreak of war that led Republicans finally to adopt the Unionism most often attributed to them.

In company with their growing disenchantment with the Union and the proslavery policies of the federal government, most Wisconsin Republicans also advocated an extreme brand of states' rights principles. Upheld in defense of individual liberty and basic civil rights, these differed from the states' rights doctrines advocated by the South to safeguard slavery. In fact, until the eve of the Civil War, support for states' rights became a

{ *Preface* }

test of party loyalty and a requirement for political advancement that nearly shattered the Republican coalition.

One final note. Historians of antebellum America in recent years have come to a greater understanding and appreciation of the richness and complexity of the nation's politics and political system. It was not too long ago that scholars focused almost exclusively on the importance of national issues, and especially presidential contests, in shaping the political identity of nineteenth-century voters. Today, so-called "new political historians" have called attention to the significance that cultural differences, particularly those rooted in ethnic and religious backgrounds, have had in determining the ways in which Americans responded to their political world. Indeed, many argue that ethnocultural issues, most often played out in local and state political contests, caused the destruction of the Jacksonian party system and forced the partisan realignment of the 1850s.

I assume that ethnocultural issues played a role in the formation of political loyalties, but they did not bring down the second-party system. Prior to 1850, the political concerns that traditionally had divided the Democratic and Whig parties had been settled to the satisfaction of most Americans, while the bitter debates over slavery's expansion in the 1840s and the provisions of the Compromise of 1850 had exposed the grave danger that divisions over slavery posed to the Union. Both major parties responded by discouraging discussions about slavery, and, with long-standing national issues either dead or circumvented from 1850 to 1854, the nation's political system was thrown into a state of extreme confusion. In the midst of this turmoil, nativist fears aroused by the flood of Irish and German immigrants gave birth to the Know Nothing party, which in many locales temporarily filled the void left by a decaying political order. But it was the renewal of the slavery controversy, prompted by the passage of the Kansas-Nebraska Act, that produced the enduring political realignment that took shape between 1854 and 1856 and led to the Republican triumph in 1860. Unwilling to submit to Republican rule, the slaveholding South instead chose secession and bloody civil war.

ACKNOWLEDGMENTS

T<small>HIS</small> <small>BOOK</small> has been a long time coming and would never have seen the light of day without the help and encouragement of many good people. My friend and mentor Richard Sewell stuck with me through a career change and many years of slow progress to the completion of my dissertation. I was never prouder than the day of my Ph.D. oral examination, after which Dick congratulated me as "Dr. McManus."

Others who have helped me along the way and deserve special mention are Norm and Connie Risjord, with whom I have enjoyed many convivial hours; my good friend Joe Glatthaar, whose professional example and gentle prodding continue to inspire; Cecile Gartner McManus, who during her "summer vacation" many years ago patiently compiled much of the statistical data used in this study; and special thanks to Al "Doc" Oviatt, emeritus professor of history, Montana State University, a good friend and a great teacher.

Other friends who have put up with my idiosyncratic behavior over the years include Jim and Donna Sweet, David and Karin Shepard, Jeff and Mary Klees, Joe Lunn and Marsha Richmond, George Sweet, John and Mary Sheean, Marjorie Kreilick, Charlie Hartman and the Capital Financial–FDI crew, and my old Montana friends, Randy and Ginny Ogle. Most recently, my graduate school buddy David Blight has given me much encouragement, as have Don DeLuca and George Reuhl, businessmen and Civil War buffs whose enthusiasm keeps the fire burning, and

Russ McManus and Gary Klunder, whose companionship becomes ever more important as the years go by.

I also would like to remember my friends from the Astoria projects in Queens, New York, especially Fred Seney, Bobby and Margaret (Boylan) Slayton, Barry and Dougie Lennihan, Anthony Centrone, Paula (DiPietrantonio) Lewkowitz, Billy Russo, Diane (Kunar) and Chuck McCarthy, Johnny Tomasulo, Susan Doyle, Budgie Bogeatjes, and Gerrie (Sellito) Denkus, and to pay my respects to the memories of Kathy Carvallo, Tommy Centrone, David Slayton, David Seney, Vinny Tomasulo, and Judy Boylan.

And to my friend and business partner, Ron Perkins, and his wife, Bonnie, who have endured with patience and good cheer my efforts to combine business and academic careers. Words cannot express my gratitude and affection.

Lastly, to Sandy, Dawn, Izzy, Amy, and Chris—thanks for hanging in there with me.

CHAPTER ONE

A Redeeming Spirit Is Busily Engaged

WHEN WISCONSIN took its place as the thirtieth state in the American Union in the spring of 1848, the young republic was preparing for a presidential contest. The principal issue at stake, the status of slavery in the territory recently acquired from Mexico, had exposed dangerous sectional rifts within the nation's two major political parties, the Whigs and the Democrats. Yet it was not the first time that residents of the new state had wrestled with what a Whig journalist once had referred to as "the odious and detestable institution of slavery."[1] Wisconsin's Protestant sects, most taking slavery's immorality for granted, had been quarreling publicly for nearly a decade over the propriety of sermonizing against black bondage from the pulpit, while some itinerant abolitionists, such as the English-born Baptist minister Edward Mathews, bypassed the dispute and established churches pledged to admit only those who disavowed the right of property in man.[2]

Antislavery views also found expression outside the territory's churches. In the spring of 1840, the first Wisconsin antislavery society sprang up in the town of Burlington.[3] Several months later, E. G. Dyer, a respected physician and a hardworking friend of black fugitives, denounced slavery in a Fourth of July oration delivered to the citizens of Delavan. "American Slavery," he insisted, "cannot be sustained in a government like ours without trespassing upon the rights of the free." As evidence of this, Dyer pointed to Northern citizens incarcerated in Southern jails for speaking out against it and to those unfortunate free blacks in the North who were kidnapped and dragged southward to a lifetime of bitter servitude. He viewed America's future with confidence, however, for "a redeeming spirit . . . is busily engaged in undermining the strongholds of . . . domestic slavery, and with perseverance . . . this foul blot will be wiped from our national escutcheon—the oppressed emancipated—and every fetter severed."[4]

The link between slavery and the threat it posed to the liberties of freemen would constitute an important element in antislavery thought and rhetoric. Yet when Dyer uttered this sentiment in 1840, few people found it compelling enough to take an active part in the movement to free the nation's blacks. Most Wisconsinites had little love for slavery, but they were too "busily engaged" in trying to carve a living out of the frontier to trouble themselves about it. And in any event, few believed that agitation would serve a practical purpose.

Ten years before the formation of the Burlington antislavery society and Dyer's Independence Day speech, only 3,700 non-Indian inhabitants, 700 of whom were military personnel stationed in the territory's three forts, lived in Wisconsin. The remaining 3,000 people settled primarily in the rich lead region in the southwestern counties or engaged in the far-flung fur trade.[5] The lead district grew rapidly in the 1830s, as settlers from southern Illinois, Indiana, Ohio, Missouri, Kentucky, Tennessee, and Virginia streamed in to work the mineral deposits. A number of Pennsylvanians, New Yorkers, and New Englanders joined these Southerners, as did many immigrants from England and Ireland after 1840. A small contingent of Welshmen, Scotsmen, and Canadians and a corporal's guard of free blacks and slaves, the latter numbering eleven in 1840, rounded out the lead region's pioneer inhabitants.[6]

Despite the strictures of the Northwest Ordinance, military men assigned to Wisconsin and Southerners looking to take up permanent residence had brought these few slaves into the territory. Some, like Henry Dodge, promised freedom and "40 acres and a yoke of oxen" to bondsmen who accompanied them to the frontier and labored for a specified period of time. Presumably, the auction block was their only alternative. Other slaveholders may have followed the example of James Mitchell, a Methodist clergyman from Virginia, who returned his wife's two slaves to the South after several years residence in Wisconsin with the couple. Mitchell's action precipitated a bitter controversy within the territory's Methodist Conference and eventually led to his suspension as the sect's district elder. Whatever the means, by 1844 or thereabouts, slavery had vanished from Wisconsin.[7]

In addition to harboring the territory's few slaves, the newcomers to southwestern Wisconsin discouraged abolitionist agitation. Edward Mathews often faced threats of physical violence on his tours through the lead region. On several occasions, unappreciative audiences made him the target of "an abundance of eggs." Once, at Mineral Point, William S. Hamilton, the cadaverous son of the great Federalist leader, warned Mathews that a suit of tar and feathers awaited him if he remained in town. In Potosi, Mathews "narrowly escaped a fence rail," and in Lancaster a drunken mob serenaded him and his hosts with "Negro songs" and very nearly turned a cannon on them. As late as 1849, Ichabod Codding, the renowned Liberty party organizer and abolitionist lecturer, was showered with eggs to prevent him from addressing the citizens of Shullsburg.[8]

The early arrival of native Southerners, the temporary presence of slaves, and antagonism toward abolitionists had stamped southwestern Wisconsin with the flavor of Dixie.[9] Further east, settlement differed considerably. In 1830, the area contained few whites; a decade later twelve thousand of the territory's thirty-one thousand residents lived in the southeastern counties of Milwaukee, Racine, and Walworth.[10] Restless Yankees from New England and upstate New York comprised the bulk of the frontiersmen who laid claims to the region's extensive lakefront properties, took up farms on its fertile prairies, and plied their trades in its growing towns and villages. By 1850, more than one-half of Wisconsin's adults had been born in New York, leading some to characterize it as the younger sibling of the Empire State.[11]

Large numbers of foreign-born immigrants, primarily from the various German principalities, but including many Irish, English, Scotch, Welsh, Scandinavian, and other nationalities, joined the Yankees. Foreign immigration swelled in the latter half of the 1840s. As the decade came to a close, 36 percent of Wisconsin's 305,000 residents claimed a country other than the United States as their place of birth.[12] The greatest proportion of Wisconsin's foreign-born citizens poured into the lakeshore counties of

Milwaukee, Washington, Sheboygan, and Manitowoc. Significant numbers also wandered further south and established homes alongside the suspicious Yankees, while many English-speaking immigrants moved west into the lead region.[13] By 1850, population density and improved transportation facilities combined to push all elements of this heterogeneous mass into Wisconsin's interior. There they might make a fresh start on the abundant fertile land awaiting them.[14]

Not surprisingly, given Wisconsin's settlement patterns, antislavery sentiment first found expression in southeastern towns like Burlington and Delavan and within the area's Protestant churches. Many of the territory's Yankees had migrated from New York's "Burnt-Over District," a region swept by successive waves of religious enthusiasm during the early nineteenth century. This enthusiasm engendered a fervent desire to rid American society of all influences that counteracted man's innate goodness and frustrated his potential to bring about the physical, social, and moral elevation of mankind. Slavery was among those evils, stripping bondsmen of their humanity, desensitizing slaveowners to human suffering, and preventing both groups from achieving their full capabilities as members of the human family.[15] The problem was how to purge America of that sin.

Prior to 1840, many abolitionists had adopted the tactics of moral suasion and interrogation of prospective officeholders as the best means of undermining support for slavery. But that strategy brought limited success, and increasing numbers of abolitionists questioned its efficacy. Disenchantment finally led to the formation of the Liberty party, the first independent political organization dedicated to slavery's destruction.[16] The "Burnt-Over District" was especially receptive to the Liberty appeal, and at least some of Wisconsin's immigrants undoubtedly received their baptism in the political antislavery movement while resident there.[17]

The establishment of the Wisconsin Territorial Antislavery Society in June 1842 was a predictable consequence of the growing Yankee population and the emergence of the Liberty party. The Society demonstrated its interest in politics during the spring elections of the following year, when it joined in a "People's Coalition" with Whigs and disaffected Democrats to elect Edward D. Holton sheriff of Milwaukee County.[18] A New Hampshire native, Holton had arrived in Milwaukee in 1840, and with the help of influential friends and his own industry he rapidly rose in wealth and prominence. A deeply religious man and an ardent abolitionist, he would figure prominently in Wisconsin's antislavery movement.[19]

Encouraged by Holton's election, the antislavery society held a territorial convention in Madison on September 13, 1843, and nominated Jeduthan Spooner, a Walworth County Whig, for delegate to Congress. Unfortunately, the convention failed to consult with its candidate before making the nomination. During the campaign Spooner strongly exhorted his Whig friends to support the regular party nominee. They did. Out of 8,100 votes cast, Spooner received 153.[20]

The relative obscurity surrounding the activities of Wisconsin's antislavery men ended with the fall elections of 1843. Despite the society's miserable showing, organization quietly went forward. In November, the public was advised without fanfare that a Liberty newspaper soon would be published in the thriving village of Racine.[21] Ichabod Codding's arrival during the winter of 1844 provided further evidence that serious organizing was under way. Active in the antislavery movement for nearly a decade, Codding had been instrumental in establishing the Liberty party in Maine and Connecticut. In the wake of the Spooner fiasco, his presence must have buoyed the spirits of his like-minded but woefully inexperienced associates in Wisconsin.[22]

In February 1844, at an antislavery convention in Southport (Kenosha), Codding and several other Liberty activists from outside the territory helped found the first branch of the party in Wisconsin. The new political organization promptly proclaimed its independence from the Whig and Democratic parties and vowed to contest for all elective offices, "down to the lowest precinct level," solely on slavery-related matters.[23] Following Southport's lead, chapters of the Liberty party soon sprang up throughout the territory, even in the inhospitable west.[24]

After his successful trip to Southport, Codding moved on to Milwaukee to participate in a meeting of the Territorial Antislavery Society and deliver a series of antislavery lectures. While there, he recruited a valuable new ally, Charles Clark Sholes.[25] The conversion of Sholes was a fortunate one. A Connecticut native and an able and experienced newspaper editor, he had helped establish four Democratic newspapers over an eight-year span and was a well-known and respected figure among the territory's still small journalistic corps.[26] President John Tyler's intention to annex slaveholding Texas prompted Sholes's movement into the antislavery ranks. "This is a question big with peril to our peaceful relations abroad, and to the perpetuity of our Union at home," he editorialized in December 1843. The annexation of such an enormous region committed to the use of slave labor would give the South "permanent dominion over the federal government, and fasten the pernicious institution ever more firmly upon the nation." The Texas question thus transformed slavery from an issue of local concern "to one in which the whole North has immense interests at stake."[27]

Codding's courtship and the annexation of Texas convinced Sholes to sever his ties with the proannexationist Democratic party and to undertake the editorial duties of the promised but as yet unrealized Liberty paper.[28] On March 6, 1844, the *American Freeman* finally made its appearance in Milwaukee. It replaced Sholes's *Milwaukee Democrat* and announced its intention to advance the principles and interests of the Liberty party. After a shaky start that forced him to suspend publication of the *Freeman* for three months, Sholes moved the paper to the more agreeable environs of Prairieville (Waukesha). To bolster its precarious financial position, he sold his entire printing establishment to the newly formed Territorial Liberty Association, a joint stock company that distributed shares for ten dollars apiece. Although the *Freeman* never flourished financially during the territorial years, the efforts of the Association were sufficient to keep it alive.[29]

Under the capable management of Sholes and his successors,[30] the *Freeman* gave the Liberty organization public visibility and cohesion. It supplied the party faithful with a coherent and consistently maintained set of principles and policy objectives. As the organ of the only distinct antislavery party in the territory, the *Freeman* also set a standard Whigs and Democrats would have to consider when seeking votes in southeastern Wisconsin where opposition to slavery was most pronounced. And when some might have been tempted to abandon the Liberty party as a lost cause, it reminded them of the moral and political imperatives that necessitated its creation. In addition, the *Freeman* kept party members abreast of the antislavery movement in the rest of the country and circulated a wide variety of antislavery literature.[31] Ultimately, the importance of the Liberty party in Wisconsin lay less in its role as a political association competing for popular favor at the polls than in its ability to broadcast a specific legal and constitutional political program for the destruction of slavery. By advocating a policy that availed itself of existing institutional mechanisms to achieve the group's goals, Liberty men avoided both the anti-institutional extremism popularly associated with abolitionism and the *ad hoc* responses to slavery questions the northern wings of the major parties usually proffered.[32]

Wisconsin's Liberty men advocated political ideals developed by their national leaders.[33] They condemned slavery as a moral, social, and political evil, a sin against God and man that "ought to be immediately and forever abolished." In practical terms, this meant using every legal means available to weaken and ultimately destroy slavery. Although they admitted that complete emancipation might not come during their lifetime, Liberty supporters firmly believed slavery's days in the United States were numbered. And since moral suasion had failed to work, peaceful and constitutional means of attacking black bondage were advanced to offset the perceived tendency of the federal government, evident from the earliest days of the Republic, "to patronize, protect, strengthen, and extend the institution of slavery."[34] Completely divorcing the national government from slavery lay at the heart of the Liberty party's political program. It called for abolishing slavery in the nation's capital and all other territory under federal jurisdiction, preventing its introduction and spread into the national domain, admitting no new slave states, repealing the fugitive slave law of 1793, terminating the coastal and interstate slave trade, and prohibiting the use of slaves on national projects. In addition, appointees to federal office must be men dedicated to the principles of liberty and equality rather than slaveholders or their supporters.[35] Although Liberty men deliberately refrained from endorsing direct federal intervention with slavery in the Southern states, admitting such action to be unconstitutional and expressly antagonistic to the current of popular opinion, they stressed that their halfway measures comprised a broad field of legal and constitutional action open to persons of sincere antislavery convictions. And, they confidently asserted, depriving slavery of federal sustenance and surrounding it with a chain of free states soon would force the South to abandon the institution.[36]

Agreeing that Southern slavery was a creature of local law, Liberty men based their program on the related conviction that the national government did not possess the constitutional power to establish or uphold slavery or to deprive any man of his natural right to liberty. The Constitution was fundamentally a charter of freedom, they insisted, whose authors had suffered the continued existence of slavery, assuming that a proper administration of government and a growing appreciation of republican principles and the plain truths of the Declaration of Independence would culminate in a slave-state plan of emancipation. Yet the men to whom control of the government had been entrusted frustrated the hopes of the founders. "With storm and fury, bravado and denunciation, and all sorts of vagabond bluster about the dissolution of the Union," the friends of slavery had twisted governmental policies to suit their interests. As this slave power extended its dominion, obsequious Northern Whigs and Democrats showed a willingness to pay it perpetual homage in return for political preferment. Consequently, the slavocracy's influence now transcended the bounds of the Southern states, controlled affairs in Washington, and pervaded local government throughout the Union.[37]

Liberty party advocates lent particular urgency to their appeal by arguing that the slave power's supremacy over the nation's political affairs threatened to fasten slavery on American soil permanently and, more alarmingly, to erode the liberties of white men. "If slavery should be much longer continued," resolved Green County's Liberty men, "the rights of white people will not only remain jeopardized [but] the laboring people of the North will . . . be made slaves," and all constitutional provisions designed to safeguard personal rights and civil and religious liberty would be extinguished. Thus, the Liberty message was clear. To preserve white freedom required working for black emancipation.[38]

Despite its baldly sectional appeal, Wisconsin's Liberty organization carefully avowed itself a friend of the American Union. With fellow citizens of all sections, it viewed the Union as the linchpin of America's independence and liberty, as well as its peace, prosperity, and happiness. A severed Union was synonymous with internal decay and anarchy and was a danger both to constitutional liberty and the American example that freedom was compatible with order and stability. Moreover, a divided Union at best would remove the South from the reforming impulses of the North; at worst, it would result in unceasing wars and bloodshed between the sections. No one, black or white, would benefit from that. Hence, the Liberty party proclaimed itself true to the Union and "in favor of using all the facilities it affords" to bring about "the immediate and bloodless emancipation of the slave,"[39] although it qualified its support, fearful that, like the Constitution, the Union's purposes were being subverted by the overwhelming presence and expansion of slavery and the slave power.

Formed to protect *rights,* shall it [the Union] be desecrated to perpetuate wrongs? Established to secure equal political privileges to *all,* shall it be perverted to aggrandize the *few* and crush the *many?* Designed to defend and transmit the blessings of freedom, shall it perpetuate an untold and crushing weight of *slavery* upon millions of our free born citizens—while we look on in approving silence. Would that be patriotic and loyal? We are in favor of the *Union* with the *original principles,* without them it loses its value.[40]

So to Liberty adherents, the destruction of slavery took precedence over the continuation of a Union that mocked the cherished American ideals of individual liberty and natural rights. Indeed, slavery's priority was implicit in the very decision to support a sectional party whose goal was the ultimate extinction of black bondage. Political abolitionists would rejoice to see the Union remain intact and slavery peacefully and constitutionally removed; but if one or the other had to be sacrificed, they clearly preferred a divided nation to permanent subordination to the slave power.[41]

In their battle against slavery, Liberty spokesmen also had to contend with white fears that emancipation would unleash "a dependent, barbarous, and hostile population" in their midst. They did so by arguing that enslaved blacks, schooled since childhood to labor assiduously for their daily bread, would "be the last on the face of the earth to sit still and starve to death, or to seek subsistence by plunder." Like all people habituated to hard labor, they would be orderly and quiet citizens, especially when compared to the "lawless, mischievous population [of] non-laboring whites" often found in the South.[42]

Most antislavery activists similarly renounced the "unjust, absurd, and despicable" racial prejudice that lay near the center of white concerns and undermined all appeals and efforts to bring freedom to the nation's bondsmen, and they scoffed at the doctrines of inherent black inferiority popular in the scientific community and with most white Americans. They cited the Bible as proof that "God created of one blood all the nations of men," and they enlisted nature to support the biblical affirmation of mankind's common origins. After all, one Liberty man wrote, attempts by "distinct species . . . to commingle" inevitably failed, whereas Africans and Europeans coalesced "as naturally as . . . the English and German . . . or as any other race, or different branches of the same race." Indeed, Americans need look no further for evidence than the Southern slave quarters, for there the "bleaching process" was a pervasive fact of life. History too demonstrated mankind's innate equality. Different races in different periods dominated the worlds of art, science, and intellectual achievement, abolitionists stressed, and while Greece and Rome represented such excellence in the history of western civilization, the accomplishments of the

African nations, especially Egypt, were no less brilliant. True, the once-savage nations of Europe had long ago surpassed Africa and the other empires of antiquity, and America's blacks were now inferior to whites, but nurture, not nature, accounted for this. Because slavery and discrimination robbed them of "personal freedom and the means of intellectual and moral culture," it was reasoned, blacks could not fairly be adjudged an inherently inferior race.[43]

Along with their disavowals of black inferiority and descriptions of the virtues and habits of enslaved blacks, Liberty spokesmen demanded the immediate repeal of discriminatory laws and practices under which free blacks suffered. They condemned these as antirepublican and a disgraceful perversion of free institutions and the egalitarian ideals of the Declaration of Independence. They likewise rejected schemes to colonize blacks as another offshoot of the prejudice that assumed they could never live together as equals with whites.[44]

Although some of Wisconsin's Liberty men undoubtedly dissented from certain aspects of the party's avowal of basic black equality,[45] Sholes probably spoke for most members when he defended its war against prejudice.

> It is an object of sufficient importance . . . to justify the organization of the Liberty party, and its continued existence for the term of one century, if it were only to eradicate from our . . . communities that most unchristian and inhuman prejudice against color, and that hostility which exists against the enjoyment of civil rights by colored citizens. It is a burning disgrace in the eyes of Christendom, and an exceeding sin in the sight of Heaven, that we surpass the whole civilized world, in our disregard of the rights of the Negro, and our disposition to trample him down and to oppress and degrade him. A party is needed, and an active and strong party too, in every portion of the free states, to get up and to sustain a system of opposition to these ungodly prejudices; and to the more ungodly practices which they occasion; to get up and to sustain a tone of morals, of piety, and of public sentiment favorable to the elevation and welfare of the Negro race. Our regard for human rights must be slender and superficial in the extreme, if we can witness with unconcern the prevalent and continued violation of them, as regards our colored population.[46]

Understandably, Wisconsin's major parties greeted the entry of the Liberty upstarts into territorial politics with disapproval. Both Whigs and Democrats claimed that an antislavery party was impractical and unnecessary and that it might well work against its goals by drawing off votes from sympathetic candidates in the other parties. They suggested using moral suasion and laboring within the two-party system to bring about slavery's ultimate demise, and they advised Liberty men to disband.[47] To discourage potential converts, Whigs and Democrats often united against Liberty candidates in local elections. They also dismissed slavery questions as irrelevant and played up local issues to hold the allegiance of antislavery men. "The slaves of the South will be no nearer liberty by the election of an abolitionist supervisor, justice of the peace, or fence viewer . . . than they were before," proclaimed one bipartisan meeting, self-described as "friendly to the slave and opposed to political abolitionism at our town elections." Edward Mathews, now an enthusiastic Liberty advocate and present at the gathering, rejoined that "minor offices are the stepping stones to larger ones . . . [and] by nominating . . . Liberty men for town offices, we do much to make slavery unpopular in the towns, and when in all the towns slavery is unpopular, it will be nationally unpopular and sink to swim no more."[48] Despite their efforts, the Whigs and Democrats failed to snuff out the pesky antislavery party or to quiet discussion of the black bondage. In fact, pressure from Liberty men and national events forced both parties to define their position on slavery.

Like their political kinsmen throughout the North, Wisconsin's Whigs were more critical of slavery than their Democratic opponents.[49] They denounced it as an "odious and hated institution," as "the foulest and deepest stain upon the purity of our free institutions," and as "the curse of America upon her posterity," and they looked forward to its demise "with strong aspiration and hope."[50] Slavery was not only politically and morally repugnant, Whigs argued, but it retarded America's economic growth and prosperity and tarnished its reputation as the boasted land of liberty.[51]

Prior to 1844, Wisconsin's Whigs largely ignored slavery questions in favor of local issues important to the territory's pioneers. It was President John Tyler's bid to annex Texas that triggered discussion of the issue throughout the territory and provoked the undivided wrath of the Whigs. They condemned annexation as "the blackest scheme ever conceived by a President of this Union—the most inglorious proposition ever submitted to Congress."[52] Not only was it of dubious constitutionality, but even worse, for the first time in the nation's history, the federal government was actively involved in upholding and extending black servitude. "We are called upon as a *nation* to aid in sustaining slavery," Southport's Louis P. Harvey wrote, and "the pretence that it is a local institution tolerated by the terms of the original compact [as] the pound of flesh" necessary to secure the Union, "is, by this act, disowned." Another Whig warned sardonically that distorting the Constitution to placate slaveholders might backfire, and in the future it might "be used to enlarge the *area of freedom* in a very different manner— a manner somewhat affecting the peculiar institutions of the South."[53]

But why, Whigs asked, would the South risk arousing an unwanted and heated controversy? Madison's William Wyman answered that Southerners realized they were being outdistanced by the superior energy and enterprise of their Northern neighbors and soon would occupy a subordinate place in the nation's political affairs. Since minority status threatened to have grave consequences for slavery, Southern leaders embraced Texas annexation in a desperate gamble to preserve the existing sectional balance of power that Northern Whigs were obliged to resist.[54]

Although the Whigs never proffered a comprehensive plan to end slavery, their opposition to the annexation of Texas clearly was predicated on the belief that slavery's expansion was linked directly to its perpetuation. The South's greedy and insatiable desire to distend the institution, they cautioned repeatedly, would "bind the living body of American liberty to the dead and corrupting carcass of slavery, forever." Confine the black scourge, on the other hand, and gradually it would dwindle away.[55]

With more restrained rhetoric and less acute moral revulsion, Wisconsin's Whigs shared many assumptions regarding slavery with their Liberty party contemporaries. Nevertheless, they resolutely refused to subordinate all other questions of national import to their antislavery principles. As Rock County's Levi Alden exclaimed, Whigs "cannot abandon great principles for which they have been contending for years . . . to become political abolitionists."[56] The Whig attachment to an organic view of society formed the essence of these principles. A benign, disinterested government, they believed, should direct and coordinate America's development and progress and help improve the life and livelihood of its citizens. Constitutionally sanctioned protective tariffs would encourage the growth of American industry, safeguard it from unfair foreign competition, and keep wages high. Internal improvements and banks would facilitate intersectional communication and commerce, simplify business transactions, and bring a measure of order to the nation's monetary system. Even virtue and moral behavior would be promoted by discouraging the sale of intoxicating beverages and other unwise and unhealthy practices. Whig policies, moreover, as distinct from individual Whig opinions, would honor the constitutional compromises made in reference to slavery. And although Northern and Southern party members took distinctly different positions on slavery questions, both would exercise toleration and continue to work together to achieve their more important common goals. As the government acted "to correct vicious relations in the body politic," to facilitate and protect the accumulation of property, and to improve the quality of freedom, the territory's Whigs maintained, slavery slowly would disintegrate.[57]

The tug of party loyalty and their devoted attachment to the Union further restrained Whigs from adopting a more vigorous antislavery stance. The Liberty party's platform, although constitutional and legal, horrified them because of the fatal impact it could have on the continued harmony and fraternity of the states.[58] Race prejudice likewise handicapped many sincerely repulsed by slavery. Western Wisconsin, home to many Whigs, harbored few men sympathetic to blacks.[59] Further east, party members occasionally spoke out on behalf of "the free people of color among us who are still the slaves of an unjust and tyrannical public sentiment." But party divisions on racial matters usually prescribed circumspection.[60] Finally, contempt for the Democrats and their principles of unrestrained individualism and minimal government tempered the antislavery zeal of Wisconsin's Whigs.

> We look upon modern Democracy . . . with its low trickery and reeking corruption—its loud and vaunting professions of pure principles and exalting truths, coupled with its glaring inconsistencies and dangerous deceptions in practice—its exclusive American feelings in word, and its practical devotion to British interests in the work of breaking our manufacturers by introducing the ruinous policy of free trade—its pretended regard for the free voice of the people, with its iron-wrought machinery of party discipline . . . its affectation for order, with its progress toward anarchy, misrule, and the wildness of unrestrained licentiousness, *as the embodied falsehood of the age,* comprising and surpassing all the dangers that are felt or dreaded from the existence of slavery. Whatever strength we have . . . we are

determined to use against this deadly foe of free institutions. When we have time to fix upon an individual evil as the solitary object of our hostilities, we may take up slavery.[61]

Compared to Liberty party professions, Whig antislavery rhetoric was ambivalent and revealed an unwillingness to contemplate an antislavery political union damaging to sectional and party harmony. "Slavery among men in the North is universally conceded to be an evil," one Whig pronounced, and "the only question is—which is the most speedy and practical way of eradicating it?" A Madison Whig, claiming to be "antislavery to the core," echoed this attitude. He asserted that the only difference between Whigs and Liberty men "is, not whether slavery is an evil, and inconsistent with our civil and religious institutions, for in this we agree, but over the best and most practical mode to get rid of the evil."[62] Thus, Whigs would remain doubtful allies in the antislavery cause as long as they held other principles above their aversion to slavery.

Wisconsin's ruling Democratic party spoke with two distinct voices on the slavery issue. One group, under the influence of arguments alleging the inherent inferiority of blacks, contended that they inevitably fell under the domination of whites whenever the two races lived near one another; thus, they could never coexist as equals. Short of defending slavery outright, they expressed resignation to natural laws obligating whites to "guard . . . protect, feed and clothe the Negro race" in return for faithful labor, and to "the decree of God, that the Negro should be the servant of the white man." Not surprisingly, these Democrats fulminated against emancipation efforts. America's slaves fared better under the paternal care of their white masters, they affirmed, than free blacks who as a rule were incapable of taking care of themselves. Liberate the Southern slaves, and an army of impoverished blacks would be coerced northward "to die on our highways from starvation, or be kept alive by the labors of white men." As such, abolition would alter only the form but not the fact of black subordination, and they ultimately would have to be separated from whites, presumably colonized, for their own good.[63]

Unsympathetic to moral arguments respecting black servitude or the bondsmen's plight, Wisconsin Democrats resigned to slavery's existence concluded that it was an institution best left alone, and they fretted about the impact abolitionist agitation might have on the bonds that united them to their Southern brethren. They vehemently denounced the Liberty party for launching a vindictive crusade against the slave states, the success of which would bring about "the destruction of our time-honored Constitution . . . [and] our glorious Union." Wisconsinites were urged to disregard the mad rantings of the abolitionists and to commiserate with the white people of the slave states who bore directly the oppressive burdens of the black evil.[64]

If some Democrats raised no specific objection to slavery, another group, perhaps a majority, branded it a violation of natural and divine law and a glaring contradiction to the party's professed dedication to individual freedom. And though these Democrats boldly predicted that slavery eventually would fall victim to the progress of their party's liberating principles, like the Whigs, they advanced no specific program to hasten the institution's demise.[65] Most also were hampered by prevailing racial prejudices, although an outspoken minority expressed disgust at such attitudes. Christopher L. Sholes, brother of the Liberty leader and a prominent antislavery Democrat, and Marshall M. Strong, an influential party chieftain from Racine, voiced the sentiments of this pro-black group. They avowed black men to be as naturally endowed in intelligence and ability as whites, and they blamed slavery and discrimination for reducing the nation's blacks to an inferior state. Raise them up from their enforced degradation and grant them the blessings of freedom and education, these Democrats insisted, and blacks would develop their potential as individuals in much the same way as whites did.[66]

Whatever their differences regarding slavery or blacks, Wisconsin's Democrats shared a common ideology in most other respects. Unlike the Whigs, who would employ government to enhance the quality of freedom and direct economic growth in America, Democrats believed unfettered freedom to be the birthright of all white males. Its protection required circumscribing the powers and functions of government to bare essentials. The party's attachment to minimal government and strict constitutional construction bespoke its determination to safeguard individual liberty and equality against state encroachment, as well as its opposition to Whig interventionist policies. Chartered banks, protective tariffs, and similar government legislation, Democrats argued, inevitably favored the interests of some members of society over others. The best way to preserve equal opportunity and to promote the general welfare was to restrain the heavy hand of government and allow natural laws to bring about a competitive, self-reliant socioeconomic order that bestowed its fruits fairly and equitably. "When the force of law is in no particular applied to bolster up a class, or create a fictitious value for anything," one Democrat declared, "everything will find its true and natural level," and those who by their labor produced the most would have the most, while those who produced nothing would have nothing.[67]

Since all men cherished individual liberty and feared abuses of power, Democrats championed popular movements that promised to restore people's natural rights, expand the area of freedom, and overthrow despotism. In their view, these American principles were making unprecedented and ineluctable strides throughout the world and were destined soon to eliminate all forms of tyranny. Nearer home, Americans themselves were acting as freedom's agents as they expanded westward and planted their republican institutions. This ebullient faith in freedom's progress convinced most antislavery Democrats to give blinking approval to the annexation of Texas. Christopher Sholes, for one, dismissed slavery in republican Texas as unimportant because it was "under the control of a . . . power which legislation cannot reach nor territory permanently effect." With the spread of free principles, he asserted confidently, slavery's doom became ever more imminent. Thus, "The hopes of those who seek to perpetuate slavery by this annexation and the fears of those who anticipate that thereby it will be perpetuated . . . [were] alike groundless," for "There is no power under heaven that can perpetuate slavery in these United States . . . or for any great length of time delay its abolition."[68]

Sholes's logic did not impress Marshall M. Strong. Annex Texas with slavery, he insisted, and the accursed institution would be immeasurably strengthened and Southern power and ascendancy in national affairs assured. Even disunion would be preferable to such a misfortune.[69] But Strong's remonstrances fell on deaf ears, as most Democrats enthusiastically welcomed Texas into the Union and shrugged off any misgivings with the excuse that slavery was a fact there that no one, least of all the federal government, could do anything about. With no viable alternative, party loyalty stilled questioning consciences.[70]

Finally, the shared belief that slavery was a local institution, outside of federal jurisdiction, and the frightening specter of disunion, which, Strong notwithstanding, nearly every Democrat loathed to contemplate, further checked Democratic antislavery agitation. As Sholes stated, whatever the virtue of Liberty party principles, if unchallenged in the North, they would embitter sectional relations and, if enacted, almost certainly would lead to disunion and civil war. Under the circumstances, he warned, it would be better to let slavery die a natural death, however long it took, than to court the far greater dangers of attempting to lead it to an early grave.[71]

Although most Wisconsinites disapproved of slavery, the predominance of other principles and values combined with traditional party bonds and race prejudice to complicate the Liberty party's effort to win their votes. To secure a stake in territorial politics and an enhanced degree of legitimacy, it required an issue of local interest. Black suffrage furnished that issue, and it, not slavery itself, constituted the first practical political question of consequence to engage the attention of Wisconsin's abolitionists.

CHAPTER TWO

Negro Suffrage
Is Antislavery Work

THE IDEALISM of the Liberty party was broad enough to contain black suffrage. The denial of voting privileges stood as the most common form of legal discrimination practiced against black freemen and was a clear violation of the party's egalitarian principles. Disfranchisement implied that blacks not only were undesirable members of their communities but were incapable of exercising the rights and responsibilities of citizenship. In addition, the attitudes that deprived blacks of the right to vote in the North mirrored those same principles that in the South reduced them to servitude. Remove this distinction, Liberty men insisted, and those undemocratic beliefs that justified both discrimination and enslavement would be weakened. Thus, the crusades against slavery and for black suffrage were linked, and in the inaugural issue of the *Freeman*, Sholes announced that the principle of "no political distinction founded upon color" would be the Liberty party's motto in territorial politics.[1]

Congress passed the act organizing the Wisconsin Territory in 1836. It entitled all adult white male citizens of the United States to participate in the territory's first election and empowered the legislature to determine voting qualifications at all subsequent elections.[2] Although Wisconsin's lawmakers made minor alterations in the suffrage law two years later, none showed a desire to enfranchise the territory's foreign-born or free black residents.[3]

The suffrage question emerged as a political issue for the first time in 1844, when Governor James Duane Doty requested that the question of taking preliminary steps toward statehood be submitted to a popular vote.[4] In response to the governor's call, a mass meeting of foreign-born residents convened in Milwaukee to protest the law that excluded them from the polls and to demand that all white males living in the territory be allowed to participate in any statehood referendum. Stiff opposition to that demand surfaced in the lead region, where the population remained overwhelmingly native-born, and in several of the Yankee towns of the southeast.[5]

In early January, the Assembly Committee on Territorial Affairs took up the issue and reported a bill to permit all adult white males resident in the territory for three months to vote on the question of statehood and to participate in the choice of delegates to a state constitutional convention.[6] After several days of skirmishing, William H. Bartlett, a Walworth County Democrat and abolitionist,[7] moved to strike the word "white" from the committee report. The Assembly swiftly rejected Bartlett's audacious amendment, twenty-one to five. It then passed the whites-only bill by an equally wide margin.[8] In the Council, Edward V. Whiton, a prominent territorial Whig, similarly tried to purge the Assembly bill of its color distinction without success.[9]

Petitions favorable to black enfranchisement also came before the 1844 legislature. John C. Olin, another antislavery Democrat,[10] presented one from a group of Milwaukee citizens that was referred to the assembly's judiciary committee. As adjournment neared, the committee reported that it was inadvisable to legislate on the subject, and its request to be relieved from further consideration of the matter was approved.[11] Whiton again broached the subject in the council when he introduced a petition from "David Smith and 5 other colored men" asking that voting privileges be extended "to all persons holding Real Estate in the Territory, or taxable property to the value of one hundred dollars." The tactic of the blacks and their advocates to introduce a property qualification almost succeeded. A select committee, headed by Whiton, drew up a bill corresponding to the petition, and several attempts to kill the measure failed. But after squeaking through a third reading, Michael Frank, an ardent Democrat and outspoken opponent of slavery, changed his vote and defeated it.[12] Frank's reversal resulted from an unwillingness on the decisive roll call to link suffrage to a property qualification rather than from hostility to black voting. Because only two days remained on the legislative calendar, he also saw nothing to be gained by pressing the matter since the assembly undoubtedly would reject any proposal to enfranchise blacks.[13]

Black suffrage fared even worse at the 1845 legislative session, as several petitions were buried in committee.[14] In the following year, the question provoked a sharp debate when a Prairieville Democrat moved to allow black participation in yet another proposed referendum on statehood. Moses M. Strong, a fiery, ambitious Mineral Point Democrat, denounced the proposal, insisting that arguments respecting the capabilities of blacks were irrelevant, and that he personally would forever be opposed to "nigger voting." His real concern was that the South not be led to believe "that Wisconsin is favorably disposed to the abolition movement"; therefore all questions tainted with abolitionism, as black enfranchisement certainly was, ought to be avoided.[15]

Marshall M. Strong, Racine's Democratic councilman and no relation to Moses, scolded his namesake for using the "contemptuous epithet, nigger." He too questioned the expediency of raising the subject of black enfranchisement, but he could see no better reason for excluding them from the polls than Norwegians, who were pouring into the territory in large numbers. These immigrants, Strong exclaimed, whom few in the Council adjudged unfit to vote, lived in "holes in the ground" and "huts dug from the banks of the earth," and they were less intelligent, less civilized, and less familiar with American institutions than were blacks. He also denied that blacks were an inferior race, but even if they were, then all the more reason to grant them the full rights and responsibilities of citizenship as one means of raising them from their degraded state. Lastly, what Southerners might think of black voting in Wisconsin was unimportant. They had no more right to criticize or influence the actions of Wisconsin's legislature than it had to meddle with theirs, although if granting Northern blacks the franchise indirectly weakened slavery, as some of its proponents claimed it would, then Wisconsin would be remiss if it failed to extend this measure of justice at home to assist the oppressed abroad.[16]

Despite Marshall Strong's spirited defense, Wisconsin's blacks again were denied access to the polls. Four Democrats and both Whig Council members supported the measure, while seven Democrats opposed it.[17] Although no roll call was taken, it appears that all six positive votes came from southeastern councilmen, while the four southwestern district members voted as a bloc against black voting, suggesting that constituency more than party influenced the vote.[18] Nevertheless, even if a Council majority had been obtained, the proposal would have failed in the assembly. Prior to the Council debates, an attempt to strike the word white from a suffrage bill under consideration in the lower house, on the pretense of enfranchising half-blood Indians, lost by a two-to-one margin.[19]

While the legislature made short work of attempts to include blacks among Wisconsin's voters, the Liberty party struggled to secure a foothold in territorial politics. The major parties' strategy of uniting against Liberty men, dismissing their party as irrelevant, or simply ignoring them, together with the loyalty of influential antislavery Democrats and Whigs, succeeded in reducing the already tiny Liberty vote in the spring and fall canvasses of 1844. Sholes chastised the apostates, warning that the only way to preserve and strengthen the faltering Liberty organization was to adhere uncompromisingly to its principles and candidates.[20] In February 1845, in an effort to tighten organization and discipline among the territory's antislavery forces, he succeeded in bringing about the merger of the still nominally independent Wisconsin Antislavery Society and the Liberty Association, which adopted a proviso binding every member to vote only for Liberty party candidates.[21]

Reorganized, the Liberty organization began to make its presence felt in small but significant ways. By 1846, it had elected men to minor offices in several southeastern towns; in others it held the balance of power.[22] Then, after Wisconsinites finally agreed to summon a state constitutional convention in October, the legislature boosted the party's power when it apportioned convention seats on the basis of one delegate for every thirteen hundred residents, about one-fourth of whom were eligible voters. Since the southeastern counties of Walworth, Waukesha, Rock, Racine, and Jefferson would elect 51 of the 125 members, the Liberty vote could be pivotal in determining which of the two major parties captured many of those seats.[23]

The Liberty party's potential influence especially worried the Whigs, perennial underdogs to the Democrats in territorial politics.[24] If they stood fast and made a three-way contest out of the delegate elections, Democratic craftsmen almost certainly would forge Wisconsin's constitution. If they tried to unite with disaffected Democrats, as they had on occasion in the past, formidable organizational obstacles would hamper their efforts. Finally, if they courted Liberty men in districts where they held the balance of power, some of their own party members doubtless would rebel. Without any clearly attractive alternative, and with nothing to lose, the Whigs decided to woo both Liberty men and Democrats where the opportunity presented itself and to otherwise shape their appeal to accommodate local concerns.

Leading the assault on Liberty loyalties was the urbane Rufus King, grandson of the renowned Federalist leader, only recently arrived in Milwaukee from his native New York where he had been allied with the antislavery wing of the state's Whig party.[25] As the new owner and editor of the *Milwaukee Sentinel*, King, a long-time supporter of black suffrage, urged its adoption in the future state of Wisconsin; he contemptuously dismissed laws that linked voting privileges to skin color as inconsistent with free institutions and democratic principles. Echoing the Liberty position, King insisted that slavery and racial prejudice stemmed from the same misguided beliefs, and until those beliefs were repudiated by the people of the North, the South could with justice dismiss their antislavery professions as hypocritical benevolence. "There is no more effectual mode of upholding slavery," he wrote, "than for men in the free states to treat blacks as an inferior race." And, quoting his longtime political associate and former Whig governor of New York, William H. Seward, King further argued that extending the vote to northern blacks would constitute the first act in a drama that would end "without injustice to the slaveholder, without civil war . . . in the sublime catastrophe of Emancipation."[26] Following his lead, other Whig journalists in southeastern Wisconsin came out in favor of black political equality.[27]

By supporting black voting in Wisconsin, Whigs in the southeastern counties hoped the territory's Liberty men would follow the precedent set by their party in New York, which had promised to back any candidate or party adopting a prosuffrage stand in a vote to revise the Empire State's constitution that same year.[28] Whigs also publicized an appeal of New York's blacks asking voters to champion candidates, irrespective of party, pledged to fight for equal suffrage.[29] Then they asked, would Wisconsin's abolitionists waste their ballots, stubbornly adhering to a party with no prospect of success, or would they unite with Whigs in support of commonly held principles to help bring about electoral reform?[30]

Although the offer to merge seemed attractive, Liberty men greeted it with skepticism. They not only were reluctant to disband their organization, as the Whigs demanded,[31] but many undoubtedly agreed with the Democrats, who dismissed Whig pronouncements as insincere and hypocritical.[32] So, in February, at their territorial convention, they resolved to oppose any constitution that failed to enfranchise Wisconsin's blacks and pointedly reminded both Whigs and Democrats of their past indifference, which made present signs of approval from either party highly suspect. Liberty activists thus rejected union with the Whigs and resolved to place their own men in nomination.[33] In mid-March, however, they abruptly changed course.

Probably after consulting with other Liberty leaders, Sholes now urged party members to dispense with partisanship and cooperate with Whigs and Democrats friendly to "EQUAL RIGHTS AND UNIVERSAL SUFFRAGE."[34] The reasons for this shift are unclear, but King's courtship and the example of New York's party men seem to have caused rifts among Wisconsin's abolitionists. Liberty men had always placed their principles above strict party loyalty, and doubtless this made it difficult for many to ignore the opportunity to work with others favoring black equality. Self-interest likely played a role too. Constitution-making was serious business, and the convention could be expected to chart Wisconsin's direction for years to come. Like all residents, Liberty men had a stake in its work, and some understandably might be unwilling to subordinate every issue to the free suffrage question. Finally, Liberty chieftains knew their party would not win any convention seats and at best could expect only to influence the outcome of a few contests in the southeast. So to minimize party strife, they dropped partisanship in favor of trying to influence Whigs and Democrats in anti-slavery districts to endorse black voting rights, while otherwise they remained warily neutral and kept a watchful eye on events that led up to the September election.[35]

The ensuing campaign justified their caution, as the Whigs clumsily attempted to manipulate the suffrage question to their advantage. In Dane County, they initially spurned a proposed whites-only suffrage plank and easily passed a resolution that advocated the enfranchisement of all adult males. But, under pressure from the county's Democrats, who included a whites-only article in their platform, Whig spokesmen timorously backed off and denied that the resolution placed their party on record in favor of black voting.[36] In Racine County, Democratic leaders attempted to undercut the influence of antislavery men by nominating a slate of candidates to run without the benefit of a platform. Sensing an opportunity, Racine's Whigs joined angry Democrats and a handful of Liberty men in selecting a nonpartisan "People's Ticket" pledged to "universal suffrage without invidious distinctions on account of religion, birth, or color." The coalition quickly foundered, though, when three of the six Democrats placed on the ticket declined its nomination after being warned they would be drummed out of the party if they persisted in their mutiny.[37] In Democratic Milwaukee, the Whigs attempted a similar union that met with the same result.[38]

Walworth, Waukesha, and Rock County Whigs, who competed fairly evenly with the Democrats, put up straight party tickets and baited Liberty men by embracing equal suffrage. Elsewhere in the territory, Whigs usually ignored the question; only in closely contested Waukesha County did the Democracy openly espouse black voting. In the western counties, where party organization remained undeveloped, candidates ran as independents and gave no consideration to the matter. Grant County alone had forty candidates competing for its eight convention seats, and many of them were known to be antagonistic to black rights.[39]

By August, Liberty leaders had seen enough. Although a few eastern Whigs publicly embraced black suffrage, Sholes explained, they did so only where Liberty strength forced them to. When combined with Democratic hostility and the opposition of the western counties, he continued, it was apparent that the principle stood no chance of receiving either party's endorsement. Consequently, Liberty partisans would accomplish nothing except the destruction of their organization by voting for Whigs or Democrats, and until one of them endorsed the Liberty program to destroy slavery *"beyond all doubt,"* they would continue to go their own way.[40]

The Democrats rolled to an astounding victory as a result of the weakness and poor organization of the Whigs and the failure of King and his accomplices to win over the Liberty party. One hundred three Democrats and a mere dozen Whigs were elected to draw up Wisconsin's constitution. Ten successful Independents joined them, six of whom represented Grant County and leaned toward Whiggery. As expected, the Liberty party failed to elect any of its candidates.[41]

On October 5, 1846, the delegates chosen to hammer out a state charter convened in Madison. Four days later, the committee on suffrage recommended adopting an article to restrict the vote to adult white males. Supporters of black enfranchisement instead moved to submit the question to the territory's electors as a separate item, along with the proposed constitution, an idea copied from New York's convention. Referendum backers argued that this would keep the people's attention focused on the constitution itself, limit the impact of the suffrage question, and maybe even undo the territory's abolitionist party by seeming to commandeer its main issue. Although the proposal went nowhere at first, its possible benefits appealed to a number of delegates.[42]

Ten days after the whites-only article was reported, Charles Burchard, a Waukesha County Whig and the lone dissenting member of the suffrage committee, called for the enfranchisement of all adult males without reference to color.[43] His proposal drew a harsh response from extreme anti-black delegates, especially Edward G. Ryan, a brilliant but temperamental Democratic lawyer and later state supreme court justice, who pointed to New York and alleged that blacks there led sordid lives and lacked the virtues necessary to be responsible citizens or members of the nation's political family. Moreover, if Wisconsin embraced full political equality, it would become a common destination for legions of runaway slaves, an eventuality to avoid at all costs and a clear violation of sacred decrees that whites and blacks must always remain separate.[44] Other delegates seconded Ryan's position. They condemned Liberty men for constantly promoting free suffrage against the wishes of most of the territory's white residents and for threatening to withhold support for the constitution and statehood to advance their unnatural scheme. Rather than indulge this handful of annoying abolitionists, Moses M. Strong, the former councilman, proclaimed that he "would give them war—war to the knife, and knife to the hilt."[45]

In his reply, Burchard reminded his fellow delegates that blacks already possessed the franchise in several Northern states, including Massachusetts, New Hampshire, Vermont, and Maine, and none of them had been overrun by fugitives. In fact, he continued, blacks in those states had shown themselves to be fully competent to exercise the responsibilities of citizenship; to justify withholding the ballot from them simply because of the color of their skin was "a terrible, damnable doctrine." Instead, Wisconsin's representatives had a moral and political responsibility to write a color-blind constitution. To do less would violate the principle laid down by the nation's founders, one that formed the basis of America's institutions: "All men are born free and equal."[46]

Although a defender of black suffrage, Burchard carefully disclaimed having any friendship for social equality, that is, a "mingling of the races."

It "was scarcely to be looked for and repugnant to the feelings of men and . . . divine providence." Instead, he had taken up the cause of the blacks in spite of those feelings, solely from a devotion to republican ideals and a desire to extend to them a measure of justice.[47] Moses Gibson, a Fond du Lac Whig, stated the case more plainly. Whether or not a white man wanted "to commingle, intermarry, and eat and drink" with blacks was irrelevant to the question of civil and political rights. According to Gibson,

> The whole system of a republican government [is] opposed to depriving Negroes of the right of suffrage—the whole principle of republican institutions from foundation to capstone is opposed to infringing upon the natural rights of any man, and he could not, therefore, vote for depriving this portion of citizens of the right of voting.[48]

Warren Chase, a Democrat and leader of the Fourierist community in Ceresco (Ripon), made the case for Burchard's amendment on both principled and political grounds. Not only was equal suffrage just and right, he submitted, but its confirmation would eliminate the only issue distinguishing the Liberty party from the Whig and Democratic organizations and bring about its disappearance. Other representatives, whether or not they approved of Burchard's position, agreed that enfranchising blacks would kill the antislavery party, but fearful of local reaction, they preferred a referendum.[49]

On October 22, before taking up Burchard's suffrage article, the convention defeated a proposal to refer the issue to the people as a separate question by a fifty-one to forty-seven vote.[50] Delegates from the western counties unanimously opposed the measure. They were joined by a number of representatives from the divided eastern delegations and five others from predominantly foreign-born Washington County.[51] Although Democrats dominated the convention, partisanship seemed unimportant in the balloting. Rather, as the record of the debates suggests, a delegate's perception of his constituency's attitude probably counted most, although principle did influence some votes. Charles M. Baker, a Walworth County Democrat, summed up the feelings of several members when he expressed personal sympathy for free suffrage, but he knew his constituency opposed it. Thus, he felt obliged to respect that sentiment. For his part, Burchard voted against the measure because it needlessly encumbered the constitution and provided ambitious delegates instructed to support black suffrage with an opportunity to dodge the issue directly. Marshall M. Strong, for one, had been an outspoken advocate of black enfranchisement since 1844 but, eyeing a seat in the United States Senate, now lamely explained in opposition that he "had . . . changed his views on the subject."[52]

The delegates took up Burchard's proposal to enfranchise all adult males on the following day, and any illusions he may have harbored respecting the strength of prosuffrage sentiment were rudely demolished when it was rejected ninety-one to twelve.[53] Five of the favorable ballots came from the tiny Whig delegation and included that of Rufus King's close political associate John Tweedy. Alexander Randall, a young, aspiring political adventurer who a few days earlier had made a forceful speech against excluding blacks from the polls, stood prominent among the handful of prosuffrage Democrats. Still, most delegates, motivated by personal prejudice and the perceived antagonism of the electorate, as well as by Strong's admonition that black enfranchisement would condemn the constitution, wanted nothing to do with it. As one member intimated, the convention's work hardly seemed worth endangering for the sake of a few blacks.[54]

Despite these setbacks, the friends of free suffrage persisted. On October 26, Randall introduced yet another proposal to submit the question to the people.[55] Two weeks later, Moses Strong successfully tacked an amendment onto Randall's resolution, designed to make it "as obnoxious as he could," that declared blacks eligible for all state offices if they were awarded the vote. Since the articles relative to office holding opened all elective positions to qualified voters, his amendment was needlessly provocative. Yet many delegates voted for it simply to forestall further debate on the question and get on with other business.[56] Finally, on the last day of November, Randall's proposal passed fifty-three to forty-six. The margin of victory came from seventeen eastern county representatives who had been either absent or in opposition when the question first came to a vote.[57] The latter group included Burchard, who now realized that a referendum was the best that could be obtained, and three Democrats who represented predominantly immigrant constituencies, in apparent retaliation against the successful efforts of western members to raise the residency requirement in the proposed suffrage article from six months to one year.[58] By contrast, the antireferendum coalition remained largely intact, losing only the six votes but picking up two others from representatives who earlier had cast proreferendum ballots. So, for motives ranging from principle to expediency to revenge, Wisconsin's voters would be given an opportunity to express themselves on the merits of black political equality.

In mid-December the labors of the convention came to an end. Popular debate quickly indicated that the proposed constitution had many enemies.[59] Whigs and commercially minded Democrats, including Milwaukee's Democratic postmaster and political boss, Josiah Noonan, denounced the article prohibiting banking and paper money. Marshall M. Strong, who had resigned from the convention in protest over a provision recognizing the rights of married women to retain independent ownership of their property, added his voice to the forces opposing ratification. Still other men objected to the clause that exempted the forced sale of forty-acre homesteads, not exceeding $1,000 in value, in civil cases arising over the inability of a person to repay a contracted debt. Liberty partisans scorned the obnoxious suffrage article excluding blacks and denounced the representatives who had espoused it. Some eastern Whigs also condemned the anti-black clause, with Rufus King once remarking that bad as the banking article was, "Still more glaring and reprehensible is the . . . course pursued by the majority on the vital question of the Right of Suffrage."[60]

Among the Democratic editors, only Christopher Sholes forthrightly supported both the constitution and black political equality. In an address to Liberty men, he claimed that despite the whites-only suffrage article, the democratic principles embedded in the proposed charter represented "one step towards a practical and universal recognition of the grand principle of human brotherhood" and would hasten the inevitable triumph of equal rights. James C. Bunner of the *Racine Advocate* also gave a terse, guarded endorsement of black suffrage.[61] The remainder of the Democratic press extolled the controversial document and worked feverishly to counter the opposition of Whigs, Liberty men, and contumacious Democrats. When they mentioned the black suffrage proposition at all, it usually was in tones of thunderous condemnation.[62]

On April 6, 1847, Wisconsinites trooped to the polls and soundly rejected the constitution 20,233 to 14,116. Black suffrage fared no better. Only 69 percent of the men registering an opinion on the constitution bothered to cast a ballot on the question, and they defeated it 15,959 to 7,704.[63]

To no one's surprise, voters in the southwestern counties of Grant, Iowa, and Lafayette repudiated black enfranchisement overwhelmingly, 6,216 to 205. Further east, in the lakeshore counties of Washington, Milwaukee, and Manitowoc, strongholds of foreign-born citizens, nearly 2,500 ballots were counted against black voting rights and only 700 in favor, with most of the prosuffrage support coming from the city of Milwaukee, which still boasted a significant Yankee population.[64] Dane and Green counties in southcentral Wisconsin, which were the destination of increasing numbers of foreigners and which lay contiguous to the lead district and remained under its influence both politically and socially, also provided heavy anti-suffrage majorities.[65]

Prosuffrage sentiment was concentrated largely in the southeastern counties of Racine, Walworth, and Waukesha. Those Yankee enclaves accounted for 44 percent of the pro-black vote, while Fond du Lac, Dodge, and Jefferson counties, likewise settled mainly by natives of New York and New England, but lately joined by many Germans, also gave small majorities in favor of the proposition.[66]

An analysis of the 1847 referendum returns and the 1848 governor's contest furnishes insight into the partisan responses to the suffrage question (see tables 1 and 24).[67] True to their party's principles, Liberty men overwhelmingly favored black political rights. At its peak between 1847 and 1848, the party had won the allegiance of just over one thousand men, virtually all of whom recorded prosuffrage ballots. Whigs furnished about half of the prosuffrage total, Democrats almost a third. The higher level of Whig support coincided with the party's response to race-related issues in other Northern states and with the editorial favor a few southeastern newspapermen evinced.[68] A handful of nonaligned men also seem to have contributed votes friendly to the proposition. As anticipated, more Democrats than Whigs opposed black voting, the former recording approximately three-fifths of the antisuffrage ballots, although proportionately, only slightly more Democrats expressed anti-black opinions.[69]

Among the nearly eleven thousand men who abstained on the suffrage question, Democrats outnumbered Whigs two to one. In part, the abstention rate can be attributed to the roll-off phenomenon common to referenda, particularly when a proposition is submitted on a separate ballot. This was the case in 1847. Other nonvoters, unable to reconcile the principle of political equality with their racist attitudes, chose to take no position on the question. Finally, the greater Democratic abstention rate might have been the result of the reticence of most party leaders and editors.[70]

The black suffrage debates and popular vote graphically illustrated that most white men did not consider the issue important enough to abandon traditional party ties or readjust values, whatever they thought about blacks or slavery. Indeed, the debates revealed that racist attitudes prevailed even among supporters of black enfranchisement. Edward Whiton summed up this seeming contradiction when he observed that it was not a question of whether all of the human race were of

> the same common stock. . . . An answer to that question would in no manner change the rights of the parties concerned . . . if it were conceded that though they were black, they were nevertheless men . . . [then] they were entitled to all the privileges of the elective franchise as other men.[71]

Marshall Strong had said much the same thing when he earlier alleged that Norwegians occupied a lower rung in the scale of humanity than Wisconsin's blacks but nonetheless deserved the franchise.[72] In short, political and civil rights were perceived as quite distinct from personal beliefs, and the dilemma confronting many Wisconsinites was whether blacks were entitled to political equality in spite of their alleged inferiority. The 1847 referendum demonstrated that in most cases racist attitudes prevailed over egalitarian principles.

The rejection of the constitution did not diminish Wisconsin's desire for statehood. At the behest of Governor Henry Dodge, a special session of the legislature met in October and scheduled an election for delegates to a new convention that would assemble in mid-December. The Whigs hoped that hostility to the continuing Mexican War, President James K. Polk's veto of a much desired rivers and harbors bill and widespread dissatisfaction with the unseemly behavior of many Democrats at the first meeting would help boost their representation.[73] In September, their spirits were raised when John Tweedy bested Moses M. Strong in the race for Congress to become the first Whig to win a territory-wide election. Anticipating defeat, Tweedy had absented himself from the territory on personal business during the campaign. Moreover, late in the contest, Beriah Brown, the sharp-tongued editor of Madison's *Wisconsin Democrat*, distributed a broadside throughout the western counties in which Tweedy, by virtue of his support for black suffrage at the convention, was characterized as "the champion of the abolitionists" and an enemy of the Union. Not to be outdone, an industrious Grant County Whig circulated a leaflet that described

Strong's resolution to allow black office holding as evidence of his support for black equality, concealing, of course, his motive for introducing the measure.[74]

Tweedy's unexpected victory gave the territory's Whigs ample reason to rejoice, although astute political observers noted that many eastern Democrats disliked Strong intensely and decided to sit out the election rather than vote for him.[75] Indeed, the most noteworthy aspect of the congressional election was the precipitous decline in voter participation. Sixty-four percent of the eligible electorate had participated in April's vote on the constitution, fewer than 40 percent bothered to cast ballots for a territorial representative. So Tweedy's success resulted more from Democratic apathy and disaffection rather than from a sudden conversion to Whiggery.

Nevertheless, in a campaign that was a model of propriety compared to the first one, the Whigs improved their standing significantly, electing twenty-three of the sixty-nine delegates to the second convention.[76] This air of decorum carried over into the convention itself, which was far more disciplined and workmanlike than its predecessor. Although sharp debates were common, delegates showed a marked willingness to compromise on disputed points by removing or modifying the objectionable features of the first document, and subordinating partisanship to their desire to shape a suitable constitution.[77] That reasonable atmosphere extended to discussions of the black suffrage issue.

Two weeks after the start of the convention, a motion to remove the word white from the proposed suffrage article was rejected without debate, although supporters mustered a respectable twenty-two votes in its favor.[78] Experience Estabrook, a Walworth County Democrat, then recommended that the state legislature be empowered to enfranchise blacks at its discretion. Territorial lawmakers already possessed this authority, he explained, and his proposal would permit the state to act just as expeditiously whenever the people requested the change. Moreover, a grant of legislative authority would avoid troublesome referenda and the time-consuming procedures necessary to amend the constitution. Estabrook also remarked that he had upheld the whites-only clause in deference to popular opinion, but if a majority came to favor the abolition of "this odious distinction," it should not be held in check by constitutional prohibitions. Majority rule was the true issue indeed, others acknowledged, adding that many men favored eradicating the color line in voting booths due to their democratic principles and not because they were abolitionists.[79]

Opponents of Estabrook's measure turned his majoritarian principles around and asserted that democracy would be poorly served if the convention should in any way countenance black suffrage, given the recent expression of popular opinion. It was more important to fashion an acceptable constitution, they maintained, than to encumber it with provisions likely to bring about its rejection.[80]

After some confusion, the delegates voted down Estabrook's amendment by a slim thirty-five to thirty-four margin.[81] Once again, party affiliation played a minor role in the decision of individual delegates to support or oppose the measure. The Whigs split fourteen to nine in favor of the proposal, while the Democrats voted twenty-three to twenty against it.[82] All nine opposition Whigs and sixteen of the twenty-three antisuffrage Democrats represented areas that had returned heavy antisuffrage majorities in April. A few Democrats from prosuffrage districts, like Augustus C. Kinnie from Sugar Creek in Walworth County, bucked "the expressed opinion of their particular constituents," insisting that they "should be governed by the will of the . . . whole territory" rather than local prejudices. Several members from closely divided areas probably followed their own personal predilections and cast negative ballots.[83] The prosuffrage vote followed a similar pattern, with most members strictly adhering to home sentiment. A handful of Whigs and Democrats, most notably Rufus King and James T. Lewis, ignored local opinion and voted in favor of black suffrage.[84]

The attempt to provide for future black enfranchisement without having to secure a constitutional amendment continued despite the defeat of Estabrook's resolution. George Gale, Walworth County's leading Whig, proposed that the legislature submit the suffrage question to the voters every four years. Upon gaining popular approval, blacks would be authorized "to vote for all offices, and be eligible for all offices that [are] elective." The office-holding clause was included in good faith, Gale noted, and not "for the purpose of making the subject odious," as Moses Strong had done in the previous meeting.[85]

After removing the extraneous office-holding stipulation and empowering the legislature to extend the vote to blacks at any time, subject to popular consent, Gale's amendment passed thirty-seven to twenty-nine. Five Democrats who had voted against Estabrook's proposal switched their stance and helped carry the measure, while only two delegates who had favored it, including Gale, who was upset with the changes made in his compromise formula, moved into opposition.[86] Louis P. Harvey, former editor of the Whig *Southport American* and now a Rock County representative, probably provoked the Democratic shift when he warned that the revised article "went to the utmost limits of concession," and further modification or rejection would instigate a renewal of the agitation.[87] After deleting the words "colored suffrage" to make the substitute more broadly acceptable, it was adopted overwhelmingly. In its final form the article read:

> That the legislature may at any time extend by law the right of suf-frage to persons not herein enumerated; but no such law shall be in force until the same shall have been submitted to a vote of the people at a general election, and approved by a majority of all the votes cast at such election.[88]

Rufus King introduced the only other black rights issue to come before the convention when he requested that the judiciary committee consider incorporating into the Wisconsin bill of rights an article that prohibited all state and local officials from offering official assistance "for the arrest and imprisonment of any person claimed as a fugitive from slavery."[89] King's proposal closely resembled the policy of state noncooperation in the rendi-tion of runaway slaves that Massachusetts and Pennsylvania had enacted into law following the 1842 decision of the United States Supreme Court in the case of *Prigg v. Pennsylvania;* however, his wish to include it in Wis-consin's bill of rights represented a sharp break with precedent.[90] Edward Whiton, now a well-known champion of black equality and one of the most respected lawyers in the territory, backed King and argued that the article was both constitutional and proper and was worthy of the conven-tion's serious consideration. Although the judiciary committee adopted the resolution, it issued no recommendation and the matter died.[91]

On February 1, 1848, Wisconsin's second constitutional convention adjourned. Popular discussion of the proposed charter suggested that most people were satisfied with its work.[92] Only the Liberty party broke through the chorus of praise to condemn "the God-dishonoring, liberty-hating, man-crushing document" for harboring the "infamously black word white."[93] But little other opposition surfaced, and Wisconsinites rati-fied the second constitution 16,759 to 6,384. On May 28, 1848, President Polk signed the bill admitting Wisconsin into the Union.[94]

Although the new state's blacks failed to win political equality, they still possessed greater legal rights than their fellows in most other Northern states.[95] They were allowed to accumulate property, serve on juries, hold public and private meetings, petition the legislature, testify against whites, send their children to public schools, pursue any occupation, and marry whom they chose. And since blacks were excluded from the polls and ineligible to serve in the state militia, they also were exempt from the poll tax payable in labor from all male citizens and from service with local road crews.[96] Moreover, by confronting Wisconsinites with the incongruity between their republican professions and their racial prejudices, Liberty men, along with like-minded Whigs and Democrats, made future black enfranchisement a less cumbersome process than it otherwise might have been.[97] Still, both blacks and abolitionists were disappointed in the convention's refusal to adopt equal suffrage. Marginal political support and the defeat of the principle epitomized the frustration Liberty enthusiasts experienced throughout the North in the years before statehood. Whigs and Democrats treated them seriously only when their votes could spell the difference between victory or defeat; otherwise they were met with indifference or scorn.

Yet, the Liberty party's real importance lay in devising a convincing legal and constitutional method of abolishing slavery, which in modified form would be embraced by succeeding antislavery coalitions. And in states such as Wisconsin, where most residents disapproved of slavery as a matter of principle, even if they failed to sustain it in practice, it was hoped that changed circumstances eventually would bring about the triumph of Liberty ideals. In the year Wisconsin joined the Union, events appeared to be moving in a favorable direction.

CHAPTER THREE

This Movement Is More Radical Than the Leaders Themselves Dare Avow

In MAY 1846, the United States declared war on Mexico. Three months later, David Wilmot, one of several northern Democratic congressmen upset with the economic and patronage policies of President James K. Polk's administration, as well as their party's increasingly pro-Southern tilt, offered an amendment to a presidential request for an appropriation with which to negotiate a territorial cession from Mexico. If passed, the Wilmot Proviso would have banned slavery from any land acquired from Mexico in the peace treaty. The proviso, along with antiwar sentiment and intraparty feuds, combined to politicize sectional jealousies and ignited a revolt among antislavery Democrats and Whigs throughout the North that led to the formation of the Free Soil party.[1]

Throughout 1846 and 1847, Wisconsinites were engrossed in the statehood question and manifested only passing concern with outside events. Yet the intensifying sectional controversy left its mark. The territory's Liberty men branded the Mexican War as a Southern-instigated land grab designed to expand and perpetuate slavery, and they applauded the nation's growing hostility to its spread. Although the Wilmot Proviso fell far short of their more comprehensive antislavery policy, it was considered a significant step toward "concerting and prosecuting measures for [slavery's] speedy overthrow."[2]

Meanwhile, outside Wisconsin, a number of Liberty party chieftains were searching for a credible presidential candidate for the upcoming election in 1848. John P. Hale was their favorite. An antislavery Democrat from New Hampshire, Hale had broken with his party over the Texas annexation and Mexican War issues and won election to the United States Senate with the support of Democrats, Whigs, and Liberty men. In October 1847, Liberty delegates from all the Northern states met in Buffalo and chose the reluctant Granite State politician as their standard-bearer.[3]

Hale's nomination satisfied most party members, but many in Wisconsin criticized the Buffalo convention for not selecting a known Liberty party leader. Reflecting this sentiment, the *American Freeman* cheerlessly placed Hale's name at the head of its column but refused to be considered pledged, although about one-third of Wisconsin's political abolitionists felt Hale's thunderous attacks on slavery in the Senate justified his selection. At a tumultuous meeting in January 1848, the two sides adopted a compromise resolution that applauded his stance and promised to back him wholeheartedly if he would publicly espouse Liberty principles.[4]

Smoldering party divisions flared up again in April. At the territorial Liberty Convention, friends of Hale attempted without success to win his endorsement. Then, five days after the meeting broke up, defiant Liberty men from several northern counties reconvened in Fond du Lac and pledged their support to the congenial New Hampshire man.[5]

By early summer, the battle over Hale's fitness as a candidate dwindled in importance as a movement to unite the North's antislavery forces on a platform of slavery restriction gathered momentum. New York's Barnburner Democrats, dissatisfied with their party's nomination of Lewis Cass for president, chose former president Martin Van Buren to head their ticket, adopted a strongly worded pro–Wilmot Proviso platform and invited all opponents of slavery's extension to join them. Conscience Whigs in Massachusetts, Ohio, and elsewhere in the North reacted similarly after their party nominated the Louisiana slaveholder Zachary Taylor for president. To cap things off, Ohio's Liberty leaders, in league with antiextensionists from other parties, called for a nonpartisan national convention to meet at Buffalo on August 9 and 10.[6]

Wisconsin's political abolitionists responded cautiously to the proposed meeting. Amidst rumors that a coalition was in the offing, the same April convention that declined to embrace Hale also unanimously rejected a resolution "to unite with any and all parties who will pledge themselves to carry out the Wilmot Proviso."[7] As the prospects for an antislavery union brightened, Liberty men began to have second thoughts. Edward D. Holton, the influential Milwaukee businessman whose antislavery credentials were unimpeachable, privately worried that unless the North forged "a thorough and effective organization . . . to resist the encroachments of the slave power," Southern determination inevitably would carry slavery into the newly acquired territories of California and New Mexico, with calamitous consequences for the nation's future. As such, he ruefully concluded, the weak, largely ineffective Liberty party must give way to a broader movement. Public rumblings intimated that most Liberty supporters now shared Holton's anxiety, if not his disposition toward a coalition. Accordingly, as June drew to a close, party chairman Charles Durkee asked antislavery partisans to assemble in Southport on July 19 to hammer out a response to the Buffalo invitation.[8]

Bucking the coalition movement, the *American Freeman,* now published in Milwaukee under the direction of Sherman M. Booth, urged Wisconsin's Liberty men to reject the Wilmot Proviso because its adoption would permit "slavery to live and run riot forever throughout the entire South." Sharply criticizing the Ohio abolitionists who had issued the Buffalo call, Booth argued that the Liberty organization had been founded "not simply to prevent the further *growth* of slavery, but to *put it out of existence.* . . . The reasons adduced in favor of restricting slavery, apply with tenfold force in favor of abolishing it." And regarding Durkee's request for the Southport meeting, the editor cynically replied:

Let us have a full representation so that if we have *principles* to *sell,* we can make a *clean transfer,* and renounce all pretensions hereafter to the name of Liberty party. If expediency and not principle is hereafter to govern, let us say so boldly, and make the best bargain we can *openly.* That will be *free trade* with a vengeance.[9]

An active abolitionist for a dozen years, the passionate Booth had arrived in Milwaukee on May 19, 1848, just ten days before statehood.

Thirty-six years of age, a New York native, and a Yale graduate, he had helped organize the Liberty party in Connecticut with his friend Ichabod Codding. A sharp businessman and a forceful, eloquent, and engaging writer, Booth would soon turn the *American Freeman* into one of the most popular and profitable newspapers in the state and establish himself as its most influential antislavery leader. Unfortunately, as his first month in the editorial chair indicated, Booth also was contentious, domineering, and tactless in dealing with friend and foe alike, and his personal behavior was far from beyond reproach. By early July, his angry, uncompromising remarks and his alleged support of federal abolition of slavery in the Southern states themselves brought forth cries for his removal from the paper. Fearful that Booth represented a threat to the party's already fragile unity, the state's Liberty leaders asked him to spell out party principles as he understood them; if his ideas proved unsound, presumably he would be shunned by the state organization.[10]

Taking the hint, Booth denied that he favored direct federal intervention with slavery in the Southern states and dutifully recited his devotion to orthodox Liberty doctrines. Nevertheless, he repeated his objection to the proposed free soil alliance because it appeared to rely on the Wilmot Proviso to the exclusion of all other Liberty principles, particularly those that advocated a complete separation of the federal government from slavery and the bestowal of "equal rights . . . to all men of whatever color or condition." Adopt those and he gladly would entertain fusion.[11]

Booth's response appeased Liberty coalitionists and helped avert a confrontation at Southport. Indeed, delegates attending the two-day session agreed to participate in the Buffalo meeting almost without debate and with only one dissenting vote, although lengthy heated discussions erupted pertaining to the conditions necessary to secure their approval of its proceedings. In the end, they defeated a resolution that linked resistance to slavery's expansion with federal nonintervention and instead passed a substitute introduced by Booth that proclaimed: "The Liberty party of Wisconsin can sustain no candidate for the Presidency or Vice-Presidency except those who are not only pledged against the extension of slavery, but are also committed to the policy of abolishing it, and of protecting the equal rights of all."[12]

Since Liberty dogma equated abolishing slavery with the withdrawal of federal sustenance from it, both resolutions actually conveyed the same meaning. More important, coalitionists were put on notice that a clear commitment to slavery's eventual destruction, and not simply to the Wilmot Proviso, would be necessary to win Liberty favor.[13] In addition, although not explicitly stated, Wisconsin's abolitionists expected the Buffalo convention to endorse black equality.

The Southport get-together adjourned in good spirits. No longer burdened by indecision and discord, Liberty men grew more appreciative of the prospective union as the Buffalo meeting neared. Even Booth, though still a bit wary, approvingly wrote of coalition spokesmen now openly discussing "the evils of slavery in all its phases . . . as a thing accursed and doomed to destruction." He concluded, "This movement is more radical at the bottom, than the outward manifestation of it—than the leaders themselves dare avow."[14]

The events of 1846–1848 also had a significant impact on Wisconsin's Whigs and compelled them to reconsider the place of slavery in their hierarchy of values. Polk's unabashed drive for Mexican territory appalled them, and they denounced the war in terms similar to those Liberty men employed. As one Whig concisely put it, "The present war is for the sole purpose of perpetuating slavery."[15]

In their criticism of the Administration's war policy, Whigs were careful to support measures designed to bring the war to a successful and honorable close. But they steadfastly insisted that slavery must be outlawed from all territory squeezed from Mexico, and they expressed determination to arrest its spread despite threats to the Union. "The question of the extension or non-extension of slave territory is now made emphatically *the question*," the state's Whigs proclaimed in 1848. "Regret it as we do—deplorable as it is, it is an issue between the North and South . . . between the Whig and Democratic parties, and whatever may be its consequences upon the Union of the States and government, *it must be met*."[16]

Whigs attached great importance to antiextension for several reasons. For one, many considered "the old issues which divided the parties . . . dead." Election rhetoric notwithstanding, the passage of the Walker tariff in 1846 signalled the abandonment of protection and the acceptance of duties for revenue only. Moreover, no one seriously hoped to resurrect the national bank, general laws of incorporation were becoming standard practice, a mixed currency found wide approval, and all parties in Wisconsin supported government appropriations for internal improvements.[17] Consequently, Whigs, for reasons of political expediency and principal alike, reordered their priorities.

Equally important, slavery's presence in America had always troubled Northern Whigs more than Democrats,[18] and this split carried over into Wisconsin. Slavery, Whigs maintained, was "utterly inconsistent with the principles of free government and incompatible with the interests and prosperity of free institutions." They had tolerated its continued existence, however, out of respect for the constitutional compromises relating to the peculiar institution and the "sacred and inviolable" rights of the states. Furthermore, since Great Britain had forced slavery on America, compassion for the people who shouldered the "dreadful black burden" demanded that antislavery impulses be restrained. Yet, Whig endurance had been predicated on the assumption that "the patriotism and philanthropy of the American people" and enlightened public sentiment eventually would bring about slavery's peaceful extirpation. It was clear now that in this notion they had been mistaken. Unless Southern leaders were stopped, Whigs claimed, they would continue to hatch plans to extend slavery and seek permanent control of the federal government. Levi Alden, a staunch Rock County Whig, summed up the significance of the slavery extension issue when he wrote that it would be "more decisive of the future . . . of this country—of its future prosperity—in fact of its very existence politically, than any which has ever before been agitated." And, while neither Alden nor any other Whig wanted to increase sectional animosity,

> It had become impossible for the North any longer to be a willing, or even a tacit participator in the extension of slavery. . . . [The Northern States] have already indulged the South too much in this particular—they have compromised principle . . . until to do so anymore would . . . be criminal. . . . It is time for the North to speak out on this subject, her fiat should be put calmly yet firmly and unalterably that she will not permit any further extension of slavery while her States remain an integral part of this Union. And if this question becomes an issue between the North and the South, the sooner it becomes so the better.[19]

Yet to suppose that Wisconsin's Whigs believed disunion to be inevitable, or that they no longer sought to cooperate with the South, would be wrong. They firmly believed that the South stood to lose more from a divided Union than the North did; a spirit of mutual understanding would serve to mitigate sectional tensions and in time would accomplish the goal of preventing slavery's spread. Therefore, confident that moderates prevailed in the slave states, Whigs advised Northerners to overlook the secessionist cries certain to flow from the mouths of Southern hotheads if their schemes to expand slavery failed. Present a firm, united front on the extension issue, Whigs predicted, and self-interest and popular opinion would oblige refractory slaveholders to return to their senses.[20]

A keen awareness of prickly Southern honor and political reality in the slave states also balanced the resolve of the Whigs. To a man, they affirmed that the Constitution empowered Congress to prohibit slavery in the territories. Nevertheless, for the sake of national peace, most were willing to waive the Wilmot Proviso if an intersectional accord to circumscribe slavery could be worked out. Accommodationist Whigs actually cheered Taylor's nomination as a step in the right direction. The Louisianan's expressed disinclination to use the veto, coupled with Northern control of Congress and Southern Unionism, they rationalized, would temper Southern fears of a direct federal attack on slavery and lead to its confinement. Yet, if their optimism proved to be unrealistic and sectional amity deteriorated, Whigs were prepared to resist slavery's advance at all costs, content that they had gone as far as they could to reconcile each section's needs without further compromising principle or the national interest.[21]

Along with other Northern party men, Wisconsin's Whigs occupied a difficult position. Faced with the declining relevance of the old issues, they banked their party's future on its ability to achieve a satisfactory solution to the problem of slavery; ultimately the extension issue amounted to just that. To arrest slavery's growth, in their view, meant in due course to kill it. But if slave state associates refused to work with them, or if other Northern Whigs succumbed to Southern threats, they would be confronted with the choice to compromise or quit the party. The Whig dilemma suggests the enormous difficulty of harmonizing profoundly held but contradictory principles and loyalties. Desperate to preserve national and party unity and avoid sectional extremism if possible, Whigs at the same time were determined to stand firm on the grave question that faced the country. Within a few years, the course of events would oblige them to embrace straightforward sectional politics and finally resolve those conflicting values, but in 1848, most Whigs continued to adapt their antislavery ideology to the demands of majoritarian politics and party loyalty.[22]

Wisconsin's Democrats also struggled with the extension issue, although they defended Polk's war and regarded the exaction of territory from

Mexico as just compensation for having drawn the United States into the struggle. Still, supporting the war did not mean approving slavery's spread. Quite the opposite. "A very proper distinction" must be made, declared William Cramer of Milwaukee's *Weekly Wisconsin*, "between the annexation of Texas with slavery then and there existing, and its extension to new territory, where it does not now exist."[23] Yet, while the war dragged on, the state party generally refrained from committing itself to a specific policy with respect to the extension question for fear of running afoul of the Polk administration. Indeed, in March 1848, Democrats successively tabled a pro–Wilmot Proviso resolution introduced in the legislature and "hooted down" a motion to endorse the principle at their state convention.[24]

Simmering tensions finally surfaced two months later when the Democrats nominated Lewis Cass for president and, indirectly at least, subscribed to his doctrine of popular sovereignty. As enunciated by the Michigan Democrat in December 1847, popular sovereignty meant allowing the citizens of each territory to settle the question of slavery themselves. Even if Congress had control over slavery in the territories, Cass maintained, exercising that power would be inadvisable, even oppressive. Democrats concerned about the extension controversy's potential impact on sectional relations and their personal and party fortunes found popular sovereignty appealing. It seemed an eminently reasonable solution to the slavery problem that promised, if accepted by the North and South, to remove the issue from Congress and reunite the Democracy's warring factions. Moreover, since popular sovereignty did not specify at what point in territorial development the people might make their determination, it permitted party leaders in both sections to manipulate it to their best advantage.[25]

Nevertheless, Wisconsin's Democrats gave Cass a lukewarm reception. Some, like Horace Tenney, editor of Madison's *Wisconsin Argus,* strongly affirmed Congress's absolute constitutional authority to regulate territorial affairs and to prohibit or authorize slavery as it saw fit. A longtime foe of slavery, Tenney supported the Wilmot Proviso and doubted that popular sovereignty alone would guarantee freedom in the territories.[26] Still other Democrats resented Cass's opposition to federally financed internal improvements, deemed vital in a frontier state,[27] and the role he played in denying former president Martin Van Buren renomination in 1844. Beriah Brown, Tenney's crosstown rival, and still an influential party editor and an inveterate enemy of "abolitionist fanatics," scolded the nominee's critics and assailed the Wilmot Proviso as "a mere abstraction," "a dangerous

{ *Political Abolitionism in Wisconsin, 1840–1861* }

humbug." The Constitution did not empower Congress to enact legislation regarding slavery in either the states or the territories, he alleged. Final jurisdiction rested with the people, and local law rather than congressional fiat, with one exception, in fact had determined the status of slavery in the past. This practice, Brown believed, ought to be retained.[28] Most Democrats ultimately joined Brown and endorsed popular sovereignty for practical reasons. The Wilmot Proviso, reasoned Green Bay's Charles D. Robinson, whether constitutional or not, "draws a line directly between the free and slave states, and its advocates declare for and seek an issue between the North and South"; therefore its implementation would be an unsound, possibly dangerous policy. Better to rely on popular sovereignty than personal preference, he cautioned, and trust actual settlers to keep slavery within its present bounds.[29]

Whatever their differences, most Cass Democrats, hoping to limit defections to the prospective Free Soil union, expressed confidence in popular sovereignty's capacity to check slavery's advance and keep their party and the nation united. Several reasons account for their optimism. In 1829, Mexico had abolished slavery in the territory later ceded to the United States. Therefore, Cass men argued, since all laws in place at the time of the American conquest remained in force, free soil rebels were importuning Congress to proscribe "an evil which exists in reality, only in their hot bed brains!" Slavery had never taken root in free territory, party loyalists insisted, and nothing suggested that circumstances would be different in the Mexican cession. Finally, if additional assurances were needed, the harsh climate and barren terrain prevailing in the newly acquired lands was incompatible with plantation agriculture and forever would prevent the establishment of slavery.[30]

A few defenders of congressional sovereignty advanced a slightly different argument to justify their endorsement of Cass. With the former Mexican territory already free by law, they claimed, slavery could be admitted only by affirmative action of the federal government. Consequently, as long as the North held the balance of power in Congress, slavery would be kept out, since congressional inaction would be tantamount to preserving the status quo, freedom. For this reason, these Cass supporters criticized Democratic insurgents for unnecessarily upsetting party harmony, asserting that a congressional ban was unnecessary, unwise, and impolitic.[31]

Finally, in a practical bid to retain the allegiance of the party's antislavery faction and to rebuild its tarnished image after earlier repudiating the Wilmot Proviso, Wisconsin's Democratic-controlled legislature in June overwhelmingly passed a free soil resolution. In addition, it instructed Wisconsin's first United States senators to use their influence to prevent the introduction of slavery into the national domain.[32]

Although Cass Democrats in Wisconsin went to great lengths to build a case for party solidarity on the antiextension principle and to publicly avow their opposition to slavery,[33] they steadfastly refused to provoke the South and clearly placed a higher value on reconciling national differences than on directly acting upon their antislavery beliefs. Indeed, the transcendent importance of the Union, more than anything else, kept Wisconsin's Democratic party from shattering in 1848. Time and again, its chief spokesmen reproved disenchanted party men for needlessly fanning sectional passions by demanding the rigid application of the Wilmot Proviso and threatening to build up a Northern antislavery party. Not only did these "politically insane" renegades exhibit a "criminal disregard for the rights, interests, and feelings of our Southern brethren," they brazenly ignored the risk that their actions might lead to a bloody civil war. All things considered, most Cass partisans, though they truly wished to bottle up slavery, concluded that the peace and harmony of the Union were far more important than slavery's prohibition from New Mexico and upper California or "its total extinction in the South."[34]

Despite the efforts of party regulars to discourage apostasy, numerous Democrats jumped on the free soil bandwagon. Marshall M. Strong, the sometime friend of black equality, believed that the perpetuation of America's free institutions depended upon the success of the budding antislavery union. "We are in a second revolution," he wrote, "and it devolves upon us to carry out the cause of liberty . . . commenced by our fathers to [bring about] the downfall of slavery everywhere."[35] Strong, who alone had denounced his party's designs on Texas four years earlier, now voiced sentiments many Democrats shared. Local party leaders from the southeast, including Warren Chase, Alexander Randall, James Bunner, and Christopher Sholes, repudiated Cass's nomination and bemoaned their party's failure to embrace the Wilmot Proviso. In addition to these seasoned antislavery Democrats, the free soil crusade won grudging converts like George W. Crabb, the virulently racist editor of the *Rock County Democrat*, who backed the movement only because Cass was clearly unpopular in his district and not because he wanted to change his party stripes. Indeed, by focusing primarily on slavery in the territories rather than on the institution itself, the Wilmot Proviso provided a platform broad enough to attract proponents of black equality, racists concerned mainly with the rights of white laborers, and men whose instincts were both anti-black and antislavery. Allow slavery to expand, some Free Soilers feared, and white workers would be barred from the West because of their unwillingness to toil alongside lowly blacks and their inability to compete with slave labor.[36] So the problem facing the proposed alliance in Wisconsin and elsewhere was to construct a platform and a working relationship satisfactory to the movement's various friends. A step in that direction occurred on July 26, when Democratic rebels and a handful of Liberty leaders and Whigs met in Janesville. In a cooperative spirit, they chose delegates to the Buffalo Free Soil convention.[37]

On August 9, some twenty thousand Free Soilers descended upon Buffalo. While antislavery orators stirred the assembled crowd, coalition leaders from all parties acted behind the scenes to strike an acceptable compromise. They arranged to nominate Martin Van Buren and the Massachusetts Whig Charles Francis Adams for the presidency and vice-presidency. In return, as Booth rejoiced, the delegates adopted a platform that was "all the Liberty party, as such, ever demanded." Although it did not forthrightly avow abolitionist intentions, the platform did endorse the principle of completely divorcing the federal government from slavery wherever it possessed the constitutional authority to do so. In addition, the convention advocated a congressional ban on slavery's spread and embraced the assumed policy of the founding fathers, "to limit, localize, and discourage slavery."[38]

On one important matter, Booth did exaggerate the continuity between the Liberty and Free Soil parties. In deference to prevailing racist attitudes, the Free Soil program deliberately avoided all mention of black rights. Still, it is easy to make too much of this tactical omission. Liberty men had always argued that moral suasion was the best antidote for racial prejudice and that discriminatory laws fell within the jurisdiction of each state. Consequently, these "remnants and effects of the Slave system" were individual and local, not national concerns. True, by evading the issue altogether, Free Soilers chose the expedient path and missed an opportunity to place the moral force of their party on the side of justice. Yet, disregarding the issue of black equality in the national platform was the only way the party could have brought together its diverse factions. Even so, the platform did not preclude state branches of the organization from taking up the question, and when Wisconsin's Free Soilers convened in late September to nominate presidential electors, they adopted a resolution that applauded Van Buren's "fidelity to the great principles of republican equality, displayed years ago in his advocacy of *free suffrage,* to the citizens of New York, irrespective of color." So, when Booth and other Liberty men claimed to have acted consistent with their principles after enrolling in the Free Soil army, they were largely correct.[39]

After returning from Buffalo, Wisconsin's Free Soilers entered the presidential campaign. As the only party expressly committed to the Wilmot Proviso, they had high hopes of capturing the votes of Wisconsinites determined to block slavery's advance. Indeed, their zeal and apparent vigor stunned their opponents, who appeared lethargic by comparison. As one Milwaukee Whig mournfully commented, "The free soilers . . . are making an impressive show of strength. . . . They feel confident of carrying the State and count up large majorities in all the South Eastern Counties. The Whigs and Cass men are very quiet and NOT enthusiastic for their cause."[40]

To counter Free Soil enthusiasm, both major parties tried to outdo each other in their antislavery professions. Whigs angrily upbraided Free Soilers for stealing their thunder and endeavoring "to ride into power on Whig principles." To prove the point, they nominated candidates for the state's congressional seats who were pledged to resist the extension of slavery. At the same time, local Whig clubs demanded that the Wilmot Proviso be rigidly applied even though the national organization officially stood uncommitted to it; in Columbia County, party men went so far as to endorse both Taylor and the Buffalo platform! Democrats displayed equally passionate devotion to the principle of curbing slavery's expansion, although in the second congressional district, which encompassed the southcentral and western counties, they foolishly dismissed the Wilmot Proviso as an "impracticable abstraction" and then kept silent on the question during the campaign. Other Democrats showed more discretion. Most ignored the Proviso but at least proclaimed their support for free territory.[41]

Zachary Taylor and the national Whig organization won the presidential chair, but Cass carried Wisconsin with 15,081 votes; Taylor and Van Buren trailed with 13,747 and 10,418, respectively. Of the Free Soil total, 49 percent came from the four predominantly Yankee counties in the southeast that made up the first congressional district,[42] and the vote was sufficient to elect the erstwhile Liberty leader, Charles Durkee, to the

United States House of Representatives. The second district contributed 24 percent of the Free Soil tally and the northern third 27 percent. Of the twenty-one counties included in the second and third districts, Rock, Jefferson, Dodge, and Fond du Lac, all Yankee strongholds, contributed 57 percent of the ballots won there by Van Buren. Thus, the Yankees of eastern Wisconsin provided nearly 80 percent of the Free Soilers' support, while areas containing foreign-born majorities and the lead district manifested little sympathy for the third party.[43]

An analysis of the partisan makeup of the Free Soil coalition, based upon the 1848 governor's contest and the presidential returns, reveals that over five thousand Democrats, 50 percent of the antislavery party's total vote, supported their old party chieftain Van Buren (see table 2). An unexpectedly large number of Whigs, about 3,300, also voted the Free Soil ticket, as did virtually all of the state's Liberty men and some 600 electors of unknown party background. The popular military hero Taylor also picked up the votes of about 1,250 Democrats, while Cass captured nearly twice as many gubernatorial abstainers as the Whigs.

In the state legislative races, Free Soil candidates won three senate and fifteen assembly seats, only one fewer in each case than the Whigs, but far below the Democracy's twelve and thirty-five places in the upper and lower houses respectively. Overall, the Free Soil showing in Wisconsin was impressive and attributable largely to Democratic alienation from the national organization, its distinct antislavery message, and growing exasperation with Southern dictation of national affairs.

If one simply equates antiextension with antislavery sympathies, all three parties in Wisconsin seemed equally opposed to slavery. But neither major party officially endorsed the Proviso, and Cass Democrats in particular, while insisting that "we are all free soilers," qualified their stand with an unwavering Unionism. Many Whigs, on the other hand, although they hoped their statesmen would rise above sectional prejudices and bring about a mutually satisfactory solution to the territorial debate, were prepared to face down the South rather than give in to its proslavery demands. Consequently, even though most stood by their party in 1848, unconvinced that a more confrontational approach was necessary, Whigs seemed like better prospects for a future antislavery coalition.[44]

In contrast to their opponents, Free Soilers offered an easily distinguishable antislavery program and ideology. With the old issues obsolete, they maintained, "the only practical political question now . . . is whether . . .

slavery shall be extended into territory now free." Although their national platform said nothing about abolition, Wisconsin's Free Soilers repeatedly made it clear that their success not only would prevent slavery's spread, but also seal its doom in the Southern states. Consequently, Christopher Sholes wrote, "We are abolitionists."[45]

Without question, enmity toward slavery constituted the essence of Free Soil ideology. Free Soilers called slavery "a sin," "a deplorable evil," "a great wrong upon the rights of man . . . [and] our republican institutions," whose early end was eagerly anticipated. Consistent with widespread popular sentiment, they agreed it was a local institution beyond the reach of federal power, but insisted that the nation's founders had tolerated slavery's prolongation under the firm belief that its death was inescapable and that their program sought only to complete this grand object.[46]

Free Soilers similarly believed that emphasizing slavery restriction rather than straightforward abolitionism made practical sense because it presented Northern voters with a way to attack slavery without violating the "sacred compromises of the constitution." Still, as they tirelessly explained, the substantive issue transcended the mere extension or nonextension of slavery; the very future of the nation hung in the balance. "The question . . . involve[s] the continued existence of the republic," they affirmed, because "if an evil as great as . . . slavery is allowed to spread itself wherever it chooses . . . [it] must destroy the foundation and fabric of our government."[47]

The antislavery convictions of Free Soilers were closely related to their view that the operation of republican principles in the North had given rise to a prosperous and dynamic region of enterprising freemen. This contrasted with the South, where the deadening influence of slavery had bred "sloth, listlessness . . . inequality . . . and the general social disparities of the worn out governments" of decadent Europe. Because of their differences, a collision was inevitable. "Republicanism and slavery cannot exist together," Free Soilers solemnly declared, and the American people at some point would be forced to choose between the two. For that reason, slavery must not be permitted to move West with the national government's acquiescence, if not its formal approval; otherwise the South soon would "rule the country for slavery and spread it . . . where it pleases." The only alternatives for Northerners then would be submission or revolution.[48]

Faced with such a grave prospect, Free Soilers scolded timid antislavery men who remained incapable of abandoning longstanding party ties. Democrats especially incurred their wrath. Their reliance on popular sovereignty and natural and Mexican laws to keep the territories free bordered on sheer lunacy. Such laws had not prevented slaveholders from illegally moving to Texas with their human chattels, Free Soilers reminded all who would listen, and did anyone really think they would behave differently in New Mexico and California? Besides, the South never had required federal legislation creating slavery in the national domain, it had asked only that the territories be organized without reference to the institution. With the question left open, Southerners undoubtedly would carry their bondsmen west. And, once established, slavery became untouchable as its needs shaped territorial institutions and drove free laborers out. Before long, "slave state after slave state will come thundering at the door of the Union for admission," Free Soilers warned, and Congress, having left the question in the hands of the people, would be obliged to receive them without protest. So enactment of the Wilmot Proviso was absolutely necessary, and to contend otherwise constituted an utter falsehood.[49]

Although the territorial question clearly dominated Free Soil thought, the party also exploited the growing antisouthernism of the electorate. "Has not the North suffered indignities enough to make the blood of the most phlegmatic boil?" Marshall Strong fumed. "Are we bound by party ties, when the South not only disregards them, but says [it] will violate acts of Congress, the Constitution, and even dissolve the Union? The path of duty . . . is as plain as a sunbeam to me. . . . [We must] put down forever this most damnable slavocracy." Many men shared Strong's animosity and expressed determination to resist the slave power's "insolence, arrogance and dictation."[50]

In their critique of slavery and defense of their national platform, Free Soilers were mindful of the concerns of self-interested whites. They cited southern laws and practices designed to protect slavery at the expense of individual and civil liberties and suggested the same fate would befall Northerners if the slave power gained ascendancy in the territories and the nation. For this reason, Wisconsin's major parties, especially the Democrats, were guilty of betraying the interests of free white laborers by resisting passage of the Wilmot Proviso and threatening to place them in direct contact and competition with slavery. Free Soilers also wooed voters indifferent to the plight of the nation's blacks by advocating free homesteads. Christopher Sholes, the policy's chief proponent, deemed "every landless individual, every depressed laborer, every victim of the oppressions of monopoly, every immigrant . . . seeking a home within our limits" entitled to free land. If adopted along with the rigid restriction of slavery, he vowed, homestead legislation would prevent large accumulations of property, help build up a nation of independent freeholders and cripple the plantation system and other forms of land monopoly. At the same time, it would close the gap between rich and poor, substitute free for slave labor, and lead to the speedy emancipation of America's slaves.[51] While implicitly pandering to the racial prejudices of potential converts, the Free Soil cry for free land nevertheless plainly linked white self-interest with black freedom, just as the Liberty party had. So, whether they wanted to or not, Free Soilers warred on behalf of the nation's blacks.

The decision of Free Soil Whigs and Democrats to join Liberty men in a sectional political coalition also signalled for many the abandonment of uncritical Unionism. They realized agitation might produce serious consequences, but they questioned the wisdom of preserving a Union devoid of its moral basis and decried the "blind idolatry" of those who overlooked the injustices committed in its name. Like the Whigs, Free Soilers doubted that the South would ever dissolve the Union; but, they insisted, slavery compromises no longer were possible, and no amount of intimidation would abate their resolve to place slavery on the road to extinction. If disunion should result, so be it. As a chastened Christopher Sholes now wrote:

> Of what possible use can be our Union, when all the objects for which that Union was conceived have been sacrificed. . . . If nonsense and highfalutin about stars, stripes, glorious constellations, and all that kind of trash will save the Union, this editor can bear it all upon his own shoulders, but we apprehend the welfare and happiness of the people depends on a Union which requires a different kind of Savior. . . . If the Government is to be overrode by Slavery—if it is to be administered for the benefit of a slave aristocracy and labor is to be crushed and degraded and ground to the earth—it is a matter of very little importance to the great masses whether it is under . . . or out of the Union. Instead of the Union first—the Union last—the Union forever, we should cry, *Freedom* first—Freedom last and Freedom forever! Freedom is the *soul,* the Union is the form, and we had better seek to preserve the soul pure, then we may rest with confidence that the form will correspond.[52]

With few exceptions, Liberty men and Free Soilers held remarkably similar attitudes toward slavery and favored identical programs to eradicate it over time. Yet the territorial controversy did not give rise to the Free Soilers' antislavery attitudes; it reinforced preexisting ideals and provoked thousands of men to reorder their values.

In respect to blacks, both Liberty and Free Soil party men likewise found much to agree on, despite the fact that Free Soilers, unlike their predecessors, rarely discussed them publicly. Practical political considerations and the overwhelming importance of the extension issue prescribed caution. But most of Wisconsin's Free Soilers, when given the opportunity, countenanced measures aimed at mitigating black oppression. Nearly 68 percent of Van Buren's followers had cast prosuffrage ballots in the 1847 referendum, compared to 5 percent who opposed it and 27 percent who abstained on the question. Moreover, the Free Soil movement appears to have drained the Democracy of its entire free suffrage constituency, while the Whigs lost half of theirs, signifying that it attracted the state's least prejudiced and most ardent antislavery men (see table 3).[53] The prosuffrage bias within the party underscores the moral purpose underlying its crusade and contradicts the idea that bigotry and indifference to the suffering and oppression of blacks prevailed among its membership. Racism and apathy certainly existed, and these dulled the moral edge of the movement. But to an impressive extent, the high standards the Liberty party established remained intact.

CHAPTER FOUR

A Party Separate and Distinct

WISCONSIN'S FREE SOIL PARTY captured 28 percent of the votes cast for president in 1848, elected former Liberty man Charles Durkee to Congress, and won nineteen seats in the state legislature. Nationally, 10 percent of the voters sided with the Free Soilers, and only Massachusetts, Vermont, and New York approached the percentage total supplied by Wisconsin.[1] The third party's showing in the state stunned Whig and Democratic leaders, and shortly after the election they expressed interest in a merger. The Free Soilers encouraged them at their state convention on January 11, 1849, when they affirmed their readiness to unite and cooperate with any party or party members willing to adopt their principles. These included the Buffalo platform, "free and impartial suffrage," including "all men without distinction of color," as well as land limitation, free trade, direct taxation, popular election of all federal officers, and a reduction in America's military forces.[2]

The Whigs responded coolly to the invitation. The Free Soilers' slavery resolutions comprised sound Whig doctrine, agreed David Atwood, editor of the party's Madison organ, the *Wisconsin Express*. Other measures, however, especially the free trade and direct taxation planks, reflected the

55

party's largely Democratic makeup, and could never be countenanced by true Whigs.[3] The influence of former Democrats like Christopher Sholes and Warren Chase within the Free Soil party also bothered Whigs, especially after the warm reception it gave them at its January convention. Finally, basking in the glow of Taylor's success, in control of federal patronage, and convinced that the 1848 contest greatly rearranged party ties in Wisconsin, Whig leaders believed they might yet build an organization capable of successfully competing against the shaken but still formidable Democracy, without resort to any formal coalition.[4]

With Whigs out of the picture, Free Soilers were obliged to turn to the Democrats. At first, they had good reason to be hopeful. Party leaders, among them Moses M. Strong, agreed that Free Soilers and Democrats held many ideas in common and therefore must unite, a sentiment echoed by Democratic editors.[5] Only Beriah Brown publicly decried the fusion movement. Wisconsin's loyal Democrats had repudiated the Wilmot Proviso, he raged, and yet many party leaders were prepared to sell out to an abolitionist faction whose strictly sectional appeal threatened both national Democratic integrity and the safety of the Union. Those traitors, he admonished, must be firmly repudiated.[6]

Despite Brown's warning, the coalition movement gathered steam, and soon he was forced to soften his opposition. So, when the Free Soilers formally invited a merger in early January, the combative editor cheerfully agreed to cooperate, although he remained adamantly opposed to their antislavery platform.[7] Still, whatever their differences, all Democrats clearly agreed on at least one thing: The Free Soil organization would have to be dissolved in order to achieve a successful combination.[8] That was the situation when the state legislature convened in January.

The Free Soilers, or, as they now called themselves, the Free Democrats, wasted no time in testing the antislavery professions of the Cass Democrats. In mid-January, Samuel D. Hastings, an old Liberty man elected as a Free Soiler to the assembly, introduced a battery of antislavery resolutions. These instructed Wisconsin's United States senators and requested its House members to use their influence to completely disassociate the federal government from slavery, to oppose the admission of any more slave states, to ban the institution from all federal territories, and to disavow all legislation that favored slavery and slave labor over free labor. The ultimate goal of these measures, Hastings made plain, was gradually to rid the nation of that stain "upon our free institutions," slavery.[9]

On January 27, the assembly took up the Hastings resolutions. A united Democratic majority and the hopelessly divided Whigs immediately struck out the one on slavery and slave labor.[10] A short but heated debate followed over a Democratic amendment that asked Congress to indemnify slaveowners who voluntarily liberated their bondsmen and settled them in a portion of the Mexican cession to be set aside for their exclusive habitation. Enoch Chase, a Milwaukee Whig, condemned the measure as impractical and unjust, since free blacks had proved themselves to be conscientious members of their communities fully capable of living in harmony with whites. Slaveholder intentions to carry their bondsmen into the territories and to secure a stranglehold on the federal government constituted an issue of far greater importance, Chase declared, for if they succeeded in their plans, the Union would lose its value and inevitably shatter. Ignoring Chase's impassioned protest, Democrats and a handful of Whigs easily passed the compensated emancipation and colonization resolution.[11]

Two days later, John Wells, a Waukesha Free Soiler who on the earlier votes had sided with the Democrats, proposed a substitute to the Hastings resolutions. His proposal instructed Wisconsin's representatives to demand application of the Wilmot Proviso in the acts that organized the territories of California and New Mexico and to use their influence to prevent admission of new slave states and abolish slavery in the nation's capital. Eager to lay aside the slavery issue, the assembly speedily adopted the Wells substitute with only one dissenting vote.[12]

In the senate, a select committee on slavery modified the assembly's handiwork and called for the divorce of the federal government from slavery and its permanent confinement within the existing slave states, which won approval in a fourteen to two vote. Yet passage did not come easily, as conservative Democrats repeatedly tried to weaken the committee resolutions. The assembly later concurred thirty-four to twenty-four, although Democrats once again proved to be reluctant allies, opposing the senate version by a two-to-one margin.[13]

Democratic reliability on slavery issues received two further tests during the 1849 legislative session. In mid-March, Isaac P. Walker, one of Wisconsin's United States senators and a Democrat, provoked the state's lawmakers when he introduced a bill organizing the governments in California and New Mexico without reference to slavery. Overcoming the opposition of many Democrats, the assembly enacted a resolution that condemned Walker's action and demanded his resignation.[14] The Walker bill split Senate Democrats as well; when it passed ten to six, they cast five of the opposing ballots.[15] Finally, on a Free Soil bill to refer the question of black suffrage to the people, a majority of the Democratic legislators refused, and only undivided Free Soil support and help from friendly Whigs saved the measure.[16]

The ambivalent course of Assembly Democrats did not bode well for a union with Free Soilers. Christopher Sholes, elected to the state senate as a Free Soiler, expressed disgust at the attempts of Cass men to defeat the spirit of the Hastings resolutions. Booth, too, was aware of the Democracy's reluctance to take a bold antislavery stand. They had turned their eyes southward, he claimed, and would support only inoffensive declarations that did not "smack too much of *raw head and bloody boned Abolitionism.*"[17]

Despite their dissatisfaction with Democrats in the legislature, most Free Soilers believed that an acceptable union still might be possible. Democratic leaders, they realized, would have preferred to avoid the slavery issue, but they "dared not risk their popularity with the people." Thus they were forced to contend with the genuine concerns raised by the extension controversy and the popularity of the Free Soil appeal or, once again, risk large-scale defections. That danger became plain early in 1849, when Free Soilers and Democrats came together in Waukesha, Winnebago, Fond du Lac, and Dodge counties and endorsed both the Free Soil platform and a state fusion convention.[18] Yet, obliged as they were to take some antislavery ground, party chiefs understood that the ceaseless agitation of "abolition fanatics" sickened most rank-and-file Democrats. As one put it, old abolitionists such as Booth, Codding, and Durkee belonged "to a party separate and distinct," and no true Democrat could entertain "such an *extended* union as will include them."[19] At the same time, these conservatives unhesitatingly invited Van Buren Democrats disenchanted with the abolitionists back into the party, and before long a strategy designed to woo them and shun the hard-core antislavery men began to take shape.[20]

Early in the legislative session, the Democratic caucus appointed a committee to come up with a slavery platform acceptable to all party men. All but forgotten, the committee, ten days before adjournment and to everyone's surprise, issued an endorsement of the Free Soil program adopted in January, excepting the land limitation and equal suffrage planks. Headstrong Free Soilers, supposing this to be an offer of union, refused to budge; it was their entire platform or nothing. On March 30, after several days of inconclusive negotiations, Democratic lawmakers from the southeastern counties, where the pressure to fuse was strongest, along with a handful of Free Soilers, bypassed the committee and adopted the complete platform. They also recommended that the parties meet in a joint convention on September 12 to bring about a formal union.[21]

Despite the claims of Wisconsin's Free Soilers, this seeming coalition was an illusion, and to conclude, as did one historian, that on April 1 they found themselves joined to the old line Democracy is mistaken.[22] The Democratic caucus had never empowered the committee to discuss, much less to consummate, a union with them. And one can scarcely imagine the Democratic leadership accepting the Free Soil platform, equal suffrage plank and all. In fact, it was assumed that the legislature's adoption of the antislavery resolves in February made the continued existence of the committee unnecessary; thus, its preadjournment meeting and announcement came without caucus approval. As for the rump March 30 conference, fewer than one-fourth of the Democratic members of the legislature were present, and of those, at least half disavowed its outcome.[23] Regardless, Free Soilers embraced the March 30 resolutions, hopeful that the Democratic chieftains soon would be forced to do the same.

At first, the Democratic state committee met the call for a joint convention with complete silence. Undeterred, Free Soilers in late May publicly asked the Democrats to meet as scheduled on September 12 to bring about a merger based on the principles adopted at the March meeting.[24] Finally, on June 27, the committee responded, firmly rejecting an alliance because of the differences and jealousies certain to arise over specific policies and candidates; it instead set a regular party meeting for September 5. In addition, it bid all Democrats who had backed Van Buren to return to the party without fear of censure or dishonor.[25]

Free Soil leaders were incensed, but they remained convinced that most Democrats favored a coalition based on antislavery principles and would rebel at the leadership's obstinate behavior.[26] George Hyer, a Waukesha Democrat and influential party newspaper editor, reinforced their optimism when he called his party's action suicidal. Along with other Democrats, he petitioned Free Soilers to reschedule the joint convention for September 7 and promised that major defections would follow if Democratic leaders failed to join the fusion movement. The Free Soilers obligingly went along with this request.[27] As a result, Democrats in Waukesha, Winnebago, and Dodge counties promptly chose delegates to the regular party convention who were forbidden to participate in its nominating process and were instructed to demand its postponement until the seventh.[28] Similarly, in Rock, Walworth, and Marquette counties, Democrats and Free Soilers promoted a party merger and expressed confidence that "hundreds, aye, thousands, who voted for Cass and Taylor . . . will join the Free Democrats" if the regulars balked.[29]

Despite those hopeful signs, serious problems beset the Free Soil desire to fuse. Democrats, for all their internal squabbling, retained longstanding party ties that the leadership could exploit. Indeed, many Van Buren backers seemed eager to rejoin the party, seduced by the claim that no meaningful difference separated them any longer from Cass men. Meanwhile, Free Soilers were obliged to rely on the continued urgency of the antislavery issues that had dominated the 1848 presidential campaign to keep their coalition intact, while both Whigs and Democrats vied to weaken it with antislavery professions of their own. Within the Free Soil party, Conscience Whigs groused about the free trade plank and the unabashed attempt to join with the Democrats, whereas Liberty men, riled by the Democratic rebuff, now expressed hostility toward any combination with that "proslavery organization."[30]

With those factors in mind, Booth concluded in early August that the problems of balancing the needs of the party's disparate factions were insurmountable and further efforts to merge with the Democrats futile. He encouraged true antislavery men to remain within the Free Soil coalition and blasted Democratic equivocation on slavery issues, citing as evidence the party's rejection of the Hastings resolutions and its broad-based antipathy to the Wilmot Proviso. If the Democracy adopted any antislavery planks, Booth cautioned, they would be expedient measures only, calculated to win votes, not genuine expressions of principle, and he accused Democrats like Hyer, a "known Cass Man," of conspiring to destroy the Free Soil party with false professions of friendship.[31]

Amidst this political disarray, Wisconsin's Democrats came together as scheduled on September 5 and conducted a meeting that proved to be a model of clever efficiency. In order to "relieve the tender consciences" of delegates instructed not to meet on the fifth, they quickly agreed to adjourn to the following day, and before breaking up, they soundly defeated a resolution that endorsed the Wilmot Proviso.[32] Alarmed at the turn of events, several representatives from the southeast spent the balance of the day trying to drum up support for the Free Soil platform, only to be rebuffed by party men from the state's western counties.[33]

When the delegates reconvened the next morning, they chose a conservative ticket headed by the inoffensive incumbent, Nelson Dewey, to lead them in the upcoming campaign. Then, after a fierce disagreement, a committee appointed to study the feasibility of endorsing the Free Soil program struck a deal that allowed delegates from antislavery districts to adopt it and all others to ignore it, as they wished. So, when the committee dutifully reported back a resolution endorsing the Free Soil platform, only fifteen of the sixty-two delegates were on hand to pass it "without a dissenting vote." Commenting on the ruse, Rufus King aptly observed, "The Free Soil resolutions of the Hunker convention were passed for *Buncombe* . . . under false pretenses," and, he hoped "the counterfeit is so bad that nobody will be taken in by it."[34] Still, most Democrats seemed satisfied with the result; conservatives had their candidates, antislavery men had their platform, and the question of a coalition had been completely ignored. That was how matters stood on September 7 when twenty-two Free Soilers and eighteen Democrats, most of whom had already attended their party's convention, came together at Madison.

Led by Alexander Randall, the Democrats wasted no time in moving that the Free Soilers endorse the regular ticket and disband since the necessity for a separate organization no longer existed. Although critical of his party's decision to call a separate convention, Randall deemed it unwise and improper "to allow a mere question of etiquette to divide them when they were united in principle." The Free Soilers rejected the proposal, insisting they would name their own candidates. The Democrats then resubmitted the motion to disband, along with an offer to appoint a committee to secure a public declaration of support from the Democratic nominees for the Free Soil platform. Angry Free Soilers rejected this overture and repeated their determination to nominate their own men. Randall and thirteen others then immediately stormed out of the meeting and reassembled at a nearby hotel where they blessed the handiwork of the Democratic meeting and pledged to rejoin the party if its candidates would openly uphold the antislavery resolves. The Free Soilers, meanwhile, adjourned for the day.[35]

The following morning, Randall and his allies reappeared at the convention and made one last attempt to convince the Free Soilers to break up. Once again they failed, although the Free Soilers, at Booth's direction, shifted ground and proclaimed theirs a union meeting called to nominate a joint ticket. That provoked a final withdrawal by the Democrats, whereupon the Free Soilers nominated Nelson Dewey for governor and his running mate, Benjamin Hunkins, for secretary of state. Men of unquestioned antislavery principles filled out the balance of the "fusion" ticket, while the platform backed a complete separation of the federal government from slavery and declared that Free Soilers would spurn the advances of any party whose candidates were not expressly pledged to fight its expansion into every part of the national domain.[36]

Booth's change of heart apparently came as a result of pressure from Free Soil Democrats such as James Densmore, an Oshkosh "abolitionist and proud of it," who remained convinced that many voters continued to favor a merger despite the action of the Democrats. Moreover, Beriah Brown had privately assured Booth and Warren Chase that Dewey would turn down the union nomination; he produced a letter from the candidate as proof. Unwilling to risk further party disruption, anxious to court popular favor, and armed with Brown's pledge, Booth acquiesced. As promised, several days later, Dewey and Hunkins declined the joint nomination.[37]

Practical political difficulties frustrated the efforts of Democrats and Free Soilers seeking to merge, but splits over questions of principle assured failure. One Whig editor neatly summarized the problem.

> In regard to the cardinal point of union, the Wilmot Proviso, there is nominal and apparent agreement, yet what a real wide discrepancy of feeling and sympathy and interest underlies their mutual assent to the naked doctrine. . . . The Free Soilers regard the Wilmot Proviso of paramount importance, overruling all questions of legislative policy . . . it is the cornerstone of their political system. They do not give to it simply the cold assent [as] merely an abstraction or a measure which, though right in itself, is yet but of little consequence. . . . They regard it as a vital principle to be upheld at every sacrifice, which no consideration of political advantage should allow them in the least degree to compromise. . . . They regard it as vital to the interests and destiny of the country. . . . The old Democracy look upon the Proviso more in its political than its moral bearing, more as a matter of policy than principle. They have no deep sense of the immense evil and wrong of slavery and hence they care rather to keep themselves free from censure and politically right on the question, than to take a single step looking to the ultimate extinction of this

evil. . . . They will only move in the direction of freedom as they are carried by the irresistible current of public *sentiment* not moral sentiment . . . and hence their course will be vacillating, inconsistent, and uncertain, exhibiting an entire dereliction of principle.

To this Christopher Sholes responded, "Amen."[38]

With fusion dead, Free Soilers labored to repair the divisions within their ranks. At a mass meeting held in October, they replaced Dewey and Hunkins with Warren Chase and Edward Holton and once more affirmed their willingness to join with any man or organization dedicated to antislavery politics.[39] But the misleading incorporation of free soilism into the Democratic platform and the effective isolation of "unassimilable abolitionists" greatly hampered their exertions. With the assistance of Randall and others who by this time had rejoined the party, Democrats successfully neutralized the charge that their antislavery resolves were bogus by publishing brief statements from the candidates supporting the Free Soil platform and discounting the need for a third party. Moreover, to produce the greatest impact, these assertions were broadcast one week before the election to coincide with the release of a Free Soil address that detailed the disingenuousness of their opponents.[40] The popular Randall further frustrated Free Soil efforts to sustain their fragile coalition when he took to the stump on behalf of the Democratic nominees. Overall, the Free Soilers received an impressive lesson in political management from the Democrats, and as the campaign drew to a close, many observers declared the antislavery party dead.[41]

Largely ignored in the struggle, the Whigs scrambled to take advantage of the situation. At their September 11 convention, they adopted an unambiguous platform pledged to "the rigid and invariable application of the antislavery clause of the Ordinance of 1787 to every law organizing a new territory or creating a new State" and to the abolition of slavery wherever Congress was empowered to act, such as in the nation's capital. By taking a clear antislavery stand, the Whigs hoped to regain the loyalty of their Van Buren rebels and even attract the support of disgusted antislavery Democrats.[42] But they failed.

The Democratic ticket captured all the state offices by impressive margins (see table 4). Dewey received three thousand more votes than Cass had, while the Whig tally fell nearly two thousand from the preceding year. For the Free Soilers, the election was a disaster; from over ten thousand votes in 1848, they dropped to thirty-seven hundred in 1849, a decline of 64 percent.[43]

In the three-way race for president in 1848, the Democrats had picked up only 38 percent of the votes cast; in 1849 their candidate for governor captured 53 percent. Equally striking was the number of eligible voters who sat out the 1849 contest. In the 1848 presidential and gubernatorial elections, 62 and 57 percent, respectively, of the total electorate cast ballots; in 1849 participation plummeted to 44 percent. A closer analysis of the returns shows that most abstainers from the previous year's presidential contest also stayed home in 1849. Nearly five thousand Van Buren supporters, twenty-three hundred Cass men, and eighteen hundred Taylor Whigs joined them on the sidelines. The most interesting result indicates that the Democrats failed to regain the loyalty of their Free Soil defectors; fewer than one out of five rejoined the party and cast ballots for Dewey in 1849. On the other hand, the incumbent did pick up support from most of the Taylor Democrats and about two thousand 1848 nonvoters, while nearly all of the Free Soil and Whig votes came from men who had backed their presidential ticket in the previous year.

The referendum on whether to extend the franchise to Wisconsin's blacks had been lost amidst the confusion and maneuvering for party advantage in 1849. Although ostensibly committed to free suffrage due to their supposed endorsement of the Free Soil platform, no one seriously believed that the Democrats favored black voting, and both the party's standard-bearers and the press ignored the issue during the campaign. The Whig platform likewise neglected the question, though several party editors did take up the matter. Levi Alden denounced the "double dealing, dodging, disingenuous" Democratic position and urged voters to grant this "long oppressed, down trodden race" political equality. Rufus King asked Wisconsin to "rise superior to the prejudice which in many of her sister states still withholds this simple act of justice from the colored man." Another Whig deemed it "the height of folly and injustice that the tincture of African blood should cut off a man from this privilege of his born equals, and from the natural equality, unity and brotherhood" rightly his. Free Soilers, embroiled in their struggle with the Democracy, rarely mentioned the referendum, but when they did, they uniformly supported it.[44]

The overall inattention to the issue during the campaign carried over to the ballot box. More than sixty-eight hundred men cast ballots in favor of the measure; slightly more than fifty-two hundred voted against it. But more than thirty-four thousand voters had participated in the election for governor, and the state board of canvassers, quoting Wisconsin's constitution, ruled that the proposition had lost because it did not receive the required "majority of all votes cast." Booth complained that this interpretation nullified the results "by a back-handed blow," but his protest was ignored.[45]

In this manner, Wisconsin's few blacks once again were denied the franchise.[46] The returns indicate that the prosuffrage ballots came from Free Soilers, along with some Whigs and others who chose not to participate in the governor's contest (see table 5). Since those who joined the Free Soilers in 1848 had overwhelmingly supported black suffrage in 1847, it is likely that those who shunned the general election but voted prosuffrage came from their ranks. Dewey men contributed nothing to the prosuffrage tally, but they did provide about one-quarter of the antisuffrage total. The data also suggest that nearly two-thirds of the opposition votes came from men who sat out the governor's race, most of whom probably were Democrats upset with their party's dalliance with the Free Soilers.

Wisconsin's Democrats had good reason to crow about their victory in 1849 and the ease with which they had outmaneuvered the Free Soilers. Yet their inability to win back most of the rebellious Van Buren men, coupled with the dramatic decline in turnout, raised questions about the future direction of politics in the state. Nonvoters constituted a substantial portion of the eligible electorate. If mobilized, they could become the nucleus of an anti-Democratic coalition. Furthermore, by 1849, Wisconsin's Whigs could furnish vocal but mostly ineffective opposition to the ruling Democrats, a fact not lost on Free Soilers, whose own party lay in shambles. Antislavery leaders could only bide their time and hope the course of events would provide an opportunity to fashion a more cohesive political union dedicated to ending American slavery.[47] As 1850 dawned, they once again saw grounds for hope.

CHAPTER FIVE

The Principles of the Free Soil and Whig Parties Are Identical

WISCONSIN'S FREE SOIL PARTY suffered a devastating blow in 1849. Yet, its leaders responded to the setback with equanimity. Although critical of the Democracy's duplicity in the recent campaign, they seemed satisfied with its putative antislavery platform; however, they warned that any future deviation from it would trigger a rebellion among the state's voters and bring it down once and for all.[1] The Democrats, still savoring their recent triumph, must have had a good laugh at the Free Soilers' expense.

The election also hurt the Whigs. They not only had failed to overcome the Democracy's political domination, but worse, their support among the state's voters actually declined. Whig fortunes were destined to sag further as a result of the continuing sectional controversy in 1850.[2]

In an attempt to quiet agitation over the status of slavery in the Mexican cession, President Zachary Taylor urged Congress to acquiesce in California's wish to form a state government and to treat New Mexico, whose citizens soon were expected to apply for statehood, in the same way. With both likely to organize as free states, the North, it was believed, would welcome the president's plan, while the South, due to the absence of the hated Wilmot Proviso, would grudgingly go along. Instead, the crisis intensified as Southern leaders demanded greater protection for slavery and threatened disunion if their demands were not met. As an alternative to Taylor's recommendations, the aging Whig senator from Kentucky, Henry Clay, proposed a wide-ranging compromise of the outstanding issues. Among other things, he offered to admit California as a free state, abolish the slave trade in the nation's capital, organize the territories of New Mexico and Utah without reference to slavery, and replace the Fugitive Slave Act of 1793 with a more severe law.[3]

Wisconsin's Whigs rallied around the president's plan. It would permit California and New Mexico to bypass the territorial stage and gain immediate admission to the Union as free states, without reference to the Wilmot Proviso. Clay's proposal, if enacted, would keep the status of slavery in the territories in suspense for an indeterminate period and provide an opportunity, albeit a small one, to plant it in New Mexico and Utah. Although they had no desire to irritate the South unnecessarily, the state's Whigs were determined to confine slavery within its present bounds. As the normally temperate editor of the *Wisconsin Express* put it:

> We can *never* concede that the peculiar institution is right . . . that traffic in human beings is humane. . . . We have compromised too long . . . it is now time that a limit be set to our concessions. . . . If the Union is divided, it is the act of the South . . . urged on by a headstrong determination . . . to either rule or ruin. We love the Union, but we *hate* slavery, and while we have no desire . . . to interfere with this institution in the slave states, we do demand . . . no more slave states shall ever be admitted into the sisterhood.[4]

The Taylor wing of the Whig party appeared ready to meet the Southern threats of disunion in 1850 head on. Whether the administration's scheme would have succeeded and the South been forced to back down remains conjectural since the president suddenly died in early July.[5] Still, one thing is clear: For many of Wisconsin's Whigs, the free soil antislavery position had become more important than the Union, a trend first evident in 1848. Much like Liberty and Free Soil stalwarts, they had ruefully concluded that continued concessions to the South could lead to slavery's

{ *Political Abolitionism in Wisconsin, 1840–1861* }

spread and perpetuation and even to the erosion of individual liberty and republican ideals in the North. Millard Fillmore, Taylor's replacement and a compromise advocate, placed these party men in the uncomfortable position of having to back Clay's plan or be set adrift by the national administration.[6]

While Wisconsin's Whigs tried to accommodate themselves to the new situation, Democrats bided their time, testing the political winds. By early July they had set their course, confidently expressing the view that America's vast western territories would forever remain free. That position, combined with their increasing fears for the safety of the Union, led them to dismiss the Wilmot Proviso as unneeded and swung them firmly into the procompromise camp.[7]

The Free Soilers followed the proceedings in the nation's capital with distaste. They denounced the New Yorker Fillmore for his unequivocal opposition to the application of the Wilmot Proviso, in favor of the Cass doctrine of federal nonintervention, and they blasted Democrats for their blind idolatry of the Union. The South needed the North infinitely more than the North needed the South, Free Soilers insisted, and would quickly recant if it ever attempted the folly of disunion. "The Union must *stand*," Sherman Booth roared. "Put that down as a fixed verity. Shall it stand with honor or shame, with Freedom or Slavery? That is the question for men of this generation to answer."[8]

By mid-September, now under the guiding hand of Senator Stephen A. Douglas, an Illinois Democrat, the last of the compromise measures had passed both houses of Congress and received Fillmore's signature. Three months later, in his annual message, the president urged all Americans to support the settlement as "final and immutable."[9]

At best, it would have been difficult to fashion any permanent legislative settlement of the slavery issue. Yet, what became known as the Compromise of 1850 did result in a short-lived truce between the North and South, though the slavery issue was hardly dead.[10] Throughout the North, the Fugitive Slave Law was the most damned of the compromise measures. It denied alleged fugitives the right to a trial by jury, to sue for writs of habeas corpus, or to bring witnesses to testify on their behalf. Equally bad, federal judges were authorized to appoint commissioners to try cases under the law, and they in turn were empowered to command the citizens of any state to assist in its execution. Consequently, whites could be enrolled as slavehunters against their will and prosecuted for obstructing enforcement of the act, while free blacks were stripped of all protection against false claims and unjust imprisonment.[11]

Wisconsinites of all political persuasions denounced the Fugitive Slave Law unsparingly. "Beyond a question," wrote Horace Tenney, it is "the most despotic act ever adopted in a republican government—a monument to tyranny—and a libel on civilization." Byron Paine, a young Free Soil lawyer, likewise condemned the act as "an unhallowed usurpation of the dearest rights that God has given to his creatures."[12] In Milwaukee, blacks staged a public meeting, their first ever in Wisconsin, to express their anger at the passage of the infamous law. They resolved "to come forward at any alarm given and rescue our fugitive brethren even unto death." To back up their words, Booth noted approvingly, the city's "colored people are armed to the teeth, and go armed about their daily work. . . . The first kidnapper who lays hands on one of them, we expect will be shot dead."[13]

In addition to robbing citizens of basic civil liberties, many Wisconsinites considered the measure an unconstitutional encroachment upon the reserved rights of the states. They contended that the Constitution committed the free states to act in good faith in the recovery of fugitives, and it empowered them, not the federal government, to set the terms of compliance. As usual, Booth stated the matter most bluntly. "Congress has just as much right to legislate on runaway horses," he wrote, "as it has to legislate on runaway slaves."[14] Even Beriah Brown, the staunchly conservative Democrat and bitter racist, agreed that while the Constitution granted Congress legislative prerogative regarding alleged escapees, in this case it had clearly overstepped its mandate.

> Under the regulations of the slave states, an hereditary state of bondage is recognized, under those of the free states, no individual, black or white can be deprived of his liberty. . . . The black man is entitled under the laws of the free states to the same rights as the white man, and the state . . . is pledged to [his] protection. . . . To place the black man under martial law in time of peace, to hold him subject to accusation and imprisonment for no crime, to take from him the dearest rights guaranteed to every man, is literally to extend the slave laws over the free states, is an infringement of our state sovereignty and individual rights, is pledging the Union to slavery and mak-

ing every citizen North and South, in effect, a slaveholder. . . . The law . . . makes us a party to slavery in its most odious form—the hunting down of men . . . with ropes, chains and bloodhounds. . . . We demand its repeal . . . we wash our hands of the curse.[15]

Despite this widespread revulsion, three years of sectional controversy and concern for the Union's safety tempered popular reaction to the Fugitive Slave Law. Racism, too, played a role. One lead district Democrat frankly stated a preference to see "the whole negro race annihilated" rather than witness the destruction of the Union and the Constitution, an immoderate sentiment undoubtedly shared by others.[16] Yet, Wisconsinites generally seemed willing to live with the law, never expecting a summons to join in a slave hunt or aid in any fugitive's rendition. Indeed, many privately pledged to assist runaways whenever the opportunity arose.[17] As such, enforcement in Wisconsin could prove troublesome, perhaps impossible.

Still, the Fugitive Slave Law helped keep the political antislavery movement alive throughout the North, especially as national leaders exerted pressure on local Whigs and Democrats to disavow "any useless agitation of the slavery issue" and to endorse the compromise as a final settlement of the question.[18] In Wisconsin, state newspapers spotlighted the law with vivid accounts of blacks on the run and extensive coverage of the more celebrated fugitive slave cases. The publication of Harriet Beecher Stowe's *Uncle Tom's Cabin*, beginning in June 1851, hailed as "one of the great events of the year" by a Rock County Free Soiler, poignantly reminded readers of the horrors of slavery and the desperation of bondsmen in flight. Itinerant black speakers, including at least one avowed runaway, ranged through Wisconsin's towns lecturing on the plight of the slave.[19]

The state's lawmakers also focused attention on the measure. During the 1851 legislative session, the Senate affirmed Congress's constitutional right to legislate on the issue but requested the removal of provisions of the 1850 law understood to be dangerous to personal freedom. In the Assembly, Wyman Spooner, a former Liberty man turned Free Soiler, introduced an amendment to the Senate resolution denying Congress any legitimate jurisdiction in the matter of fugitive slaves, such authority being reserved to the states, and instead called for the law's complete repeal. After some delay, an attempt to kill Spooner's amendment failed, but in the rush to adjourn it seems to have been buried purposely.[20]

Senate and assembly voting on the Fugitive Slave Law resolutions revealed a clear partisan split. A majority of the Democratic lawmakers opposed both the senate and the Spooner versions; Whigs favored them by nearly a two to one margin; and Free Soilers unanimously endorsed them. As in the past, legislators who represented the southwestern and heavily immigrant counties fronting Lake Michigan provided most of the anti-resolution votes, while southeasterners were nearly unanimous in support of the petitions requesting either repeal or modification of the law.[21]

In the following year, a senate committee composed of three Whigs and one Free Soiler recommended passage of a resolution similar to the one Spooner had introduced in the previous session. The preamble contained a major difference. It maintained that:

> The leading principles on which the government of the United States is founded and which are the foundation of all republican governments are the liberty of speech, and the press; the right of the people peacefully to assemble and express their views on all questions connected with the government . . . and the right of the majority to rule; and if a state of facts exist . . . which forbid the people . . . from expressing, in language of reprobation, their detestation of a law abhorrent to freemen—then is our republicanism but a name, and . . . our government the rankest despotism on earth. And if the only ligament which binds the states is unconditional submission to any and every law, however unjust and odious . . . as a sort of condition precedent to the continuance of the Union, then the bonds that bind us together are but ropes of sand, and our boasted union is not worth preserving.[22]

Although the preamble further suggests evidence of an increasing unwillingness in Wisconsin to sacrifice long-cherished rights and freedoms as the price of Union, its high-sounding sentiments failed to win the legislature's approval. With a presidential contest in the offing, reluctant lawmakers from both parties tried to downplay slavery issues and quietly laid the declaration to rest, although the senate did agree to have five hundred copies of the resolution printed for distribution.[23]

Unceasing labor by Wisconsin's Free Soilers also kept slavery concerns in the public eye in the immediate aftermath of the compromise's passage, despite their party's weakened condition. As James Densmore, an ardent antislavery Democrat, sighed, there no longer seemed "life enough to sustain" an independent antislavery party.[24] Even Booth for a time appeared uncertain of the future. "Shall we join and endeavor to mould the [Democratic] party and prevent it going for Cass in 1852," he quizzed the Ohio Free Soiler, Salmon P. Chase, "or still maintain a separate organization. That's the question!"[25] Disregarding the party's woes, many Free Soilers kept the faith. "Medicines may be administered which will protract the final dissolution and death of slavery," Christopher Sholes insisted, "but the struggle, however protracted, can only end in the death of that institution." Likewise, Charles Durkee, Wisconsin's Free Soil congressman, confidently predicted "that the time is not distant when there [will] . . . be an irresistible current from the masses in favor of freedom."[26]

Booth's indecision did not last long. With congressional races looming in 1850, he and Sholes offered one last time to merge with the Democrats, conditioned upon their willingness to support Durkee's reelection effort. As expected, the Democratic leadership ignored this proposition and treated the Free Soil leaders, as Booth disgustedly wrote, "as dogs and outcasts."[27] This approach was repeated throughout the North, he noted, as the Northern Democracy reaffirmed its compact with Southern party members. "The Central Committee at Washington has decreed it . . . and Southward the party is bound to go."[28]

Spurned by the Democracy, Booth organized a petition drive, urging his friend Durkee to seek reelection as an independent candidate. More than two thousand voters signed the call and persuaded the popular incumbent to run again.[29] Five hundred Whigs, disenchanted with the compromise and recognizing the futility of fielding a candidate of their own, were among the petitioners. Rufus King and John Tweedy engineered additional Whig aid when, at the party's district convention, they pressured delegates to nominate Tweedy who, as planned, declined the honor. Upon reconvening, the Whigs failed to make any nomination, as "an enthusiastic expression from *every* delegate . . . to give Mr. Durkee a cordial support" prevailed. Although a few grumbled about being sold to the abolitionists, most Whigs rallied to the Free Soiler's assistance and helped carry him to an easy victory.[30]

Free Soilers returned the favor in the western second congressional district when they backed the anticompromise Whig incumbent, Orsamus

Cole. In that case the coalition proved unavailing. The Democrats nominated a popular opponent of the Compromise of 1850, Ben Eastman, who triumphed handily.[31]

Chaos ruled in the northern third congressional district. James D. Doty, the incumbent Democrat and one of Wisconsin's founding fathers, had angered party regulars with his protariff views. For this he was unceremoniously dumped at the district convention. In response, he decided to campaign for reelection as an independent. Whigs and Free Soilers, hopelessly outgunned in the overwhelmingly Democratic north, used Doty's antislavery record as a pretext for throwing him their support. At least five disgruntled Democratic editors joined them. Coalition efforts, along with the incumbent's personal popularity, overwhelmingly returned him to office.[32]

Despite the presence of several popular congressional candidates, only 52 percent of the eligible electorate bothered to vote in 1850. To enliven interest in politics and unify their ranks in preparation for the 1852 presidential contest, the Democrats took vigorous steps. They established newspapers that preached adherence to traditional party principles and replaced editors who refused to toe the line. Between 1847 and 1852, the number of party newspapers climbed from eleven to twenty-five, with most of the increase coming after 1850. In order to arouse political enthusiasm among the state's burgeoning foreign-born population, they organized county level committees to distribute party literature prior to elections.[33] Democratic unity received a further boost in mid-1852 when Horace Tenney and Beriah Brown, editors of Madison's two contentious party newspapers, ended their longstanding feud. At the behest of Josiah Noonan, Milwaukee's Democratic boss, the two journals were consolidated under the ownership of Brown and Tenney's former associate, Stephen D. Carpenter.[34]

Capping the drive to bring about greater harmony and reestablish the primacy of established party ideals, Wisconsin's Democracy began to shed its antislavery garb. At the 1851 legislative session, the Democratic majority overwhelmingly voted to rescind the 1849 resolution censuring Senator Walker.[35] Several months later, Walker himself gave a rousing and well-received speech in Milwaukee endorsing the compromise measures.[36] At its state convention, the party firmly repudiated "all extraneous issues and sectional tests of party faith as pernicious, clannish, and disorganizing in their tendency." It also embraced a resolution from the 1836 national platform that denounced all forms of abolitionism as inevitably tending "to diminish the happiness of the people and to endanger the stability and permanency of the Union."[37] With free soilism purged from the party, Democrats celebrated the return to the "Glorious old National Democratic Charter." "We are free," the editor of the *Kenosha Democrat* rejoiced: "Free from sectional tests—free from the heresies of free soil—free from degrading compromises with a selfish enemy."[38]

As Democrats returned to their roots, Free Soil leaders in 1851 looked to nurture the relationship established with Whigs the previous year. Since Whigs had little hope of overturning their opponent's statewide majority and refused to be muzzled on slavery questions, the strategy made sense. Whigs, to be sure, mindful of Southern threats to break up the Union, discouraged agitation, but they refused to surrender their right "to discuss and strive to amend or repeal . . . any or all laws which do not suit them." The Whigs deferred to no man or party in their love of the Union, Rufus King observed, and short of violating personal liberty or abandoning the territories to slavery, they were prepared to make any sacrifice to preserve it.[39] Encouraged, Free Soilers issued a call to all men, without reference to party, who were opposed to the Fugitive Slave Law, to the extension of slavery, and "to the insolence of men of any section of the Union who dictate to us on what subjects we shall or shall not discuss," to come together at a mass convention in Madison on September 17.[40]

At this largely Free Soil affair, Booth, Edward D. Holton, Byron Paine, and other former Liberty men overcame the objections of leery Democratic Free Soilers and succeeded in nominating Leonard J. Farwell, a popular antislavery Whig, for governor.[41] They filled out the rest of the ticket with Free Soilers, reaffirmed the party's 1849 platform, and condemned the Fugitive Slave Law as antirepublican and subversive of individual liberty. Finally, the convention enthusiastically promoted the notion that the nation's founders fully expected "that under a proper administration of the General Government, slavery would cease to exist at an early period."[42]

After the convention, it remained only for the unwilling Farwell to accept the nomination. Booth spent several days at the candidate's Madison home trying to convince him to accept the bid, especially since the Whigs also were expected to place his name before the people. Convinced that the Democrats were unbeatable, Farwell would have preferred to be left to his business pursuits. In the end, he was prevailed upon to await the outcome of the Whig convention before announcing his decision.[43]

The so-called mass meeting's nomination of Farwell placed the Whigs in a quandary. If they seconded his candidacy, they would be open to the charge of having surrendered their organization to the Free Soilers; if they did not, the Democrats undoubtedly would elect their man. Rufus King, probably after discussions with Booth, boldly called on the chairman of the Whig party's state organization either to call off the upcoming convention and work for the election of the nonpartisan candidates or to convene and disband without making any nominations.[44]

Ignoring King, the Whigs assembled as scheduled on September 24 and proceeded to name A. L. Collins for governor. Collins, the party's nominee in 1849, had no desire to head another hopeless cause and declined the tribute. Frustrated, the delegates turned to Farwell who reluctantly agreed to run.[45] The Whig platform endorsed traditional party measures, opposed the extension of slavery, and pointedly upheld the "unquestionable right of every citizen to canvass the merits of every enactment, and if found to be unjust, oppressive, or of doubtful expediency, to advocate their modification or repeal."[46] Like the Free Soilers, the Whigs then completed their ticket with party loyalists. In a comment that contained more than a little truth, one Democrat exclaimed, "Married—at Madison, on Wednesday, September 24th, by Gen. Rufus King & Co., the Universal Whig Party to the Woolly-Headed Abolition Party, all of Wisconsin."[47]

Farwell's candidacy provided the only link in 1851 between Free Soilers and Whigs who otherwise deliberately ignored each other during the campaign, perhaps fearful that the appearance of too close a union might alienate some party members. Instead, they concentrated their fire on the Democrats. The Whigs also played down the slavery issue and urged voters to support a referendum on the establishment of state banks. Since most political observers expected the bank question to win easily, they noted, it made sense to elect a governor who would enact laws necessary to organize them. Farwell was such a man. "With slavery the Governor of this State can have nothing to do; with the BANK question he may have much."[48] Free Soilers, meanwhile, hammered away on the slavery issue and labored to retain the loyalty of antislavery Democrats who hesitated to support Farwell, committed as he was to Whig economic programs, unless he publicly aired his views on slavery. Taking matters in hand, Booth drafted a letter to Durkee, over Farwell's signature, that confirmed his opposition to slavery's extension and the Fugitive Slave Law and his support of measures to abolish "slavery wherever it exists under the exclusive jurisdiction of Congress."

Farwell gave Booth permission to publish the letter, and it seems to have satisfied the uneasy Democrats.[49]

Whigs and Free Soilers cheered when Farwell squeezed out a narrow victory over his Democratic rival, and opposition candidates wrested control of the assembly from the Democrats for the first time in the state's brief history. Whigs won thirty-one assembly seats, Free Soilers six, and the Democrats thirty, but the Democrats retained a two-to-one majority in the senate. As expected, the bank issue easily passed. Although Whigs and Free Soilers were pleased with the election results in the gubernatorial and assembly contests, they hardly could lay claim to a resounding victory. The popular Farwell ran six thousand votes ahead of the other Whig candidates for state office, while the Free Soilers polled fewer than three thousand votes, a decline of more than 25 percent from 1849. Moreover, the combined Whig and Free Soil tally did not put Farwell over the top. He required the support of about three thousand "sore headed Democrats" and a handful of men voting only in the governor's contest to eke out his win, although the Whig nominee's popularity and Democratic efforts helped raise voter participation slightly from 1849.[50] The Whig achievements in 1851 failed to mask its persistently weak position in Wisconsin politics, particularly compared to the robust if factious Democracy, and the Free Soilers continued to struggle for their political life.

The Free Soilers were hurt further when, shortly after the 1851 election, Rufus King and other friendly Whigs came under pressure from the Fillmore administration to mend their coalitionist ways. A procompromise paper was set up in Milwaukee to compete with King's *Sentinel,* and it frankly advised both Whigs and Democrats who were disenchanted with their party to join the abolitionists, as they "alone can sympathize with you."[51]

King took the hint and withdrew from the Free Soil embrace. Three weeks after the administration paper appeared, he downplayed slavery's significance in the recent election. "The Whigs of Wisconsin let the slavery question alone," he truthfully stated, and they "commended their candidates to the people on . . . local issues," most notably the bank question.[52] King then publicly rebuffed renewed Free Soil advances to enact a formal union with the Whigs, even though many would have welcomed it.[53] Booth took the snub with unusual grace, fully aware that the pending presidential election made any concert of action unlikely. He counseled patience and the continuation of an independent Free Soil course for the foreseeable future, confident that old party ties were unraveling and that the slavery issue soon would mold them into some new form.[54]

Booth's prediction came one step closer to reality as a result of the 1852 presidential contest. At their national convention, Democrats enthusiastically championed the compromise measures as a final solution to the slavery issue and nominated the inoffensive Franklin Pierce for president. Smelling victory, Wisconsin's Democratic leadership, united as never before, eagerly touted Pierce's candidacy and overwhelmed the party's few dissenters.[55] The Whig convention turned out to be a raucous affair. It selected the aging military hero Winfield Scott as its standard-bearer and approved a procompromise platform resolution. Because Southern Whigs distrusted Scott and Northern Whigs disliked the platform, the party's sectional rift deepened and it ran a listless campaign. In Wisconsin, Whigs angrily repudiated the compromise resolution and made only halfhearted efforts on behalf of Scott.[56] Like the Democrats, Free Soilers enjoyed an agreeable convention. This time they nominated John P. Hale for president and drafted an antislavery platform similar to that of 1848. The other parties refused to engage them in a serious debate over slavery, however, and in Wisconsin, frustrated Free Soilers denounced the supporters of "Slavery Ticket—No. 1" and "Slavery Ticket—No. 2." The Whig failure to again back Durkee's reelection effort most infuriated them. They accused Milwaukee's Whigs of placing a candidate in the field solely to enhance the chances of Daniel Wells, the Democratic nominee, whose business ties placed him in a better position to boost the city's commercial prospects.[57]

Pierce handily carried Wisconsin and the nation. In the state, he received 33,658 votes to Scott's 22,240 and Hale's 8,842. Turnout was the same 62 percent it had been in 1848. To the bitter disappointment of Free Soilers, Durkee failed to win a third term to Congress, as the Democrats swept to an easy victory in all three districts. Free Soilers did make a respectable showing, though, and promised to remain a political force within the state. Whig reverses nationwide irretrievably sundered the party, perhaps nowhere more than in Wisconsin. In his typically forthright manner, Booth declared that the Whig party "is blotted from the political map, and henceforth ceases to be a political organization." The earthy Democrat George Hyer said much the same thing when he exclaimed, "All there is left of the Whig party is a few feathers and a pair of epaulets. Scott's *rear* was entirely shot off. It wasn't much of a fight after all."[58]

As their anger over the alleged complicity of Milwaukee's Whigs to thwart Durkee's reelection effort subsided, Free Soilers began to explore the possibility of taking advantage of Whig decrepitude. They encouraged political abolitionists to subscribe to party newspapers and organize local clubs throughout the state as the most effective way of spreading anti-slavery dogma and winning new converts.[59] At their well-attended state convention in January 1853, Free Soilers took steps to tighten their organization and reaffirmed their determination to remain an independent party.[60] By contrast, the Whigs were an unhappy lot. As summer neared, several of their editors floated the possibility of a coalition in the upcoming fall elections.[61] A handful of Democrats, disgusted with their party's suppression of the slavery issue, joined them. As one stated, "None have so kicked, cuffed, reviled, abused, insulted, slandered and outraged Free Soil Democrats as has the Hunker party of this State."[62] At first, Booth sounded unimpressed with the overtures. As a prerequisite to merging, he asked for the complete dismemberment of the Whig organization and the adoption of the 1852 Free Soil platform. He also advocated independent Free Soil nominations for the upcoming state campaign, whatever the Whigs might do.[63] Christopher Sholes tempered Booth's haughty attitude, and he counseled antislavery men to be more realistic in their demands and to treat the friends of union with greater respect.[64]

Early coalition efforts focused on the proposed renomination of Farwell. Free Soil and Whig editors warmly backed him, although it was rumored he would not run again due to the personal and financial sacrifices the governorship required.[65] The likelihood that Free Soilers and Whigs at the very least would unite behind the incumbent became clear when both called state conventions to meet in Madison on successive days in June, several months earlier than usual.[66] Only Farwell discouraged the prospective arrangement.

On June 7, a mere thirty-nine Whigs convened from fewer than half of Wisconsin's assembly districts to hear the governor absolutely decline to be a candidate again. The confused delegates informally nominated him anyway and adjourned without naming a ticket. They also ignored Free Soilers who attended the melancholy gathering to feel them out on the fusion question. Few now doubted, as one the observer reported, that "the great Whig party of Wisconsin is no more."[67]

The following day sixty-three hearty Free Soilers assembled in the capital city. Several of them made strenuous efforts to convince the convention to abstain from making nominations, hoping yet to make an arrangement with the Whigs, but their proposal fell on deaf ears. With Farwell out of the picture and the Whigs moribund, the delegates had little incentive to pursue a coalition. Instead, they chose the old Liberty man, Edward D. Holton, to head their ticket on an antislavery platform.[68]

Free Soilers pursued their independent course, convinced that Whigs could be absorbed into the antislavery coalition without concessions on principle. The influential Whig Horace Greeley lent encouragement in his *New York Tribune,* when he warmly commended Wisconsin's party leaders for avoiding nominations and urged them to coalesce with the Free Soilers. Farwell himself, it was whispered, had told antislavery friends that "the Whigs ought not to have called a convention or even talked of nominating." In Milwaukee, Rufus King denounced the Democrats for their abandonment of free soilism and declared himself in favor of fusion. Even David Atwood, chairman of the Whig state central committee, spoke approvingly of the antislavery ticket and expressed no desire to "reanimate dead bodies."[69]

The prospects for a union were dampened in mid-August when, under pressure from conservatives, the Whigs issued a call for a meeting on September 14. Although in essential agreement on slavery questions, these conservatives continued to attach greater priority to Whig economic issues. For that reason, they repudiated the coalition movement because the Free Soil economic creed contained too many Democratic ideas "and as such has no business to be embraced by the Whigs."[70]

While the Whigs struggled desperately to survive, internal warfare broke out among the Democrats. Josiah Noonan, Milwaukee postmaster and party chieftain, was laboring to thwart the upstart William A. Barstow's attempt to seize control of the organization. As Wisconsin's secretary of state between 1849 and 1851, the charismatic Barstow had used his position to build up a personal political following independent of Noonan. Relations between the two rapidly deteriorated in 1852, when Noonan had Barstow arrested on his way to the Democratic national convention to compel payment of a $300 loan contracted several years earlier. After the presidential contest, Barstow, along with prominent Democrats such as Beriah Brown and former Governor Dewey, tried without success to have Noonan removed as postmaster. They then initiated impeachment proceedings against Circuit Judge Levi Hubbell, one of Noonan's closest friends and political allies, charging him with more than fifty offenses, including one of "inducing females interested in suits before his court to submit themselves to be debauched by him."[71]

On September 7, the battleground shifted to the state Democratic convention. Barstow was the leading contender for the party's gubernatorial nomination, along with A. Hyatt Smith, president of the Rock River Valley Union Railroad, and Jairus C. Fairchild, a former state treasurer and Noonan's favorite. After twelve ballots, Smith, whose railroad interests competed with Noonan's, threw his support to Barstow and gave him the nomination.[72] Barstow's triumph intensified the Democratic split. Alexander Randall, the erstwhile Free Soiler and a friend of Noonan's, openly rebelled, while Brown's short-lived partner at the *Argus and Democrat,* Stephen Carpenter, complained that "a more contemptible ticket could not be picked."[73] The Democratic platform did not reflect these divisions; basically it restated the 1852 party positions, including a reendorsement of the Compromise of 1850.[74]

The Whigs reconvened as scheduled on September 14. If anything, the second meeting was more pathetic than the first. Only twenty-six delegates from twelve of the state's thirty-six counties bothered to show up. Nevertheless, they went ahead and picked candidates pledged to "uphold the old and well-known principles of the Whig party" and oppose the extension of slavery and the Fugitive Slave Law.[75] Very few observers took the conservatives seriously, although it was suggested that they had named candidates merely to abet the defeat of any Whig–Free Soil union.[76] And the Democrats understood the advantages of keeping these Whigs in the race. George B. Smith, one of Barstow's intimates, hearing rumors of renewed coalition efforts, asked the Democratic candidate if he could fix it so that the Whig nominee, Henry Baird, "will stand firm."[77]

Smith's intelligence proved correct. Milwaukee's powerful Whig faction, which had boycotted the September meeting, had quietly been laying the groundwork for a People's Mass Convention to be held at the upcoming state fair in Watertown.[78] To Booth, Rufus King acknowledged that the conservatives had acted "neither wisely nor well in making a nomination, [but] they can at least plead in extension of their error that they followed the example of the Free Soilers," who earlier had placed their own ticket in the race. He also asserted that issues of substance no longer divided the two parties, making it "highly desirable that they should act together." As to the process of effecting a union, King swept aside the demand that his party disband and march under the Free Soil banner. "Party ties . . . have lost much of their prescriptive authority in this State," he explained, "but party prejudices still linger." He suggested a coalition bearing a new name.[79]

Booth happily agreed. On the evening of October 5, the two men met privately and completed the arrangements. Although evidence is scarce, it appears that they agreed to place Farwell before the people, in order to appease conservative Whigs, and then replace him with Holton.[80]

The next morning, state fair goers in Watertown found a call posted around the village asking those opposed to the Democracy's candidates to gather at a nearby schoolhouse to select a People's ticket. Utter confusion resulted. Democratic leaders attending the fair packed the meeting place with their supporters and forced an adjournment. At 7:00 P.M., with John Tweedy in the chair, the meeting finally came off. But Democrats continued their disruptive tactics and blocked every attempt to nominate a fusion ticket. Outmaneuvered, Booth and King, who so far had maintained a low profile, retired with a small number of coalition leaders to a friend's law office for a secret caucus. Taking matters into their own hands, they disingenuously announced that the People's convention had chosen the incumbent governor as its favorite.[81]

As expected, Farwell rejected the so-called nomination. A committee appointed at Watertown then named Holton to head the ticket. Three Free Soilers and five Whigs filled the remaining slots. With the exception of Baird, all of the regular Whig and Free Soil nominees then stepped aside in favor of the People's candidates. And, with a single exception, every Whig and Free Soil newspaper, along with one Democratic journal, supported the new coalition. Most significantly, Holton won over western Whigs who, some feared, might reject the well-known abolitionist's candidacy. In a speaking tour through the lead district, he successfully quieted their misgivings and helped organize local support.[82]

Unlike the Liberty and Free Soil parties, the People's coalition did not have its roots in opposition to slavery. It arose in 1853 to fill the vacuum created by the demise of the Whig party and the realization that the old national issues were dead. Local issues dominated the canvass. The People's candidates tried to mobilize voter dissatisfaction with government corruption and high taxes with a promise to restore republican purity to the administration of the state's affairs.[83] That appeal might have found wider support if the temperance issue had not intruded. At a special session in June, the state legislature reluctantly agreed to hold a referendum on whether to ban the sale of intoxicating beverages in Wisconsin. None of the parties took a stand on the question as leaders and editors announced their positions as principle or local circumstance demanded. The People's movement became strongly identified with the ban, however, much to the chagrin of Whigs, when influential Free Soilers publicly recommended it. King and others would have preferred to ignore the issue altogether, while the Democrats adroitly manipulated the issue to accommodate local prejudices. In Milwaukee, with its large immigrant population, Barstowites staunchly opposed prohibition; in the northern and western counties, they claimed to be its friend.[84]

The Democratic strategy on the liquor question and insufficient time to organize led to the defeat of the People's ticket. Barstow captured 30,542 votes to Holton's 21,918 and Baird's 3,364. Interestingly enough, neither the temperance issue nor dissatisfaction with alleged corruption and spoilsmanship stirred the enthusiasm of Wisconsin's electorate. Fifty-two percent of the state's eligible voters chose to remain home on election day, nearly the same proportion as in the two previous contests for state officers. Only 46 percent bothered to vote on the liquor question, with a slight majority in favor of a ban.[85] Counties and towns with large numbers of German and Irish residents tended to be heavily against the ban on alcohol; those with the fewest immigrants favored it. Yet, neither large nor small concentrations of foreign or native-born citizens were good predictors of turnout. Seventy-one percent of the people in Manitowoc county and 62 percent of those in Milwaukee county were born overseas, primarily in Germany, but only 37 percent and 53 percent, respectively, turned out to vote on the liquor issue. More than 85 percent of Portage and Richland county residents were native-born, but 38 percent and 33 percent took the time to vote on temperance. Eighteen counties contained more than one-third foreign-born men and women. In these counties average turnout was 46 percent, although those with the largest concentrations of Germans displayed a slight tendency to turn out in greater numbers than counties with the fewest foreign-born citizens. Nevertheless, using turnout as a measure of interest, neither the governor's race nor the liquor question generated any more excitement than had been shown in earlier elections.[86]

In the state contest, the Democrats succeeded in mobilizing the bulk of their 1852 constituency. They also gained several thousand prior nonvoters and new electors, probably mostly foreign-born residents alarmed over the liquor issue and a handful of Free Soil Democrats upset with their party's marriage to the Whigs (see table 6). Nearly 80 percent of Hale's supporters rallied to the People's standard. The rest either abstained or voted for Barstow. Less than one-half of the Scott Whigs favored the union, while 40 percent did not vote at all. About 13 percent stood by the conservative Baird. The People's coalition failed to make inroads among the Democrats, although it did show surprising strength among former abstainers and, perhaps, some newly eligible voters.

The 1853 election convinced all but the most obstinate Whigs that their party was dead. It also gave a boost to the friends of fusion as western Whigs for the first time rallied behind the candidacy of an avowed abolitionist, eroding in part the intrastate sectionalism that hampered prior coalition efforts. Shortly after the campaign, both Whig and Free Soil leaders hinted that a more permanent union based on opposition to slavery might be in the offing. Christopher Sholes, sensing a turn in national affairs, wrote that antislavery men would soon unite to rescue the government from the slave power and thus complete "the mission of the Free Democracy as an independent party." Even the conservative Whig *Janesville Gazette* confessed that "the principles of the Free Soil and Whig parties are identical," and a union likely. David Atwood agreed.

> It must be admitted that there are numerous indications in the present condition of parties pointing to such a state of things in the future. . . . The ostensible issues have become matters of fancy. . . . A great majority of the people are opposed to the extension of slavery; the humbug of "saving the Union" is beginning to be appreciated in all quarters. . . . If slavery can be restricted within its present limits, it must inevitably decline. Southern fanatics are unquestionably aiming at its introduction into Nebraska and New Mexico. It is against these designs that we wish to see the Free Soil sentiment of the North united.[87]

Shortly after Atwood penned this article, Stephen A. Douglas introduced a bill to organize the Nebraska territory without restrictions on slavery.

CHAPTER SIX

We Must Unite
or Be Enslaved

As THE YEAR 1854 began, the political situation in Wisconsin was muddled. The People's coalition offered no binding principles or ideological appeal to take to the voters, while bitter factionalism and internal battles for party control split the majority Democrats. What shape the future political landscape might take was anyone's guess. The federal government's approval of the Kansas-Nebraska Act and the dramatic rescue of a fugitive slave held in a Milwaukee jail helped shed some light.

Stephen A. Douglas, the ambitious Unites States senator from Illinois, submitted his bill to organize the Nebraska Territory in early January. After nearly five months of turbulent proceedings, it passed both houses of Congress and was signed into law by President Pierce. The act repealed that part of the Missouri Compromise of 1820 that prohibited slavery above 36°30' north latitude and permitted settlers of the newly organized territories of Kansas and Nebraska to decide on slavery themselves.[1]

The federal government's endorsement of popular sovereignty and the abrogation of the Missouri Compromise once again thrust slavery and the sectional controversy to center stage in the nation's politics. Many Northerners truly feared that the peculiar institution was intended to take root in

85

one of the territories. As one alarmed Wisconsin diarist noted, the "slavery monster shall spread his wings over our intire [*sic*] Republic" unless northerners resisted this latest outrage of Douglas and the slave power.[2] Joseph C. Cover, a lead district Whig leader and newspaper editor, predicted that the act would abolitionize the entire North and bring about slavery's early demise.[3]

Wisconsin's Free Soilers wasted no time in trying to exploit the issue. Shortly after the bill's introduction, they encouraged state residents to overwhelm their representatives in Congress with anti-Nebraska petitions; the response was enthusiastic. In more than thirty anti-Nebraska meetings, thousands of angry Wisconsinites adopted resolutions that denounced the measure and instructed their congressmen to vote against it.[4] In late January, Sherman Booth asked for a nonpartisan state convention to meet in Madison and formulate a response to this brazen "attempt of the Slave Power to desecrate every foot of free territory . . . with the curse of slavery."[5] For several reasons, the call for a statewide meeting initially met with little enthusiasm.

For one, most Democrats kept silent on the matter, presumably awaiting direction from their national leaders. When it came in February, Democrats were urged to rally around Pierce and the Nebraska bill as a manifestation of party loyalty and to rely on the west's physiographic characteristics and the benign influence of popular sovereignty to keep slavery out of the territories. Trying to put the best face possible on the repeal of the Missouri Compromise, some even falsely insisted that the 1820 settlement actually had impaired freedom's spread by insulating territories below 36°30' north latitude from the democratic tendencies now prevalent throughout the North. Josiah Noonan, the administration boss in Wisconsin, also used the patronage whip unsparingly to weed out anti-Nebraska sentiment and sternly warned the unconvinced to maintain "an expressive silence" on the issue lest they contribute to a new wave of sectional animosity that threatened to convulse the nation and destroy the Union. By early March, reluctant Democrats began to fall in line.[6] Although administration backers failed to suppress all internal opposition to the Nebraska bill, surprisingly few Democrats publicly disavowed the new test of party faithfulness. Most dissidents seem to have muzzled their objections and looked to work from within to correct the party's alleged proslavery leanings.[7]

The state's Whigs also responded coolly to the idea of a convention. Without exception, they denounced Douglas' bill as a scheme to introduce slavery in the territories, but they remained unwilling to see their party absorbed by the Free Soilers. When Rufus King reprinted Booth's call without comment, party conservatives, worried that they would have limited influence in any coalition managed by those two, publicly scolded him for supposedly conspiring once again to sell out to the abolitionists. Other Whigs opposed the meeting, imagining that the Nebraska controversy might give new life to their party.[8]

Important local issues such as railroad land grants, temperance, and corruption in state government also occupied the attention of state residents and suppressed enthusiasm for a convention. Finally, and probably most decisive, with the North generally hostile to the Nebraska measure, few believed it actually would succeed in the House of Representatives. As one Democrat succinctly stated, "Its passage was not . . . looked for by the people."[9]

In spite of the lukewarm response to his appeal, Booth continued to press for a mass protest meeting. Unexpected help came when a federal marshal arrested a hapless black, Joshua Glover, near Racine on the evening of March 10. A Missouri runaway, Glover had escaped to Wisconsin from his owner, Bennami Garland, two years earlier. Finding work as a millhand, Glover, by all accounts, was considered "a faithful laborer and an honest man." On the night of his capture, he had been drinking and playing cards in his home with two black acquaintances, Nelson Turner and William Abby. Unknown to Glover, Turner had betrayed his whereabouts to Garland and unlatched the door to allow him entry along with his accomplices. After a short but violent struggle, Glover was bound, thrown into a wagon and carted off to the Milwaukee county jail.[10]

On the morning after Glover's arrest, citizens of Racine held a mass meeting on the public square. They adopted resolutions demanding a fair trial for Glover and promised to use force if necessary to free him.[11] In the meantime, word of Glover's seizure had reached Booth. Acting quickly, he mounted his horse and rode through Milwaukee's streets shouting that slavecatchers were in town and that an indignation meeting would be held that afternoon at the county courthouse. Booth then persuaded a county judge to issue a writ of habeas corpus on the fugitive's behalf, but the sheriff refused to serve it on the grounds that Glover was held in federal custody and not subject to local authority.[12]

Later that day, more than five thousand people jammed the courthouse grounds to protest Glover's arrest. After a vigilance committee selected to obtain a writ of habeas corpus returned empty-handed, the crowd grew restive. At about 5:00 P.M., Glover's self-appointed attorney condemned the seizure in a fiery speech and suggested they take the law into their own hands. Booth followed and advised against a forcible release, but after local officials refused a demand to deliver Glover, the crowd rushed the jail, smashed in the door and whisked him away to freedom. One reporter was moved to write of the affair, "We regret to . . . inform the friends of Glover that it was deemed unsafe for him to remain in this Republican country, and that by this time he is safe in Canada, under the protection of a monarchy."[13]

For Booth's alleged role in the rescue, a United States commissioner had him arrested on March 15. Two days later, at a preliminary hearing, he was released on bond for later trial, but not before he regretfully denied taking a direct role in liberating Glover, immodestly claiming that the need for his voice against the Nebraska bill had restrained him. Then, amidst wild cheering, he went on to say that rather than see one fugitive returned to slavery, he would prefer to "see every Federal officer in Wisconsin hanged." Booth had voiced similar sentiments just before his arrest, warning that "every U.S. Judge and Marshall . . . [would] be treated to a wet bath or a coat of tar and feathers," if necessary, to safeguard habeas corpus and jury trial rights. "If the time has come when we are called on to yield these sacred rights," he proclaimed, "then . . . the time has come for revolution."[14]

Coming amidst the tumultuous congressional contest over the Nebraska bill, the Glover affair brought the slavery controversy closer to home and intensified the growing distrust of federal authority.[15] At a crowded "Anti-Slave Catchers Mass Convention," convened in Milwaukee on April 13, those in attendance renewed the argument that the Fugitive Slave Act represented an unjust seizure of power by the national government and a threat both to individual freedom and states' rights. They also endorsed the famed Virginia and Kentucky Resolutions of 1798, authored by Thomas Jefferson and James Madison, that had provided a thoughtful defense of state prerogatives, as well as of civil liberties thought to be under attack by the administration of President John Adams. These proclaimed that whenever the federal government transcended its constitutional mandate, "Its acts are unauthoritative, void and of no force."[16]

Booth's extremism and popular support for the rescue horrified Wisconsin's Democrats. Countenance the willful destruction of public property and the flagrant violation of federal law, they warned, and soon security for both whites and blacks would be imperiled. "We might as well bid welcome to anarchy."[17] Whigs, on the other hand, began to rethink their opposition to a mass convention and a new antislavery coalition, even though they disliked seeing "the laws of the land trampled upon, and the mob triumphant." Because of the Senate's recent passage of the Nebraska bill, characterized as a violation of the public faith and a renunciation of the solemn bisectional covenant embodied in the Missouri Compromise, most excused the angry citizens who actively resisted the Fugitive Slave Act. As Charles Holt, the conservative Whig editor of the *Janesville Gazette* approvingly wrote, "the attempted repeal of the Missouri Compromise has so exasperated many [Northerners] that they consider themselves absolved from the obligation to enforce the fugitive slave law."[18]

Seizing the moment, Free Soilers skillfully tied the Glover affair to the House battle over the status of slavery in Nebraska. Riding a wave of popularity, Booth renewed his call for a fusion of all men opposed to the further extension of slavery, and by late April he appeared to be gaining ground among Whigs. In his *Grant County Herald,* Joseph Cover proclaimed that Whig and Democratic harmony had been irreparably shattered, and from this some new political organization soon would arise. David Atwood and Horace Rublee, of the *Wisconsin State Journal,* agreed. "There is no use in trying to keep up the old political parties," they asserted; "New combinations are inevitable."[19] Booth applauded this progress and asked for further encouragement from all Whigs. After several false starts, during which union backers labored to appease headstrong conservatives and a few diffident moderates,[20] the signal Booth awaited finally arrived. On May 18, the *State Journal* printed an unambiguous endorsement of "a union of men opposed to slavery should the Nebraska Bill become law."[21] Four days later the House passed the measure and on May 30 it received Pierce's signature.

Now Booth patiently waited, supposing Whigs would take the initiative after House approval. When they did not, he once again proposed a state convention. On the day the bill became law, Rufus King at last broke the Whig silence. He observed that a nonpartisan meeting had been summoned in Ohio "to determine what action should be taken . . . in view of the passage of the Nebraska Bill," and he asked if all the free states should do the same.[22] One week later, King urged that the coming congressional elections be conducted without reference to party distinctions and all issues save slavery laid aside to facilitate an anti-Nebraska coalition.[23] Christopher

Sholes and two Democratic editors, E. B. Quiner and John Walworth, joined him. Finally, on June 9, Booth, on behalf of "many citizens," formally invited

> All men opposed to the Repeal of the Missouri Compromise, the Extension of Slavery, and the Rule of the Slave Power . . . to meet at *Madison, Thursday, July 13,* to take such measures as may be deemed necessary to prevent Future Encroachments of the Slave Power, to Repeal all Compromises in favor of Slavery, and to establish the Principle of Freedom as the Rule of the State and National Governments. The time has come for the Union of all Free Men for the sake of Freedom. There is but one alternative. We must *unite* and be *free,* or *divide* and be *enslaved* by the praetorian bands of the Slaveholders and their Nebraska allies.[24]

King endorsed Booth's call the following day. On June 12, Atwood and Rublee did the same.[25] Holt followed, but with a warning; if Booth and King staged a repeat performance of the "cattle show" held in Watertown the previous year, he would withdraw his support. Most other Whigs quickly laid aside lingering doubts and fell in line, although some in the lead district continued to balk. They sympathized with the goal of unifying the state's anti-Nebraska men but feared that "party hacks, place seekers, spoilsmen," and the *"vegetable remains of two or three defunct parties or factions"* would control and manipulate the convention for their own selfish purposes.[26]

As Free Soilers, Whigs, and a few antislavery Democrats took tentative steps toward cooperation, Governor Barstow and Josiah Noonan renewed their war for control of the Democracy. During the final weeks of the Nebraska debate, the governor and Beriah Brown journeyed to Washington and tried without success to pry the Pierce administration loose from its attachment to Noonan. While they were in the capital, the Milwaukee boss made arrangements with Horace Tenney to establish an anti-Barstow paper in Madison to compete with Brown's *Argus.* Shortly after their return, Barstow and Brown publicly broke with the administration, contending that "support of the Nebraska Bill . . . is not a test of Democracy." Although they never explicitly came out against the act, Barstow and Brown clearly were trying to rally anti-Nebraska Democrats, fed up with Noonan's dictation, and conservative Whigs, opposed to fusion, with assurances that popular sovereignty would secure the territories for freedom and keep the Union intact.[27]

With Barstow and Noonan doing battle, preparations for the mass convention proceeded with enthusiasm. Delegates were chosen at meetings held throughout the state. Train and steamship fares were reduced for men coming from the populous lakeshore counties, and keepers of hotels, public houses, and other businesses eagerly anticipated the influx of free-spending conventioneers. Minor preconvention skirmishes between Whigs and Free Soilers over the role each would play in the new coalition were transcended by the need for mutual forbearance and compromise in order to bring about a successful union.[28] Finally, on July 13, as delegates poured into Madison, spokesmen from all three parties met informally to iron out remaining differences over procedural and organizational matters. Leaving nothing to chance, they hoped the gathering would come off without a hitch.[29]

By early afternoon, upwards of one thousand people had arrived,[30] forcing an adjournment from the assembly's chambers to the east lawn of the capitol building. Taking the advice of the *State Journal*'s editors, Booth, King, and other party bosses remained in the background to give the impression that new men were in control of the convention, but behind the scenes they wielded considerable influence. At their urging, John Walworth, the Democratic editor of the *Monroe Sentinel*, was named to preside over the meeting to emphasize its nonpartisan character, in spite of the overwhelming numbers of Whigs and Free Soilers. Another conciliatory gesture included the appointment of a Democrat, Rhenodyne A. Bird, and the Whig, Charles Holt, to chair the resolutions committee, which then sought Booth's blessing before presenting its report to the delegates. Similarly, Myron and Harlow Orton, prominent conservative Whigs from Dane county, were permitted to address the gathering along with the radicals Booth, Charles Clement, Hiram McKee, and the recent Wisconsin immigrant and abolitionist, William Abijah White. Myron Orton's speech, a "laboured eulogy" to the Whig party, provoked the only note of dissension when the Free Soiler James Densmore let go with a loud hiss at the mention of Henry Clay and Daniel Webster. Otherwise, the convention rolled along with impressive smoothness and efficiency.[31]

The delegates created a state central committee of nine headed by the newcomer White to coordinate activities in the state and make contact with similar organizations that were springing up around the North. They also selected five men, including two prominent Germans, to oversee the establishment of foreign-language newspapers and to court Wisconsin's considerable foreign-born population. Most importantly, the resolutions committee deliberately avoided divisive issues such as land distribution and homestead legislation and reported a set of distinct antislavery measures that the delegates unanimously adopted. And, probably following the suggestion of meetings held earlier in Ripon, Wisconsin, and Jackson, Michigan, and of thirty or so anti-Nebraska House members, they took to calling themselves Republicans.[32]

The Republican platform sprang from the Free Soil platforms of 1848 and 1852, which in turn had Liberty party parentage. It called for the confinement of slavery to its present borders, the admission of no more slave states, the exclusion of slavery from all territories under federal jurisdiction, the prohibition of human servitude in any future land acquisitions, the restoration of freedom to Kansas and Nebraska, and "the repeal and entire abrogation of the Fugitive Slave Law." It also asked party members to support only candidates for office who were fully committed to the Republican antislavery platform and to the goal of delivering "the Administration of the government back to . . . first principles," a familiar way of advancing the supposed policy of the founding fathers "to limit, localize, and discourage Slavery" and bring about its gradual extinction peacefully and constitutionally. No other alternative existed; continued Southern domination of the federal government had forced Republicans to battle over "freedom or slavery as a political issue." In conclusion, the new party invited all men, whether foreign-born or native-born, to join in the struggle.[33]

Amidst wild cheering, Wisconsin's first Republican convention came to an end, its members pledged to return home and begin the mundane task of preparing for the upcoming congressional campaign. By August, organizational meetings at the local level were being held around the state. The shift of nearly the entire leadership of the Whig and Free Soil organizations and the experience of working together in prior years facilitated the movement into the new party. The unification process stalled only in Walworth County, where stubborn conservatives dominated the Whig party, and Free Soilers, who outnumbered them, foolishly snubbed them in selecting candidates for local office and drove many into the welcoming arms of the Democracy. The enthusiasm manifested for the new party in the lead district more than offset the Walworth county split. By late August, Cover and George Bliss, influential editor of the Whig *Mineral Point Tri-*

bune, counted themselves in the Republican column along with the rest of the Whig leadership and the region's few Free Soilers.[34]

The efforts of local Whigs and Free Soilers to bury party differences and merge also bore fruit in the congressional nominating conventions. In the southeastern district, Free Soilers dominated the coalition, and four of them, Booth, Charles Clement, Christopher Sholes, and Wyman Spooner, competed for the spot. A plurality of the delegates favored the controversial Booth, but King, fearful that Booth's selection would alienate many Whigs, used his considerable influence on behalf of Spooner, who alone among the candidates had belonged to that party prior to 1848. After five unsuccessful attempts to choose a nominee, Sholes and Clement rewarded King's persistence and swung their support behind Spooner. Sholes, commenting on the nomination, proclaimed that now "our union is perfect." Booth took the rejection calmly, even after the *State Journal* compared him unfavorably to Spooner, stating that the former Whig was "a zealous opponent of slavery without being a brawling fanatic, and is progressive without being crazy."[35]

In the western region, Republicans had no trouble selecting a candidate. Few Free Soilers lived there, and the convention's choice fell between two Whigs, Cadwallader C. Washburn, whose brothers Elihu and Levi already represented Maine and Illinois in Congress, and former representative Orsamus Cole. The popular Washburn easily won the nomination, and except for a soundly quashed attempt to amend the Madison convention's call for the repeal of the Fugitive Slave Law to a demand for its modification, the meeting was thoroughly friendly.[36]

Charles Billinghurst, an anti-Nebraska Democrat and editor of the *Burr Oak,* and James Shafter, the Whig party's congressional nominee in 1852, were the Republican hopefuls in the heavily Democratic north. After seven informal ballots, the party convention remained almost evenly divided between the two men. Shafter then rose, thanked the delegates for their support, and withdrew in favor of Billinghurst. The erstwhile Democrat promptly received the party's endorsement and the gathering broke up in high spirits.[37]

The choice of a Free Soiler, a Whig, and a Democrat to represent the new party in its debut was fortunate. It helped unite all factions behind the candidates and platform and allowed Republicans to enter their first campaign brimming with confidence and enthusiasm. By contrast, internal feuding as usual threatened Democratic harmony. Daniel Wells, the party incumbent representing the southeast, had his work cut out for him. A warm friend and supporter of Noonan's, he reluctantly had voted against the Kansas-Nebraska measure because his constituency was thoroughly "disaffected on that question."[38] By combining his anti-Nebraska vote with careful attention to and encouragement of the district's administration supporters, Wells entered the party convention in early October an overwhelming favorite. With Noonan's backing, an effort to unseat him by friends of Barstow was thwarted easily. Just as important, the convention heeded Wells's advice to be "wily as serpents and harmless as doves" on the slavery question. It adopted a resolution that opposed slavery's extension "by all constitutional means" and extolled popular sovereignty as "the only true basis" upon which to achieve that goal. This "time serving milk and water position" did not entirely satisfy administration men, but political reality and the advantage of appearing to be both anti-Nebraska and pro-Pierce proved irresistible; Wells entered the contest with most of the party behind him. The incumbent further enhanced his reelection chances by instructing his followers in Walworth County to nominate dissident Whigs for local office in exchange for their support. Finally, with Noonan and George Paul holding the president's followers in line, Wells took to the stump to shore up his support among anti-Nebraska Democrats, and on election eve, he circulated a pamphlet strongly critical of Douglas's bill.[39]

Only an all-out effort kept the Barstow and Noonan factions tenuously allied behind Wells; otherwise the feud took a painful toll in the district. Both sides nominated candidates for local and state offices, and in the governor's home county of Waukesha, where antiadministration sentiment was strongest, Barstow's champions openly disavowed both Pierce and Wells. Noonan retaliated by convincing his friend, the popular and opportunistic ex-Free Soiler Alexander Randall, to run for a seat in the state assembly against the governor's personal choice. In spite of the Democracy's problems, party loyalty, hard work, political skill, and an overconfident Republican coalition helped reelect Wells comfortably.[40]

Democrats in western Wisconsin did not fare so well. Supporters of the president hoped to unseat the popular incumbent, Ben Eastman, an unrepentant anti-Nebraska man.[41] At the party convention, Eastman took a slight lead in early balloting over his nearest competitor, a Barstow supporter, while the pro-Nebraska candidate ran a distant third. On the second day of the meeting, Otis Hoyt, the administration's choice, began to pick up strength; on the twenty-third ballot he overtook Eastman but still remained short of a majority. Seizing their chance, party regulars secured an endorsement of a set of resolutions sustaining both Pierce and Nebraska. Eastman interpreted that as a personal rebuke and, along with the entire Green County delegation, promptly abandoned the meeting. The remaining delegates then gave the nomination to Hoyt.[42]

Hoyt's selection and the pro-Nebraska platform did not sit well with the district's Democrats. "The report of the doings of the . . . convention has reached this place," exclaimed one Rock county man, "and it is no go. . . . Democrats will not submit to such doughfaced dictation." Only Noonan's organ, the *Wisconsin Patriot,* backed Hoyt, but Dane County's Democrats, under Barstow's control, refused to endorse his candidacy. To make matters worse for the unfortunate Hoyt, Eastman bolted the party in favor of Washburn,[43] and the Pierce administration blocked passage of a rivers and harbors bill highly popular in the southwestern counties. As Joseph Cover put it:

> The Homestead Bill, River and Harbor Bill, Pacific Railroad Bill— all were for the special benefit of white laboring men—and consequently failed. Such bills as those repealing the Missouri Compromise and for the recovery of fugitive slaves, were full of *niggers,* and they went through like Croton Oil.[44]

With so many obstacles, few people expected Hoyt to win. The popular Washburn handily defeated him, capturing 60 percent of the vote.[45]

Democrats in northern Wisconsin faced similar problems. The incumbent, John Macy, had favored the Kansas-Nebraska bill at first, but strong opposition back home led him to pair off on the measure when the final vote came. For this act and his ties to Barstow, Pierce Democrats under the lead of Charles Robinson, the pugnacious editor of the *Green Bay Advocate,* sought to dump Macy in favor of an unqualified Nebraska man at the district's nominating convention.[46] Macy won renomination anyway, then spurned his opponents by deliberately refusing to take a stand on the Nebraska question or express support for the president. Because of Macy's renegade behavior, a number of administration men walked out of the meeting in protest, and with Noonan's blessing, placed an avowed Pierce and Nebraska candidate in the race.[47] The slavery issue and local political rivalries crippled the Democratic effort in the North and left them to the mercy of the Republican coalition. So in spite of their overwhelming numbers, the Democrats suffered another crushing defeat.[48]

The success of the new party was remarkable. It elected two congressmen, won a majority of the seats in the state assembly, and nearly captured the senate as well. Three months later, the Republican legislative majority then picked the old abolitionist, Charles Durkee, to serve in the United States Senate in place of the incumbent Isaac Walker.[49]

Nearly half of the Republican vote in the 1854 congressional races came from men who had backed the People's coalition in 1853 (see table 7). Since Whigs had cast 50 percent and Free Soilers 35 percent of the People's ballots, it is highly likely that they also made up the bulk of this portion of the Republican tally. About half of 1853's conservative Whigs moved into the Republican camp, constituting about 5 percent of the new party's support, while Democrats formed another 7 percent.

Republican candidates also attracted a rather large number of votes from men who had sat out the election in 1853; those voters comprised close to 40 percent of their support.[50] Whigs and Democrats who failed to show up in 1853 undoubtedly cast some of these Republican ballots. But how many? By comparing the election returns in the 1855 judicial and gubernatorial contests with 1854's congressional totals, at least one inference can be drawn (see tables 8 and 9).

An analysis of these races suggests that the 1854 coalition remained largely intact the following April. About 90 percent of those who voted the Republican ticket in 1854 did so again in the spring election for state supreme court justice; the Democratic candidate for the judgeship picked up 82 percent of his party's congressional ballots. In the 1855 governor's campaign, held in November, the returns suggest that 15 percent of the men who voted Republican in 1854 crossed over to the Democrats. If this is true, Democrats actually made up 20 to 25 percent of the Republican vote in 1854,[51] but most of them returned to the Democracy one year later.

The overall Republican coalition in 1854 seems to have been made up of roughly 40 percent Whigs, 25 percent Free Soilers, 20 percent Democrats, and 15 percent prior nonvoters.[52] Democratic support in 1854 did not vary much from 1853; nearly 80 percent of its vote came from party loyalists, 10 percent from supporters of the People's coalition, 5 percent from disaffected Whigs, and 5 percent from nonvoters.

Outrage over the Kansas-Nebraska Act and the Glover rescue, as well as the emergence of a political union dedicated to combating the slave power and its northern allies, did not translate into increased voter turnout. Only 47 percent of the eligible electorate in Wisconsin bothered to vote in 1854, suggesting that the political passions unleashed sparked only a partial electoral revolution. Several possible explanations for this exist. For one, in spite of the genuine consternation brought on by the decade-old territorial controversy and the accompanying sectional conflict, slavery so far had failed to obtain a foothold anywhere in the West. That simple fact, plus the widespread belief that the North's superior industry, talent, and drive would safeguard the territories for freedom, probably quelled much unease. "Slavery can never go to the new territories," one Democrat insisted. "This is the only point of practical importance in the controversy about which the masses care a fig."[53]

Apathy and alienation undoubtedly contributed to the low turnout as well. Not only had slavery failed to expand, but old party issues ceased to be important. The growing sense that politicians lacked principles and cared only for "spoils . . . the *fat office*," added to the problem.[54] Consequently, many men did not feel compelled to vote. During the 1854 campaign, Willet S. Main, Dane County's Democratic sheriff and a relatively attentive chronicler of local and national events, expressed this indifference. "One week from today our election comes off. Candidates are hard at work. I . . . do not feel much interest in the result. May the right triumph." Reluctantly, Main showed up and voted a split ticket, but he added, "I don't care but a little how the [election] goes."[55] If party activists like Main felt this way, it is not surprising that a majority of the state's eligible voters stayed home on election day.

Finally, simple confusion almost certainly augmented the abstention rate. The withering away of the Whigs, the numerous coalition efforts, the interminable power struggles within the Democratic party, all of these must have left many perplexed. In an apt comment, Willet S. Main mused:

Politics is pretty well mixed. Hards and Softs, Barnburners, Wooleys & Silver Greys, Republicans, Whigs and Nationals, Nebraska and anti-Nebraska, all in friction, yes and Know Nothings, all appear to be mixed in a heterogeneous conglomerated mass of fusion. No one can tell where he belongs or what his politics are.[56]

Nevertheless, the 1854 election did foreshadow a change in the making. The Republican coalition united Free Soilers and most Whigs, and it attracted enough Democrats, abstainers, and new voters to achieve impressive election victories. Success at the polls also bolstered Republican confidence and acted to counter the Democratic charge that the party would founder once the furor over Nebraska subsided, although as 1854 came to an end, it was not yet clear if the Nebraska bill and the fugitive slave controversy would be enough to sustain the organization. "The truth is the people of the North are incapable of any lengthy and persistent effort in behalf of justice and right," Cadwallader C. Washburn anxiously noted. "They rouse up and become indignant for a time but gradually settle down and acquiesce in whatever imposition may be placed upon them."[57] Between 1854 and 1860, however, events would give shape and substance to the Republican appeal and help usher in a new and final chapter in the politics of antislavery. First, though, the party and its distinctly antislavery message had to contend for political supremacy, not just with its Democratic opponents, but with the emergent force of nativism.

CHAPTER SEVEN

This Thing
Called Know Nothingism

BETWEEN 1847 AND 1855 Wisconsin's population grew from 210,546 to 522,109. Nearly 200,000 of the state's inhabitants had been born abroad, with the majority claiming either Germany and Ireland as their place of birth. Men and women from the British Isles, Norway, British America, and a scattering of people from other countries made up the rest of the burgeoning foreign-born population.[1]

Wisconsin was not alone in experiencing that tide of immigration. Poverty-stricken families fleeing Ireland, along with politically and economically disenchanted nationals from Germany and elsewhere in Europe, swamped the nation during those years. Not only did the size of that new wave of immigration dwarf prior surges into America, but its composition was different. Large numbers of the new emigres were Roman Catholics, and in many locales they were greeted with suspicion and hostility.[2]

Anti-Catholic prejudice had deep roots in Protestant America. Occasionally, animosity led to outbreaks of violence, most notably the burning of the Ursuline Sisters' school outside Boston in 1834 and the murderous Philadelphia riots a decade later.[3]

Extreme anti-Catholicism lay quiescent for several years after 1844. Toward the end of the decade, however, native-born Protestants began to view the growing number of immigrants with alarm. Throughout the country, their churches, newspapers, and religious societies warned of the dangers the alien menace posed to the Republic. Catholics, it was said, remained slavishly devoted to the pope, a foreign potentate who represented values totally at odds with those of republican America, and they could not be trusted to embrace the institutions of their adopted homeland. To counter that threat, organized Protestantism undertook the job of converting and educating the immigrants to American religious and political values and of containing the spread of their heathen ways.[4]

Nativist fears of the growing Catholic menace took a turn for the worse in the early 1850s when Whig policymakers looked to the foreign-born Catholic vote to save their failing party. At the prodding of leaders like William Seward, United States senator from New York, Whigs attempted to seduce those traditionally Democratic voters into supporting Winfield Scott's candidacy. The strategy failed miserably. The Catholic vote remained solidly Democratic and their party's appeal to the papists galled nativist Whigs who either switched parties or sat out the election altogether.[5]

America's Catholic bishops fueled nativist anxiety in the following year when they condemned public schools, with some justice, as inherently anti-Catholic. They cited the refusal to use the Catholic version of the Bible in the schools as evidence of that discrimination, as well as the derogatory manner in which textbooks and teachers referred to the Church of Rome. Failing to reform the public school system, America's Catholics campaigned vigorously to secure public funding for their own schools.[6]

The school controversy and the increasingly aggressive Catholic clergy and laity panicked many lower- and middle-class Protestants. President Franklin Pierce heightened their fears when he appointed the Catholic James Campbell as his postmaster general, it was widely perceived, to placate the nation's "Roman Legions." Even less well received was the 1853 trip of the papal emissary, Archbishop Gaetano Bedini, to the United States. After adjudicating a conflict over church property, he toured the country, with unfortunate results. Nativists denounced Bedini as a violent foe of republican institutions and cited as evidence his role in suppressing the Italian uprisings in 1848 and 1849. His real mission, they maintained, was to create papist secret societies dedicated to the destruction of American liberty. Enraged nativists dogged his every step, and his journey through the states often met with violence.[7]

The temperance movement likewise created friction between nativists and immigrants. Drunkenness and its attendant social problems concerned many Americans. The enactment of prohibition laws, it was hoped, would arrest alcohol abuse and instill proper moral values and social behavior, particularly among the Irish and Germans, for whom drinking was socially and culturally acceptable. Not surprisingly, anti-Catholicism and prohibitionist attitudes often went hand in hand. Prohibitionists scored their first victory in 1851, when Maine outlawed the sale of alcoholic beverages in the state, permitted the search and seizure of suspect property, and subjected offenders to fines and imprisonment.[8] Many northern states soon followed Maine's example.

Anti-Catholic bigotry lay at the core of nativist sentiment in the first half of the 1850s, but many viewed the foreign invasion as dangerous in general. Protestant and Catholic immigrants, with their different customs, values, and language, it was thought, threatened the social, economic, and political fabric of American life. Many, particularly the Irish, arrived in extreme poverty and drained local resources set aside to aid the poor. Oftentimes, out of desperation, they resorted to criminal acts and swelled local jails. American workmen especially feared that the influx of foreigners would depress wages, lower their standard of living, and limit upward mobility and opportunity. Nativist observers claimed that the immigrants also threatened the purity of American political institutions, since their unfamiliarity with the nation's electoral traditions and practices made them easy targets of corrupt politicians. Thus, foreigners were blamed for most of the ills that afflicted American politics and were looked upon as threats to republican institutions and government.[9] Out of this maelstrom of intensified ethnocultural rivalry the Know Nothing party emerged.

The Know Nothing party, so-called because its members pleaded ignorance when questioned about its principles, exploded onto the national political scene in 1854 and for a time contended with the newly emergent Republican organization as the Democracy's major opponent. Indeed, the party's rapid growth was phenomenal. From a minuscule organization in 1850, it claimed four years later to have ten thousand local lodges and a national membership of more than one million. Although antipathy to foreigners, and especially Catholics, was the one common denominator binding its members, the party also appealed to a genuine reformist impulse that swept America in the early 1850s. At the same time that traditional party battles faded into irrelevance, nativists censured both Whigs and Democrats not only for failing to address issues the huge number of immigrants raised but for exacerbating the problems in their shameless pursuit of office and foreign votes. The system's unresponsiveness in turn bred an impatience with politics-as-usual and self-serving party hacks and a desire for new leadership to tackle the issues head on and reaffirm that the "American" people indeed were the locus of power.[10] The Know Nothing political program promised to do just that. It called for an overhaul of the nation's naturalization laws, greater restrictions on officeholding and voting rights, and political reforms designed to drive corrupt party bosses and officeholders out of power. Voter dissatisfaction with the political system, the foreign threat to the nation's social and economic order, and the reemergence of the slavery issue combined to break the enfeebled Whigs and force a realignment of the already-shaky second-party system. But in 1854, it remained a toss-up whether the politics of nativism or antislavery would bring about a new and lasting coalition to challenge the Democrats.[11]

The relations between Wisconsin's native and foreign-born citizens reflected many of the same problems that gripped the rest of the country, most especially other Northern states. They battled over the use of the Bible in common schools and whether to teach children in the language of their native country rather than in English, and they marveled at each others' outlandish behavior and traditions. Unalloyed religious bigotry also created tension between Catholics and Protestants, as did disputes over dancing, gambling, smoking, Sabbath-breaking, and drinking. From time to time violence broke out. One notorious case involved both a murder and a lynching and led to unusually strained relations between Germans and nativists in Milwaukee and its vicinity.[12]

Politically, the temperance issue caused the greatest animosity, at least in part because it embraced so many of the cultural and religious questions that divided Wisconsin's diverse population. In 1849, the Wisconsin legislature took the unusual step of requiring liquor dealers to post a one thousand dollar bond, making them responsible to communities and individuals for damages their sale of intoxicants caused. The law was ignored, however, and soon calls for repeal were heard, especially from the state's mushrooming German population. Instead of bowing to such pressure, the lawmakers strengthened the statute, but lax enforcement again prevailed.[13]

When the attempt to encourage responsible use of liquor proved to be a failure, temperance advocates in Wisconsin, reflecting national trends, turned their hopes to complete prohibition. In 1853, legislators, eager to keep the liquor question out of politics, reluctantly gave the state's voters the choice of whether a prohibitory law should be passed. By a narrow margin, they endorsed the idea. Those Wisconsinites who had come from the northeastern part of the United States, nearly all of them Protestants, supported prohibition more than any other element of the population. So did natives of Great Britain, Norway, and British America. The increasingly influential Germans, along with the Irish, just as predictably opposed it.[14] The liquor issue remained controversial until mid-1855 when Governor Barstow put the issue to rest by vetoing legislation that prohibited the sale of intoxicating beverages.[15] By that time, however, Know Nothingism had emerged on the national political scene, and in Wisconsin, it temporarily threatened to tear apart the state's newly formed Republican party.

The Know Nothing, or Native American, party's appeal varied from state to state in 1854. Irish men and women, fleeing their famine-stricken homeland, had overrun Massachusetts, leading fearful natives to elect a Know Nothing governor and legislature and all of that state's congressmen. In New York, only the masterful tactics of Thurlow Weed, the state's Whig leader, brought a narrow victory to that party's candidate for governor over his Democratic and Know Nothing opponents. Further west, Know Nothings dominated the fusion movement in Indiana and played an important but less significant role in Ohio, but they had little input in Illinois. Throughout the North, the 1854 elections presented a confused picture as the tottering Jacksonian party system received a mortal blow, and nativism thwarted the attempts of anti-Nebraska men to organize a new party in a number of crucial states.[16]

Wisconsin was somewhat different. Most residents, both native and foreign-born, had been in the state less than ten years and together had contributed to its growth. Still in a formative stage, Wisconsin lacked the political, social, and economic traditions the older states in the East had. So in spite of their divisions and the genuine animosity that surfaced, a spirit of accommodation also existed. The state constitution best expressed this openness by granting suffrage to all immigrants who had lived in the state one year and had declared their intentions to become American citizens. Nativism also ran into a wall of angry opposition from Wisconsin's Liberty and Free Soil men and antislavery Whigs.[17] Fusion on an antislavery platform also came easier in the state due to the perennial weakness of the Whigs and the party's earlier experience of working with the Free Soilers. All of these factors, combined with the large number of potential voters of foreign birth, effectively forestalled any attempt to set up a viable Know Nothing organization in Wisconsin and minimized the possibility that either the Republicans or Democrats would adopt nativist political goals. In fact, both parties went out of their way to condemn Know Nothingism.[18]

Still, many native-born Wisconsinites found at least a part of the nativist appeal compelling. Those who entered Know Nothing lodges in the state probably did so more to reaffirm nationalist values they believed were threatened by massive immigration than to circumscribe the political rights of foreigners. In short, the state's Know Nothing and other nativist organizations may have been little more than fraternal orders for overzealous and concerned Wisconsinites to assert their Americanism. That may explain why such staunch Republicans as Rufus King and David Atwood[19] could consistently and vigorously denounce Know Nothingism, maintain the primacy of Republican antislavery principles, and still be under suspicion of harboring nativist sentiments and belonging to the secret order.[20] Many Wisconsinites undoubtedly sympathized with nativist concerns; but those were not more important than their opposition to slavery and had little to do with their decision to embrace the Republican party.[21]

Nevertheless, several thousand hard-core Know Nothings did make their homes in Wisconsin. They followed the national party line and demanded a naturalization law that required the foreign-born to live in the United States for twenty-one years before they could become citizens and that proscribed them from holding public office. They also endorsed ballot-box and educational reform and denounced the unruly Sabbath day behavior of the heathens from abroad.[22]

Whatever the party's attraction, Know Nothingism did not figure prominently in Wisconsin's 1854 elections, in spite of Democratic charges that Republicans would rob adopted citizens of their religious and political rights. Indeed, led by Sherman Booth, Republicans actively denounced nativism, courted the immigrant vote, and invited foreign-born residents to their first state convention. At the county level, Republicans expressed a strong dislike of all organizations that intended "to array one class of our fellow men against another for any difference of nationality or creed," and they insisted that their party drew its strength from the notion that all men, "without regard to clime or color," were entitled to "equal and exact rights and justice." Consequently, no man who claimed to be a Republican could be a Know Nothing. By emphasizing their antislavery creed and downplaying nativism, Wisconsin's Republicans largely succeeded in defusing the issue in their first run for office.[23]

The party's success in sidestepping the Native American appeal came to an abrupt end early in 1855. The Republicans opened themselves to charges of Know Nothingism and angered the state's immigrants when they pushed for a prohibition measure in the state legislature. Governor Barstow's veto of the 1855 prohibition bill made him a hero, especially among the Germans and undoubtedly many native-born tipplers as well. The Republican infatuation with temperance faded in June when Maine's state militia, called out by the state's fanatical prohibitionist governor, Neal Dow, crushed a riot in Portland. A growing backlash against Maine lawism all but buried temperance as a meaningful issue in Wisconsin for the remaining prewar years, but Republicans could not shake off all suspicions of harboring nativist prejudices.[24]

Rumors that the Know Nothings were organizing to manipulate Republican nominations for state office in the upcoming fall elections posed a greater threat to the party. Booth cautioned Republicans to be on their guard against the attempts of the "dark lanterns boys" to pack local meetings and nominate their own men as candidates to the convention; he also warned that he would not endorse anyone who belonged to the secret political order.[25] Moreover, to minimize the possibility that Know Nothings would dominate the state convention, Booth petitioned the state Republican committee to call for a mass meeting instead of one composed of locally selected delegates. Erstwhile Whigs, such as Rufus King, Charles Holt, and David Atwood, instead preferred a much smaller gathering to check the nativist influence. Ultimately, both sides agreed on a basis of representation that would permit more delegates than the Whigs wanted yet not be an open meeting.[26]

Booth's suspicions proved to be well founded. In early July, John Lockwood, the organization's head in Wisconsin, distributed a private directive that urged lodge members to turn out en masse and seize control of the local Republican caucuses. He also instructed them to nominate "none but members of the Order to the Convention" and to delay acting for any candidates seeking state office until the leadership designated an acceptable ticket. Lockwood urged the same action in the Democratic caucuses wherever some prospect of success existed, but clearly the Republicans were his main target.[27] Know Nothing tactics included posting new times for party caucuses, usually without notice; placing ads for meetings without giving details about time or place; and distributing this information only to local lodges. Often, they simply attended the meetings as Republicans. In some villages, this deception worked. "I hasten to inform you," one Lake Mills Know Nothing wrote Elisha Keyes, the order's Dane county chief, that "Brother G. L. Linsley and myself were appointed delegates to the [Republican] State Convention. No Booth men from this district. May God speed the right."[28]

With Know Nothings working to take control of the Republican coalition, a worried Booth decided, to everyone's surprise, to seek the party's nomination for governor. As the rank-and-file's apparent favorite, he asked: Who better to check Know Nothing designs and affirm the primacy of the party's antislavery principles?[29] Booth received encouragement from many friends in Wisconsin as well as from antislavery papers like the *Chicago Tribune,* which maintained that his election would inspire the North and unambiguously establish both the Republican commitment to states' rights and its opposition to the further spread of slavery.[30] Others were less sanguine. James Densmore, a former Free Soil Democrat who now edited the *Elkhorn Independent,* praised Booth's labors in the antislavery movement and agreed that his election "would be the greatest rebuke Wisconsin could give the Slave Power." Nevertheless, over the years the hotheaded editor had stomped "on the toes of hosts of politicians" and gained many personal enemies, a fact that, coupled with his belligerent personality, made him a decidedly unattractive candidate. Densmore believed the amiable and respected Edward Holton, an old abolitionist himself, stood a far better chance of success.[31]

Most ex-Whigs agreed with Densmore, adding that Booth had overestimated his personal popularity. Some, resenting his influence and overbearing manner, threatened to desert the party rather than back him. Many concluded that his "nomination would be injudicious and inadvisable."[32] Commenting on the squabble provoked by Booth's candidacy, Joseph Cover probably spoke for most Republicans with his frustrated assertion that the nominee chosen was unimportant, as long as he was not "a doughface or a demagogue . . . a halfway man . . . [or] a pussy footed pusillanimous little skunk who is afraid of his shadow and believes the union in danger unless . . . [it] becomes a potatoe patch of niggers."[33]

So Republicans faced two problems in 1855: Know Nothingism and the discord created by Booth's candidacy. The Know Nothing threat particularly vexed them because, as a secret society, its true strength and political appeal was unknown. Often, they tried to wish the nativist phenomenon away, dismissing it as "a diversion," "a side issue," "a minor question," compared to the all-important question of slavery. But Know Nothings shrewdly tried to undermine the Republicans by challenging both the growing influence of Catholicism in American politics and the extension of slavery.[34] In the weeks prior to their September 5 nominating convention, Republicans vigorously attempted to counteract Know Nothingism and dissociate their party from the secret organization. They denounced the Know Nothing demand for proscription of immigrants and Catholics as contrary to cherished republican principals and to the "right of every man, without distinction of birth, to the privileges and immunities . . . guaranteed by the Declaration of Independence." They similarly chastised Democrats for arousing the fears of native and foreign-born Americans with their cries "against papal and foreign influence" to divert attention from the slavery issue. Lastly, they blamed the ethnic and religious violence sweeping the nation's cities on fanatical Know Nothing and Democratic demagogues whose rhetoric inflamed tempers and led to the bloody street battles. Rather than yield to those attempts to stir up "the fires of jealousy, hate and proscription," Republicans invited all men, irrespective of "what land gave you birth, or in what manner you choose to worship," to join their crusade.[35]

The Republican denunciation of Know Nothing principles sprang from expediency as well as conviction. Given the size of Wisconsin's immigrant population, any overt appeal to nativism was politically unthinkable, yet many anxious citizens found it compelling, and Republicans found it impossible to ignore. Even Booth, who continually heaped scorn on "the despotism of Know Nothingism," openly welcomed nativist support as long as Republican principles remained paramount.[36]

Recognizing that the struggle for control of the Republican party largely transcended personalities and centered on the relative importance of its antislavery ideals versus nativist fears, Booth, in an effort to defuse the tension created by his candidacy, dropped out of the race for governor. He urged his supporters to concentrate on securing the nomination for state office of Republican candidates who were committed to the original party platform and, if possible, to prevent the dismemberment of the coalition.[37] Just hours before the Republican state convention was called to order, Booth and others came together in a hastily convened "mass meeting" to spell out their objectives. They proclaimed their unwillingness to support any Know Nothing for state office and demanded a categorical renunciation of the organization by their party.[38] "If the Republican Convention take decided ground against secret political organizations and nominates a ticket of capable men, free from the taint of Know Nothingism, it shall have our cordial support," otherwise, it would meet with "our most decided·opposition."[39] Amidst that uncertainty, the convention came together the same afternoon.

It is impossible to determine the number of Know Nothings present at the Republican convention. Some knowledgeable politicians flatly asserted that "they . . . secured a decided majority of the delegates," and had even selected their own ticket, so confident were they of dominating the meeting, while others claimed their number was far less.[40] Whatever the truth, John Fox Potter and A. H. Spain, representing Republican antislavery activists, immediately provoked a battle when they spoke against seating D. E. Wood, a Fond du Lac Know Nothing who earlier had attended the party's national convention in Philadelphia and vowed to block any proposal "which gives the sanction of this convention to the principle of Know Nothingism." In the heated debate that followed, Potter, Spain, and others firmly stood their ground, finally prompting Wood to come forward to announce that he held Republican principles above "those of any other political organization" and would support all of its nominees, including foreign-born citizens. Wood's declaration broke the deadlock, satisfying even Booth.[41] Before proceeding with the nominations, Byron Paine, a Milwaukee abolitionist, introduced the following resolution, which won unanimous approval.[42]

That the fundamental principles of the Republican Party are based upon the equal rights of all men, that those principles are utterly hostile to the proscription of any on account of birth place, religion or color, and that this convention is opposed to all secret political organizations which favor such proscription or adopt secret measures or take upon themselves obligations inconsistent with the Republican faith, and with fair and honest action as members of the Republican party.

The convention then went on to select a ticket headed by Coles Bashford, a temperance advocate and alleged Know Nothing who vehemently denied being a member of the organization.[43] Of the remaining seven nominees, three were well-known political abolitionists in no way associated with the nativist movement, and one was a German-born newspaper editor and antislavery activist. Former Whigs and Democrats rounded out the ticket, none of whom had any known connection to the Know Nothings. Indeed, Elisha Keyes, Dane County's leading Know Nothing, later admitted that except for the protesting Bashford, they had failed to win a place on the Republican ticket for any of their favorites.[44]

The Republican platform similarly failed to placate nativists. In addition to the antiproscription plank, it disavowed "all sympathy . . . with the Know Nothing organization" and reaffirmed the party's antislavery resolves of 1854.[45] But Know Nothings did enjoy some success in the selection of state central committee members, securing at least four of its nine seats. Although no direct evidence exists, it appears that antislavery men agreed to share control of the committee, convinced that nativism as a political force would quickly fade away. In the meantime, the American leadership might be counted on to work, presumably with discretion, on behalf of the Republican candidates. As Booth put it, "If Know Nothings choose to support our ticket, let them. If Hunkers choose to support it, let them. In so doing they aid Republicanism, not Know Nothingism, not Hunkerism. Let us, then, not fight on a false issue, but carry the war into Africa."[46]

The convention broke up in a spirit of harmony, and Booth especially was pleased with himself for laying the groundwork that kept the Republican organization intact and true to its principles. Even his most conservative critics within the party commended him for restraining "that anti-Republican and dangerous secret organization known as *Know Nothings* . . . his course throughout the Convention was such as met the approval of every true Republican."[47]

The Democrats meanwhile displayed their usual factional infighting. Allegations of widespread fraud, mismanagement, and corruption in the awarding of state contracts, in the use of state funds, and in the sale of state lands added to their problems. Nevertheless, delegates to the party's convention nominated the charismatic and popular Governor Barstow for a second term and reaffirmed the national platform of 1852. Conspicuously avoiding any mention of "color,"[48] they also attempted to distance themselves from the Know Nothings by declaring their hostility to "every political organization which is bound together by secret pledges, or which seeks to proscribe any class of our citizens upon account of their religious creed, or the place of their nativity."[49]

Despite their efforts, Democrats too came under attack for harboring supposed Know Nothings. In fact, during the party convention one delegate even accused Barstow of being a member of the secret order.[50] With both parties trading wild charges of Know Nothingism, the campaign quickly deteriorated, and bitter, personal invective replaced reasoned discussion of the issues. The attacks got so bad that Booth finally was moved to apologize to his readers, only half in jest, for "devoting so much space to the dissection of such an insignificant ass," David Gillies, the Know Nothing editor of the *Milwaukee Daily American,* whose "ears are too large and prominent." Gillies had embarrassed the Republicans with a public endorsement of their ticket and provided gleeful Democrats fresh ammunition with which to step up their attacks.[51] The Know Nothings, in fact, worked diligently on behalf of their ambivalent allies. All around the state, particularly in the rural areas, they bent their efforts to bring about a Republican victory.[52]

In a contested result, Bashford managed to eke out a win over the Democratic incumbent. He did not take office, though, until nearly five months later when the state supreme court awarded him the election after throwing out baldly fraudulent ballots that had been counted in Barstow's favor.[53] Yet the Republicans otherwise had little reason to be pleased with the results. The remainder of their ticket was defeated, running between 600 and 3,300 votes behind Bashford. They also lost heavily in the assembly and gained a slim one-seat majority in the Senate.[54] Men who had supported Republican congressional candidates in 1854 delivered as much as 70 to 80 percent of Bashford's tally (see table 9). The rest came from a large block of voters who had abstained in the prior year's contest. The new governor ran poorly in counties with the highest percentage of foreign-born residents,[55] but he picked up support from those in which the native-born predominated. Bashford's total vote also jumped nearly 11 percent from 1854's Republican ballots.[56] The southcentral counties of Dane, Rock, and Walworth, reputedly the centers of Know Nothing strength in the state, provided 50 percent of the increase. Nearby Jefferson, Green, Columbia, and Fond du Lac counties, where the "dark lantern boys" supposedly had large, active lodges, supplied another 40 percent.[57] Most of the thirty-three hundred vote fall-off in the totals between Bashford and the German-born Republican candidate for state treasurer, Charles Roeser, also came from those counties.

The Democratic vote reveals several surprises. Most of the Democratic defectors to the Republicans in 1854 returned to their traditional party loyalty in 1855. But less than half of the Democrats who stayed with the party in 1854 voted the Democratic ticket in 1855,[58] perhaps in protest against the alleged corruption of the Barstow administration and the bitter factionalism that divided the leadership. Barstow's veto of the prohibition law and the party's courtship of the foreign vote also may have alienated some Democrats. But a large bloc of new voters and earlier nonvoters helped offset those losses, and the total Democratic vote actually surged 32 percent from the prior year. The returns indicate that counties with large concentrations of foreign-born residents provided a substantial portion of the increase,[59] although Barstow picked up impressive new support all across the state. Charles Kuehn, the German-born Democratic candidate for state treasurer garnered the largest statewide tally, outpolling Barstow by nearly three thousand votes and confirming that the Know Nothing threat and the popular antiprohibitionist governor brought out the state's immigrants in record numbers.[60]

Nativists undoubtedly put Bashford, the reluctant Know Nothing,[61] over the top, but they backed off from the other Republican nominees in the state and local races.[62] In their post-election analysis, Republicans posited several reasons for the defeats, including voter apathy, overconfidence, an uninspiring set of candidates, and inattention to the details of local organization. Most often, the Republicans attributed their setback primarily to the "venomous and life-destroying sting" of Know Nothingism and declared their intention to be free in the future from all suspicion of having any affiliation with that organization. The Know Nothings,

Republicans insisted, had overestimated their own strength, and after "fairly begriming us with their filth," scared away many men who otherwise supported Republican principles.[63]

There probably was some truth in that. Many Free Soilers and Wisconsin followers of the New York Whig leader, William H. Seward, had a long history of opposition to nativist bigotry and may have boycotted the 1855 election in protest against the Republican strategy of castigating Know Nothings while accepting their aid. Know Nothings, meanwhile, although working for the antislavery ticket, undoubtedly resented the Republican rejection and denunciation of nativist principles in their platform and campaign. Thus, when the Know Nothings after the election announced their intention to run an independent ticket in future campaigns, Republicans cheered and hoped it would bring an end to the murky alliance. "Religious bigotry and intolerance has never taken root here," they argued, and it must be forthrightly renounced by Wisconsin's antislavery men. William A. White, chairman of the party's state central committee, summed up the Republican position when he optimistically stated that "side issues [such] as Know Nothingism and other kindred tomfooleries" would not influence future elections. Rather, they would be focused on "the plain issue of freedom and slavery."[64]

The Republican determination to purge its ranks of Know Nothings became evident in January 1856. A party legislative caucus directed White to ask suspected state central committee members if they belonged to "the American organization or any other likely to become antagonistic to the Republican party in the approaching Presidential campaign." He was to tell them that "any other reply than a negative shall be considered affirmative" and subject to caucus action.[65] The Know Nothings responded with a charge that the question be put to all committee members and that their answers be made public.[66] Hoping to circumvent the inquiry, they believed the Republicans would not want to openly admit that Know Nothings held influential positions within the party. Although the caucus did back off, in a face-saving gesture it demanded the resignation of D. E. Wood. Wood refused. He claimed to have "conscientious scruples about surrendering" the trust confided in him by the Republican party, and he would step down only "at the request of a State Convention or of a majority of the State Committee." He added that the Republican and Know Nothing parties "agree, in the main, on the slavery issue," and it required their united action to be brought to a satisfactory conclusion.

Outmaneuvered and unwilling to suffer further embarrassment, Republicans temporarily dropped the matter after warning the Native American leadership that they would not be allowed to serve two masters much longer. Either they would abandon the Know Nothing organization without equivocation or the Republicans would abandon them at the next state convention.[67]

The election setback and the bickering about Know Nothing influence combined to reopen the factional rifts repaired at the September convention. Booth, as usual, was in the eye of the storm. With both parties claiming victory in the governor's race, former Whigs accused him of scheming to undermine Bashford's chance for election owing to his frustrated ambition and personal friendship with Barstow. Booth denied the charge and chided them for regarding "the Republican party as organized and existing [solely] for the benefit of Whigs."[68]

With the increasingly bitter dispute threatening to blow the Republican coalition apart, the state central committee summoned delegates to a convention on March 12 to iron out their differences and choose presidential electors. To counteract what he thought would be an attempt by Know Nothings on the committee to assume control of the party, Booth instead called for a mass meeting to convene at a later date when Republicans had a better idea of who the presidential candidates might be. He also urged the party rank and file to resist the ruse of *"mere wire working politicians"* to impose their will and to "repudiate Know Nothingism . . . and set the party on the highway to public confidence and certain victory." Booth's ploy seemed to work; the March 12 convention was canceled.[69]

Over the next few weeks, Booth became more strident in his demand for a mass meeting. In early April, the committee answered by inviting each assembly district to send two delegates to Madison on June 4 to select presidential electors and effect a "thorough reorganization of the Republican party in the State." Since most Know Nothings lived in counties close to the capital city, it was reasoned, they were more likely to exert disproportionate influence in a mass convention than in one where all districts were guaranteed equal representation.[70]

Frustrated by the committee, Booth and his allies decided to imitate 1855 and hold a mass meeting in Madison on the same day as the regular convention in an effort to steer Republicans away from Know Nothingism. Failing that, they threatened to quit the party and run their own ticket.[71] Booth also pleaded privately with committee member John Fox Potter to change his mind and support the call. "If you would it would restore harmony, put an end to doubts, & Kill Know Nothingism, if you oppose we are split and gone up."[72]

A few days later White publicly challenged Booth's threat to set up a separate organization. He made it clear that he and Potter had originated the idea for a delegate meeting and added that "the difficulty with Mr. Booth seems to be, that everyone who does not think as he does becomes immediately a Know Nothing. I do not yield to Mr. Booth either in my zeal in the antislavery cause, or my opposition to the proscriptive course of the Know Nothings." Neither would he yield to anyone his "right to act as I think best, without dictation." The popular White's offensive worked. Most Republican editors and leaders rallied to his support and denounced Booth for playing into Democratic hands with threats to split the party if he was not made "permanent captain and leader." Even Christopher Sholes lambasted his old ally for exploiting the Know Nothing scare to avenge his failure to win the gubernatorial nomination in the previous year.[73] Rebuffed, Booth backed off and meekly promised to embrace the regular convention's course as long as Know Nothings did not control it. He was applauded for this "change of programme," but the bitterness the controversy engendered lingered.[74]

As it turned out, events in Kansas and the nation's capital would soon eclipse nativism's political appeal. By the time Wisconsin's Republicans met on June 4, the slavery question was once again "the all absorbing business." Writing to his friend Potter, the amiable Moses M. Davis exulted that Republicans no longer needed to "step out of our way to give fight to an organization [Know Nothing] that is quite dead."[75]

CHAPTER EIGHT

Freedom and Liberty
First, and
the Union Afterwards

ON MAY 21, 1856, between seven hundred and eight hundred heavily armed proslavery "border ruffians," led by Samuel Jones, the belligerent sheriff of Douglas County, Kansas, rode into the free-state town of Lawrence. Meeting no resistance, they destroyed the offices and presses of the two local newspapers, burned the home of the free-state governor, and set fire to the finest hotel in the territory, confiscating its store of liquor. One proslavery man died, crushed by a collapsing wall of the burning hotel.[1]

Republican editors throughout the North took immediate advantage of the propaganda value the "Sack of Lawrence" provided. They painted a wildly exaggerated picture of murder and devastation visited upon free-state settlers by Southern marauders bent on planting slavery in the territory.[2] The townsmen had been "butchered," "slaughtered," "shot down in cold blood," it was reported, while women and children were forced to flee "from their blazing homes" lest they too fall victim to the "ruthless invaders."[3]

The attack on Lawrence and the widespread coverage it received in the Northern press represented the culmination of nearly two years of turmoil in the unfortunate Kansas territory. Settlers had divided primarily over disputed land titles, but owing to the well-publicized efforts of antislavery societies to help people the territory and the equal determination of proslavery forces to keep free staters out, Kansas became the "fighting point" where the North and South vented years of frustration and anger over the slavery issue.[4]

Antagonism surfaced even before the Kansas-Nebraska Act emerged from Congress, when Eli Thayer, an enterprising Yankee and foe of slavery, announced grandiose plans to assist free-state settlers who wished to move West. To meet that threat, proslavery Missourians encouraged slaveowners to take up homes in Kansas to insure that the future state would be "moulded by our private and domestic institutions." They also joined secret societies designed to discourage free-state migrants and threatened to resort to "the last argument" if peaceful persuasion failed.[5]

The determination of these Missourians to protect their "homeland" was made clear in November 1854, when hundreds of them crossed into Kansas and illegally participated in the territory's election for a delegate to Congress. Erastus D. Ladd, a Kansas resident who hailed from Wisconsin and was a prolific correspondent for the *Milwaukee Sentinel,* voiced the fears of many Northerners when he wrote that the violence and fraud attending the voting was "part of a grand nefarious scheme . . . to make Kansas a Slave State."[6]

Ladd's warning seemed right on the mark when, in March of the following year, five thousand whiskey-swilling Missourians, led by their hotheaded United States senator, David Atchison, poured into the territory and elected a proslavery legislature. After stealing the election, the lawmakers promptly passed draconian statutes that stripped slavery's opponents of their basic civil rights. Anyone who spoke against the institution or circulated abolitionist literature committed a felony; anyone who gave refuge to fugitive slaves or encouraged them to flee their masters could be punished by death; and no man could hold public office in Kansas who refused under oath to affirm slavery's legitimacy. The legislature gave weight to this enactment when it expelled its few antislavery representatives.[7]

In response to that slave code, free-state men set up a rival government in Topeka, adopted an antislavery constitution, and took preliminary steps toward statehood. As the year 1855 came to a close, matters in the territory had reached an impasse; its settlers seemed impossibly divided.[8]

The Republican press unquestionably embellished the news from Kansas for propaganda value and twisted the truth for political advantage. To focus only on the distortions, however, risks minimizing both the disturbing events that did occur and the genuine alarm with which contemporaries received them.[9] In Wisconsin, Republicans greeted the reports from the territory as a vindication of their opposition to popular sovereignty. In countless editorials and numerous Freedom for Kansas meetings held throughout the state, they seized upon the ballot box frauds and the laws of the "bogus pro-slavery legislature" as evidence of the doctrine's failure. Rumors of violence committed by the "ignorant mercenaries of slavery" against free-state Kansans also were broadcast in all their gory details. Southerners, it was argued, believed they could bring their slaves with them into the territories, and "once there, [they] *cannot be removed by future legislation.* This, of course, would make Kansas and Nebraska slave states for good." What was worse, the Pierce administration, which was "utterly subservient to the Slave Power," sided with the South.[10] All these acts, Republicans claimed, flaunted the ruthless determination of slaveowners to establish "slavery as the law of the land and arbiter of the destinies of this Republic" and posed a direct threat to "the perpetuity of our republican institutions." Horace Rublee and David Atwood, in the *Wisconsin State Journal,* grimly articulated the conclusion many state residents reached. "Kansas has become the battleground of freedom. On her soil a struggle that has been impending for years has begun. . . . [It] must end in the destruction of slavery . . . or its ascendancy upon the American continent."[11] So by the time Sheriff Jones and his band of "Missouri cutthroats" marched into Lawrence, thoughtful Northern citizens could readily accept that proslavery thugs intended to reduce it "and all other abolition towns to ashes" and murder or banish all "men guilty of belonging to the free state party."[12]

As the reported outrages in Kansas mounted, many Republicans became convinced that force might be necessary to bring peace and freedom to the territory. Free-state Kansans, they contended, had just grounds to resist the imperious attempts of proslavery interests to snuff out their rights, and they called upon the citizens of Wisconsin to send them "thousands of rifles and powder and balls." At a Milwaukee meeting of the Kansas Emigrant Aid Society, antislavery radicals such as Sherman Booth and Edward Holton joined with well-known conservatives and moderates, including John Tweedy and Rufus King, and publicly pledged Sharps rifles to assist the free-state settlers. In other towns, Edward Daniels, whom the society had sent to investigate the goings-on in Kansas, openly asked for weapons. A resort to arms, possibly involving civil war, it was alleged, remained "the only means of redress left."[13]

The vocal Republican support for a violent resolution to the territory's problems seemed to satisfy a need to stand up to the South. For too many years, Southern hotheads had browbeaten the North with threats of disunion if their demands were not met. Republicans drew the line in Kansas; here Northern rights would be sustained at all costs. Cyrus Woodman, a conservative ex-Democrat and lead district businessman, gave voice to this hardening antisouthernism. He rejoiced that "at last there is a *North*."

> I was always called a *proslavery* man up to the time of the repeal of the Missouri Compromise. I thought I had got low enough in the dirt to satisfy the South then, but to be kicked after I was down was a little more than I could stand, and now if Kansas comes into the Union as a slave state it will be without any help of mine.[14]

The Kansas troubles drove an ever-deepening wedge between the North and South and blessed the Republicans with an issue to advance the fortunes of their fledgling party. Yet, the Kansas ruckus alone did not promise success. The political confusion that attended the breakup of the second party system, along with resurgent nativism and the rise of the Know Nothings still vied for the electorate's attention. Moreover, much of the news from the far-off territory was contradictory, sensational, and open to question. An electrifying event in the nation's capital proved to be decisive in forging a durable and successful coalition.

The day after the Lawrence raid, Senator Charles Sumner of Massachusetts, while working on constituent matters at his seat in the nearly empty Senate chamber, suffered a brutal and bloody beating at the hands of Preston S. Brooks, a congressman from South Carolina. Sumner had provoked Brooks several days earlier when he delivered a speech entitled "The Crime Against Kansas," in which he scathingly rebuked the Pierce administration and the South for attempting, no matter the cost, to plant slavery in the territory. Sumner also fired a tasteless personal onslaught against South Carolina's aging senator, Andrew P. Butler, a relative of Brooks.[15]

The assault on Sumner shocked and infuriated Northerners, especially after the South greeted it with boastful approval and returned the unrepentant Brooks to his seat in an uncontested election. In Wisconsin, Rufus King snapped that Brooks should "be treated like any other dog and shot at sight," while other indignant Republicans urged their representatives in Washington to arm themselves "and be prepared for any emergency." John Fox Potter, running for Congress in the southeastern district, warned that if elected he would suffer no insult, "And the man who interferes with me in debate, I will blow his lights, liver and innards as far as powder and ball can do it."[16]

Most important, the attack on Sumner persuaded many that a truly "malevolent and violent spirit prevailed Southward," and unless checked, it threatened to undermine "the liberties of the people in the North."[17] It also lent credibility to the endless horror stories flowing out of Kansas and the Republican contention that Southern slaveowners and their friends would stop at nothing to achieve their goals. "I don't know of any despotism more to be dreaded than what the poor Emigrants at Kansas have witnessed within the last two years," wrote one Wisconsin Republican. "And . . . the *outrage* upon a *Massachusetts Senator has no parallel in the history of our country.*"[18] Seizing the opportunity, Republicans quickly linked the two issues as irrefutable evidence of Southern determination to retain a stranglehold over the national government and "extend, strengthen and render permanent that shameful institution," slavery. The Kansas atrocities now had a counterpart in Washington where "brute force has been appealed to, to silence Free Speech." Rufus King equated it to an attack on northern rights and manhood.

> Will the Free States of the Union submit any longer to be dragooned, insulted, and outraged by the minions of slavery? Shall we not at least stand up for our own? Is there not spirit and manhood enough left in the North to vindicate the Freedom of Debate, the Liberty of Speech, and the personal inviolability of our representatives in Congress? Will not Wisconsin record her protest against each and every phrase of Border Ruffianism, and renew her pledge of devotion to the cause of Right, Humanity and Freedom?[19]

Throughout the North, "Bleeding Kansas" and "Bleeding Sumner" profoundly influenced the political landscape, dimming Democratic hopes of an easy victory in November's presidential contest, dramatically boosting Republican prospects and self-assurance, and effectively destroying Know Nothing expectations of becoming a durable national political organization.[20] Indeed, slavery had already exposed deep divisions among Northern and Southern Know Nothings. At its national meeting in 1855, the organization split over the issue; it did so again, this time fatally, early in 1856. In Wisconsin, the Know Nothing party, as distinct from the nativist appeal, had never really taken hold. The size of the state's foreign-born and Catholic population created an insurmountable roadblock to Know Nothing political success, while the unrelenting opposition and influence of antislavery men in the Republican party all but insured that its political program would never find an acceptable home there. And, in spite of the fears the immigrants raised among the native-born, the shared experience of taming the Wisconsin frontier helped blunt those concerns, as did strenuous Republican efforts to court foreigners who held pronounced antislavery principles, especially German Protestants.

So by 1856, crushing political liabilities, along with the violence in Kansas and the attack on Sumner, persuaded most nativists within the state that slavery presented a far greater threat to them than "honest and intelligent foreigners" and was now the all-important question.[21] And Republicans were prepared to take them in, on one condition. "We gladly welcome all to the Republican party and platform," Rufus King wrote. "ALL, whether native or foreign-born, American, Whigs, Democrats, or no party men, Catholics or Protestants, who agree and will act with us, *in resisting the aggressions of slavery.* And provided they make *that* the paramount issue, we neither ask, nor care whether their sentiments on other political topics concur or conflict with ours."[22] Sensing the drift of events, the editor of the *Milwaukee Daily American* proclaimed,

> Whigs, Democrats, Americans, Abolitionists and Republicans are clustering in one conglomerated mass, in which past political differences are forgotten, while the great and overpowering issue of liberty of speech, freedom of the press, and the inviolability of the spirit of the Missouri Compromise is thrust upon the people of the North.[23]

As the year wore on, many Know Nothings, including the *American's* editor, made their way into the Republican ranks.[24]

With the Know Nothings neutralized, Wisconsin's Republicans labored to patch up their differences and grasp the political opportunity Sheriff Jones and Congressman Brooks had provided.[25] A chastened Sherman Booth dropped his opposition to the call for a delegate convention, which came together as scheduled on June 4. The meeting, all later agreed, was a harmonious one where "the best feelings prevailed."[26] Charles Roeser, for example, one of the German Republicans who had signed the summons for a mass convention with Booth, played a prominent role. He served on the resolutions committee with antislavery stalwarts John Fox Potter and Byron Paine and was named to the state central committee. Together they drew up a decidedly radical platform. It declared that "the great and only issue which now divides the parties of this nation is that of freedom and slavery," and it called on the federal government to protect the individual rights of all settlers in the territories. It also summoned Congress to repeal the fugitive slave law, to admit no new slave states into the Union, and to abolish slavery wherever it constitutionally was empowered to do so. The party then "thoroughly purged itself of all affinity with Know Nothingism," professing that "all men, irrespective of nativity or religion, are entitled to equal rights," and it unqualifiedly condemned "all secret political organizations as dangerous to our political and civil rights."[27] The delegates adjourned in high spirits, brimming with confidence.

The presidential campaign of 1856 generated great enthusiasm in Wisconsin and the nation. "Politics is all the rage nowadays," observed Willet S. Main. "The excitement never ran higher than at present. It outdoes 1840 by a long shot."[28] The Republicans nominated John C. Frémont, a national hero without an embarrassing political past, and adopted antislavery resolutions every bit as radical as Wisconsin's. The Democrats placed James Buchanan before the people on a platform that made support of the Compromise of 1850 and the Kansas-Nebraska Act a test of party orthodoxy. A veteran of forty years with the Democracy and hailing from the critical state of Pennsylvania, Buchanan had been conveniently abroad as the nation's minister to England during the bitterly divisive Kansas-Nebraska debates. Pliant, conservative, and controlling a powerful political organization in his home state, he was viewed as a perfect candidate for the times.[29]

With the campaign underway in earnest, Wisconsin's Democrats attempted to stem the Republican tide by cynically manipulating the nativist issue and insisting that Frémont's election would lead to disunion. In an effort to shore up their support among the state's immigrants, they assailed Republicans for admitting former Know Nothings. At the same time, in order to undermine his strength among nativists, they accused Frémont of being a Catholic. Exasperated Republicans denounced the Democrats for dodging the slavery issue and for their hypocritical regard for civil and religious liberty, so amply contradicted by their objection to Frémont "on the ground that he belongs to the Roman Catholic Church."[30]

Ethnocultural concerns probably won the Democrats few votes in 1856, but they likely earned some with their argument that Republican success would force the slave states out of the Union. "Its platform is a declaration of war upon the South and its institutions," they warned, and it is "full of treason against the Union."[31] Although Democrats carefully swore their opposition to slavery's extension, their Unionism clearly outweighed their antislavery professions.[32] "Dissolve the Union and where are we?" they asked. "Constant strife and warfare over what are now common possessions," "anarchy, blood . . . and destruction," all of these would accompany a dismembered Union and inevitably lead to the loss of individual liberty and the destruction of the Constitution.[33] For that reason, Democrats contended, no one could belong to the Republican party, "and be anything else but a disunionist."[34]

The absolute Unionism of the Democrats drained their antislavery position of all moral content. Whatever they felt about slavery, most stood by the core doctrine of their party, popular sovereignty, ostensibly a middle ground between Northern and Southern extremism, which by upholding the right of territorial residents to decide slavery's fate without interference from Congress seemed to be a truly democratic solution to the problem.[35] To counter the Republican charge that uprooting slavery would be impossible once it gained a foothold in the west, Democrats insisted that few slaveowners would move into territories already free. Thus, "We may safely concede to it [slavery] a right to extend, when we know it has no power to do so."[36]

The Democratic claims failed to win Wisconsin. Frémont received 56 percent of the vote and turnout was the highest yet recorded in a statewide contest. Nearly 119,000 voters showed up at the polls, an increase of 48,000 from the previous year, and comprising about 80 percent of the eligible electorate. Indeed, more Northern voters registered an opinion in the 1856 contest than in any other between 1848 and 1860,[37] and although

Buchanan won the election, Frémont rolled up majorities in all but five Northern states and captured one-third of all the ballots cast.[38] In Wisconsin, the Republican tally increased a remarkable 83 percent from 1855, while the Democratic total jumped 43 percent. Unsurprisingly, the returns show that both parties obtained substantial support from prior nonvoters (see table 10). They made up as much as 44 percent of the Republican and 33 percent of the Democratic electors.[39] The Wisconsin experience was not unusual though, as both organizations picked up substantial numbers of new voters throughout the North.[40]

Frémont also retained the backing of nearly all of Bashford's supporters from 1855, while Buchanan won about 85 percent of Barstow's voters, suggesting that disenchantment with traditional party politics and leaders still ran deep among some Democrats. But Democratic alienation did not translate into gains for the Republicans, as those voters chose to abstain rather than support Frémont. In fact, the Republican success with Bashford loyalists and previous nonvoters in 1856 stands in stark contrast to their failure to win over Democrats. It appears that except for a few holdovers from 1854, the bulk of Wisconsin's anti-Nebraska Democrats had either rejoined the party by 1856 or simply did not vote, a pattern followed in most Northern states.[41] After protesting passage of the Kansas-Nebraska Act, they came to embrace popular sovereignty as the best solution to the bothersome slavery question, and few, it seems, ever felt that their separation from the party would be permanent.[42]

As in earlier elections, in 1856, counties with large foreign-born populations went overwhelmingly Democratic. Counties with native-born populations turned in equally disproportionate majorities for Frémont. Most of the state's Scandanavian and English-speaking residents, except the Irish, apparently backed Frémont, who also won over some German Protestants; but the Republicans received a meager return on their efforts to attract immigrant voters, especially Germans, and were understandably disappointed.[43] Nevertheless, the Kansas and Sumner outrages completed the political revolution in Wisconsin, which Republicans nourished with a compelling antislavery interpretation of national events. The resulting party appeal, or ideology, was broad enough to attract radicals who were motivated primarily by the moral dimension of the antislavery crusade, moderates who hoped to confine slavery and place it on the road to extinction, and a small number of conservatives who were alarmed about the political and economic consequences Southern domination of federal affairs might have on the nation's future.[44] All those factions toiled in an uneasy alliance for the success of the Republican political program, united in the conviction that the "Slaveocracy" was conspiring to undermine liberty in the free states. "The great and living issue of the day in American politics, is resistance to slavery oppression," they preached. "It is upon this rock that the Republican Party is founded."[45]

First developed by Liberty men, the idea of a slave power conspiracy rested in the belief that slaveowners, with the help of corrupt Northern Democrats "anxious for a little pay,"[46] dominated all branches of the federal government and looked to retain their mastery by planting slavery throughout the American West. Moreover, the despotic conspirators plotted to extend their reach to include Mexico, Cuba, Central America, and in time, even the free states themselves.[47] The fundamental issue, then, was simple: "Shall the National Government be devoted to slavery, using its patronage, purse and power to increase and extend it, or shall its sympathies and support be on the side of human freedom, meting out to every man those rights set forth in the Declaration of Independence."[48]

The image of the slave power controlling the federal government frightened Republican loyalists. It combined their loathing of slavery and the shameful contradiction it presented to their deeply held democratic values with their great fear that unless control was wrested from the slave-owning oligarchs, the liberties of Northern whites would be snuffed out. Christopher Sholes expressed that sentiment best.

> We have been endeavoring for a long time to convince the people that slavery was more than a mere question of black or white, that it was not confined to the proposition whether a man with a dark or black skin should or should not be owned. But it was a question involving liberty in all its length, breadth, height and depth, *and* slavery in equal extent. It was a most natural, indeed an inevitable result of the dominance of the slavery sentiment at Washington.[49]

In making their case, Republicans often pointed to the South itself, where fewer than "500,000 slaveowning aristocrats" ruled the region with an iron fist and kept both blacks and the poor white majority under their absolute control.[50] They did so out of necessity, Republicans maintained, because slavery could not withstand the glare of free criticism. And while these "slavocrats" professed adherence to political liberty, they suffered no word to be written or spoken against the peculiar institution and enforced a rigid proslavery orthodoxy backed by "the most odious police regulations." They also declared themselves children of enlightened idealism, yet suppressed freedom of conscience and the free transmission of "the great leading ideas of the age," out of fear that "they might engender a thought against slavery." In short, Southern liberty, progress, and prosperity had been sacrificed to safeguard slavery. And now, Republicans warned, the slave barons stood ready to destroy the American Union, its republican institutions, and all remnants of individual liberty.[51]

Southern leaders and spokesmen added to Northern worries with public declarations that America's republican experiment had failed and that slavery was "the *natural and normal* condition of the laboring man, *whether white or black*."[52] Republicans denounced these "madmen" and their color-blind defense of slavery, along with their abandonment of the revolutionary principles of the nation's founders, as evidence of slavery's inability to coexist with freedom. And they grimly accepted the slaveowners' contention that ultimately "one must give way and cease to exist [while] the other must become universal."[53]

Those circumstances of Southern life and thought, as Republicans understood them, where "slavery overrules everything," intensified their growing anxiety over the slave power's preeminence in national affairs and the notion that "a deep laid scheme for the overthrow of popular liberty" existed.[54] Skillfully cultivating growing resentment of the South's overbearing tendencies, most Wisconsin Republicans deemphasized the horrors the slave system imposed on its black victims and played down "extending the claims of liberty as a right beyond the pale of our own race." They focused instead on the growing anxiety and "prudential selfishness" Northern whites felt with respect to their own freedom.[55] The party's accent on white self-interest represented a realization that laboring on behalf of enslaved blacks alone would not bring political victory. Wisconsinites had to be convinced that if the slave power was not stopped, no one's freedom in the long run would be saved. In knitting together their antislavery coalition, the Republicans succeeded, as their Liberty and Free Soil forebears had not, because they were able to shift the electorate's attention from blacks, who were "only an incident of the strife," to anxieties about their own liberty and the future of free institutions in America.[56] And it was within that framework of deepening unease and suspicion about the ultimate goals of the slave power that they responded to events in and after 1856.

Self-interest, fear, anger, idealism; all of these and other emotions motivated men to embrace Republican doctrine. Yet the party's success would have been impossible were it not for the prevailing sentiment among its members that slavery was inherently wicked and "at war with all the best interests of humanity."[57] Most had always hated the institution, but few had been moved to active resistance until forced by circumstances and the conviction that slavery, the source of Southern attitudes, power, and prestige, lay at the bottom of the increasingly divisive sectional strife. "Slavery is the direct cause of the present exasperated state of feeling between the different portions of the Union," Governor Coles Bashford claimed in an address to the Wisconsin legislature. "It is the only brand of dissension which threatens permanently the peace of the country and endangers the perpetuity of our Republican institutions."[58] In a solemn Independence Day editorial, the *Wisconsin State Journal* tied Republican resistance to the "Aristocrats of Bondage" to their underlying antislavery feelings.

> The most prominent and dangerous evil in our national fabric . . . is that of Slavery; an evil so odiously intrusive that it forces itself more persistently upon the attention, on this day, than upon any other; as if by contrast with the principles and memories which consecrate our national anniversary, to become tenfold more hideous and deformed. It is a specter that will not be put down even upon this festal day. It is the discord that mars all our music, gives the lie to all our professions, and makes us feel like a nation of hypocrites in the midst of our rejoicing. Against this evil . . . the people who earnestly and really believe in the Declaration of Our Independence must unite. It must be walled in . . . or anarchy and disaster are in store for us. Already its influence has entered the free states, our best men are proscribed for their devotion to liberty; and we must either conquer or become mere serfs ourselves to a slaveholding oligarchy.[59]

The Republican party's hostility toward the slave power and slavery found political expression in its uncompromising opposition to the further spread of black bondage, which symbolized the twin desires to confront Southern imperiousness and see slavery eventually driven from the country. "That water will run down hill is no more certain than that slavery must die unless allowed to spread itself over new territories," ran the commonly accepted belief in antebellum America. "Expansion or death is its inevitable law. And nobody knows this better than the Slavery propaganda."[60]

Wisconsin's Republicans expounded the expand-or-die theory so often that no informed observer could question their commitment to the ultimate extinction of slavery.[61] As the 1850s drew to a close, nearly all them would agree with the party editor who explained, "We oppose the extension of slavery because it is in itself morally and politically wrong." And, those "opposed [to] its extension from such principles must of course see that if slavery is wrong in one place, it was equally wrong in another, if wrong in a territory, it would also be in a State. And so seeing it must beget a desire to have it abolished everywhere."[62] This willingness to take whatever legal and constitutional steps were necessary to hem the institution in and bring about its slow but inevitable death clearly distinguished the Republican appeal from the popular sovereignty doctrine of Northern Democrats and made slaveowners understandably edgy.[63]

The party's antiextension message also exploited the widespread Northern belief in free labor's superiority over slave labor. Free labor, so the thinking went, encouraged diligence and hard work and brought about increased productivity and prosperity. It rewarded the honest, independent laborer and wage earner with an opportunity to raise himself economically and socially and to move into the ranks of the "middling class."[64] By contrast, the slave labor system stifled enterprise and initiative. It spawned poverty, ignorance, and a "moral miasma" that affected not just its obvious victims, the enslaved blacks, but the South's laboring white classes as well. With labor of all sorts viewed with disdain, the region's "poor white trash" had little hope of improving their lot in life. Even lowly blacks looked down upon these "degraded and brutish . . . white men who labor." Allow slavery into the territories, Republicans warned, and these same attitudes and conditions would take root and drive out industrious Northern settlers who would never agree to labor alongside bondsmen or place limits on their social and economic mobility. "Free labor and slave labor are antagonistic to each other," they insisted, and "the states of this Union must ultimately be all free or all slave."[65]

The territorial issue therefore had profound political, social, and economic implications for Republicans that went directly to the heart of the

future course of the nation. Slavery's expansion would insure its perpetuation and Southern preeminence in national affairs, and it would discourage
Northerners from taking up homes in the West. With so much at stake,
Republicans had to risk all to keep slavery penned up. Carl Schurz, the
German-born antislavery activist, predicted that unless slavery's advance
was arrested, the unavoidable contradictions between it and freedom would
bring about "a crisis more violent than any we have seen yet, and will en-
velop Slavery, and Union, and progress, and prosperity, in the flames of a
universal conflagration."[66] Yet, while Republicans understood the dangers
of confronting the South, few in 1856 could have comprehended the ultimate bloody consequences.

In defending their stand against slavery, Wisconsin's Republicans
linked their cause to that of the nation's founders.[67] The fathers, they
argued, looked upon slavery as an unmitigated evil, strictly local in character, and entirely incompatible with the genius and principles of the new
American government. They had tolerated its continued existence temporarily for the sake of national unity, but they looked forward to the day
when republican ideals and the good sense of the American people would
bring about its demise.[68] Thus, the founders had adopted a national constitution based upon individual liberty and the natural rights of all men,
and they deliberately avoided all mention of slavery within the charter "as
one would the existence of a loathsome disease." Early efforts to end the
importation of enslaved blacks and to keep slavery from overspreading
the national domain gave additional substance to their professions.[69] But
Southern slaveholders and their Northern lackeys in the Democratic party
had frustrated the founders' desire to remove the contradiction between
the fundamental principles of American government and the institution of
slavery. The Republican goal was to complete the job their revolutionary
predecessors had started: "To confine slavery within the narrowest limits
and to promote its gradual abolition by local legislation."[70]

The reopening of the slavery controversy and the emergence of the Republican party, as the Democracy tirelessly pointed out, did in fact pose
a genuine threat to the slaveholding South and the American Union. Well
before the outbreak of formal hostilities, Wisconsin's Republicans had
concluded that a showdown of some sort with the South was probable.
"The battle between Aristocracy, Slavery and Despotism, on the one side,
and Liberty, Republicanism and Equality, on the other . . . can no longer
be conciliated by compromise or suppressed by the threats of dissolution of

the Union. We must choose between resistance and submission."[71] Republicans chose resistance. Indeed, the decision to embrace the party suggests they had already decided its antislavery appeal took precedence over the Union, and they began to coalesce around a policy of absolute Unionism only in the year prior to the election of 1860, and especially after the South repudiated its legitimate outcome and brought on the secession crisis and war. Before then, the state's Republicans had never matched their steadfast refusal to bow to the slave power's demands with a well-defined policy of what they would do if the South did attempt to secede. But continued Southern aggression, most had concluded, irretrievably ruptured the good faith shown by the North in smoothing out past disagreements and left no choice but to resist further compromises on slavery questions, regardless of the consequences to the Union.[72] One Watertown Republican angrily voiced this shift in values.

> I say, drive slavery from the whole country, and drive the South from the Union. . . . Let the South take charge of herself. . . . Once I thought calculating the worth of the Union a political heresy, not to be thought of, much less to be tolerated in any person, but the problem has been forced on us by Southern knaves and Northern traitors.[73]

The Kansas outrages only increased the resolve of Republicans. The Union had done nothing to protect the civil rights of the free-state settlers from proslavery sympathizers, they protested, and further attempts to placate them would lead only to greater demands later on. "The threats of secession have lost their power to force freemen from their position in the maintenance of right and justice," Republicans defiantly proclaimed. They were prepared to wage "unconditional warfare" against the South until either slavery or "the political connection between the free and the slave states is destroyed."[74]

Republican willingness to risk disunion rather than back down was predicated on the notion that stopping slavery and preserving Northern rights superseded threats to the unity of the American states. The Union, they cried in terms reminiscent of their Liberty party forebears, had been formed to advance freedom and individual liberty. Instead, in recent years it had been manipulated to bolster human bondage. The greater danger, then, was not that the Union would be dissolved, but that it would become an agent of oppression and tyranny. And "when the Union fails to accomplish the purposes for which it was framed, its perpetuity ceases to be desirable." The *Wisconsin State Journal* best summed up this position. "Slavery is so repugnant to free men; so utterly at war with all the principles which we are taught to venerate . . . so unjust, overbearing, and inhuman, that should it acquire an absolute . . . predominance in the nation, disunion would be the only course left for the free states."[75]

Other Republicans agreed and resolved that only the eventual destruction of slavery could save the Union.[76] Former Liberty men and other antislavery radicals had no problem with that position; they had always maintained that combating slavery took precedence over the Union. It is also likely that some Republicans without identifiable party antecedents or a history of political activism held their antislavery principles above their attachment to the Union.[77] The alienation of past Whigs, on the other hand, had been brewing for many years. The emergence of the territorial issue in the 1840s, the growing domination of the slave power in national councils, the dissolution of their party and political connection to the South, and their unquestioned hostility toward slavery all combined by the middle of the decade to erode Whig dedication to the Union.[78] Democratic Republicans seemed to have been most steadfastly Unionist, but they were few in number and spoke with more than one voice.[79]

To be sure, no Republican looked forward to a breakup of the Union. Most often they rationalized their unyielding refusal to make any further concessions to slaveholders on principle and blithely dismissed secessionist bombast as "simply ridiculous, and not entitled to the slightest consideration." It was all bluff and had "never been serious, never." Dissolution, after all, would render the fugitive slave law inoperable and require significantly higher taxes in the South to help police the peculiar institution and maintain a new government. "The South is too well aware of its dependent position, ever to dare the step," Republicans optimistically explained. "She may cry disunion, but dissolve she never will."[80]

On occasion, Republicans seemed willing to let the slave states go. If the triumph of antislavery principles and men proved unpalatable, "Let the door be open for them to pass out." The South's obstreperous behavior had pushed Northern patience to the limit, and if it should choose to leave, "we are willing it should make the attempt."[81] Frustrated and angry Republicans themselves sometimes threatened disunion if they failed to wrest control of the government from the slave power. Some even thought that the South's efforts to expand slavery revealed a plot "to *drive* the *North* out of the Union." Make no mistake about it, John Fox Potter declared, "This is the key to their whole policy. What seems suicidal to [us] looks like immortality to these scoundrels."[82] Other Republicans did take threats of secession seriously though, and they vowed to resist any attempt to the death. The slave states' legal and constitutional rights to retain slavery would not be contravened, but those Republicans would never consent to "speculate upon a contingency in which disunion could be justifiable, or even excusable." Force, they cautioned, would be employed to bring back "every state that forgets its loyalty."[83]

The Republican party was to a great extent the legitimate offspring of Liberty and Free Soil parents. Its appeal drew on the various shades of antislavery thought advanced over the years, and it differed primarily in its emphasis on the slave power conspiracy to subvert free institutions and individual liberty.[84] Aided by events that seemed to substantiate their allegations, Republicans reordered the components of the antislavery agenda and blended those into a convincing whole.

The Republican achievement was to forge a durable coalition of men persuaded by its claims and in substantial agreement with its national goals, in spite of the different assumptions and viewpoints they may have brought into their evaluation of the growing crisis. That broad commitment to the party's national program did not carry over to state matters. Early on, nativism threatened to rupture the party, but the greatest danger to Republican harmony in Wisconsin came from the explosive state's rights issue. Divergent attitudes toward blacks also came to the surface, but those were comparatively minor and never imperiled party unity.

CHAPTER NINE

The Dangerous Doctrine
of Nullification

In wisconsin, the Republican party's avowal of states' rights stemmed
from the Joshua Glover rescue and Sherman Booth's subsequent legal en-
tanglements with the federal government for his alleged role in the affair.
On May 26, 1854, Booth, free on bail, disclosed his intention to challenge
the Fugitive Slave Law when he turned himself in to federal authorities
and was returned to jail. His attorney, twenty-six-year-old Byron Paine,
then applied to state supreme court judge Abram D. Smith for a writ of
habeas corpus. The timing of Booth's move was purely tactical, since on
two earlier occasions the opportunity to apply for a writ and receive the
judgment of the full court had been available. He seems to have waited
until intersession, hoping that Smith, a Democrat and well-known opponent of the act, might be persuaded to pronounce against it. On the
May 29, Booth's counselor made his case to the judge.[1]

In a lengthy argument, Paine asked the court to overturn the Fugitive
Slave Act because the Constitution did not grant Congress the power
to legislate on the matter. Furthermore, the law condemned alleged fugitives to slavery without a jury trial, and it vested judicial power in court-
appointed commissioners unrecognized by the Constitution. Paine also

presented an exhaustive refutation of the 1842 United States Supreme Court decision in the case of *Prigg v. Pennsylvania,* which strongly affirmed federal jurisdiction in the execution of the Constitution's fugitive slave clause and, in his view, improperly transferred control over these cases from the states to the national government. He further insisted that state courts could intercede on behalf of citizens imprisoned under national authority and denied that the federal government was the final judge of the limits of its own powers. To concede these points would lead inevitably either to unspeakable tyranny or the "terrible ordeal of revolution."[2] One week later, to the delight of most of Wisconsin's antislavery men, Smith sustained Paine's reasoning, discharged Booth, and declared the law unconstitutional and void.[3]

Stunned federal officers then applied to Smith for a writ of certiorari, hoping that the full court would reverse his ruling. Instead, on July 19, it affirmed his decision. Two days later, acting under an order of a United States district court judge, federal officials rearrested Booth.[4] Paine again applied to the state supreme court for a writ of habeas corpus. This time the justices denied his request, asserting that there was a major difference between a warrant issued by a federal court and one by a commissioner exercising extrajudicial authority. They acknowledged that the federal judiciary had assumed jurisdiction in the case, and they would await the outcome.[5]

In January 1855, after a contentious trial, Booth was found guilty of abetting Glover's rescue and violating the Fugitive Slave Act.[6] The state supreme court now granted the editor's application for a writ of habeas corpus. On February 3, the state judges reaffirmed their earlier judgment and overturned the federal court decision.[7] All three justices agreed that Wisconsin possessed the right to inquire into the reasons for the imprisonment of its citizens and to release them if they were found to be held illegally. Otherwise, they argued, the state would be powerless to safeguard individual liberty and would have no claim upon their citizens' loyalty. That ruling was consistent with current legal thinking, since the issue of federal judicial supremacy as it related to the powers of the states on questions of habeas corpus jurisdiction remained unsettled and controversial.[8] In the case of Booth, the judges claimed that his discharge was required because the warrant made out for his arrest contained deficiencies, in that Garland had not laid title to Glover in precise accordance with the act's provisions. As Smith noted, the act operated in restraint of freedom; therefore its application required "strict technical exactness," including the issuing of warrants. Consensus did not extend beyond that one issue, though; on other questions, the justices expressed widely divergent opinions.[9]

Associate Justice Samuel Crawford declared himself satisfied that the constitution empowered Congress to legislate upon the matter of fugitive slaves. He based his conviction on the Supreme Court's ruling in *Prigg* and on the belief that the Court possessed ultimate authority over all constitutional issues. The Wisconsin bench had "to yield obedience . . . for upon such questions we are subordinate."[10]

Chief Justice Edward Whiton also bowed to the Supreme Court's superiority and acknowledged the right of Congress to enact fugitive slave legislation. But, he maintained, in the *Prigg* case the court neither entrusted specific legal powers to commissioners appointed by federal officials to hear fugitive slave cases, nor did it directly refuse jury trials to alleged escapees. Lacking federal guidance, it fell to the state supreme court to judge the constitutionality of those two provisions of the 1850 statute. Moved by that logic, Whiton concluded that Congress had exceeded its mandate, and he proclaimed the Fugitive Slave Act void.[11]

Smith delivered a far more sweeping opinion than either of his colleagues. Influenced by the states' rights philosophy expounded in the Virginia and Kentucky resolutions and, although never directly cited, the writings of the South Carolinian, John C. Calhoun, he found that the Fugitive Slave Act violated the Constitution and that Congress lacked authority to legislate on the subject.[12] The American people, Smith argued, operating through their states, had forged the constitutional compact, which clearly specified all powers delegated to the federal government and reserved to the states all powers not expressly bestowed. This system of divided sovereignty permitted both federal and state authorities, as codepartments in a unified system of government, to fully exercise their rights and to act as checks upon each other. And, according to Smith, a careful reading of the fugitive slave clause, one of the comity provisions of Article 4 of the Constitution, disclosed nothing that either inferred or implied a grant of power to the federal government on the matter. Besides, he asked: Did anyone really believe that the nation's founders would have adopted this provision without opposition or debate if, in its enforcement, they thought the national government would be allowed, in every county in every state, to appoint officials invested with judicial prerogatives and answerable neither to state courts nor to local police regulations? Or that federal lawmakers would be permitted to suspend the writ of habeas corpus and the right to a jury trial and to send "the whole military and naval force of this Union" uninvited into any state in pursuit of a runaway slave? "The idea is preposterous," Smith insisted. "The Union would never have been formed on such a basis. It is an impeachment of historic truth to assert it."[13]

In regard to the *Prigg* case, Smith bluntly declared that the Supreme Court had overstepped its constitutional grant and should reexamine its 1842 decree. He also criticized the Court for urging the need for a federal statute to force Northern states into compliance with the fugitive slave clause, assuming they would otherwise neglect their obligation, solely for the convenience of slaveowners and the safety of their economic interests.[14]

Although Smith went on to encourage state officers to acquiesce cheerfully in every privilege constitutionally exercised by federal officials, he likewise exhorted them to resist every assumption of power "not expressly granted or necessarily implied in the federal constitution." Like Paine, Smith championed the prevailing antebellum view that the states reserved the right to determine the conditions and extent of civil liberties within their jurisdiction and to check the unauthorized use of federal power, and he flatly rejected the notion that any branch of the national government, including the judiciary, could define the extent of its powers. As such, state judges, bound to resist federal intrusions upon the reserved rights of the states and to guard the liberty of their citizens, could invalidate both congressional laws and judicial determinations that violated the constitutional compact.[15]

In order to calm the fears of those who imagined that his states' rights philosophy would lead to "dissension, disruption and civil warfare," Smith emphasized that the collisions inherent in a system of divided sovereignty signified strength and vitality, not weakness. They encouraged investigations into the correct and legitimate boundaries of federal and state sovereignty and served to restrain both, "quietly and almost imperceptibly . . . within their true and proper limits." Indeed, submission to unconstitutional enactments posed a far greater danger to national peace and unity, Smith warned, than resistance to the unlawful manipulation of power. If left unchecked, the abuse of power soon would become "so deeply and firmly rooted that the only remedy is revolution."[16]

The decision of Wisconsin's supreme court to release Booth from custody after he had been tried, convicted, and sentenced before a federal tribunal for violating a federal law was unprecedented. It represented a bold act of defiance to the national government and to the still-controversial doctrine that the United States Supreme Court was the final arbiter of constitutional questions. Moreover, Smith's opinion embraced a form of states' rights and nullification that few Southern zealots ever had contemplated. As one antislavery editor chuckled, "We shall be curious to see how this new application of an old doctrine will be relished by the ultra states' rights men of the South." The new application he referred to was "judicial *nullification*," which was distinctly different from Calhoun's position that only a state convention, as the original contracting party to the Constitution, could resort to nullification when the general government exceeded its powers.[17]

Wisconsin's invocation of states' rights also differed from the South's in another important way. South Carolina had originally embraced states' rights principles to safeguard its economic interests. Thereafter, the South took up states' rights, to block national interference with slavery within the slaveholding states, and state sovereignty, with decrees such as the Fugitive Slave Act, to demand federal protection for the rights of slaveowners outside the state jurisdictions in which they had been granted.[18] To counteract Southern aggressiveness, Wisconsin, along with other Northern states, employed states' rights to defend individual liberty from legislation regarded as unconstitutional. Most often, resistance took the form of personal liberty laws designed to thwart enforcement of the Fugitive Slave Act. To many antislavery men, this form of state interposition represented a middle ground between revolution and absolute submission to a proslavery federal law that overturned fundamental civil rights.[19] Consequently, Wisconsin's use of states' rights to secure personal liberty more truly represented the philosophy embodied in the Virginia and Kentucky resolutions than did the South's, which in increasingly provocative ways shaped the doctrine to justify perpetuating and expanding slavery.[20]

Paine's brief and Smith's opinion won praise in antislavery circles throughout the North. Both were reprinted in pamphlet form and reported brisk sales, particularly in the East. Paine received congratulatory letters from antislavery advocates such as Charles Sumner and Wendell Phillips, while Smith was invited by "numerous and prominent citizens of New York" to attend a banquet in his honor. One of them, Horace Greeley, editor of the influential *New York Tribune*, headed his account of the court's decision with the words, "Glorious Wisconsin."[21] Similarly, most members of Wisconsin's Republican party championed Smith's pronouncement as evidence of their resolve to take on the slave power, both at home and in Washington, whereas the state's Democrats condemned it with equal fervor.[22] Still, a determined Republican minority rejected Smith's case for the supremacy of the state judiciary, and in the years before the onset of war, that principle split the party leadership and became the litmus test for political preferment.

The state court decision quickly influenced the political direction of the newly formed Republican coalition. Shortly after winning two of Wisconsin's three seats in the House of Representatives in November 1854, its unity was tested for the first time in the balloting for United States senator. The choice fell to a joint vote of both houses of the state legislature where the Republicans, in league with a few holdover Whig senators and a handful of anti-Nebraska Democrats, commanded a razor-thin majority. Senate Democrats, with nothing to lose, at first refused to consent to a joint session, chancing that delay might help their favorite, Byron Kilbourn, if the opposition failed to unite behind a candidate.[23] The strategy nearly worked as determined Free Soilers looked to avenge Charles Durkee's unsuccessful bid for reelection to Congress in 1852, while Whigs stood fast behind their own nominee, Orsamus Cole, also a former House member. Just when it appeared that the coalition would fly apart, with a number of Free Soilers threatening to back Kilbourn, the Whigs gave in and Durkee received the caucus nod. On February 1, 1855, the joint session finally convened, and Durkee, after a tough fight, secured the necessary majority.[24]

Two days after Durkee's election, Wisconsin's high court overturned the decision of the federal district court in the Booth case. With Justice Crawford up for reelection in April, former Whigs saw an opportunity to assert themselves after the rebuff they received in the senatorial contest. They likened the election to a referendum on the state court's decision and inferred that the Democrat Crawford's return would be construed as an endorsement of the Fugitive Slave Act. For this reason, and although Crawford was a competent judge, Republicans had to field a candidate against him. Other party chieftains agreed and also promised to name a Whig.[25]

With the judicial election scheduled for April 3, there was no time to convene a nominating convention, so the Republican caucus in the state legislature assumed responsibility for choosing a candidate. Ex-Whigs Timothy Howe and Orsamus Cole competed for the appointment. A former state legislator and circuit court judge, the highly regarded Howe was suspected of upholding the final authority of the national Supreme Court on constitutional questions; therefore he was unacceptable to Booth and the states' rights faction, while Cole's appeal straddled both partisan and ideological lines. As a one-term Congressman who represented Wisconsin's conservative southwestern district, the lifelong Whig had voted against the Fugitive Slave Act. Furthermore, he had forthrightly backed Smith's states' rights position from the beginning, and just days before had been the losing choice of Whig Republicans to represent Wisconsin in the United States Senate. In closed-door meetings, Republican lawmakers debated the merits of both men, finally settling on Cole and rejecting Howe because of his supposed "federal views."[26]

Campaigning on behalf of "State Rights, State Sovereignty, and the personal liberty of all our citizens," the popular Cole received enthusiastic support from most Republicans. With less eagerness, Democrats rallied behind Crawford and criticized their adversaries for opposing him because of "his opinions upon *one political question*" and for introducing partisan issues into a judicial election. But their efforts were unavailing; Cole won a surprisingly easy victory, picking up 55 percent of the vote, although voter turnout dipped to 42 percent of the eligible electorate. Not unexpectedly, Crawford picked up most of his support from voters who had supported Democratic congressional candidates in the previous year's balloting. However, the unusual cohesion of the still new Republican coalition provides striking testimony of the extent of popular party support for the states' rights position (see table 8). With good reason Republicans cheered Cole's election and declared the Fugitive Slave Act dead in Wisconsin.[27]

For the remainder of 1855 and most of 1856, Know Nothingism and preparations for the 1856 presidential contest held the attention of Wisconsin's Republicans. Although their party failed to win the White House, they swept to an impressive statewide triumph, rolling up huge majorities in the legislature and bringing the states' rights issue back to center stage.[28] Once again, a joint ballot of both houses would choose a United States senator, but this time Republican control would assure an easy victory, or so it was thought. Timothy Howe, hoping to avenge his earlier defeat, was the clear front-runner, with influential ex-Whigs Horace Rublee and Rufus King rumored to be working quietly on his behalf. Most other erstwhile Whigs and the few Know Nothings in the legislature also favored him.[29] Equally auspicious, opposition to Howe was scattered over no fewer than eight other candidates, only one of whom, the long-time abolitionist Edward D. Holton, commanded any meaningful support. But Durkee already represented the "original abolitionists," and even Holton conceded that his nomination would seriously compromise party unity. For that reason, his backers seemed disposed to back anyone "willing to stand firmly on a sound antislavery platform," and Holton himself, the scuttlebutt went, was prepared to withdraw his name whenever the caucus majority found a satisfactory candidate.[30] James R. Doolittle, a former Democrat and recent convert to the Republican cause, was the only other candidate expected to mount a serious challenge to Howe, but he was believed to be constitutionally ineligible for the post.[31] So all appeared bright for Howe's chances, with one keen observer claiming that two-thirds of its members were ready to endorse him and another that his "election seemed a near certainty."[32]

Only Sherman Booth and the states' rights bloc stood between Howe and a senate seat. Recognizing his strength and conceding that "on the Slavery question he is a decided Republican," Booth at first seemed willing to endorse Howe if he would stand by the principle of the state court's preeminence. Although hopeful that the Green Bay Republican would "promptly and cordially sustain the [court's] decision," he warned that Howe's refusal to bend to "the sentiment of the . . . party on this vital issue" would kill his chances.[33] Two weeks before the scheduled caucus gathering, the two men met privately in an attempt to avert a split, but Howe steadfastly denied the authority of state courts to issue writs of habeas corpus on behalf of residents charged with violating federal law. Moreover, on the question of the appellate jurisdiction of the national judiciary, he feebly claimed that he had not yet formed an opinion. Howe's rejection of this "well defined and clearly expressed doctrine of the party," an exasperated Booth reported, should eliminate him from consideration. "In short, he denies the doctrine of State Rights, and the authority of the State Judiciary to protect the lives and liberties of our citizens from Federal usurpation and outrage." Commenting on Howe's prospects without Booth's backing, one Democrat pronounced him "dead as Julius Caeser! D——d by the good offices of General Booth who has wiped him out as easily as you would brush a fly from the window sill."[34]

Howe's stand did seriously hurt his position within the party and induced Booth to actively fight his selection. Equally damaging, it forced many of his Whig allies to reluctantly abandon him. "The time has come when I see no middle ground on the issue before the country," one wrote.

"We must either acquiesce in federal usurpation and passively yield our rights to the dictation of the slave power, or we must assert the Jeffersonian doctrine of state sovereignty and actively sustain our rights as a free people."[35] When caucus members came together on the evening of January 15, their disarray became apparent on the first ballot. Howe received a mere twenty-two votes to Holton's sixteen and Doolittle's ten; the rest were scattered among five other hopefuls. Disturbed at the turn of events, Howe partisans warned that to make states' rights a test of Republican orthodoxy imperiled party unity. They agreed that most Republicans stood by the doctrines and the decision of the state tribunal, including many who supported Howe, but these were not contained in the national party platform and could not arbitrarily be added by the Wisconsin organization.[36] Other caucus members thought otherwise.

After another poll revealed that an impasse had been reached, the caucus adopted three resolutions and asked the candidates to respond to them.[37] The first pledged the party to revitalize the republican creed bequeathed by the founding fathers and to resist unjust seizures of power by the federal government; the second endorsed in full the states' rights precepts of the Virginia and Kentucky Resolutions. The last and most important declared the need to sustain the right of Wisconsin's court to shield its citizens from the application of unconstitutional enactments, such as the Fugitive Slave Law, free from federal judicial scrutiny.[38]

Two days later the caucus reconvened and examined the candidates' replies. Predictably, Holton wholeheartedly endorsed all three propositions. Howe, in a curious bid to placate states' rights men and party nationalists, warmly approved the Republican mission statement, the constitutional doctrines of the Virginia and Kentucky Resolutions, and the authority of state tribunals to render final judgment on the reserved rights of the states in order to safeguard their citizens from unauthorized national legislation and judicial decrees. But he also cautioned against an overly zealous regard for states' rights that earlier in South Carolina had bordered on treason,[39] reiterated his belief that writs of habeas corpus issued by state courts on behalf of federal detainees were unlawful, and once again excused himself from offering an opinion on whether the Supreme Court could review the decisions of state judges.[40]

The caucus then reviewed Doolittle's response. Endorsing the first two resolves without qualification, he also championed liberal accessibility to habeas corpus and declared that the failure of the Fugitive Slave Law to provide alleged escapees a jury trial clearly violated the constitution. Doolittle went on to expressly repudiate the idea that "the decision of one supreme court is absolutely binding upon another supreme court," arguing that all jurisdictional disputes between state and federal authorities ultimately must be resolved peaceably by an appeal to the people, "the highest of human tribunals." He took it for granted that the national government would respect state decrees backed by public opinion and that it would never attempt to enforce its will by resort to arms.[41]

Doolittle was also careful to distinguish between Wisconsin's stand in 1854 and South Carolina's in 1832. In his view, the Carolinians had openly violated the Constitution when they attempted to repeal and nullify the tariff laws of the United States and threatened to secede from the Union. Wisconsin, on the other hand, upheld its "rights as a sovereign State *in the Union,*" and did not seek to vindicate them "by going *out of the Union.*"[42]

Howe's stand on the habeas corpus issue and his attempt to dodge the question of the appellate jurisdiction of the federal courts failed to satisfy states' rights men and doomed his candidacy. His remaining supporters made strenuous efforts on his behalf, but to no avail. After Holton withdrew from the race, the scattered forces of the remaining candidates coalesced around Doolittle. On the sixth ballot, he received a bare majority of the caucus votes and later was elevated by the Republican legislature to the Senate.[43]

Howe's defeat bitterly disappointed his supporters. They accused states' rights men in the legislature of inflaming passions against him and threatening to quit the party if he was chosen. Booth especially came under fire for allegedly misrepresenting Howe's position on the states' rights question and introducing "trumped-up and false issues" to prejudice the lawmakers against him. Rublee especially denounced him as "a malignant and unscrupulous calumniator" who looked to dictate party principles and shut out all men from positions of influence who did not bow to his demands.[44]

Howe's opponents viewed matters differently. They applauded Doolittle's election as a vindication of states' rights, which alone promised to "redeem the country from the tyranny of the slave power concentrated in the federal government." It also was touted as a triumph of independent party men over the designs of power-hungry politicians who worked in secret to control party affairs.[45] A few antislavery radicals reproved Booth for his harsh and unrelenting attacks against Howe, and at least some thought that Holton would have been selected if he had exercised greater prudence.[46] Still, Doolittle was warmly received by most Republicans, and all were asked to put aside their differences and work for the success of the party.[47]

Two weeks after naming a United States senator, Republican lawmakers once again tackled the states' rights issue—this time in the form of a proposed personal liberty law. Its aim was to give effect to the decision of the state supreme court in the Booth case and to make the Fugitive Slave Act all but unenforceable in Wisconsin. Free Soilers first forced a debate on this question during the 1853 legislative session, when a committee report argued that Wisconsin's citizens needed an ordinance to shield them from the unjust application of the 1850 Act and other proslavery measures enacted by the national government. The majority Democrats frustrated that early effort though, as well as others made in 1855 and 1856.[48] In control of both houses of the 1857 legislature, Republicans now confidently expected to put a law on the books. Their proposal would require state officers to do everything in their power to obtain the freedom of all men or women arrested or claimed as runaways; this included granting writs of habeas corpus and jury trials. In addition, anyone who made false accusations or submitted inaccurate testimony would be subject to stiff fines and a minimum of one year in prison, and depositions presented by the prosecution would be inadmissable as evidence.[49]

A senate majority of twelve to seven passed the bill in mid-February. Republicans cast all twelve favorable votes and only one against it.[50] The assembly amended the senate's handiwork to include a provision that directed the state to fully reimburse any citizen of Wisconsin prosecuted under the Fugitive Slave Act and banned the sale of any real or personal property to enforce a judgment secured under it. Dubbed the "Booth Relief" provision, fifteen Democrats joined forty-eight Republicans in approving the amended version, the former hoping to embarrass their opponents with the "infamous clause . . . to pay Booth for breaking the law."[51] But senate Republicans refused the bait. They struck out the relief clause and returned their original bill to the assembly where it passed forty-seven to thirty-one.[52]

Most Republicans praised the personal liberty law for erecting the barrier "of State Sovereignty to protect citizens of Wisconsin from the aggressions of the Slave Power," although a few, most notably Timothy Howe, groused about it in private. Predictably, the state's Democrats denounced the law as an act of treason against the constitutional compact between the states.[53] As chance would have it, Chief Justice Whiton's term of office was coming to an end in April 1857, and in his bid for re-election, Wisconsin's voters once again would be given an opportunity to express themselves on the states' rights issue. Interest in the contest intensified greatly when, one month before the election, the United States Supreme Court delivered its judgment in the case of *Dred Scott v. John F. A. Sanford*.[54]

Two weighty questions were before the federal judges. Could Dred Scott bring suit in a federal court? And was Scott, a Missouri slave who had temporarily resided in Illinois and Wisconsin, made free as a result of their prohibitions against slavery? The Court majority ruled that American blacks were ineligible for United States citizenship or any of its rights and privileges. This included the right to sue. Further, they declared unconstitutional the Missouri Compromise restriction of slavery above 36°30' north latitude.[55]

The Dred Scott decision outraged Republicans. They condemned it as an unjust abrogation of the sacred accord reached in 1820 and a monstrous injustice to the nation's free blacks. It now permitted slaveholders to carry their bondsmen into all the territories; next they would demand entry into Wisconsin and the other free states.[56] The judgment also reinforced the Republican conviction that the slave power controlled all branches of the national government and lent added importance to Chief Justice Edward Whiton's bid for reelection. If they wished to protect the individual liberty and basic civil rights of all their citizens and check the growing centralization of power in Washington, wrote one routinely temperate Republican editor, Wisconsinites should stand behind their court and their legislature and return Whiton to his post. This would show the rest of the nation that they at least "remain a free people."[57]

Democrats depicted the contest for chief justice as a referendum on the "dangerous doctrine of nullification" and a test of the state's devotion to the Union.[58] But Whiton's personal popularity and broad Republican regard for the court's stance and the personal liberty law led to a smashing victory. Attesting to the widespread interest in the contest and its significance, the incumbent received 57 percent of the ballots cast amidst a record turnout for a state election. The vote also reveals that cross-over voting was insignificant; public party positions accurately reflected and reinforced the opinions of the electorate (see table 11).[59]

In his evaluation of the election, Horace Rublee reported that "every friend of state rights, every opponent of slavery extension, of the nationalization of slavery, of the recent daring encroachments upon the reserved rights of the states" could take great satisfaction in Whiton's triumph.[60] Rublee's good friend Timothy Howe did not agree. From his Green Bay home, he looked with increasing displeasure at the direction the Republican party was taking. Booth's success in engineering his defeat was especially galling, although he readily admitted that most Republicans backed the party's unofficial states' rights position. Nevertheless, in early March, Howe publicly declared his intention to steer the party away from states' rights and nullification if possible at its fall convention. He also threatened to abandon the organization if it continued to proscribe men from high office who rejected the doctrine.[61]

Most Republican leaders resented Howe's threat to desert the party and vowed to resist him at the state convention.[62] Not unexpectedly, Booth plotted to foil Howe's plan "to take over the party." He advised calling a mass meeting on June 17, the anniversary of the Battle of Bunker Hill, both to protest the Dred Scott decision and to show support for Wisconsin's judiciary and legislature. In the weeks prior to the gathering, Booth and other organizers worked hard to obtain backing for the meeting from the state's leading Republican officeholders and editors and to bring in nationally known speakers. In both efforts they were successful.[63]

The weather on June 17 was terrible. Rain blocked travel in the rural districts, and towns such as Fond du Lac reportedly were under water. Nonetheless, between eight hundred and twelve hundred enthusiastic conventioneers jammed into the Madison meeting hall to hear the wealthy New York abolitionist, Gerrit Smith, and the grim-faced Kansas "freedom fighter," John Brown, give well-received speeches. Nearly every Republican leader in the state attended, although Howe and Rublee were conspicuously absent.[64] The meeting proceeded without a hitch and unanimously endorsed distinct antislavery and states' rights resolutions denying that the Constitution sanctioned slavery or gave Congress any power to legislate on its behalf. They also expressed alarm at the slave power's domination of every branch of the federal government, most recently displayed in the Dred Scott decision, the principles of which, "if carried out, would introduce and perpetuate slavery in every free state in the Union." The concluding resolutions affirmed each state's obligation to guard the liberties of its citizens and pledged Republicans to stand by Wisconsin's judiciary and legislature in the legitimate exercise of their reserved rights, "At all hazards and in all emergencies." In keeping with the spirit of those sentiments, the delegates denied that the states were obliged to return fugitive slaves and that, in Wisconsin at least, all people were presumed free. For that reason, slavecatchers could expect to be prosecuted as kidnappers and would suffer the severe penalties prescribed in the state's personal liberty law.[65]

The convention adjourned in good spirits. Harrison Reed, an influential and perceptive Republican editor from Menasha, probably spoke for most when he wrote that the meeting's success should remove any doubts about the resolve of the Republican party to defend the people of Wisconsin from acts of "federal aggression and official usurpation." Even Rublee, who claimed that the press of business had prevented him from attending, deferred to popular sentiment and backed the resolutions. And, while Booth disputed charges that political considerations had inspired him to call the meeting, the tone of the resolutions clearly indicated that Howe's bid for ideological and political control of the party faced tough going.[66]

In the weeks prior to the state Republican convention, scheduled for September 1, Howe continued to caution the party against taking a stand that would force him and his supporters out.[67] The meeting began inauspiciously when, after several ballots revealed that none of the principal candidates had any prospect of gaining the support of a majority of the delegates, Booth's allies joined with those of Alexander Randall and nominated the former Free Soil Democrat to head their ticket over Howe's favorite. Matters did not improve when, in his acceptance speech, Randall resolved to "resist to the extreme limit of the executive power of the state, each and every attempt at aggression or usurpation by the federal government upon the reserved rights of the states."[68] Satisfied that his position within the party was secure, Booth, in a show of party unity, agreed to Howe's appointment as chairman of the platform committee.[69] The harmonious facade crumbled when the committee delivered its report. In addition to reaffirming the party's antislavery principles and its opposition to the Dred Scott decision, Howe insisted on inserting a resolution that bound the party to "maintain this creed—this whole creed—and nothing but this creed," in order to protect him and his partisans from being proscribed from future political favor because of their refusal to endorse Smith's states' rights position. Booth exploded at the blatant attempt to back away from a principle supported by most Republicans and declared that his followers would quit the party if it adopted the Creed Resolution. They were willing to forego formal approval of the states' rights faith, he explained, but they demanded the right to continue publicly advocating the doctrine and, based on it, to withhold or grant political preferment to anyone. Realizing that the resolution would lose badly if it came to a vote, Howe wisely retreated, seemingly content that the party at least officially had not gone on record in favor of states' rights and nullification.[70]

The year 1857 found Booth at the peak of his power in the Republican party. Howe's attempt to promote himself and his "federal principles" had been blocked, and even though states' rights and nullification were not embraced as fundamental Republican doctrine, politicians looking to advance within the party could not ignore them. Yet Booth continued to make enemies with his uncompromising tactics and volatile personality, while Howe, equally vain and determined, at least did not provoke similar personal animosity. In fact, even though most Republicans refused to swallow his "old federal politics," Howe remained well liked and respected.[71]

The wrangling between the two factions subsided during the 1857 campaign when, for the third time in less than a decade, the state's voters were asked to rule on the question of black suffrage.

CHAPTER TEN

A Little Matter
of Justice

THE REPUBLICAN APPEAL did not concentrate directly on the evils of the slave system itself; it emphasized instead the slave power's threat to the security of traditional republican values and freedoms in the North. Most party members agreed they could be of little immediate help to enslaved blacks, but they did expect the triumph of their party and principles, especially slavery's containment, would someday drive slavery to its grave.[1] Still, they did not ignore the plight of blacks.

When Wisconsin's Republicans addressed questions relating to race, they often warned that the "selfish indifference" of Northern whites might someday come back to haunt them. "The great principles of Republican Government" embraced all men, most insisted, and to withhold any man's rights because of the color of his skin would degrade the ideal of basic human equality and breed contempt for the concept of individual liberty.[2] And many within the party had long taken a principled stand against slavery in the South and prejudice in the North. Rufus King, for example, claimed to look forward to slavery's destruction not simply on moral grounds, but because it would lift "the African from the statutory level of a beast, up to the dignity of complete manhood."[3] The questions of black suffrage and colonization provide insight into Republican racial attitudes and the limits of the party's commitment to equal rights, just as they had for the Liberty and Free Soil organizations.

The ruling against enfranchising blacks in 1849, despite the favorable popular vote, had not brought an end to the matter. Free Soil representatives, joined by friendly Whigs, continued to press the legislature early in the decade to resubmit the suffrage question to the voters, only to be thwarted by the Democratic majority.[4]

In 1855, Wisconsin Republicans revived the issue when their state convention unanimously proclaimed that the party's principles were "utterly hostile to the proscription of any on account of birth place, religion, or color."[5] With new hope, a group of Milwaukee blacks resolved to circulate petitions throughout the state requesting the legislature to "adopt such measures as will secure us this God-given right." At its 1856 session, the Republican senate acted favorably on their petitions, but the measure failed in the Democratic Assembly.[6]

Undeterred, free suffrage advocates continued to pressure the legislature, especially after both houses came under Republican control in 1857. Once more, the senate passed a bill enfranchising blacks, subject to approval by the state's voters. In the assembly, the judiciary committee took up the bill for consideration, and on March 2 Joseph Trotter Mills, a fiercely independent abolitionist and Republican legislator from the lead-district town of Lancaster, delivered its opinion.[7]

Mills amended the senate bill by calling for universal suffrage, irrespective of color or sex. "Vulgar prejudices" and "hereditary hatred" had for too long denied free blacks the privileges they were entitled to, he claimed, but science and the growing acceptance of libertarian principles were eroding "the unmanly dogma that human rights are qualities of color." As for narrow-minded men who retained the pretensions of a "cutaneous aristocracy," they embodied "stubborn conglomerates of obsolete ideas . . . men born in an age to which their natures are not adapted." With regard to sexual discrimination, Mills declared that legal and cultural strictures kept women from realizing their full potential, and he called for the repeal of all laws that denied them participation in "the discussions of questions in which their happiness and destiny are involved." Only then would they enter the real world, and "hollow compliments and rose-water flatteries . . . [would] be exchanged for a pure admiration, and a well grounded respect, when we see [them] nobly discharging [their] part in the moral and intellectual struggles of the age."[8]

Mills was sincerely dedicated to universal equality, but he also had a practical reason for uniting the questions of black and women's suffrage. The first issue alone would not sufficiently excite popular participation, he believed; combine the two, and every voter in the state would turn out.[9]

The assembly passed Mills' version of the senate bill and referred it back there for reconsideration. But the senate balked. Enfranchising blacks was one thing; enfranchising women was quite another. The senate re-passed its own original bill, which the assembly ultimately accepted.[10]

During the months between passage of the suffrage resolution and the state party conventions, Democrats made a determined effort to insure that their opponents would be unable to avoid the "nigger question" in the coming campaign. Black suffrage was a cardinal principle of the Repub-lican party, they insisted, daring it to proclaim so publicly.[11] At their own convention, held in late August, the Democrats made it clear where they stood on the issue, proudly proclaiming, "We are unalterably opposed to the extension of the right of suffrage to the Negro race, and will never con-sent that the odious doctrine of Negro equality shall find a place upon the statute books of Wisconsin."[12]

In response to Democratic goading, a number of Republican journal-ists took up the challenge. In defense of black voting, many asserted that in recent years the unwarranted prejudices of the whites "have yielded to sober reason" and the biblical proclamation that "God . . . hath made of one blood all men."[13] Others were ambivalent, admitting their inability to completely overcome "early imbibed prejudices" and their lack of desire to associate with blacks. Nevertheless, even they insisted, "No man can be a true Democrat or true Republican who would deny it [the vote] to any man on account of color, creed, or birthplace."[14]

At their September meeting, Republicans declined to take a direct stand on the suffrage question; instead they again approved the antiproscription plank adopted in 1855. Vague though it was, the Democrats took advan-tage of the resolution and claimed it to be, in reality, an endorsement of black political equality.[15] Chiding the Republicans for feebly attempting to disguise their position, the Democrats crudely insisted that the party had "swallowed the nigger whole, wool, boots, breaches, and all."[16] The Democrats also tried to capitalize on white fears and hatred of blacks with hysterical fulminations against the "absurd and revolutionary" Republican belief that they could be raised from their "condition of inferiority . . . to the white race."[17] Grant this lowly people the right to vote and Wisconsin would become "a grand asylum for the animalized free Negro hordes who curse our eastern and southern cities with their noxious existence." As their numbers increased, so too would their influence; in time they might even rule the state.[18]

The Democracy added to this bleak picture by assuring white Wisconsin that social equality and racial amalgamation naturally would follow political equality. As one Democratic editor put it:

> We want no Negro equality, for it is a physical and mental impossibility . . . it would degrade and brutify our race, giving Negro husbands and Negro progeny to our fair daughters and sisters—We religiously believe it an insult to our creator to suppose that he ever designed such disgusting amalgamation. The very thought would be unnatural, offensive, and revolting to our natures. That such would certainly occur was no imaginary matter . . . we have not given ourselves up to barren speculation, but statements made on facts.[19]

Finally, in an appeal to the prejudices of Wisconsin's large foreign-born population, Democrats asserted that their Republican opponents cared more for blacks than for them and would subordinate their needs to those of the state's black inhabitants.[20]

The Republican candidates for state office, probably by mutual agreement, chose political expediency over principle by responding to these race-baiting tactics with complete silence. Democrats, in turn, reminded voters that Alexander Randall had introduced and supported the proposition on black suffrage finally adopted by the 1846 constitutional convention. Likewise, Samuel Hastings, the Republican choice for secretary of the treasury, was a well-known abolitionist agitator and "friend of the Negro," while James McMynn, the party nominee for superintendent of public instruction, also was accused of harboring prosuffrage sentiments.[21]

Unlike the candidates, most Republican editors publicly stood foursquare in favor of black voting. At least twenty-nine party journals supported the measure and twelve mounted FOR EXTENSION OF SUFFRAGE on their bannerhead; only three opposed it, and two failed to take a position. The party's broad editorial approval led one Democrat to insist, with only slight exaggeration, "Every organ of Shanghaiism [Republicanism] in the state of Wisconsin without a single exception, has taken strong ground in favor of Negro suffrage." As a result of this support, another crassly declared, "All real Republicans . . . must toe the mark and go the whole figure. No grimaces, no wretchings, no distortion; but go the whole figure and swallow the whole nigger."[22]

A number of Republicans responded to the Democratic charge that black enfranchisement was a party issue by insisting instead that it was a simple matter of principle and justice.

> It is of little use to blind ourselves by party feeling or prejudice against color. . . . We have no right to deny to any the natural rights we claim for ourselves or to follow our prejudices at the expense of our principles. . . . We ask every good citizen . . . to divest himself of prejudices and act from principle, and in casting his vote consider its effects upon the country, and especially upon that unfortunate class who are now oppressed and deprived of all the rights of manhood.[23]

Others boldly asserted that the platform did indeed endorse the measure. Rufus King warmly professed, "No portion of the Republican platform receives a more cordial assent from us" than that advocating free suffrage.

> To every word of it, we give our ready support, for every word is right. We do not believe that any man should be deprived of his rights . . . because of the color of his skin. . . . We are glad the word *color* is in the Republican platform, and would hope to see every re-publican vote for conferring the right of suffrage upon colored men.[24]

Additional reasoning employed by Republicans to justify their stance was remarkably broad-minded. Many decried the efforts of Democrats to stir up racial hatred among Wisconsin's immigrants. If they would deny blacks basic rights due to their alleged inferiority and ignorance, it was asked, what would prevent them from doing the same to the thousands of foreigners who "cannot read their ticket" at the polls? Republicans implored their foreign-born friends to reject these coarse Democratic appeals and vote in favor of black suffrage as a just standard that would help safe-guard the rights of all. "Far better is it to open the national gates wide and let in to full citizenship, without conditions, all nations and tribes, than to cherish the idea of exclusiveness of political communities," contended the South Carolina–born abolitionist William H. Brisbane.[25]

Republicans also appealed to cherished principles of the American Revolution to promote their position. They reminded voters that since the property of blacks and whites was taxed equally, both should enjoy the privilege of choosing their legislators. After all, "Is not the maxim of taxation and representation a correct one?" Blacks also were subject to the laws of the United States and the state of Wisconsin and therefore deserved "a voice in making the law and regulating its penalties." In short, the state's blacks asked only for that which was theirs by natural right, one lead district Republican argued. "No special pleading as to color, or race, or religion can destroy such right."[26]

Party leaders also recalled that many blacks had fought and died defending the nascent republic during the Revolution and the War of 1812. They retold the story of Crispus Attucks's bravery at the Boston Massacre and Andrew Jackson's tribute to his black troops at New Orleans. They also asked whites "hitherto indifferent upon the question of colored suffrage" to reflect on "whether some small degree of consideration is not due from those who are enjoying the blessings of liberty here to a race of men who helped win those blessings for [them]."[27]

To the Democratic scare that Wisconsin would be inundated with free blacks and runaway slaves if equal suffrage passed, many Republicans countered with an attack on the very notions underlying those concerns. Denying that blacks were an "inferior, ignorant, wicked, and debased race," they pointed to those residing in their own towns and inquired, "Can a more thrifty, peaceable, industrious, intelligent class of citizens be found?" Moreover, in states where blacks already possessed the franchise, "They have asserted this right quite as intelligently and quite as much for the public good as any of those . . . who have a hysterical spasm whenever they happen to think of free suffrage."[28] If some blacks appeared to fit the stereotype, it was not because they were of a lower order of humanity, naturally suited to a condition of political and social subordination to whites. Rather, it was a result of the "inhuman tyranny of the white race of America, who have . . . held them in the deepest, darkest bondage the world ever saw."[29] For all these reasons, Wisconsin's voters had a duty to discard their unfounded race prejudice and confer upon blacks all the rights they were entitled to. After all, "In our essential rights we are a common brotherhood," a self-evident truth contained in "the first proposition in our political catechism. . . . All men are created equal."[30]

The Republican response to the amalgamation bugbear was more circumspect. Spokesmen dismissed the Democratic argument that black political equality would lead to amalgamation as "senseless" and "all twaddle." The two issues were unrelated, and it was more important to help raise blacks from their lowly state than to fear social equality.[31] Besides, the much-feared "bleaching process" was far more common in the female slave quarters of the South than in the free North.[32] Nevertheless, most party members probably agreed with the editors of the *Janesville Gazette* who explained that interracial marriages were wrong and in bad taste, but in Wisconsin at least they were sanctioned by law. And legitimacy, they maintained, was an improvement over the immorality and excesses practiced in the South.[33] Considering the explosiveness of the amalgamation issue, Wisconsin's Republicans approached it in a manner that was understandably cautious but far more civil than the simple repugnance expressed by Democrats.

Republican editorial opposition to equal suffrage was concentrated in the western counties, which had a long history of being unsympathetic to either abolitionism or blacks. Joseph Cover, editor of the influential *Grant County Herald* and one of the party's founders, claimed that the west originally was home to many hard-core Democrats.[34] As a result, Whig and Republican leaders in the region had been forced to broadcast their principles in the "most attractive, strongest and entertaining" manner possible. For Republicans especially, that meant focusing on popular opposition to the extension of slavery into the western territories, in the hope they would attract white settlers only. Accordingly, Cover extolled these as "the watchwords of Republicanism":

> No slaveholders and no niggers in the territories—white men must own and forever occupy the great west. Nigger slaves shall not be allowed to work among, associate, nor amalgamate with white people. Democrats must go to the old slave states if they want to own and live among niggers. These are Republican ideas . . . against the progress of Negro slavery, Negro amalgamation, Negro association, and every other infernal Negro business.[35]

Cover's racist appeal was equally explicit regarding suffrage. He denounced the proposition and accused the Democratic nominee for governor, James Cross, who had once signed a petition requesting the legislature to submit the question to the people, of favoring black equality and of being a representative of the "Negro loving northern Democratic Governors" allied with the slave power of the South.[36] Cover's sentiments regarding the "Negro business" were acclaimed by the Democrats, and the *Herald*'s editorials marked it as "an intelligent Republican paper . . . occupying the ground we do." They urged the editor to reevaluate his party affiliation and join the side whose principles were most like his own.[37]

Republicans and Democrats were not alone in voicing their opinions on the suffrage question. Wisconsin's blacks demonstrated their increasing political sophistication by sending their own speakers around the state to rally support for the measure. Predictably, the Democratic press ridiculed their efforts and referred to them in highly disparaging terms. Republicans, on the other hand, spoke of them with considerable respect. One editor, for example, found much to praise in a speech given by Milwaukee's Byrd Parker: "Mr. Parker is a ready and powerful speaker and well did he defend the rights of his race. We think those who heard him, and whose reason is not perverted by political prejudices, will admit that if Mr. Parker was put on a level with *some* white men he would be by no means *elevated.*"[38]

Despite the backing of the Republican press and the efforts of Wisconsin's blacks, few expected the proposition to pass. Widespread popular opposition within both parties, most people believed, was insurmountable. William Brisbane regretfully expressed this view when, on the eve of the election, he confided to his diary, "I feel uncomfortable to know that there are many connected with the Republican party who are so prejudiced against the Negro as to vote against a measure [black suffrage] so just and right."[39]

The black suffrage resolution went down to defeat, 45,157 to 31,964.[40] In the general election, Alexander Randall captured the governorship by fewer than 100 votes out of 90,000 cast, while two other Republican candidates also eked out narrow victories. Jubilant Democrats won four state offices and confidently predicted the rapid demise of the "nigger party."[41]

Although the state's blacks were once again denied "this measure of justice," an examination of the results indicates that a solid majority of Republican voters supported the proposition, while a much larger proportion of Democrats voted against it (see table 12). Republicans accounted for nearly 95 percent of the prosuffrage tally and 14 percent of the antisuffrage ballots. Looked at another way, about two-thirds of all Republicans who participated in the governor's race favored black political equality, only slightly less than the proportion of the party's legislators who had favored submitting the question to the electorate. Democrats, on the other hand, cast 78 percent of the anti-black ballots and only about 4 percent of the prosuffrage votes.

Further analysis reveals that most antisuffrage Republicans were found in western Wisconsin. Cover's home county of Grant alone contributed nearly 30 percent of their number. The western counties of Pierce, Dunn, Eau Claire, Jackson, and Bad Ax also gave Republican and antisuffrage majorities, as did Adams, Wood, Portage, and Marquette in the central part of the state. The prosuffrage Republicans were concentrated in the Yankee and Yorker counties located in the southeast and north-central parts of the state, while huge antisuffrage majorities were registered in the Democratic lakeshore counties of the east, where large numbers of German and Irish voters lived.[42]

The returns also indicate that many men who cast ballots for their party's candidate for governor failed to vote on the suffrage question. Fully 20 percent of Randall's supporters abstained on the issue; nearly 18 percent of his opponent's backers did the same. Abstention in some cases probably resulted from an absence at the polls of tickets asking participants to take a stand. Simple apathy undoubtedly explains a portion of the inaction as well. Other Republicans may have suffered from conflicting pressures to disavow their prejudice against black political equality and, in the case of a few Democrats, even to oppose equality when, in principle, they did not.[43] In any event, it seems reasonable to conclude that some Republicans and Democrats were questioning long-held racial attitudes, or at least did not hold them strongly enough to vote against blacks.

About 8 percent of the antisuffrage vote appears to have come from non-participants in the general election. Some of those men likely sat out most contests, but found themselves sufficiently aroused by the suffrage issue to get out and register their objection. Other than to speculate that they harbored a profound antipathy toward blacks, little can be said of them. Another group of opponents may have been disaffected party men. The Democratic party, feuding as usual, contained a highly dissatisfied faction. While he served as a Democratic legislator from Milwaukee,

James Cross had been a trusted associate and defender of former governor William Barstow, who suffered still from the taint of the corruption that had aided in his narrow defeat in 1855. Yet Barstow continued to wield great power within the party, struggling as usual for control with his rival Josiah Noonan. Amidst rumors that he had manipulated the selection of delegates to the party's state convention in order to insure the selection of Cross, a group of disgruntled Democrats met in Milwaukee in early September and resolved not to be bound by his nomination.[44] Shortly after, a committee appointed at the meeting published a report that traced the corruption of the Barstowites. It called on all party members "to come forward and join in such reformatory measures as shall secure the triumph of Democratic measures and men."[45]

Most Democrats dismissed the reformers as "soreheads," but several noteworthy defections did occur. Edward G. Ryan, high in party circles, scorned the nomination of Cross; Samuel "Pump" Carpenter, a friend of Noonan's and editor of the *Wisconsin Patriot,* denounced the nominee and demanded the party be "cleaned out—all the filth and excrescences cut off and thrown away. Until this is done, we cannot and *ought* not to succeed."[46] In October, a "Reform Democratic Convention" gathered in Milwaukee and nominated its own slate of candidates. The delegates proclaimed "undiminished confidence in the democracy, integrity, and ability of President Buchanan . . . and the Democratic party," but they condemned the state organization as hopelessly corrupt. It had to be repudiated and rebuilt in order to compete effectively with the "Black Republicans." The convention also circulated an address to the state's Democrats.

> We . . . appeal to you, that duty and a high sense of right and justice, require the rejection of Cross. He stands as the representative of an organization repudiated by the people and no longer worthy of the name Democrat. His election would be to continue the abuses which he has so zealously defended, and a re-enactment of the frauds which have so grossly injured the State. He is not a Democrat because he is not an honest man. . . . He is unworthy of your confidence.[47]

The Democracy received another jolt when the *Milwaukee American,* the state's Know Nothing paper, lent its support to Cross. This hardly could have set well with Wisconsin's foreign-born community, particularly when the *American* ran long articles that slandered the Republican nominee for lieutenant governor, Carl Schurz. Seeing an opportunity, the reformers placed Francis Heubschmann, a prominent German-born Democrat residing in Milwaukee, at the head of their ticket.[48]

Democratic disaffection lends credence to the possibilities that many antisuffrage ballots came from persons who did not vote in the general election and that the bulk of those men probably were Democrats. Moreover, an examination of the returns at the township level, where these figures are available, seems to confirm this. In Washington, Manitowoc, Milwaukee, and Ozaukee counties, some men undoubtedly showed up at the polls to cast antisuffrage ballots but did not vote in the gubernatorial contest. All four of the counties were Democratic strongholds, where Cross received between 66 and 82 percent of the votes cast.

A few prosuffrage ballots were cast by nonparticipants in the governor's contest. Perhaps 200 of those came from the city of Racine's fourth ward and may have been cast by nativist former Whigs upset about the selection of the crafty ex-Democrat Randall and the German-born Schurz to head up the Republican ticket. A few Garrisonian "non-resistors," characterized by their ardent opposition to slavery and their refusal to participate in a political system deemed immoral and corrupt, may also have voted for free suffrage.[49]

Similarly, little information exists about the eligible voters who sat out the election entirely. A comparison of the gubernatorial turnout with the 1856 presidential returns indicates that twenty thousand Republicans and eight thousand Democrats stayed home in 1857 (see table 13). Yet it would be a mistake to assume that the Republican decline came as a result of the widespread editorial support for black voting rights. In fact, the 1857 turnout in the governor's contest nearly equaled the record showing in the recent judicial contest. Moreover, the Democrats maintained a consistently higher level of participation in statewide contests than their opponents when results were compared to the presidential campaigns.[50] Most commentators blamed the lower turnout on overconfidence and the harsh economic times that prevailed then. "The money pressure is the chief matter which absorbs the public mind," observed Kenosha Republican Michael Frank, "so much so that it seems impossible to get up any enthusiasm on the election."[51] Republicans like Frank expressed great concern over "the apathy of the people," and in their postelection commentary they scolded the "potato diggers" in their party who stayed home and tended to business rather than show up at the polls.[52] All in all, the most that can be said about nonvoters in 1857 is that they did not sufficiently fear the consequences of black political equality, so vividly detailed by the Democratic press, to go to the polls and record an opinion.

The presence of blacks seems to have had no impact in determining whether a county or township would support or oppose the suffrage measure. Racine and Milwaukee counties contained the largest numbers of blacks in the state; the former voted in favor of black suffrage, the latter against it. In the twenty-four counties where the bulk of Wisconsin's black residents lived, Republican prosuffrage forces scored victories in eleven, while Democratic antisuffrage partisans triumphed in nine.[53] An examination of the township returns likewise reveals no meaningful patterns. Thus, partisan affiliation and racial attitudes were probably much more influential in shaping a voter's response to the suffrage question than were a few neighboring blacks.

Commenting on the results, some Republicans publicly rebuked the party leadership for treating the suffrage issue so gingerly because of "a difference of opinion." It was deemed "*expedient*," they complained, "to slur it over with the single word color . . . because a small part of the Republican party are not sufficiently free from an unreasoning *prejudice* to accord this simple justice to the colored man." But it was wrong, they insisted, to labor "for the freedom of four million blacks in the South" and at the same time refuse "the boon to four hundred in Wisconsin. . . . We are tired and disgusted with this type of policy."[54]

The state's blacks also deplored the results of the referendum and promised to hold "one hundred anti-Slavery conventions" throughout Wisconsin for the purpose of "indoctrinating the people . . . into the true principles of Democratic Republicanism."[55] But there is no evidence that any of those meetings occurred, or that the cries of the dissident Republicans were heeded.

Wisconsin blacks suffered a third disappointing setback in their effort to achieve political equality in 1857, and although a solid Republican majority had backed the proposal, the opposition of many signified that the deep humanitarian strain of the earlier antislavery parties had been weakened. This makes sense because the Republicans embraced a much wider and larger segment of the state's population than its forebears. Yet, what is remarkable is not that it harbored racially biased persons, but that so many of them seem to have shed at least some of the common prejudices of the day and backed equal suffrage.[56]

In general, the Republican party in Wisconsin and other northern states attracted men whose attitudes towards blacks were substantially more moderate than those in the Democratic organization. However, it is interesting to compare the response of neighboring Iowa's Republicans to a referendum on black suffrage held just three months earlier.[57]

As in Wisconsin, the Hawkeye state's Republican leadership kept mute on the proposition, not wanting overt support to engender a racist backlash against a new constitution it strongly favored and that would be voted on the same day. But unlike Wisconsin, Iowa's Republican editors, with very few exceptions, failed to endorse the measure, thus leaving it to fend for itself. Without significant backing, the proposition suffered an overwhelming defeat, with perhaps 25 percent of the Republicans who showed up that day casting prosuffrage ballots and fully half abstaining. Yet the unwillingness of Iowa's Republican elites to support black political equality probably only partly explains why party members in the two states voted differently on the issue. With slaveholding Missouri as their neighbor to the south, many Iowa Republicans, undoubtedly torn between their lifelong racism and their republican idealism, worried that too much racial tolerance would attract large numbers of fugitives and free-state black settlers into the state, fears the Democrats attempted to capitalize on. Also important, Iowa contained far fewer residents who might be predisposed toward black suffrage than did Wisconsin. More than twice as many Yankees and Yorkers settled in Wisconsin than in Iowa, and they provided a solid core of political and moral support for both antislavery radicalism and racial broad-mindedness.[58]

Colonization, which gained a small popular following as the decade rolled to an ominous close, also provides some insight into Republican attitudes toward blacks. Earlier colonization schemes had won few friends among antislavery advocates. Liberty men and Free Soilers, more often than not, repudiated colonization as nothing more than a proslavery plot to intensify racial animosity and rid the nation of free blacks, thereby throwing up further barriers to future emancipation. Some Free Soilers, it is true, endorsed voluntary emigration, assuming that a separation of the races into different climates was inevitable and desirable, but rarely did they invoke degrading and demeaning racial stereotypes to support their position.[59]

Among Republicans, colonization found champions in Francis P. Blair, Andrew Jackson's old crony, and Wisconsin's own United States senator,

James R. Doolittle. Both former Democrats, Blair and Doolittle pressed the Republicans to embrace colonization in order to broaden the party's appeal and increase its chances for success in 1860. Their plan, which looked to purchase land and establish free black colonies in Central America, also gave an added dimension to the slavery extension issue. By encouraging the voluntary emigration of "our colored men of African descent," they declared, the ambitious Southern strategy of spreading black bondage southward would be frustrated, and the dream of building a "Slaveholding Empire" permanently blocked. "It is outflanking them," Doolittle claimed. "It is posting a strong and faithful force in their rear [that] would sooner die than let slavery go there." Coupled with the Republican efforts to curb slavery's expansion in the American West, the institution would be hemmed in on all sides, ultimately resulting in its "extinction by peaceable means without any infringement upon the rights of the states where it exists."[60]

Colonization advocates also asserted that nonslaveholding whites in the border slave states might jump on the Republican bandwagon if they were convinced that manumitted slaves would be removed from their communities. They were emancipationists, they staunchly maintained, who hated blacks as much as slavery. Adopt colonization, Doolittle confidently predicted, and "our friends in Missouri, Maryland, Delaware, Kentucky and Virginia" would quickly "Republicanize these States!"[61]

The Republican endorsement of colonization served the party's interests in other ways. It deflected the increasingly virulent Democratic claims that a Republican triumph would result in social equality and entice swarms of freed blacks to emigrate North. Similarly, it played on the longing of many whites to rid the nation of both slavery and blacks and to place it "under the sole dominion of the white race."[62]

Yet, pandering to racist attitudes comprised only one theme in colonizationist rhetoric. More often than not, Wisconsin Republicans spoke sympathetically about the degradation blacks endured as a result of the slave system, and they deplored "the oppressive and infamous black laws of the free states." Some national figures, including Blair, were even moved on occasion to question the racist assumptions that justified the continued enslavement of blacks. It is not, the Missourian noted, "that the white races are . . . necessarily superior to the black . . . the relative superiority or inferiority is rather the result of circumstances and climatic influence than of natural endowment." Still, even if it were found that whites were superior, it did not follow that their inferiors should be reduced to involuntary servitude or denied the basic rights of citizenship.[63]

Thus, most Republican colonizationists justified separating the races as the best means both to safeguard white freedom from the "aggressive and acquisitive spirit of the slavery propagandists" and to insure that blacks would obtain all the "rights and privileges of settlement and citizenship" denied them in the United States. It would, they insisted, eliminate "the obstacles interposed to the freedom and equality of the blacks here, from the prejudices against color, by opening up a place where they can enjoy the rights and privileges of freemen."[64] After all, it was the unreasoning prejudices of the whites, according to some spokesmen for black removal, that posed the one insurmountable obstacle to emancipation. Hence, colonization offered the nation an answer to two troubling questions. How shall "the foul blot of slavery be peacefully and satisfactorily" eliminated? And, equally important, "What shall be done with the Negroes if they are emancipated?"[65]

For all of the discussion of colonization, and despite Doolittle's prominence among its advocates, the issue seems to have inspired little popular enthusiasm in the North or in Wisconsin. This was due to the sheer impracticality of the venture, and as Sherman Booth put it, to "the non-emigrating character of the Negro."[66] Nonetheless, the colonization debate did force many Republicans to confront the monumental challenge abolition and racial prejudice posed, and undoubtedly it nurtured their dual longing to remove slavery, *the cause* that for years had engendered increasing sectional hatred, as well as the nation's unloved and hapless blacks.[67]

Republican differences over the questions of black suffrage and colonization never threatened party harmony in the same way that the states' rights issue did. Indeed, the battle between states' rights men and party nationalists for control of the Republican organization ended only with the outbreak of the Civil War.

CHAPTER ELEVEN

It Looks Like
Civil War Is Inevitable

THE REPUBLICAN PARTY'S STRENGTH and durability in the prewar years lay in the diversity and adaptability of its appeal; men who held different opinions found some aspect of it sufficiently compelling to justify their support. But the glue that held the coalition together was the increasing fear of the slave power, its desperate attempts to secure "an absolute and firmly grounded predominance in the nation," and the dire implications that held for the future of individual and civil liberty in America.[1] The advent of the newly elected Democratic president, James Buchanan, greatly added to Republican concerns.

A seasoned politician, Buchanan assumed office in 1857, confident that he could bring about a peaceful resolution to the sectional controversy.[2] His administration got off to an inauspicious start, however, when two days after his inauguration, the United States Supreme Court delivered its decision in the Dred Scott case; that decision set off a firestorm of criticism, including accusations that Buchanan and the justices had conspired with other friends of slavery in formulating an opinion designed eventually to legitimize the institution everywhere.[3]

Buchanan's problems were just beginning though. When he took over the White House, he was convinced that popular sovereignty honestly applied in the territories would end sectional quarrels. In Kansas, still the main trouble spot, free-state settlers in early 1857 outnumbered slave staters by a two-to-one margin. The president, like most politicians North and South, believed that in a fair vote Kansans would opt for freedom. But in taking that stand, Buchanan failed to credit Republican hostility to the doctrine, especially in light of the fraud and violence that had so far discredited it. And with an eye on the Dred Scott decision, he also rejected the Republican party's continued insistence that Congress itself should act to keep the territories free. Consequently, as a matter of principle, Republicans could be counted on to fight him every step of the way. Yet, if the administration's strategy worked, and Kansas was admitted as a free state, their appeal might have been seriously weakened. A greater danger to the president's plan lay in the growing alienation of Northern Democrats since the Dred Scott case. That decision put a decidedly Southern spin on the meaning of popular sovereignty when it declared that neither Congress nor a territorial legislature could exclude slavery from the territories.[4]

In Kansas, meanwhile, an election for delegates to a state constitutional convention was underway. Free staters, fearful that widespread fraud again would accompany the balloting and negate their majority, yet bind them to its outcome, refused to vote. To no one's surprise, slave-state men carried the day. Meeting in the proslavery town of Lecompton, the delegates fashioned a constitution and asked residents to adopt it with or without slavery, as opposed to the accepted practice of submitting the entire document for approval. A provision permitting slaveholders already in Kansas to retain their bondsmen proved equally controversial, since slavery would obtain a foothold in the new state no matter what the voters decided.[5] Buchanan found himself in a tough situation. If he endorsed the Lecompton Constitution, he risked alienating Northern party men; if he did not, Southern Democrats would rebel. Leaning toward the proslavery view anyway,[6] the president resolved to throw the full weight of his administration behind Lecompton. In the process he broke up the Democratic party.

Stephen A. Douglas deserted Buchanan and joined the Republican opposition to the Lecompton "swindle." The integrity of his cherished principle of popular sovereignty was at stake, he believed. The people of a territory should be free to determine all of their "domestic institutions,"

Douglas insisted, not just slavery, and the proposed constitution did not permit them to do even that. Southern Democrats stood with the administration and vilified Douglas for his apostasy. The ensuing battle in Congress convulsed the nation for months as Buchanan ruthlessly wielded the patronage whip to bring shaky Northern Democrats in line. But his attempt to ram it through Congress came up short.[7] Finally, in the spring of 1858, weary lawmakers narrowly passed a compromise measure that essentially offered Kansans statehood if they accepted Lecompton with slavery and denied it to them if they did not. This time free staters showed up at the polls and buried it once and for all.[8]

Democrats in Wisconsin watched events unfold in Kansas and the nation's capital with dismay. Party leaders, especially administration appointees to local office, were reluctant to buck the president.[9] But Douglas, the champion of genuine popular sovereignty, had broad support among the Democracy's rank and file, and like him, they spurned Lecompton and pressured the leadership to follow suit.[10] The first crack came early in January 1858, when a mass meeting of Janesville Democrats formally rejected the administration position and backed the recusant senator. "In sustaining Douglas, we sustain ourselves, our party and the Union," they announced.[11] One week later, a Democratic legislative caucus gathered in Madison, and participants endorsed the Illinois leader's course. In March, ignoring warnings from administration backers that they would be committing political suicide, Milwaukee's Democrats met and did the same. Amidst enthusiastic cheering for Douglas, they proclaimed popular sovereignty to be "the foundation of our institutions . . . a Charter of Independence from God to man."[12] Before long, Buchanan could count only five of Wisconsin's Democratic newspapers in his corner.[13]

Republicans everywhere thrilled to the sight of Democratic unity shattering. They applauded the principled defiance of Douglas, and they complimented Northern Democrats for refusing any longer "to eat the dirt" their Southern masters dished out. Some antislavery leaders even thought Douglas might convert to Republicanism, and from a practical point of view, that prospect was attractive. But most party men in Wisconsin and elsewhere in the North still profoundly distrusted Douglas, even as they encouraged his spirited attacks against Lecompton.[14] More important, the state's Republicans resisted Lecompton for reasons quite different from those of the Democrats. Those reasons once again revealed the wide gulf in party attitudes toward slavery and the sectional contro-versy, and even alone, they would have posed an insurmountable barrier to any alliance.[15]

Northern Democrats held that popular sovereignty, honorably em-ployed, would keep slavery within its present bounds and Congress out of the quarrel without disrupting the Union. Buchanan also believed that, but when he embraced Lecompton, he exposed himself to the charge of aban-doning principle and caving in to the demands of the proslavery members of his administration. The Wisconsin party would have none of that. Yet the doctrine of popular sovereignty, even though it might work to hem in the peculiar institution, was not inherently antislavery. It made no distinc-tion "between one domestic institution and another," and it concerned itself primarily with the "question of whether the people shall have the right to frame their own laws." As one Democrat stated, "We don't believe that slavery has anything to do with the admission of Kansas."[16]

Republicans objected to popular sovereignty precisely because it held both freedom and slavery "to be equally national." The Republican posi-tion that Congress possessed the right to restrict slavery's growth implied that it had only a local sanction and reflected a national policy of disap-proval. Republicans also voiced the wish that in time the slavery question would be peacefully disposed of and the nation everywhere would be free.[17]

The combination of Dred Scott and Lecompton provided the state's Republicans with fresh evidence of the slave power's influence in all branches of the federal government.[18] Indeed, a sense of foreboding now permeated the party's ranks as the possibility of finding a nonviolent reso-lution to the slavery conflict seemed increasingly remote. To many, vio-lence seemed not just likely, but inevitable. "The future certainly looks dark and I fear there is no light except through the flames of civil war," wrote the Portage antislavery man, Moses M. Davis. "For one I am ready for the worst."[19] In knowledgeable circles, it was even rumored that if Lecompton passed, war would break out immediately. Northern Republican governors were supposedly gathering "all the state arms" in their capitals in antici-pation of a fight. Secret bands of men allegedly were armed and ready to march on Kansas. Slave insurrection, the scuttlebutt went, would be en-couraged to keep the South busy with "home matters."[20] One furious Green County Republican actually looked forward to a bloodletting. "This na-tion has become so corrupt in administration of its general government . . . that nothing but the cleansing influence of a sacrifice of blood will purify its political elements" and bring about a reaffirmation of "the doctrines of the Declaration of Independence." As an adjunct to the coming civil war, he looked forward to seeing Buchanan hung along with "the servile spawn of cringing lickspittles" who supported him.[21]

The passions aroused by the latest acts of the slave power further steeled Republicans in their determination to rescue the national government in spite of renewed Southern warnings of secession. "We have been governed by our fears long enough," protested Michael Frank, and they would not be swayed from their "conviction of right by this threat." Unlike the Democrats, they would risk disunion rather than sit passively and watch slaveowners and their friends "crush out the liberties of the people."[22] Moreover, with the principle of imposing a congressional ban on slavery's spread declared unconstitutional by the Dred Scott case, some argued that the party had to foreswear moderation and strike directly "at the root of the evil, slavery."[23] Failure to take action could result in its legalization, "*without exception,* in every one of the United States," as slaveowners, backed by federal court decisions, demanded the right to carry their bondsmen into every state and territory.[24] One Republican grimly forecast that the bitter national divisions would "have no finality until slavery is abolished. . . . Whatever may be done by slaveholders or their northern . . . servile supporters to extend slavery and perpetuate it, and prevent discussion or agitation, there can be no peace under such a system of outrage and wrong."[25]

Although the federal judiciary and the Buchanan administration appeared to hand the Republicans a dazzling political opportunity in their quest to drive the Democrats from national power, they first had to confront the problems of maintaining local party unity and contending with the competing ideals and aspirations of ambitious politicians. And, as the Republican setbacks in Wisconsin and elsewhere in 1857 had shown, the Democratic party, in spite of internal quarrels, Dred Scott, Kansas, and the nation's economic woes, remained a formidable foe. Future political success would require a well-drilled organization and "men filled with common principles . . . a common zeal, and determined to overthrow the common enemy."[26] From 1858 through early 1861, Republican chieftains throughout the North worked to improve party organization and iron out their differences; Wisconsin was no exception.

The newly elected governor, Republican Alexander Randall, began his administration with a vigorous denunciation of slavery and a defense of states' rights. Then, at the urging of his good friend and deposed Democratic boss of Milwaukee, Josiah Noonan, Randall asked the state's lawmakers to investigate the 1856 land grant to the La Crosse and Milwaukee Railroad. Rumors that legislators in that year had been "bought and sold like slaves in the market" and Noonan's desire to embarrass backers of his rival, William Barstow, prompted the call.[27] Republican unity nevertheless began to unravel shortly thereafter when Booth and other party leaders upbraided the governor for appointing several former Democrats to minor state offices. The choice of Samuel Bugh, head of the state lunatic asylum under former governor Barstow and a pro-Nebraska Democrat, as the school land commissioner, was particularly galling. They reminded Randall that he himself had once branded Bugh as guilty "of the rankest corruption and fraud" while serving in his earlier post. The governor's retort that he had selected Bugh and others because "he wanted to" did not help matters. In an "Address to the People of Wisconsin," German Republican editors denounced him for appointing "corrupt opponents of Republicanism . . . while true and good men were unceremoniously thrown aside." Of the major Republican papers, only Madison's *Wisconsin State Journal,* the recipient of lucrative state printing contracts, firmly backed the governor.[28]

Republicans likewise divided over the true extent of the railroad land-grant corruption that was being uncovered. Some Milwaukee party men who were involved directly in the scandal—or were friends of Democrats like Byron Kilbourn, who, along with other officials of the La Crosse and Milwaukee Railroad had engaged in wholesale bribery of the legislature—tended to downplay the issue; meanwhile, friends of the governor in Madison lauded his manly efforts to expose the frauds.[29] Allegations that the editors of the *State Journal* had won printing jobs as a result of inside information on their competitor's bids also riled many Republicans,[30] and in the northern counties, Timothy Howe battled Moses M. Davis, a staunch antislavery and states' rights man, to a standstill in his bid to control the party in his home district.[31]

Alarmed at these increasingly bitter quarrels, Horace Tenney, the former Democrat who now was chairman of the state Republican committee, solicited opinions from the other committee members regarding the advisability of calling a convention to patch up divisions and strengthen party organization at both the state and local levels. Committee members agreed that a meeting was necessary, but they were unsure whether a dele-

{ *Political Abolitionism in Wisconsin, 1840–1861* }

gate meeting or a mass convention was more appropriate. In the interests of harmony, they finally decided to hold a delegate convention but to invite all Republicans interested in attending who might help the party "by their presence and counsel." One member also suggested that party editors get together and hammer out "an agreement to let each other alone and give their blows to the common enemy."[32]

Only Booth balked at the call, arguing that the party did not need any "doctoring just now," and fearing that the gathering might seek to impose "new articles of faith" or fall under the sway of self-interested "political tricksters" unhappy with his influence. Broad support for the meeting led Booth to quickly change his mind and give it his grudging approval.[33]

Booth's concern seems to have been well founded. In August, the *Wisconsin State Journal* stepped up its attacks on the Milwaukee editor, accusing him of being in league with the "Railroad Corruptionist" Barstow and unworthy of the support of the Republican masses. Booth's detrimental impact on party harmony, stemming from his imperious personality and mercurial temper, also laid him open to the charge of being one "of the deadliest enemies of the Republican party in this state." Although evidence is sparse, it appears that supporters of the governor looked to undermine Booth's authority within the party and consolidate power in their own hands. As Noonan put it to Tenney, "[Booth] means the destruction of Randall and all his friends in the State Administration. . . . Who will you have at the state convention that will drop him down?"[34]

Booth did not endure the assault quietly. Downplaying his disagreements with the governor, he levelled his most vicious criticism at "Rublee, Tenney and Co." He vilified the *State Journal*'s editor for "his attempted forays upon the state treasury in the matter of the public printing," and he denounced Tenney as "the man who first broached corruption in the state by deliberately proposing to buy up Barstow and the Balance."[35] Booth further accused this "Madison Clique" of trying to use the state patronage to gain control of the party. They were unprincipled men, he claimed, who viewed politics as "a mere game of chance, in which the shrewdest trickster and the most accomplished blackleg is sure to win."[36] Unless the *State Journal* ceased being a mouthpiece for this gang, he warned, a competing Republican paper in Madison would "become a political necessity."[37]

It was in this atmosphere of growing ill will that the Republicans came together in early October. The designs of Booth's foes emerged early as they tried to railroad him out of the convention, claiming he had been selected as a substitute delegate and had no real standing at the meeting. But the attempt failed, and amidst continuing tension the delegates proceeded to revamp the party.[38] In order to boost turnout, they established county canvassing committees obliged to identify Republicans in their home districts and personally encourage them to get out and vote. The delegates also reaffirmed the party's devotion to the national and state platforms of 1856 and 1857, and they vowed "to use all constitutional and proper means to restrain the already preponderating influence of the slaveholding interest in the national legislature . . . and oppose all further extension of the slavery of the African race upon this continent." The meeting concluded by appointing Booth and several other party radicals to draw up an address that emphasized the importance of the upcoming congressional elections for circulation around the state.[39]

The address turned out to be a comparatively moderate document, produced, it would seem, to appeal to all party members and minimize their differences. The Buchanan administration, it claimed, had forsaken the republican ideals upon which the American government was founded when it declared the Dred Scott decision "to be the supreme law of the land" and "slavery the ruling and paramount interest in our national policy." It also accused the national administration of using its patronage to buy up the votes of the people's representatives, in much the same way Wisconsin's Democrats did, and it closed with a plea to support the Republican party and "the cause of human liberty."[40]

Wisconsin's Democracy, handicapped by its usual factional problems—including the now-well-known fact that Noonan was helping the Republicans—still commanded considerable popular support, and it made a vigorous effort to recapture the congressional seats lost to its opponents in 1854 and 1856. Backing Douglas, with his insistence upon an honest application of popular sovereignty in the territories, the party covered the state with its most popular speakers.[41] But hard work could not overcome the Lecompton and corruption issues, and the Republicans once again carried the day, retaining two of the three congressional seats.[42]

The efforts of both parties to get out the vote in 1858; the excitement generated by the Kansas troubles, coupled with Douglas's bid for reelection to the United States Senate; and the Randall administration's evenhanded way of dealing with the railroad land grant scandal boosted turnout to 68 percent of the eligible electorate, by far the highest percentage yet recorded in a nonpresidential contest for national office in Wisconsin (see tables 14 and 15). An analysis of the returns indicates that party lines in 1858 held firm. Most of the additional backing each received came from 1857's nonvoters, many of whom undoubtedly had cast ballots in the 1856 presidential race and returned to the same party in 1858. In short, while turnout fluctuated from year to year, few voters appear to have crossed party lines when they did show up at the polls.[43]

The unity displayed by Republicans after the October convention was fundamentally a public relations ploy for use during the election campaign, and, predictably, it began to break down after the votes had been tallied. Lead district Republicans accused Dane County leaders, including the *State Journal*, of secretly working on behalf of the Democratic challenger to incumbent Republican congressman Cadwallader C. Washburn, because he had failed to secure money for a Madison post office, and with seeking the election of Madison Democrats to the state legislature in order to guarantee their votes for unpopular capital expenditures.[44] In the northern district, states' rights Republicans, many of whom had become disenchanted with House member Charles Billinghurst for his alleged conservatism, reportedly stayed home on election day rather than back his failed reelection bid.[45]

On March 7, 1859, in the midst of this renewed bickering, Chief Justice Roger B. Taney delivered the decision of the United States Supreme Court in the Booth case. Four years earlier, just after Wisconsin's high court had nullified the ruling of the federal district court and freed Booth, the United States attorney general applied to the federal Supreme Court for a writ of error. It was allowed by the federal court, but the state court directed its clerk to reject the writ and "to enter no order upon the journals or records of the court concerning the same." The attorney general then convinced the Supreme Court to accept a certified copy of the state court's proceedings, which had been handed in with the application for the writ, as the basis upon which to adjudicate the case.[46] The state's refusal to deliver an official record of the proceedings, coupled with the jurisdiction it had asserted over a district court of the United States, placed it in direct conflict with the national judiciary. According to Taney, the state court's assertion of supremacy over the federal courts in constitutional disputes represented a novel proposition that, "if it could be maintained, would subvert the very foundations of this Government." Thus, he found Wisconsin's supreme court in error on every point at issue, and he affirmed the preeminence of the federal judiciary in unambiguous terms. The judicial power the Constitution conveyed to the federal government, the Chief Justice wrote, "covers every legislative act of Congress, whether it be made within the limits of its delegated powers, or be an assumption of power beyond the grants in the Constitution." For this reason, the United States Supreme Court was invested with ultimate authority in all constitutional controversies arising between the states and the federal government. "So long . . . as this Constitution shall endure, this tribunal must exist with it, deciding in the peaceful forms of judicial proceeding the angry and irritating controversies between sovereignties, which in other countries has been determined by the arbitrament of force."[47]

After upholding the supremacy of the federal judiciary, Taney made short work of the decision of Wisconsin's court. States were not empowered to conduct investigations into the imprisonment of persons held for violations of national law or to issue writs of habeas corpus on their behalf, he argued. Indeed, federal officials were duty bound to refuse state-issued writs "and to call to [their] aid any force that might be necessary to maintain the authority of law against illegal interference." Accordingly, the decision of the federal district court in the Booth case was final, "and neither the regularity of its proceedings nor the validity of its sentence could be called into question in any other court." In essence, Taney's ruling annulled the right of a state to protect the liberty of its citizens or even to inquire into the reasons for their detention.[48] As for the closely reasoned and well-documented arguments of Judge Smith and Byron Paine in respect to the unconstitutionality of the Fugitive Slave Act, the chief justice decreed in one sentence that it "is, in all of its provisions, fully authorized by the Constitution of the United States."[49]

Taney's proclamation electrified the state. Wisconsin's legislature immediately took up and passed a joint resolution that denounced the Supreme Court's assumption of sovereignty as an unconstitutional and arbitrary act of power that, unless checked, threatened to prostrate "the rights and liberties of the people" before unrestrained federal tyranny, and it declared the ruling "without authority, void, and of no force."[50] The lawmakers went on to adopt almost verbatim the Kentucky Resolution of 1798, arguing that the states had brought the Constitution and the federal government into being, so they alone possessed the right to adjudicate disputes over the powers granted and reserved to each, and when necessary, to interject "*a positive defiance* . . . of all unauthorized acts done or attempted to be done."[51]

Wisconsin's "Resolves of '59" represented yet another unprecedented rebuke to federal authority. Republican legislators displayed continued strong support for the state's position when they cast all sixty favorable votes and only four of forty-eight no votes on the measure in the senate and assembly.[52] Most party members cheered on their lawmakers and urged them to stand fast against that latest manifestation of federal tyranny. If Wisconsin bowed to the decision, one angrily intoned, "It would cease to be free, and its people . . . only fit to be slaves."[53]

The Supreme Court's decree also enlivened the campaign to replace Judge Abram D. Smith, whose term of office was coming to a close early in 1859. Elected to the state court as a Democrat in 1853, the Republican hero had fallen on bad times. In testimony before the committee appointed to investigate the LaCrosse and Milwaukee Railroad scandal, former governor William Barstow had accused Smith of unlawfully accepting bonds from its promoters, a charge the justice vigorously denied. Still the kingpin of the state's Democratic party, Barstow supposedly hoped to discredit Smith and avenge his decision favoring Coles Bashford in the disputed 1855 gubernatorial contest.[54] In February 1859, he and his henchmen powwowed in Madison and resolved to place a candidate in the field against Smith. They selected William Pitt Lynde, a conservative Democrat well known for his views opposing the decision of the state court and favoring the Dred Scott decree and other proslavery enactments of the federal government.[55]

The Democratic decision to contest Smith's seat placed Republicans in a quandary. Although the investigations into legislative fraud and corruption uncovered evidence of some Republican complicity, the party had emerged relatively clean compared to the Democrats. Randall's publication of the entire committee report and the nomination in 1858 of candidates to office who were untainted by scandal also helped the Republicans. So in spite of their respect for Smith, some believed that he could not truly represent both "the Republican *character*" and its principles and that his nomination might harm the party's image and fail to rally the rank and file.[56] Smith understood the problem and hoped to sidestep it by running as an independent, but the Democratic nomination forced Republicans to consider putting up a man of their own.[57]

On February 15, the Republican legislative caucus met to consider its options. Booth and the German-born Carl Schurz were in attendance and lobbied hard for a state convention, hoping to gain the party's official endorsement of the states' rights position and a candidate committed to it. Governor Randall recommended supporting Smith as an independent candidate rather than making any formal nomination. The caucus ignored both suggestions and, instead, nominated Byron Paine, Booth's defense attorney, in Smith's place; it concluded that it was too late to call a convention and inappropriate to name anyone tainted by scandal.[58] But Paine, citing his close personal friendship with Smith, turned down the nomination and temporarily confused his supporters. Some remained interested in fielding a candidate, while others now urged against naming anyone, preferring to promote an independent Smith against the Democratic nominee.[59] Booth then decided to turn his influence against Smith. "In the present temper of the public mind," he wrote in the *Free Democrat*, "the Angel Gabriel could not be elected judge with ten thousand dollars of Land Grant Bonds in his possession." Booth expressed appreciation for Smith's efforts on his behalf, but to permit him to run as a Republican would be "the height of folly and madness. . . . [He] stands no more chance of being elected than he does of being struck by lightning." The election should turn on principles, he argued, not on men.[60]

The Republican caucus reconvened on March 3 and, prodded by Booth, again chose Paine. Apparently Booth had convinced the reluctant candidate that Republicans would refuse to rally around Smith, and only Paine's candidacy could vindicate "the position of the [state] Supreme Court in resisting the unconstitutional and tyrannical encroachments of the Slave Power in Congress." Booth also hinted that Smith would drop out of the race if the party selected Paine.[61]

With the nomination out of the way, Republicans put forth a show of unity with the publication of "An Address to the Republican Electors of Wisconsin," written by Horace Rublee, Rufus King, and Booth.[62] In it they charged the Democrats with nominating Lynde for the single purpose of overturning the decision of the state court. Equally bad, his election would be construed as an endorsement of the Fugitive Slave Law, the Dred Scott decision, and the iniquitous behavior of the Buchanan Administration in Kansas. Paine's triumph, on the other hand, would alert the nation of Wisconsin's firmness in upholding states' rights and individual liberty against "the despotism of the Slave Power."

The Slave Power, which rules the federal government, never permits the appointment of a Federal Judge unless he is known to be devoted to the interests of Slavery, and will sustain all its encroachments upon the rights of the States and the liberties of the people. The States, unless they are prepared to surrender their own sovereignty and yield implicit obedience to the usurpations of the Federal Courts, should elect men to judicial stations who will maintain the rights of the States and the liberties of the people against all encroachments of the Federal Government, whether attempted by Federal enactments or the decrees of the Federal courts. . . . The election of a [State] Supreme Court Judge is more important to the protection of life, liberty and property, than any other election by the people. We can live under the administration of a despotic President, protected by a firm, independent, liberty-loving Supreme Court. But when this last defense of the people's liberties, and the rights of a sovereign State are surrendered to the Slave Power, the sun of Freedom has set, and the darkness of Despotism overshadows the last bulwarks of liberty.[63]

Four days after Paine's selection, the Supreme Court ruling in the Booth case reached Wisconsin. In a long and stirring speech delivered in Milwaukee and warmly received by Republicans throughout the North, Carl Schurz proclaimed, "If the people of Wisconsin had forgotten the question at issue in the impending judicial election, the Supreme Court of the United States took care to remind us of it. . . . It is the question of State Rights." Citing the doctrines of Jefferson, Madison, and Calhoun, Schurz warned that in the absence of any curbs on federal power, political control inevitably would accumulate in the hands of a centralized and despotic state, and would result in the elimination of individual liberty and constitutional government. He also dismissed dissenters such as Howe, who referred to states' righters as advocates of disorder and disunion, asserting that conspiracies against freedom could not be displaced without a struggle. Indeed, clashes were both welcome and "*inevitable,*" and if the Union could not withstand the scrutiny of a freedom-loving people, then it would be better to disband. Schurz concluded with a stirring exhortation that urged Wisconsinites to defend their rights on April 5 with a vote for "STATE RIGHTS AND BYRON PAINE."[64]

And vote they did. In an exciting contest, Republican editors from all corners of the state took up Schurz's cry, and Paine coasted to an easy victory.[65] In another record turnout for state office, he received 62,755 votes to Lynde's 54,525.[66] As in the previous judicial contests, the Republican vote came largely from party loyalists, augmented by a few ballots from Democrats and nonvoters (see tables 16 and 17).[67] The Democratic turnout deviated somewhat from previous elections, as identifiable party members cast only 55 percent of the total Democratic vote, with nonvoters and Republican defectors making up the rest. Indeed, about 15 percent of the men who cast votes for Paine's Democratic opponent seem to have supported Randall's reelection in the governor's race held nine months later. Those defectors numbered perhaps seventy-five hundred, but they constituted no more than 10 percent of the total Republican constituency, a fact that signified that the overwhelming majority of Republicans continued to uphold states' rights as a shield against federal laws helpful to slavery and hostile to individual freedom.[68] The drop-off in Democratic participation suggests that disenchantment with the Buchanan administration and the national organization was beginning to have negative political consequences for that party.

The Republican party's states' rights faction retained broad popular backing and continued to dominate Wisconsin's politics in early 1859, just as it had for most of the past four years. And although the party never officially incorporated state rights into its platform, the adoption of the "Resolves of '59," the address of Rublee, Booth, and King, and Paine's nomination and election, all within the span of one month, unquestionably placed the doctrine near the core of its appeal. Andrew Jackson Turner, Republican editor of the *Portage City Record*, left no doubt of this when, speaking for the Republican majority, he claimed each state was duty bound, as an act of self-defense, "To nullify any act of Congress" that usurped basic civil liberties. Jefferson's and Madison's Virginia and Kentucky Resolutions, "The soundest political gospel ever proclaimed to an intelligent people," he proudly noted, formed the source of this dogma.[69]

Still, champions of states' rights were mindful that Timothy Howe remained an irritating spokesman of a powerful "though not numerous class of Republicans" who acknowledged the popularity of the states' rights position among the party rank and file, even as they opposed it. His supporters included former Whigs such as John Tweedy, the ex-Democrat Horace Tenney, and Wisconsin's small group of erstwhile Know Nothings. Some Republican editors also shared Howe's opinion, but they felt compelled to back states' rights publicly. For that reason, Howe had a difficult time making his case to the people. In private, he despaired at the latest efforts "to involve Wisconsin in the guilt of nullification," and he once again threatened to forsake the party if it tried to force him to take his "republicanism from Mr. Calhoun, from A. D. Smith, or from S. M. Booth." The publication of the "Address to the Republican Electors of Wisconsin" especially depressed him. "Oh my God Horace! how you hurt me," Howe cried to his good friend Horace Rublee, as he spurned the editor's request either to stump the state or issue a public statement in support of Paine's candidacy. Howe understood that on occasion a political party had "to stoop a little to conquer," but never would he agree to embrace "the enormous lie" of nullification.[70]

To soothe Howe's feelings, Rublee offered to throw open the columns of the *State Journal* and provide him with a forum to fight nullification. If the party had taken too extreme an opinion on the matter, he reasoned, the sooner it could be convinced of its error the better. But, if the Republican stand against federal "usurpation and centralization" was demonstrably consistent with the Constitution, then it should be accepted without reservation. Howe rejected the offer at first. Since most Republicans opposed his "federal views," he believed, any effort to defend them would only deepen their resentment against him. But when it came to light that he had boycotted the recent judicial contest, his influence within the party sunk to new lows. So with nothing to lose, he changed his mind and chose to make one last effort to bring Republicans around to his point of view and win back his standing within the party.[71]

In the months after Paine's election, Howe published in the *Oshkosh Democrat*[72] a series of letters that restated his position on the question of states' rights and nullification. Republican papers all over the state reprinted the letters and granted Howe the opportunity to explain himself publicly, however much they may have disagreed with him. Although his efforts won few converts—indeed he was read out of the party by some— the chance to air his opinions seems to have stiffened his resolve to stay with the Republican organization and keep it from being completely won over to the states' rights viewpoint.[73]

Howe's perseverance soon paid off as circumstances combined to erode the influence of Sherman Booth and the states' rights faction within Wisconsin's Republican party. With his blistering pen, arrogant self-righteousness, overbearing tactics, and disdain for conventional party norms, Booth had driven Republicans hard to stand by their antislavery origins and to defend aggressively state prerogatives from federal authorities. Over the years, he had made many enemies who looked forward to "a day of reckoning."[74] Booth's quarrels with Randall, Tenney, and Rublee damaged his standing with some in the party; but his real decline began with the fierce attacks he made on Judge Smith, which angered some of his most avid supporters, and the highhanded tactics he used to push Paine's candidacy. "The spoiled child who rules the house and has his own way in everything, very naturally wonders what the rest of the family are grumbling about," the *Whitewater Register* observed. "Two or three applications of the birch" might well be necessary to rein in the headstrong leader. B. S. Heath, who had replaced Harrison Reed at the helm of the influential *Menasha Conservator* and was every inch the states' rights and antislavery man his predecessor had been, proclaimed it was time for "those who have blindly followed Booth's lead . . . to enlist under some other Captain now."[75]

Ongoing disputes with Randall also hurt Booth. In one instance, he waged a bitter war against the reappointment of Horace Tenney, Noonan's good friend and the party's chairman, to the office of state comptroller. Furious, Randall threatened to resign if the senate did not approve the nomination. Booth ridiculed the governor's childish behavior and urged him to withdraw and "go to the oblivion he courts and deserves." In the hope of defusing tensions and preserving party unity, Tenney wisely handed in his resignation.[76]

Relations with Booth and his followers worsened when they attempted to displace Randall as the Republicans' gubernatorial candidate in 1859. Carl Schurz, Randall's chief competitor, picked up a number of impressive endorsements, but he fell far short of the votes needed at the party's convention in September. The cagy Randall, with the advice of Tenney and Noonan and the strong backing of the *State Journal,* had wisely used the state patronage to undermine his adversaries and close some of the breaches within the Republican organization. Randall and a few of his closest confidants also ranged around the state shoring up support among local leaders, including Howe. As a result, according to one delegate, Randall secured a "packed delegation from most of the counties" before the meeting got under way.[77]

Booth's standing in the party dropped further when, just before the judicial election, he was hauled into court on a seduction charge. The editor's neighbor accused him of having had sexual intercourse with his fourteen-year-old daughter while she cared for the married Booth's children. Although Booth refused to testify at his trial and the evidence seemed to support the prosecution's charge, his attorney successfully blunted the young woman's explicit testimony by calling in witnesses to speak against her supposedly wanton character; Booth won his acquittal, but the damage to his reputation was irreparable.[78] The Democrats gleefully indulged their hatred of him, a man who for so many years had reviled them as unprincipled, immoral, and corrupt. According to Samuel "Pump" Carpenter, himself a longstanding victim of Booth's acid tongue, he was

> a walking monster—a defamer of characters a million times superior to his own—a destroyer of domestic happiness—a cancerous leech—a blotch upon the body politic—a wreaking, vile pestilence—a viper of the lowest species—a self-conceited nuisance—in short, a disgrace to his profession—a fiend in human shape—a deceitful, bigoted hypocrite—as blackhearted as a rotten potato, and as nauseating as a stinking mackerel.[79]

Some of Booth's Republican enemies were only a little less caustic and took advantage of his misfortune to unleash years of pent up frustration for having had "to yield to his dictation or [be] subject to the lash of his tyrant rod." The Republican party, the *Menasha Conservator* rejoiced, was now free "of its most fruitful source of discord and mutiny."[80]

Randall's appointment of Luther S. Dixon to complete Edward Whiton's term as chief justice of the state supreme court delivered another crippling blow to Booth and the states' rights bloc. Whiton had died on April 12, 1859, and the governor had selected Dixon as his replacement after supposedly receiving word that he was "sound on state rights," though he had signed a public address endorsing former justice Crawford's re-election to the state court in 1855, and was rumored to be a Republican "of the Judge Howe stamp."[81] Christopher Sholes soothed concerns about Dixon when he published assurances that the appointee was "a warm state rights man on the Judge Smith, Paine and Republican platform."[82]

It therefore came as a shock when on December 14, 1859, the new chief justice acquiesced in a motion filed by Wisconsin's federal attorney, on behalf of the Supreme Court, directing the state tribunal to reverse its decision in the Booth case. Dixon agreed that Congress had overstepped its authority in legislating on the return of runaway slaves, but he also maintained that the federal court possessed the final say on constitutional questions. And since the court had come down in favor of Congress, he was "bound to regard its decision." Although the motion failed because Cole voted to resist the directive and Paine disqualified himself for having represented Booth, Dixon's opinion lifted the spirits of party nationalists. Three months later, cautious but confident federal authorities rearrested Booth, who promptly requested a writ of habeas corpus. In another split decision, the court rejected the application and Booth was returned to prison.[83]

Dixon's seeming duplicity outraged most Republicans. Many accused him of misleading states' rights men into believing that he backed the position of Wisconsin's court and legislature simply to obtain the judgeship, and they looked forward to contesting his candidacy for a full term at the Republican state convention scheduled for March.[84] Others were divided over the wisdom of naming a candidate. Randall and Howe, now openly allied and backed by the *Wisconsin State Journal* and the *Milwaukee Sentinel*, claimed that the likely selection of "an out and out State Rights man" would only exacerbate party divisions at a time when the impending presidential contest required the united energies of all Republicans. Lacking Booth's leadership, states' righters vacillated at first, but when it became clear that the Democrats would assist Dixon, support for a party choice quickly gained favor.[85]

The Republican state convention began auspiciously. As expected, William H. Seward won its unanimous approval for president. Howe then attempted to turn back the growing sentiment in favor of selecting a candidate for the judgeship. He praised Dixon's stand as principled and bold, and he urged delegates to forego tying Republicans to anyone by naming a party candidate. Opposing Howe, Carl Schurz pressed them to run a states' rights man but to avoid taking any public stand on the doctrine.[86]

Schurz easily carried the day, with 137 votes in favor of a nomination, 84 in opposition. Afterwards, on the first nominating ballot, Dixon failed to receive a single ballot out of 221 cast; his few friends elected to sit out the process in frustrated silence. A. Scott Sloan, a former circuit court judge, then received the nomination after his supporters vouched for his reliability on the states' rights question.[87]

As agreed, Sloan ran without a platform in order to downplay states' rights and to conciliate all party members as they prepared for the pending presidential contest. This especially pleased Randall's supporters, who maintained with increasing frequency that the issue would "cease to be a matter with practical importance" if the Republican party gained the White House in November; they hoped to focus only on issues that Wisconsin's Republicans held in common with the party in other states.[88] Moreover, it was even hinted that Seward himself had ordered several party chieftains to drop states' rights immediately.[89]

But Dixon's December opinion and his refusal to grant Booth's request for a writ of habeas corpus, along with the Milwaukee editor's subsequent arrest, made any show of unity unlikely. Dixon's "betrayal" and Booth's imprisonment, according to one Republican, had "wrought up the public feeling to the highest pitch." Cooperation was further hampered after Dixon, as expected, was persuaded to run against Sloan as an independent at the behest of Democrats and a few dissident Republicans, solely on the basis of his decision in the Booth case.[90] A number of party men then renounced the policy of "noncommittalism" and pressed Sloan to publicly define his position on states' rights. *This knowledge the people must and will have from the candidate who receives their votes,"* the old abolitionist Charles Clement insisted.[91]

Sloan meanwhile had been corresponding with Republican leaders around the state, expressing his puzzlement at the request for an "authorized avowal of my sentiments on State Rights." He had voiced his agreement with Smith and the state legislature at the convention and acknowledged that most Republicans shared his view. Otherwise, it would have been an act of bad faith for him to have accepted the nomination. Nevertheless, although he did not think it prudent to issue a public statement,[92] in mid-March the reluctant candidate gave in and allowed one of his letters to be published. Within days, satisfied states' rights men happily endorsed the harassed nominee.[93]

Unfortunately for Sloan, the strategy failed. In a close election, he lost by 395 votes out of 116,621 cast. Turnout declined from 65 percent of Wisconsin's eligible voters in the prior year's judicial and gubernatorial contests to 61 percent. Unwilling to support either their party's nominee or Dixon, perhaps seven thousand Republicans from the 1859 judicial contest sat out the 1860 election and cost Sloan the victory. Otherwise, surprisingly little crossover voting occurred in spite of the efforts of a few Republicans to swing votes to Dixon; most of his Republican support, perhaps three thousand votes, came from his home county of Columbia and from Madison (see tables 18–20).[94] In the election's aftermath, despondent states' righters railed against the treachery of Dixon Republicans. Harrison Reed, now editor of the *Wisconsin State Journal,* suffered the harshest criticism, although he claimed to have worked for Sloan "in the teeth of the most violent local opposition." Reed blamed his defeat on Republicans who threatened to desert Sloan unless he publicly avowed his states' rights sympathies, and he pleaded with them to drop their criticism and unite for the approaching presidential contest.[95]

CHAPTER TWELVE

The End of
the Antislavery Question
Has Arrived

SLOAN'S DEFEAT signified the end of the controlling influence of the states'
rights faction within the Republican coalition. Nevertheless, before long,
its followers heeded Reed's advice and joined with their fellow Republicans
to advance the party's electoral prospects in 1860. One month after Dixon's
narrow victory, Wisconsin's Republican delegation, led by Carl Schurz,
traveled to Chicago to participate in selecting a presidential candidate.
New York's Senator William H. Seward was the preconvention favorite
and the clear choice of the state's party members, but he had made many
enemies in his long political career, a fact that combined with his reputation as an antislavery extremist to hamper and ultimately doom his
candidacy. Republican strategists, hoping to woo conservatives in the key
states of Pennsylvania, New Jersey, Indiana, and Illinois, which Frémont
lost in 1856, looked to soften the party's radical image on the slavery question and expand its appeal with overtures to the foreign-born and support
for a protective tariff and free homesteads. Even so, the platform's antislavery provisions, while more moderately phrased, reaffirmed the stand

taken in 1856: that the federal government was obliged to restrict slavery's expansion. When, on the third ballot, Abraham Lincoln of Illinois received a bare majority of the delegates' votes, it was Schurz who seconded the call to make his selection unanimous. According to Rufus King, a longtime supporter of Seward, most Republicans considered the moderate but firmly antislavery Lincoln an acceptable second choice. In addition, Lincoln's reputed moral integrity was no small matter to an electorate sick of the political scandals and corruption so common in the 1850s.[1]

With their comrades throughout the North, Wisconsin's Republicans entered the campaign full of energy. They organized torchlight processions that drew large and enthusiastic crowds, and they listened to speakers like Timothy Howe and Governor Randall trumpet the virtues of "Honest Old Abe."[2] Compared to the confident Republicans, the state's Democrats were dispirited, with small hope of carrying Wisconsin in the fall. The national party, at its April convention, had split; Northern Democrats backed the candidacy of Stephen A. Douglas and Southern Democrats that of Kentucky's John C. Breckinridge. In an exhaustive campaign tour, Douglas made a vain effort to convince voters, North and South, that the Union was in real peril and the nation face to face with impending disaster. But the Little Giant's heroics came too late.[3] Southern radicals were bent on seceding if Lincoln was elected, and Northern Republicans were just as determined to elect their man, whatever the consequences.[4]

Lincoln went on to carry Wisconsin with 56 percent of the vote and the nation with barely 40 percent. Like Frémont in 1856, Lincoln picked up the votes of nearly all Republicans who had cast ballots in the prior year's race for governor, as well as those who had supported Sloan in the April contest for chief justice of the state supreme court (see tables 21 and 22). Probably 25 percent of Lincoln's supporters had not voted in these earlier contests, while the few thousand Republicans who had opted for Dixon, the Democratic favorite for chief justice, now cast ballots for the Illinoisan.[5] In keeping with past elections, minimal crossover voting occurred. Most Republicans and Democrats either backed their party's candidate or, particularly in the case of Democrats, did not vote.

In analyzing the presidential election of 1860, some historians have charged that Republicans trivialized secessionist threats and toned down their antislavery professions to avoid scaring off potential conservative supporters. Allan Nevins, otherwise a Lincoln admirer, went so far as to accuse the Republican candidate of being "deplorably complacent" about the obvious peril confronting the nation.[6] But to focus only on the political strategy adopted in 1860 ignores the long-standing resolve of Republican radicals and moderates both to stand fast against the fulminations of Southern hotspurs and to yield no more territory to slavery. And if Wisconsin is at all representative, radicals and moderates made up a huge majority of the Republican rank and file. Lincoln's managers had to avoid alienating them too as they chased after conservative votes.[7]

In Wisconsin, most Republicans had embraced the Liberty and Free Soil precept that preserving American freedom and republican institutions took precedence over preserving the American Union. Also like their predecessors, Republicans failed to formulate a policy that specified what, if anything, they would do if the slaveholding states did attempt to secede. Instead, as the sectional crisis deepened later in the decade, Republicans continued to reject compromises on the slavery question and to dismiss the increasingly shopworn cry of dissolution.[8]

John Brown's raid on the federal arsenal at Harpers Ferry, Virginia, in October 1859 made an especially deep impression on Republicans. Brown, with fewer than two dozen followers, had planned to seize the arsenal and foment a slave insurrection in the South. Captured by Virginia authorities, he was summarily tried and hanged. Although most Republicans denounced Brown's foray into Virginia as the work of a "crack brained fanatic," his dignity and courage won their admiration; the hysterical reaction of Virginia and other slave states opened their eyes to the depths of the South's insecurity and, they thought, its complete inability to protect itself.[9] Timothy Howe, who thought Brown was crazy, nevertheless praised him for acting, "Not wisely but bravely, not selfishly but benevolently." He likewise condemned Brown's execution as another example of the savage character of slavery, similar to the beating of Senator Charles Sumner in 1856. Brown died, Howe wrote, not because he was guilty of treason or murder, but "for the simple reason *that he is opposed to slavery.*" Christopher Sholes agreed, and he added that this latest display of slavery's inherently violent spirit was "sure to increase the hatred of it" and, eventually, to kill it. Even the *Wisconsin State Journal,* which cautioned Republicans to be careful in their pronouncements lest they be accused of sympathizing with Brown, was moved to note that Virginia's "contemptible cowardice" disgusted even normally "dispassionate and conservative men," whereas Brown's courage stirred their enthusiasm.[10] Some Republicans disregarded the *State Journal*'s advice; they began to countenance slave uprisings or at least to predict that they would become more common-place, since so far all attempts to settle the slavery question peacefully had failed.[11] Others thought Brown's raid, rather than still attempts to hem in and eventually destroy slavery, would hasten "the day of deliverance."[12]

Most importantly, the John Brown affair reinforced the resolve of Republicans to remain unmoved by the South's threats to dissolve the Union and to liberate the federal government from the slave power's control. To yield now, they argued, would expose the nation and the American people to slavery's natural offspring: unceasing lawlessness and violence and the continued debasement of individual liberty and civil rights. The incident also reaffirmed the Republican conviction that the South, which had "quailed before John Brown and his seventeen miserable Abolitionists" and overreacted with fear and panic to the Harpers Ferry fiasco, required the assistance of the federal government to police slavery and would never chance secession.[13]

Wisconsin's Republicans carried these hardened attitudes with them into the 1860 presidential contest. They cautiously fended off Democratic charges that they cared nothing for the Constitution and the Union, yet they firmly rejected all calls to concede any part of their antislavery program. If anything, as the campaign evolved, Republicans grew increasingly angry at Southern attempts to browbeat the North into submission; they came to view the contest as an opportunity both to vindicate Northern rights and to save the nation's republican experiment. Southern intimidation, Republicans insisted, represented a haughty attempt to strip Northerners of the right to vote for their choice among the presidential candidates. If successful, the franchise would be reduced to a worthless privilege exercisable only under a master's watchful eye, and national elections would be transformed into nothing more than pageants without substance. In short, if the North backed down, minority rule would be triumphant, and its people would be as much slaves as were the most abject Southern bondsmen. But Republicans would have none of this, Rufus King exclaimed. They were ready to "put the courage of these fire-eaters to the test." More ominously, King warned, if Lincoln's election provoked secession, the offending states would be whipped into submission and their leaders hanged.[14]

Republicans in 1860 remained convinced that facing down the slave-owning states posed less danger to the nation's future than did the slave power's continued mastery of the federal government. Unquestionably, they underestimated the commitment of Southern radicals to secession, but even had Republicans foreseen the coming tragedy, they would not have acted differently; the stakes simply were too high. Moreover, Republicans had come to bitterly resent the South's bullying insistence that it would reject the legitimate outcome of the presidential match if it did not get its way. In the months prior to Lincoln's election, it was the growing antisouthernism of Republicans, more than constitutional scruples or a mystical attachment to the Union, that provoked a shift to King's position that secession, if attempted, must be put down with force.[15]

Even so, many Republicans for a time rejected the idea of coercing the South by a resort to arms. Unable to reconcile his states' rights principles with the alternative of compelling a resistant state back into the Union, Christopher Sholes suggested that the federal government should prepare a plan to allow the slave states to leave in peace. The *Wisconsin Daily Free Democrat,* now under the editorial guidance of none other than the former state supreme court justice, Abram D. Smith, agreed. Other Republicans also were prepared to accept disunion rather than compromise their antislavery principles or force the South into obedience. Secession rather than concession, they believed, would at least free the North from a lasting association with slavery and its ruinous influence in the national government, and it would bring about a rededication to the principles upon which the nation was founded.[16]

The secession crisis of 1860–1861, President Lincoln's unwavering Unionism, and the war itself eventually led most Republicans to blend their festering antisouthernism with acceptance of the concept of a perpetual Union, heretofore maintained most vigorously by Democrats, and the absolute authority of the federal government to uphold it.[17] On May 15, 1861, one month after the fall of Fort Sumter, Governor Randall, in an address to a special session of the legislature, proclaimed this growing Republican faith in uncritical Unionism and the party's determination to punish southern traitors.

There can be no more compromises, no settlements, no treating with rebels, no concessions; nothing now but absolute submission to the power and jurisdiction and authority of the Government of the United States. The people will never consent to any cessation of the war, forced so wickedly upon us, until the traitors are hung or driven into ignominious exile. This war began where Charleston is; it should end where Charleston was.[18]

Within two years, Wisconsin's Republicans would forsake the states' rights principles that had served them so well in defense of civil liberties in the last half of the 1850s. In 1862, somewhat grudgingly, they repealed the Personal Liberty Law; one year later, again with some reluctance, they rescinded the spirited "Resolves of '59." Timothy Howe's election to the United States Senate in January 1861, perhaps more than anything else, symbolized the conversion already in progress. Still, it bears repeating that prior to the war, Republicans from Wisconsin and other Northern states embraced states' rights in order to defy federal legislation that stripped people of their personal freedom and constitutionally guaranteed rights. After the war, they nationalized civil liberty by adopting civil rights legislation and the Thirteenth and Fourteenth amendments, thus making freedom a concern of both federal and state authorities and dividing a power once almost exclusively exercised by the states.[19] In both cases, they shared the common goal of protecting and expanding individual liberty.

In time, though, self-styled reformers and progressives, who once trusted the good judgment and common sense of the American people to advance worthwhile social and political goals, came to rely increasingly on the coercive power of the state to achieve their version of a just society.[20] Paradoxically, the American Civil War, fought in part to realize more fully the principles of freedom willed by the revolutionary generation, helped bring an end to republican idealism. In favor of the supposed security and stability that only government compulsion could bring about, Americans abdicated their revolutionary heritage.

Shortly before the 1860 campaign for president began in earnest, Stephen S. Barlow, a former Whig assemblyman turned Republican, acknowledged that "the spirit of Abolition is the soul of the Republican Party." Republicans, Barlow explained, considered slavery to be "morally and politically wrong," and for that reason they opposed its spread as the first step necessary to bring about its ultimate destruction.[21] The key to implementing the Republican program of confining slavery within its present bounds and of reconstituting the national commitment to freedom and republican institutions, Harrison Reed made clear, lay in reclaiming the federal government from the slave power. Although they contemplated no direct action against the slave states, Republicans confidently expected that their management of national affairs would, in time, bring down slavery.[22]

The political abolitionism of Wisconsin's Republicans was rooted in the antislavery doctrines first enunciated twenty years earlier by the Liberty party. Those had spelled out a legal and constitutional framework within which to attack slavery, and they formed the basis for the appeal of the later Free Soil and Republican parties. As the 1860 contest drew to a close, Charles Clement, a former Liberty party firebrand and editor of the *Racine Weekly Journal,* chose to remind voters of the Republican party's parentage and the election's significance. "The glorious result of the old Liberty party is now before the nation. The old Whig party and the old Democratic party are both dead at the feet of this Little David of the Land." The pending Republican triumph and the inevitable tendency of its doctrines, Clement happily declared, signified that the nation could at last look forward to slavery's demise. Then, and only then, he concluded, would "the object and end of the Republican party be accomplished."[23]

Barlow and Clement correctly identified the source and intent of Republican party ideals and policies. Even so, national and local events and the necessity of broadening the Republican party's popular base unavoidably led to a debasement of the moral principles that had motivated the founders of the Liberty organization. The slave power's determination to retain its hold over the federal government, and the threat it presented to civil rights in the North, moved many men unconcerned with the plight of the slave to take up the Republican cause. Yet the degree to which the ideals of the Liberty party were vitiated, as it evolved into the Free Soil party and then into the Republican party, has been exaggerated. Free Soilers and then Republicans emphasized different aspects of the Liberty party appeal, largely in response to events and to the changing perceptions of slavery's malevolent impact on the nation's social, economic, and political life.[24] As Kenneth Stampp wisely has suggested, the uneasy feeling that freedom was besieged by slavery, coupled with the unending sectional battles and growing antisouthernism of the Northern electorate, brought out the latent antislavery sentiments of many men who became Republicans. And, Stampp argues, "It would have required an exceedingly fine discrimination to enable Republicans to have negative feelings about the South, or about slaveholders, without having similar feelings about the institution that gave the South and its social elite their power and distinct identity."[25]

So before Northerners would act on their antislavery attitudes and commit themselves to a political party dedicated to eliminating slavery from American life, they needed sound reasons to subordinate other attitudes and values of importance. The decline of the issues that had divided Whigs and Democrats and the reemergence of the slavery issue, beginning with the passage of the Kansas-Nebraska Act, furnished those reasons.

The Republican party in Wisconsin, possibly more than in any other Northern state, largely retained the antislavery radicalism bequeathed by the Liberty party. Huge numbers of New Englanders and their descendants from western New York had settled in Wisconsin. Beginning in 1854, the pressure of events pushed most of those Yankees and Yorkers into the Republican organization, convinced that slavery had become a true threat to Northern values and free institutions, that the slave power's control over the national government had to be broken, and that slavery itself in time must be brought to ruin.[26] And they carried these attitudes with them into the presidential election of 1860 and beyond. Understandably, the slave states that came to form the Confederacy broke up the Union rather than become subject to Republican rule. When the war came, Badger State Republicans had no trouble finding its source. "There is no fact more obvious," wrote Joseph Trotter Mills, "than that the present war is a natural result of the institution of slavery."[27] Without it, Republicans agreed, secession and war would have been inconceivable. For that reason, permanent peace between the North and South would not be possible until America's enslaved blacks either were set free or the time for their emancipation firmly fixed.[28]

Still, mindful of the opposition within the tenuously loyal slaveowning border states and the Northern Democratic party, the cautious Abraham Lincoln emphasized the more popular goal of restoring the Union, and he moved slowly towards emancipation, finally urging it primarily as a military necessity. Until then, hardcore administration backers in Wisconsin and other Northern states worked assiduously at the local level to pacify impatient Republicans who demanded more forceful measures against slavery and to retain Democratic support for the war effort.[29] Nevertheless, even the most ardent administration men clearly desired emancipation and expected the war's progress to secure it. And though they declined to openly advocate it as a war measure, they greeted each step toward black deliverance with undisguised joy. At war's end, Willet S. Main, the longtime Madison diarist and political observer, spoke for all Republicans when he cheerfully wrote, "*Peace* once more smiles upon the land with *no slave* in all its broad domain. Thank God for it all."[30]

In concert with their opposition to slavery, Wisconsin's Republicans also manifested relatively evenhanded attitudes toward black Americans, especially when compared to the cruel negrophobia of their Democratic opponents. At the very least, most were willing to grant and defend the basic civil rights of the state's black residents. A majority would go further and grant them the franchise, manifesting their open-mindedness in an 1857 referendum on free suffrage, and once again in 1865 in even greater numbers (see table 23). True, virtually all Republicans in Wisconsin shared in some of antebellum America's prevailing racist attitudes, and unlike the Liberty men, they never formally pledged their party to black political equality. The presence of racist sentiments within the Republican party is not surprising though; the degree to which prejudice was tempered, if not altogether repudiated, is.[31]

Wisconsin's blacks finally received the vote in 1866, after the irrepressible Sherman Booth and a Milwaukee black, Ezekiel Gillespie, successfully challenged the result of the 1849 suffrage referendum before the state supreme court.[32] Four years later, President Ulysses S. Grant signed the Fifteenth Amendment, enfranchising the nation's black males in every state. Willet S. Main once again aptly noted the occasion.

The President's proclamation of the ratification of the Fifteenth Amendment was sent to Congress and to the country today. Thus the final end of the antislavery question has arrived. From slavery to the ballot is indeed an immense stride. This land is now in fact, the land of the free and the home of the brave.[33]

Main, of course, was only partly right. Blacks would endure another century of discrimination and injustice, but the men and women of both races who had worked so long for that day in March 1870 had every reason to look back with pride.

Wisconsin Election Tables

Methodological Note

IN EVALUATING WISCONSIN'S ELECTIONS for the years 1847 through 1860, I have relied on a statistical technique known as ecological regression, which provides estimates of individual voting behavior using aggregate data, in this case county-level voting returns, including nonvoters. Ecological regression permits historians to calculate changes in a political party's constituency from one election to another and to measure the stand its voters took on a specific question, such as black suffrage. Moreover, because the procedure divides the potential electorate (all adult white males) into those who voted for each party and those who did not vote in an election, it provides turnout data and a means of assessing the impact nonvoters had on an election's outcome. Nevertheless, regression analysis does make the assumption that groups behave consistently across all voting units (i.e., counties) and that any variations are random. Thus, Democrats in heavily Democratic Milwaukee County should have acted in much the same way as Democrats in Republican Rock County, a chancy assumption that reinforces the need to consider cell entries as estimates only.

I obtained Wisconsin's county-level voting returns for the years 1847–1860 from the Records of the Secretary of State of the State of

Wisconsin, *Election Return Statements from County Boards of Canvassers, 1847–1914* and *Certificates from the State Board of Canvassers, 1848–1863.* The Records of the Executive Department, *Election Certificates from County and State Boards of Canvassers, 1847–1857* also proved useful. Still, gaps appeared on occasion. I tried to fill these, often with success, by resorting to a search for missing returns in local newspapers. In addition, the number of Wisconsin's counties doubled between 1847 and 1860. When a county was partitioned, I aggregated the total votes of the new units with the old unit to derive estimates for a particular year's election; thereafter the units were directly correlated.

A county-by-county count of all adult white males, found in the 1850 and 1860 federal censuses and the 1855 state census, provided the number of estimated eligible voters in those years. I computed the eligible electorate in the intervening years simply by employing the linear technique of calculating the difference between the number of voters in 1850 and 1855, and 1855 and 1860, dividing by five and adding the result to each year's total. Since no official record of the actual number of voters exists for Wisconsin during those years, I chose to make my appraisals of voting behavior and turnout based on the estimated number of adult white males between 1847 and 1860, without attempting to correct for ineligible voters. For this reason, and taking into account the growth and mobility of Wisconsin's population, it is possible that voter turnout in any given year may be underestimated by as much as 6 to 8 percent. Nevertheless, I am convinced that further attempted refinements would in no way challenge the results given, since quantitative analysis can at best provide historians with only an impression of voting behavior and reveal consistent patterns and trends rather than precise measurements. As a tool for historians, statistical techniques complement established sources of information, such as letters, newspapers, and other archival material; they do not replace them.

For purposes of interpretation, each table's row and column cell entries add up to the marginals; that is, the percentage of the eligible electorate that voted for a party in a given year. In table 2, the results indicate that 2/22, or about 9 percent, of the Democrats who had voted for Nelson Dewey, their party's gubernatorial candidate in 1848, cast ballots for Zachary Taylor, the Whig presidential nominee, in that same year. If Taylor's total vote of 13,747 is multiplied by 9 percent, we arrive at the estimate of about 1,250 Taylor Democrats cited in chapter three. Similarly, the Republican cell entries in table 12 suggest that 19/20, or 95 percent, of the vote in favor of black suffrage in 1857 came from supporters of Alexander Randall, the party's gubernatorial candidate that year, and that 19/29, or about two-thirds, of all Randall backers favored the proposition. Finally, rounding leads to occasional minor inconsistencies between the text and the tables, while negative cell entries, a common phenomenon when a group votes overwhelmingly in one way, should be interpreted as zero.

Historians have put ecological regression to good use in recent years, most recently in William Gienapp's exhaustively researched *The Origins of the Republican Party: 1852–1856*. His statistical appendix provides the best introduction to the technique currently available. In designing the format and titles to my own tables, I borrowed extensively from Gienapp. Peyton McCrary has also employed ecological regression with success in his *Abraham Lincoln and Reconstruction: The Louisiana Experiment*, as has J. Morgan Kousser, *The Shaping of Southern Politics: Suffrage Restriction and the Establishment of the One-Party South, 1880–1910;* Stephen E. Maizlish, *The Triumph of Sectionalism: The Transformation of Ohio Politics, 1844–1856;* Dale Baum, *The Civil War Party System: The Case of Massachusetts, 1848–1876;* Peyton McCrary, Clark Miller, and Dale Baum, "Class and Party in the Secession Crisis: Voting Behavior in the Deep South: 1856–1861," *Journal of Interdisciplinary History;* Ray M. Shortridge, "The Voter Realignment in the Midwest During the 1850s," *American Politics Quarterly;* Kevin Sweeney, "Rum, Romanism, Representation, and Reform: Coalition Politics in Massachusetts, 1847–1853," *Civil War History;* and Dale Baum, "Know Nothingism and the Republican Majority in Massachusetts: The Political Realignment of the 1850s," *Journal of American History.*

Ecological regression receives a substantial technical discussion in J. Morgan Kousser, "Ecological Regression and the Analysis of Past Politics," *Journal of Interdisciplinary History;* E. Terence Jones, "Ecological Inference and Electoral Analysis," *Journal of Interdisciplinary History;* and W. Phillip Shively, "Ecological Inference: The Use of Aggregate Data to Study Individuals," *American Political Science Review.*

TABLE I

Estimated Relationships between Voting for Governor 1848 and Black Suffrage 1847 (in percentages)

	Governor 1848				
Suffrage 1847	Democrat	Whig	Liberty	Not Voting	Total Electorate 1848
Prosuffrage	4	6	1	1	12
Antisuffrage	14	10	0	1	25
Not Voting	13	7	0	43	63
Total Electorate 1848	31	23	1	45	100

TABLE 2

Estimated Relationships between Voting for President 1848 and Governor 1848 (in percentages)

	President 1848				
Governor 1848	Democrat	Whig	Free Soil	Not Voting	Total Electorate 1848
Democrat	21	2	8	1	32
Whig	-2	18	5	2	23
Liberty	0	-1	2	0	1
Not Voting	5	3	1	35	44
Total Electorate 1848	24	22	16	38	100

TABLE 3

Estimated Relationships between Voting for President 1848 and
Black Suffrage 1847 (in percentages)

	President 1848				
Suffrage 1847	Democrat	Whig	Free Soil	Not Voting	Total Electorate 1848
Prosuffrage	-1	3	11	0	13
Antisuffrage	11	11	1	3	26
Not Voting	14	7	4	36	61
Total Electorate 1848	24	21	16	39	100

TABLE 4

Estimated Relationships between Voting for Governor 1849
and President 1848 (in percentages)

	Governor 1849				
President 1848	Democrat	Whig	Free Soil	Not Voting	Total Electorate 1849
Democrat	18	0	0	3	21
Whig	2	15	0	3	20
Free Soil	1	0	5	8	14
Not Voting	3	0	0	42	45
Total Electorate 1849	24	15	5	56	100

TABLE 5

Estimated Relationships between Voting for Governor 1849
and Black Suffrage 1849 (in percentages)

Suffrage 1849	Governor 1849				
	Democrat	Whig	Free Soil	Not Voting	Total Electorate 1849
Prosuffrage	-2	2	6	3	9
Antisuffrage	2	1	0	5	8
Not Voting	23	14	0	46	83
Total Electorate 1849	23	17	6	54	100

TABLE 6

Estimated Relationships between Voting for Governor 1853
and President 1852 (in percentages)

President 1852	Governor 1853				
	Democrat	Whig	People	Not Voting	Total Electorate 1853
Democrat	23	0	0	6	29
Whig	-1	3	10	8	20
Free Soil	1	0	7	1	9
Not Voting	3	0	3	36	42
Total Electorate 1853	26	3	20	51	100

TABLE 7

Estimated Relationships between Voting for Congress 1854
and Governor 1853 (in percentages)

Governor 1853	Congress 1854			
	Democrat	Republican	Not Voting	Total Electorate 1854
Democrat	16	2	7	25
Whig	1	1	0	2
People	2	13	2	17
Not Voting	1	11	44	56
Total Electorate 1854	20	27	53	100

TABLE 8

Estimated Relationships between Voting for State Supreme Court 1855
and Congress 1854 (in percentages)

Congress 1854	State Supreme Court 1855			
	Democrat	Republican	Not Voting	Total Electorate 1855
Democrat	16	0	3	19
Republican	1	21	2	24
Not Voting	2	2	53	57
Total Electorate 1855	19	23	58	100

TABLE 9

Estimated Relationships between Voting for Governor 1855
and Congress 1854 (in percentages)

| | Governor 1855 | | | |
Congress 1854	Democrat	Republican	Not Voting	Total Electorate 1855
Democrat	8	-4	15	19
Republican	4	21	-1	24
Not Voting	13	10	34	57
Total Electorate 1855	25	27	48	100

TABLE 10

Estimated Relationships between Voting for President 1856
and Governor 1855 (in percentages)

| | President 1856 | | | |
Governor 1855	Democrat	Republican	Not Voting	Total Electorate 1856
Democrat	21	-2	5	24
Republican	-2	29	-2	25
Not Voting	13	21	17	51
Total Electorate 1856	32	48	20	100

TABLE 11

Estimated Relationships between Voting for State Supreme Court 1857
and President 1856 (in percentages)

| President 1856 | State Supreme Court 1857 | | | |
	Democrat	Republican	Not Voting	Total Electorate 1857
Democrat	23	-5	14	32
Republican	-2	32	12	42
Not Voting	2	4	20	26
Total Electorate 1857	23	31	46	100

TABLE 12

Estimated Relationships between Voting for Governor 1857
and Black Suffrage 1857 (in percentages)

| Suffrage 1857 | Governor 1857 | | | |
	Democrat	Republican	Not Voting	Total Electorate 1857
Prosuffrage	1	19	0	20
Antisuffrage	22	4	2	28
Not Voting	5	6	41	52
Total Electorate 1857	28	29	43	100

{ *Appendix* }

TABLE 13

Estimated Relationships between Voting for Governor 1857
and President 1856 (in percentages)

President 1856	Governor 1857			
	Democrat	Republican	Not Voting	Total Electorate 1857
Democrat	16	-4	21	33
Republican	4	27	10	41
Not Voting	9	5	12	26
Total Electorate 1857	29	28	43	100

TABLE 14

Estimated Relationships between Voting for Congress 1858
and Governor 1857 (in percentages)

Governor 1857	Congress 1858			
	Democrat	Republican	Not Voting	Total Electorate 1858
Democrat	21	0	6	27
Republican	-3	27	2	26
Not Voting	12	7	28	47
Total Electorate 1858	30	34	36	100

TABLE 15

Estimated Relationships between Voting for Governor 1859
and Congress 1858 (in percentages)

Congress 1858	Governor 1859			
	Democrat	Republican	Not Voting	Total Electorate 1859
Democrat	22	1	5	28
Republican	1	27	4	32
Not Voting	10	8	22	40
Total Electorate 1859	33	36	31	100

TABLE 16

Estimated Relationships between Voting for State Supreme Court 1859
and Congress 1858 (in percentages)

Congress 1858	State Supreme Court 1859			
	Democrat	Republican	Not Voting	Total Electorate 1859
Democrat	25	-2	6	29
Republican	-5	28	9	32
Not Voting	10	8	21	39
Total Electorate 1859	30	34	36	100

TABLE 17

Estimated Relationships between Voting for Governor 1859
and State Supreme Court 1859 (in percentages)

State Court 1859	Governor 1859			
	Democrat	Republican	Not Voting	Total Electorate 1859
Democrat	18	2	10	30
Republican	5	31	-2	34
Not Voting	10	4	22	36
Total Electorate 1859	33	37	30	100

TABLE 18

Estimated Relationships between Voting for State Supreme Court 1860
and State Supreme Court 1859 (in percentages)

State Court 1859	State Supreme Court 1860			
	Democrat	Republican	Not Voting	Total Electorate 1860
Democrat	24	-1	6	29
Republican	-1	27	6	32
Not Voting	8	4	27	39
Total Electorate 1860	31	30	39	100

TABLE 19

Estimated Relationships between Voting for State Supreme Court 1860
and Governor 1859 (in percentages)

Governor 1859	State Supreme Court 1860			
	Democrat	Republican	Not Voting	Total Electorate 1860
Democrat	29	-1	4	32
Republican	2	31	0	33
Not Voting	0	1	34	35
Total Electorate 1860	31	31	38	100

TABLE 20

Estimated Relationships between Voting for President 1860
and State Supreme Court 1860 (in percentages)

State Court 1860	President 1860			
	Democrat	Republican	Not Voting	Total Electorate 1860
Democrat	17	5	9	31
Republican	1	28	2	31
Not Voting	14	13	11	38
Total Electorate 1860	32	46	22	100

TABLE 21

Estimated Relationships between Voting for President 1860
and Governor 1859 (in percentages)

	President 1860			
Governor 1859	Democrat	Republican	Not Voting	Total Electorate 1860
Democrat	22	⁻4	13	31
Republican	⁻3	35	1	33
Not Voting	13	15	8	36
Total Electorate 1860	32	46	22	100

TABLE 22

Estimated Relationships between Voting for President 1860
and State Supreme Court 1859 (in percentages)

	President 1860			
State Court 1859	Democrat	Republican	Not Voting	Total Electorate 1860
Democrat	16	4	8	28
Republican	2	31	1	34
Not Voting	14	12	12	38
Total Electorate 1860	32	47	21	100

{ *Appendix* }

TABLE 23

Estimated Relationships between Voting for Governor 1865
and Black Suffrage 1865 (in percentages)

	Governor 1865			
Suffrage 1865	Democrat	Republican	Not Voting	Total Electorate 1865
Prosuffrage	-2	23	0	21
Antisuffrage	23	3	I	27
Not Voting	2	4	46	52
Total Electorate 1865	23	30	47	100

TABLE 24

Estimated Voter Turnout in Wisconsin Elections, 1847–1860

1847	Black Suffrage Referendum	44%
1848	Election for Governor	56%
1848	Election for President	62%
1849	Election for Governor	44%
1849	Black Suffrage Referendum	17%
1850	Congressional Elections	52%
1851	Election for Governor	47%
1851	Bank Referendum	43%
1852	Election for President	62%
1853	Election for Governor	48%
1853	Prohibition Referendum	46%
1854	Congressional Elections	47%
1855	State Supreme Court Election	42%
1855	Election for Governor	52%
1856	Election for President	80%
1857	State Supreme Court Election	54%
1857	Election for Governor	52%
1857	Black Suffrage Election	48%
1858	Congressional Elections	68%
1859	State Supreme Court Election	65%
1859	Election for Governor	68%
1860	State Supreme Court Election	61%
1860	Election for President	79%

NOTES

ONE *A Redeeming Spirit Is Busily Engaged*

1. *Southport American,* Mar. 2, 1844.

2. Louis S. Gerteis, "Antislavery Agitation in Wisconsin, 1836–1848," and "An Abolitionist in Territorial Wisconsin: The Journal of Reverend Edward Mathews."

3. Theodore Clark Smith, "The Free Soil Party in Wisconsin," 97–162, esp. 101.

4. *Southport Telegraph,* Aug. 4, 1840. Dyer apparently was involved in the Underground Railroad in Wisconsin and later was a stockholder in the Territorial Liberty Association. Fanny S. Stone, ed., *Racine and Racine County Wisconsin,* 426–29; and C. W. Butterfield, *The History of Waukesha County Wisconsin,* 562; Russell B. Nye, *Fettered Freedom: Civil Liberties and the Slavery Controversy, 1830–1860.*

5. Alice E. Smith, *The History of Wisconsin,* vol. 1: *From Exploration to Statehood,* 196–97.

6. Alice Smith, *History of Wisconsin,* 474–75; Joseph P. Schafer, *The Wisconsin Lead Region,* 44–56; C. W. Butterfield, *The History of Grant County, Wisconsin;* Raymond V. Phelan, "Slavery in the Old Northwest," 252–64; John N. Davidson, "Negro Slavery in Wisconsin," 82–86.

7. *Southport Telegraph,* Aug. 31, 1841, gives a good account of the disposition of Dodge's slaves. Gerteis, in "An Abolitionist in Territorial Wisconsin," 12, 258–62, 332–40, recounts the Mitchell controversy.

8. *Grant County Herald,* Apr. 23, May 13, 20, 1843; *Shullsburg Telegraph,* Mar. 13, 1849; Gerteis, "An Abolitionist in Territorial Wisconsin," 125–31, 248–53. Eugene Berwanger, *The Frontier Against Slavery: Western Anti-Negro Prejudice and the Slavery Extension Controversy,* 18–19, discusses the attitudes of nonslaveholding Southern yeomen who migrated to the old Northwest in reference to slavery, its extension, and blacks.

9. Alice Smith, *The History of Wisconsin,* 388–89.

10. H. A. Tenney and David Atwood, *Memorial Record of the Fathers of Wisconsin,* 374–75, contains a convenient record of Wisconsin's population by county, from 1836 through 1880. Alice Smith, *The History of Wisconsin,* 250, 468.

11. *Kenosha Telegraph,* Nov. 14, Dec. 19, 1843, Jan. 8, Feb. 5, 1844; *Janesville Gazette,* Oct. 25, 1845, June 13, July 18, 1846. These contain population data testifying to the preponderance of settlers from New York and New England in a number of southeastern towns, collected by one Julius P. Bolivar MacCabe. Also see, Lois Mathews, *The Expansion of New*

England: The Spread of New England Settlements and Institutions to the Mississippi River, 1620–1865, 236–47; Alice Smith, *The History of Wisconsin*, 467–73; Joseph P. Schafer, *Four Wisconsin Counties, Prairie and Forest*, 80–82; Edward Alexander, "Wisconsin, New York's Daughter State," *Wisconsin Magazine of History*, 11–30. Excluding the Wisconsin-born residents in 1850, most of whom were children, nearly 53 percent of Wisconsin's population was born in the Empire State; with Wisconsin residents included, the figure was still a very high 35 percent.

12. *Seventh Census of the United States, 1850*; Alice Smith, *The History of Wisconsin*, 470; Schafer, "The Yankee and the Teuton in Wisconsin," *Wisconsin Magazine of History*.

13. Schafer, *Four Wisconsin Counties*, 390–94; Alice Smith, *The History of Wisconsin*, 470. Cathleen Conzen, *Immigrant Milwaukee, 1836–1860: Accommodation and Community in a Frontier City*, 16–19, states that as early as 1848, the city of Milwaukee had changed from a predominantly Yankee population to one in which a majority of its residents were foreign-born.

14. Alice Smith, *History of Wisconsin*, 464–68. Joseph P. Schafer, *The Winnebago-Horicon Basin: A Type Study in Western History*, 132–92, gives information on those people who settled in Calumet, Dodge, Fond du Lac, and Winnebago counties, for example.

15. Whitney Cross, *The Burned-Over District: The Social and Intellectual History of Enthusiastic Religion in Western New York, 1800–1850*.

16. Richard H. Sewell, *Ballots for Freedom: Antislavery Politics in the United States, 1837–1860*. Theodore Clark Smith, *The Liberty and Free Soil Parties in the Northwest*, is an older, but still useful work on antislavery politics.

17. Sewell, *Ballots for Freedom*, 58; Cross, *The Burned-Over District*, 226–27; A. M. Thompson, *A Political History of Wisconsin*, 38–39; C. C. Olin, *A Complete Record of the John Olin Family*, 20–21.

18. *Milwaukee Courier*, Apr. 26, 1843; Theodore Clark Smith, "Free Soil Party in Wisconsin," 101–2.

19. Edward D. Holton Diary, Feb. 26, 1847, and passim, Edward D. Holton Papers, gives a perspective on Holton's views. Gerteis, "Antislavery Agitation in Wisconsin," 71–77, provides biographical material on Holton.

20. *Milwaukee Democrat*, Oct. 13, Nov. 17, 1843; Theodore Clark Smith, *Liberty and Free Soil Parties in the Northwest*, 59. Moses M. Strong, *History of the Wisconsin Territory, from 1836–1848*, 420, gives a breakdown by county of the returns.

21. *Milwaukee Democrat*, Nov. 10, 1843.

22. Hannah M. Codding, "Ichabod Codding," 169–96; Gerteis, "Antislavery Agitation in Wisconsin," 105–12 and "An Abolitionist in Territorial Wisconsin," 255.

23. Michael Frank Diary, Feb. 13, 1844, Michael Frank Papers; *Southport American*, Feb. 24, 1844; *Southport Telegraph*, Feb. 6, 1844.

24. *Grant County Herald*, Oct. 16, 1844.

25. *Milwaukee Democrat*, Feb. 23, 1844; *Milwaukee Sentinel*, Mar. 2, 1844; *American Freeman*, Mar. 6, 1844; Gerteis, "An Abolitionist in Wisconsin Territory," 255; John G. Gregory, *History of Milwaukee, Wisconsin*, 743.

26. Dwight L. Agnew et al., *Dictionary of Wisconsin Biography*, 326.

27. *Milwaukee Democrat*, Dec. 6, 1843 (e.g., this is one of many antiannexationist pieces that appeared in Sholes's *Democrat* between Sept. 1843 and Feb. 1844).

28. Gerteis, "An Abolitionist in Wisconsin Territory," 255. Since the Nov. announcement of the forthcoming Liberty paper first appeared in the *Milwaukee Democrat*, it may be that Sholes had already been approached about the job, but he remained uncommitted until Codding's visit.

29. Olin, *Record of the John Olin Family.* C. C. Olin obtained exclusive ownership of the *Freeman* in late 1846.

30. Ichabod Codding in Sept. 1846, followed by C. C. Olin, J. P. Plumb, and Sherman M. Booth.

31. Olin, *Record of the John Olin Family.*

32. Of course, the Liberty party did not escape the charges of being fanatical, disunionists, etc., but those charges generally were mild compared to the scorn leveled at abolitionists such as William Lloyd Garrison.

33. Sewell, *Ballots for Freedom,* ch. 4; Eric Foner, *Free Soil, Free Labor, Free Men: The Ideology of the Republican Party before the Civil War,* 73–87.

34. *American Freeman,* Mar. 6, Apr. 10, 1844; *Southport American,* Feb. 24, 1844, for Racine County Liberty resolves; David Brion Davis, "The Emergence of Immediatism in British and American Antislavery Thought."

35. *American Freeman,* Apr. 10, June 1, 1844, Sept. 9, 1845, Aug. 4, Sept. 9, 1846.

36. Ibid., Sept. 9, 1846, and Aug. 18, 1846.

37. Ibid., Mar. 6, 1844, paraded a number of antislavery quotations attributed to the founding fathers. Also see, Sept. 9, 1845, Aug. 18, Nov. 24, Dec. 2, 8, 1846, Apr. 8, 1848 and Foner, *Free Soil, Free Labor, Free Men,* especially ch. 3, as well as William Freehling, "The Founding Fathers and Slavery."

38. *American Freeman,* Sept. 9, 1845; also see Aug. 18, 1846.

39. *American Freeman,* Nov. 10, 1846, gives a good summary of Liberty thought on the Union. Also see Paul C. Nagel, *One Nation Indivisible: The Union in American Thought, 1776–1861;* Kenneth Stampp, "The Concept of a Perpetual Union"; Richard B. Latner, "The Nullification Crisis and Republican Subversion."

40. *American Freeman,* Nov. 19, 1846.

41. Ibid., Apr. 3, 10, 1844. David Potter, *The Impending Crisis, 1848–1861,* 44–50, for a brilliant discussion of the place of slavery in the northern value system. Foner, *Free Soil, Free Labor, Free Men,* 133–43, also recognizes that, among "radical Republicans" at least, the issue of slavery was of primary importance in their hierarchy of values. Stampp, "Concept of a Perpetual Union."

42. *American Freeman,* Apr. 10, 1844, Sept. 9, 1845; Winthrop Jordan's classic *White Over Black: American Attitudes Toward the Negro, 1550–1812* traces American racial attitudes to their English origins.

43. *American Freeman,* Sept. 22, Nov. 3, 1846, Sept. 17, 1847; *Madison Democrat,* Oct. 12, 1843, makes reference to some of these scientific notions. George Frederickson, *The Black Image in the White Mind: The Debate on Afro-American Character and Destiny, 1817–1914,* and William R. Stanton, *The Leopard's Spots: Scientific Attitudes Toward Race in America, 1815–1859,* are the most useful books on this topic.

44. *American Freeman,* Mar. 6, June 1, 1844, Nov. 3, 1846, Jan. 7, Apr. 7, 1847.

45. *American Freeman,* Mar. 24, 1847; Sewell, *Ballots For Freedom,* 99–101; Eric Foner, "Racial Attitudes of the New York Free Soilers."

46. *American Freeman,* June 1, 1844; also see Sept. 22, 1846, for similar sentiments.

47. *Southport American,* Feb. 24, Mar. 29, 1844; *Milwaukee Sentinel,* Jan. 13, Mar. 2, 1844; *Racine Advocate,* Apr. 9, 1844; Madison *Wisconsin Democrat,* Feb. 15, 1844.

48. *American Freeman,* Apr. 10, 17; Aug. 11, 1844; Mar. 5, 12, 19, 26; Apr. 2, 1845.

49. Leonard L. Richards, "The Jacksonians and Slavery," 99–118, gives an appraisal of Northern Whig and Democratic attitudes toward slavery. Also see Herbert Ershkowitz and William G. Shade, "Consensus or Conflict? Political Behavior in the State Legislatures

during the Jacksonian Era"; James Brewer Stewart, "Abolitionists, Insurgents, and Third Parties: Sectionalism and Partisan Politics in Northern Whiggery, 1836–1844," 25–43.

50. *Wisconsin Express,* Apr. 3, 10, 17, Sept. 4, 1845; *Southport American,* Feb. 24, Mar. 2, 9, 1844; *Fond du Lac Whig,* Dec. 14, 1846; *Grant County Herald,* Feb. 12, Nov. 6, 1847; *Janesville Gazette,* May 23, 1846; *Milwaukee Sentinel,* Jan. 9, 1845; Oct. 18, 1848.

51. *Janesville Gazette,* May 23, 1846; *Milwaukee Sentinel,* Oct. 10, 1845, Nov. 17, 1847, April 27, 1848; Ephraim Perkins to John Tweedy, April 13, 1848, John Tweedy Papers.

52. *Grant County Herald,* Nov. 11, 1843, May 4, 11, 1844. Although the *Herald* was "neutral" politically at that time, it conveyed a decidedly Whig tone, and in 1845 the paper's editors were instrumental in organizing the party in Grant County. See the *Herald,* July 5, 1845, June 24, 1847.

53. *Southport American,* Mar. 2, 1845; *Milwaukee Sentinel,* Mar. 14, 1845; Timothy Howe to Horace Rublee, August 14, 1857, Timothy Howe Papers; *Janesville Gazette,* Oct. 23, 1852. These offer retrospective views of the importance of the Texas issue. Also see Frederick Merk, *Slavery and the Annexation of Texas,* 135–47; William R. Brock, *Conflict and Transformation: The United States, 1845–1877,* 44–46.

54. *Wisconsin Express,* Mar. 20, 1845; *Janesville Gazette,* Oct. 27, 1852.

55. *Southport American,* Feb. 24, Mar. 2, 9, Apr. 13, 1844; Aug. 30, 1845; *Milwaukee Sentinel,* Sept. 13, 1844, Jan. 9, 1845; *Fond du Lac Whig,* Dec. 14, 1846; *Janesville Gazette,* Jan. 24, 1846; *Wisconsin Express,* Mar. 20, 1845; *Grant County Herald,* May 4, 1844. The "expand or die" theory is treated by Eugene Genovese, *The Political Economy of Slavery: Studies in the Economy and Society of the Slave South,* 243–70; William J. Cooper, Jr., *The South and the Politics of Slavery, 1828–1856,* 64–65, 238–44; Sewell, *Ballots for Freedom,* 190–91; Foner, *Free Soil, Free Labor, Free Men,* 311–12; Potter, *Impending Crisis,* 46; C. Stanley Urban, "The Ideology of Southern Imperialism: New Orleans and the Caribbean, 1845–1860"; and Charles W. Ramsdell's classic, "The Natural Limits of Slavery Expansion."

56. *Janesville Gazette,* Feb. 2, 1846. Also see the *Southport American,* Mar. 9, 1844, for similar sentiments.

57. *Beloit Journal,* Dec. 28, 1848, gives a good summary of Whig ideology, as does the *Southport American,* Mar. 2, 1844; Major L. Wilson, *Space, Time, and Freedom: The Quest for Nationality and the Irrepressible Conflict, 1815–1861,* 4–6; Ershkowitz and Shade, "Consensus or Conflict," 614–17; Rush Welter, *The Mind of America, 1820–1860,* 190–218; Robert F. Dalzell, Jr., *Daniel Webster and the Trial of American Nationalism, 1843–1852,* 32–34.

58. *Milwaukee Sentinel,* Jan. 9, 1845; Bet Williams to Elisha L. C. Keyes, 1847, Elisha Keyes Papers.

59. *Grant County Herald,* Dec. 12, 1846; *American Freeman,* Aug. 26, 1846; and ch. 2, for a more in-depth analysis of partisanship and race.

60. *Southport American,* Feb. 24, 1844; *Milwaukee Sentinel,* Jan. 7, 1846.

61. *Southport American,* Mar. 2, 1844.

62. *Milwaukee Sentinel,* Jan. 11, 1845; *Wisconsin Express,* Sept. 4, 1845.

63. *Milwaukee Courier,* Nov. 29, Dec. 13, 1843, Jan. 27, 1844; *Wisconsin Democrat,* Oct. 12, 1843, Feb. 15, 1844, Aug. 29, 1846. The condition of free blacks seemed to bear out this contention; John C. Miller, *The Wolf by the Ears: Thomas Jefferson and Slavery,* 84–88.

64. *Wisconsin Democrat,* Feb. 15, 1844, Aug. 26, 1846, July 31, 1847; *Weekly Wisconsin,* June 16, Nov. 3, 1847.

65. *Southport Telegraph,* Jan. 16, Feb. 12, Mar. 27, Apr. 30, July 9, 1844, Feb. 17, 1845, June 9, 1847; *Racine Advocate,* Apr. 9, 1844, Apr. 14, Aug. 4, 1846, Feb. 10, 1847; Madison *Wisconsin Argus,* Feb. 23, Mar. 2, 1847.

66. *Southport Telegraph*, Dec. 5, 1843, Jan. 16, 1844; *Racine Advocate*, Apr. 9, 1844; also see ch. 2.

67. *Wisconsin Democrat*, Jan. 10, 1846; *Southport Telegraph*, Feb. 27, Mar. 12, 19, July 9, 1844, Sept. 23, 1846; *Beloit Journal*, Dec. 28, 1848, give good accounts of Democratic ideology. Also see Wilson, *Space, Time, and Freedom;* Ershkowitz and Shade, "Consensus or Conflict?"; Welter, *The Mind of America,* 165–89, 243–44; Marvin Meyers, *The Jacksonian Persuasion: Politics and Belief.* Many Wisconsin Democrats excluded internal improvements from their list of government-sponsored evils, thus indicating that self-interest or practicality sometimes relegated ideology to a subordinate place.

68. *Southport Telegraph*, Apr. 30, May 21, June 4, July 9, 1844. The *Wisconsin Argus,* July 1, 1845, contains the proceedings of the Democratic territorial convention's endorsement of annexation, and the *Racine Advocate*, July 1, 1845, covers Racine County's meeting, chaired by Michael Frank, an ardent antislavery Democrat, and attended by others of a similar bent, which likewise welcomed the joining of Texas to the United States.

69. *Racine Advocate*, Dec. 3, 19, 1843; Mar. 20, Apr. 19, 1844.

70. *Milwaukee Weekly Wisconsin*, June 16, 1847, expressed this opinion. Also see the *Southport Telegraph*, July 9, 1844.

71. *Southport Telegraph*, Apr. 19, 1842; Mar. 19, 1844.

TWO *Negro Suffrage Is Antislavery Work*

1. *American Freeman*, Mar. 6, 1844, Mar. 20, Jan. 5, 1847, Feb. 23, 1848. Emil Olbrich, *The Development of Sentiment on Negro Suffrage to 1860.*

2. Olbrich, *Development of Sentiment on Negro Suffrage,* 26–27; Strong, *History of Wisconsin Territory,* 212.

3. Florence E. Baker, "A Brief History of the Elective Franchise in Wisconsin."

4. Strong, *History of Wisconsin Territory,* 423–25. Frederick L. Holmes, "First Constitutional Convention in Wisconsin, 1846," 229. Wisconsinites already had rejected statehood on three previous occasions and would reject it again in 1844.

5. *Milwaukee Democrat*, Dec. 27, 1843; *Southport Telegraph*, Jan. 2, 1844.

6. Strong, *History of Wisconsin Territory,* 425–26; Alice E. Smith, *History of Wisconsin,* 659. *Wisconsin House Journal, 1844,* Jan. 9 proceedings. I have used the manuscript copies of the territorial legislative journals which are irregularly paginated. When page numbers are listed, they will be noted, otherwise the date of the proceedings will be indicated.

7. *Wisconsin Democrat*, Feb. 15, 1844.

8. *Wisconsin House Journal, 1844,* Jan. 15, 16.

9. *Wisconsin Council Journal, 1844,* 144. The vote was six to five.

10. *Wisconsin Democrat*, Feb. 15, 1844.

11. *Wisconsin House Journal, 1844,* Jan. 13, 15 proceedings and 250, 258, 407.

12. *Wisconsin Council Journal, 1844,* 203, 431; Strong, *History of Wisconsin Territory,* 431.

13. Gerteis, "Antislavery Agitation in Wisconsin," 11–16, 38, discusses Frank's varied reform activities; *Dictionary of Wisconsin Biography,* 134; "Life of Colonel M. Frank," in Frank H. Lyman, ed., *The City of Kenosha and Kenosha County, Wisconsin,* 90–112.

14. *Wisconsin Council Journal, 1845,* Jan. 16; *Wisconsin House Journal,* Jan. 22; *Petitions, Remonstrances, and Resolutions Presented to the Senate and/or Assembly, 1845,* State Historical Society of Wisconsin, Madison.

15. Milton M. Quaife, *The Movement for Statehood, 1845–1846*, 94–105; *Milwaukee Sentinel*, Feb. 3, 1846.

16. Quaife, *Movement For Statehood; Racine Advocate*, Apr. 9, 1844.

17. *Wisconsin Council Journal, 1846*, 94; *Milwaukee Sentinel*, Feb. 3, 1846.

18. Quaife, *Movement For Statehood*, 105; Strong, *History of Wisconsin Territory*, 487, for list of Council members.

19. Quaife, *Movement For Statehood*, 87; Strong, *History of Wisconsin Territory*, 490.

20. *American Freeman*, Sept. 28, Apr. 9, 1845, Oct. 5, 1844; *Milwaukee Sentinel*, Mar. 22, 1845; *Southport Telegraph*, Sept. 24, Oct. 6, 1844. Voting data for the Liberty party is hard to come by for local contests. The regular party journals did not always print the returns; when they did, the Liberty vote often was left out. The *Freeman* did not print many returns either, possibly out of fear of discouraging the party faithful by the vote their candidates received; or it may be that the vote usually was so small that canvassers ignored it.

21. *American Freeman*, Feb. 12, 1845.

22. Ibid., Mar. 5, 12, 19, 26, Apr. 2, 9, 1845; *Southport American*, Apr. 15, Sept. 27, Oct. 4, 1845; *Janesville Gazette*, Oct. 4, 1845; *Racine Advocate*, Oct. 7, 1845; Strong, *History of Wisconsin Territory*, 480–81.

23. Strong, *History of Wisconsin Territory*, 510; Holmes, "First Constitutional Convention," 230–33.

24. Smith, *History of Wisconsin*, 307–67, for a description of territorial politics and the problems of the Whig party. The Whigs were slow to organize in frontier Wisconsin, and often the party served only as a temporary home for disgruntled Democrats. The Democrats, who were hurt by constant feuding factions vying for control, nonetheless were well established in the territory; they held all political appointments, commanded the patronage, attracted the best-known and most powerful leaders and had strong newspaper support. By statehood, the Whigs had organized, but by then the issues that traditionally had divided the two parties were becoming increasingly irrelevant; hence it never achieved any real electoral success in Wisconsin and was more susceptible to coalitionist efforts than in states such as New York and Massachusetts, where the party had both strong leadership and far better organization.

25. *Dictionary of Wisconsin Biography*, 206; A. A. Thompson, *A Political History of Wisconsin*, 300–302; Gregory, *History of Milwaukee Wisconsin*, 1008–9, for background on King.

26. *Milwaukee Sentinel*, Jan. 7, 16, 19, Feb. 3, Mar. 25, Apr. 20, 1846, for a sampling of King's opinions. Also see William H. Seward to King, February, 1845, Rufus King Papers, where Seward in a different context urged the enfranchisement of blacks in New York, as a means of rendering "the abolition of slavery in our own great State complete" and permanently crippling the Liberty party.

27. *Southport American*, Mar. 14, Apr. 11, 1846; *Janesville Gazette*, Apr. 11, 1846.

28. *Milwaukee Sentinel*, Mar. 10, 1846; *Southport American*, Feb. 21, Mar. 7, 21, 1846; Phyllis F. Field, "The Struggle for Black Suffrage in New York State, 1846–1869," (Ph.D. thesis, Cornell University, 1974), 50–53.

29. *Milwaukee Sentinel*, Feb. 14, 1846.

30. Ibid., Jan. 16, Mar. 16, 1846; *Southport American*, Mar. 21, 1846.

31. *Janesville Gazette*, Feb. 21, 28, 1846.

32. *Milwaukee Courier*, Apr. 8, 22, 1846.

33. *Southport American*, Mar. 14, 1846; *Milwaukee Sentinel*, Mar. 16, 1846. Unfortunately, the *Freeman* suspended publication from April through July 1846, for financial reasons. For-

tunately, the Liberty course is not obscure as a result of references made to the party by other editors.

34. *Southport Telegraph,* Mar. 24, 1846; *Southport American,* Apr. 4, 1846; *Milwaukee Sentinel,* Mar. 16, 1846.

35. *American Freeman,* Aug. 18, 1846, e.g., for the Liberty party emphasis of principles over party; *Southport Telegraph,* Mar. 24, 1846, and the *Milwaukee Sentinel,* Jan. 16, 1846.

36. Madison *Wisconsin Democrat,* Aug. 8, 15, 22, 1846; *Wisconsin Argus,* July 28, August 11, 1846; *Wisconsin Express,* July 28, Aug. 4, 1846.

37. *Southport American,* July 21, Aug. 6, 15, 22, 29, Sept. 3, 1846; *Southport Telegraph,* July 21, 28, Aug. 25, Sept. 1, 1846; *Milwaukee Sentinel,* Sept. 11, 1846.

38. *Milwaukee Sentinel,* Sept. 11, 1846.

39. *American Freeman,* Aug. 11, 18, Sept. 1, 22, 1846; *Milwaukee Sentinel,* Aug. 4, 15, 18, Sept. 11, Oct. 6, 1848; *Milwaukee Courier,* Aug. 24, 1846; *Southport American,* Aug. 29, 1846; *Grant County Herald,* July 5, 1845, July 24, 1847, for development of party sentiment in the territory's western counties; Quaife, *Movement for Statehood,* 302–56.

40. *American Freeman,* Aug. 4, 11, 18, 25, Sept. 2, 1846.

41. Florence E. Baker, "A Bibliographical History of the Two Wisconsin Constitutional Conventions," provides a list of the delegates and their party affiliation, if known.

42. *Journal of the Convention to Form a Constitution for the State of Wisconsin, 1846,* 29–30; Milo M. Quaife, ed., *The Convention of 1846,* 93, 177–79, 214, 224, 228, 250–52; Olbrich, *Development of Sentiment on Negro Suffrage,* 76; Field, "Struggle for Black Suffrage," 57.

43. *Journal of the Convention, 1846,* 67–68, 86, 90; Quaife, *Convention of 1846,* 209, 214, 221–22; Strong, *History of Wisconsin Territory,* 521.

44. Quaife, *Convention of 1846,* 214–15; Alfons J. Beitzinger, *Edward G. Ryan: Lion of the Law* (Madison, 1960).

45. Quaife, *Convention of 1846,* 215.

46. Ibid., 241–48.

47. Ibid.

48. Ibid., 217.

49. *Ibid.,* 214, 228, 240–41, 250–52; Milo M. Quaife, ed., *The Attainment of Statehood,* 386, where Chase gave a fuller explanation of his motives at the first constitutional convention.

50. *Journal of the Convention, 1846,* 90–91. Strong, *History of Wisconsin Territory,* 513–14, states that only 122 of the delegates "were ever in attendance" at the convention, and that "there was never a day when less than 13 of these were absent, and sometimes the absentees numbered forty or more . . . the highest vote ever recorded was 109 . . . the lowest 67, but it generally ranged from 80 to 100, and one fifth part of the votes were from 100–109." So the number of voting delegates on the suffrage question was not unusually low, and probably most nonvoters were absent, not abstaining.

51. *Journal of the Convention, 1846,* 90–91. Alice Smith, *History of Wisconsin,* 470, give a proportionate breakdown of the foreign and native-born populations by county for 1850. German-speaking Roman Catholics were predominant in Washington County.

52. Quaife, *Convention of 1846,* 215, 218, 222, 542–43; *Milwaukee Sentinel,* Oct. 27, 1846. Baker later would become editor of a Free Soil paper in Janesville. Burchard was probably referring to Waukesha County's delegation, whose members, irrespective of party, were pledged to support black suffrage. A. M. Thompson, *Political History of Wisconsin,* 63–65.

53. *Journal of the Convention, 1846,* 94.

54. Ibid., 228–29, for the remarks of D. A. J. Upham who said as much.

55. *Journal of the Convention, 1846,* 100.

56. Quaife, *Convention of 1846,* 412, 544–45; *Journal of the Convention, 1846,* 323.

57. *Journal of the Convention, 1846,* 90–91, 355–56, for both votes.

58. Quaife, *Convention of 1846,* 208, 218–20, 230–38, contains sketches of the speeches and attempts of a number of western delegates to impose more stringent qualifications on immigrant voting.

59. Alice Smith, *History of Wisconsin,* 664–65; Holmes, "First Constitutional Convention," 246–48; Milo M. Quaife, ed., *The Struggle Over Ratification, 1846–1847,* passim, for the popular debates.

60. Franklin J. Blair to Jairus C. Fairchild, January 10, 1847, Lucius Fairchild Papers, discusses the "Hunker" opposition to the constitution; *American Freeman,* Dec. 2, 8, 1846, Jan. 27, Apr. 7, 1847; *Milwaukee Sentinel,* Oct. 28, 1846; *Janesville Gazette,* Nov. 3, 14, Dec. 5, 1846; Quaife, *Struggle Over Ratification,* passim; P. F. Legler, "Josiah A. Noonan: A Story of Promotion and Excoriation in the Old Northwest," 135–56.

61. *Southport Telegraph,* Nov. 4, 18, 46, Mar. 24, 1847; *Racine Advocate,* Mar. 4, 1846.

62. *Rock County Badger,* quoted in the *Janesville Gazette,* Dec. 5, 1846.

63. My numbers were derived from the Records of the Executive Department, *Election Certificates from the State and County Board of Canvassers, 1847,* which vary slightly from the official figures released.

64. Conzen, *Immigrant Milwaukee,* 16–19, 28; Alice Smith, *History of Wisconsin,* 470.

65. Schafer, *Wisconsin Lead Region,* 12.

66. Schafer, *Winnebago-Horicon Basin,* contains information on Fond du Lac and Dodge Counties.

67. See the Methodological Note and Tables in the Appendix following the final chapter. Table 24 provides estimated turnout data for elections held between 1847 and 1860.

68. Ershkovitz and Shade, "Consensus or Conflict?" 591–621; John L. Stanley, "Majority Tyranny in Tocqueville's America: The Failure of Negro Suffrage, 1846," is an important article on Whig divisions over black suffrage.

69. Stanley, "Majority Tyranny," came to a similar conclusion in his New York study, that party lines on the black suffrage issue were not as tightly drawn as had been thought, as did Field in "Struggle for Black Suffrage in New York," 78–81, 101–3. About 46 percent of the voting Democrats and 45 percent of the voting Whigs cast antisuffrage votes.

70. Robert Lane, *Political Life: Why People Get Involved In Politics,* 199–201; Walter Dean Burnham, "The Changing Shape of the American Political Universe," for descriptions of roll-off and cross-pressure.

71. Quaife, *Movement for Statehood,* 101.

72. Ibid., 98–99.

73. Word of the veto did not reach Wisconsin in time to influence the first election.

74. Beriah Brown to Moses M. Strong, Aug. 14, 1847, James Holliday to Strong, Aug. 29, 1847, James Everett to Strong, Sept. 8, 1847, Nelson Dewey to Strong, Aug. 9, 1847, all in the Moses M. Strong Papers; John H. Rountree to John Tweedy, Aug. 6, 1847, Rufus King to Tweedy, Sept. 2, 1847, John H. Tweedy Papers; *Wisconsin Democrat,* Sept. 18, 1847.

75. George M. Jones to Strong, Oct. 15, 1847, Moses M. Strong Papers, echoed the widespread belief that many Democrats, especially in the East, were repulsed by Strong's tendency toward "dissipation," and that this had cost him the election.

76. Baker, "Bibliographical History of Wisconsin's Constitutional Convention," 156–59; Alice Smith, *History of Wisconsin,* 676–77.

77. Frederic Paxson, "Wisconsin: A Constitution of Democracy," 30–52; Strong, *History of Wisconsin Territory*, 564–82; Alice Smith, *History of Wisconsin*, 666–74.

78. *Journal of the Convention To Form a Constitution for the State of Wisconsin, 1847*, 64, 128, 182; no roll call was taken, but Warren Chase claimed that twenty-two had favored it.

79. Ibid., 130, 180–84.

80. Ibid.

81. Ibid., 183–85. The proposition originally passed thirty-five to thirty-four, but one delegate claimed "he had voted under a misapprehension of the question," and his request for a reconsideration was approved.

82. No party affiliation was found for three delegates; two were from western counties and voted negatively, and one was from Dodge and cast a favorable ballot. In all three cases, the votes were consistent with majority sentiment in their districts.

83. *Journal of the Convention, 1847*, 183–84 for Kinnie's remarks. Jefferson and Rock counties had closely divided constituencies, for example, the former in favor, the latter against.

84. King represented Milwaukee; James T. Lewis, future Democratic lieutenant governor and Republican war governor, hailed from Columbia County.

85. *Journal of the Convention, 1847*, 191.

86. Ibid., 192.

87. Ibid., 180–81, 193–94.

88. Ibid., 210, 604.

89. Ibid., 44, 53–55.

90. Thomas D. Morris, *Free Men All: The Personal Liberty Laws of the North, 1780–1861*, 94–129.

91. *Journal of the Convention, 1847*, 55.

92. Quaife, *The Attainment of Statehood*, 15–115, contains some of the popular debate.

93. *American Freeman*, Feb. 9, 23, 1848.

94. The vote on the 1847 constitution was significantly less than the vote on the rejected constitution. This is probably attributable to the widespread assumption that adoption was a virtual certainty and not to voter apathy.

95. Leon F. Litwack, *North of Slavery: The Negro in the Free States, 1790–1860*.

96. Richard N. Current, *The History of Wisconsin*, vol. 2, *The Civil War Era, 1848–1873*, 145–49.

97. Wisconsin's constitution provided that constitutional amendments must receive the approval of both houses of the legislature in two successive sessions and then be popularly sanctioned in a referendum. Blacks could be enfranchised by legislative approval in any one session, subject to popular endorsement.

THREE   *This Movement Is More Radical Than the Leaders Themselves Dare Avow*

1. Chaplain W. Morrison, *Democratic Politics and Sectionalism: The Wilmot Proviso Controversy;* Eric Foner, "The Wilmot Proviso Controversy Revisited"; Frederick J. Blue, *The Free Soilers: Third Party Politics, 1848–1854;* Potter, *Impending Crisis*, 20–27; Sewell, *Ballots For Freedom*, 107–65.

2. *American Freeman*, Sept. 1, 1846, Mar. 31, 1847, Feb. 2, 1848. It should be noted that Liberty men, unlike the Whigs, expressed little confidence in the expand or die theory;

slavery's restriction was but one part of the total denationalization package deemed necessary.

3. See Sewell's, *Ballots for Freedom*, 131–38, and his *John P. Hale and the Politics of Abolition*, 52–85, as well as Theodore Clark Smith's *Liberty and Free Soil Parties*, 105–20.

4. *American Freeman*, Nov. 11, 1847, Feb. 2, 9, 1848. The one-third estimate was derived from the proportion of delegates endorsing Hale at the Jan. meeting. Also see Theodore Clark Smith, "Free Soil Party in Wisconsin," 104–6.

5. *American Freeman*, Apr. 26, May 3, 1848. A pro-Hale motion never came to a vote at the full convention.

6. Blue, *Free Soilers*, 47–70; Allan Nevins, *The Ordeal of the Union* 1:189–206. In its platform, the Democracy officially ignored the extension question; the Whigs ignored all questions, adopting no platform at all.

7. *American Freeman*, Apr. 26, 1848.

8. Ibid., May 31, June 7, 14, 21, 27, 1848; Edward D. Holton Diary, June [?], 1848, Edward D. Holton Papers. The Treaty of Guadalupe Hidalgo was ratified in March. By its terms, the United States received the territories of New Mexico and California, and the Texas boundary was fixed at the Rio Grande.

9. *American Freeman*, June 7, 14, 21, 28, 1848.

10. Ibid., Apr. 5, May 31, June 21, July 5, 1848. Samuel D. Hastings made the request of Booth, undoubtedly on behalf of other Liberty leaders. Hastings himself was a Pennsylvania native and veteran abolitionist residing in Walworth County. On Booth, see Gerteis, "Antislavery Agitation in Wisconsin," 112–15; A. M. Thompson, *Political History of Wisconsin*, 57–59. Booth also had close ties to C. C. Olin, chief stockholder and former editor of the *Freeman*, with whom, at one time, he edited the *Charter Oak*, Connecticut's Liberty paper.

11. Thompson, *Political History of Wisconsin*, 57–59; *American Freeman*, July 5, 12, 1848.

12. Ibid., July 18, 26, 1848. The convention also passed a resolution endorsing Booth and the course he was pursuing at the *Freeman*.

13. Ibid., Aug. 2, 1848. Booth reiterated this point just before his departure for Buffalo.

14. Ibid.

15. The quotation is from the *Fond du Lac Whig*, Dec. 14, 1846; also see *Milwaukee Sentinel*, Nov. 30, 1846; Ephraim Perkins to John Tweedy, Apr. 13, 1848, Tweedy Papers.

16. "Address of the Whigs to the Voters of Wisconsin," *Wisconsin Express*, Oct. 12, 1848. James Brewer Stewart, *Holy Warriors: The Abolitionists and American Society*, 111–13, discusses the tendency of increasing numbers of Northerners to question traditional assumptions and loyalties as the slavery controversy heated up; Major L. Wilson, "Liberty and Union: An Analysis of Three Concepts Involved in the Nullification Controversy," 133–47, esp. 139–44, discusses the pressures on antislavery Whigs to reconcile their slavery views with their Unionism, as does Daniel W. Howe, *The Political Culture of the American Whigs*, 67–68. Whigs, it should be noted, would have preferred to see the war terminated without the acquisition of land by the United States, a position they abandoned for the most part when it became clear that the administration's expansionist goals were popular.

17. *Wisconsin Express*, Oct. 12, 1848; *Southport Telegraph*, Aug. 18, 1847; *American Freeman*, Aug. 2, 1848. Of course, not all Whigs supported this perspective, and some did try to exploit the tariff issue in 1848. Yet the idea that the old issues were dead gained increasing acceptance with men of all parties through the end of the decade and on into the 1850s.

18. Stewart, "Abolitionists, Insurgents, and Third Parties," 26–36.

19. *Janesville Gazette,* Oct. 2, 1847. Also see the *Milwaukee Sentinel,* June 29, Nov. 30, 1846, Jan. 27, Feb. 4, 1847; *Southport American,* Jan. 30, 1847; *Grant County Herald,* Feb. 12, Nov. 6, 1847; *Wisconsin Express,* Oct. 2, 1848.

20. *Janesville Gazette,* Dec. 28, 1848; *Milwaukee Sentinel,* Jan. 27, 1847; *Southport American,* Jan. 30, 1847; *Grant County Herald,* Feb. 2, June 24, 1847. For continuation of this sentiment see *Southport American,* Jan. 3, June 20, Dec. 28, 1849; *Milwaukee Sentinel,* Dec. 13, 31, 1849.

21. *Janesville Gazette,* Oct. 2, 1847, June 30, July 21, Aug. 31, Nov. 6, Dec. 28, 1848; *Milwaukee Sentinel,* July 15, 1848; *Grant County Herald,* Apr. 22, July 15, 1848; Brock, *Conflict and Transformation,* 79. William J. Cooper, *The South and the Politics of Slavery,* 226–74, esp. 238–44, discusses the Southern response to the territorial question and shows that at least some Southern leaders believed slavery never would expand into the West; thus they were willing to reach an agreement.

22. The *Weekly Wisconsin,* Aug. 9, 1848, contains references to some of the few Whig insurgents; Potter, *Impending Crisis,* 39–50; and Stewart, "Abolitionists, Insurgents and Third Parties," on conflicting values and tensions within northern Whiggery.

23. Ibid., June 16, 1847.

24. *Southport Telegraph,* Apr. 21, 28, 1848; Theodore Clark Smith, "Free Soil Party in Wisconsin," 110.

25. Potter, *Impending Crisis,* 57–59.

26. *Wisconsin Argus,* Feb. 23, Mar. 2, 1847, July 4, Aug. 29, Oct. 3, 1848; *Fond du Lac Journal,* Oct. 6, 29, Nov. 3, 1848.

27. A. M. Thompson, *Political History of Wisconsin,* 60; Theodore Clark Smith, "Free Soil Party in Wisconsin," 109–10, for Democratic opposition to Cass's stand on internal improvements.

28. *Wisconsin Democrat,* Oct. 16, 1847, July 8, Oct. 7, 28, Nov. 4, 1848, for a sample of Brown's opinions. He was also a leading spokesman of Democrats unsympathetic to moral arguments respecting slavery or the slave's plight, as outlined in chapter 1. Thus, Brown's antiproviso position is consistent with his earlier views. Also see *Potosi Republican,* Aug. 17, 1848, which was not as forthright as Brown, but nonetheless denied Congress the right to determine slavery policy in the territories. Oregon was the one exception Brown referred to, but even here, he insisted, settlers already had set the precedent by prohibiting slavery, and Congress merely took the constitutionally dubious step of affirming popular will.

29. *Green Bay Advocate,* Feb. 10, Aug. 24, 1848; *Waukesha Democrat,* July 20, Aug. 29, Sept. 19, 26, Oct. 3, 10, 17, 26, 1848; *Weekly Wisconsin,* July 5, Aug. 30, Sept. 7, 1848. Some popular sovereignty Democrats thought Congress might have the right to legislate on slavery matters for the territories, but like George Hyer of the *Waukesha Democrat,* they yielded their "personal preferences" to those of the national party and its candidates and would forthrightly abandon the proviso in 1850, as did the Democracy generally.

30. *Wisconsin Democrat,* Oct. 7, 28, Nov. 4, 1848; *Waukesha Democrat,* Sept. 19, Oct. 3, 1848; *Wisconsin Argus,* Aug. 29, 1848; *Weekly Wisconsin,* Aug. 30, 1848; *Potosi Republican,* Aug. 17, 1848, for an overview of this argument.

31. *Wisconsin Argus,* Aug. 29, Oct. 3, 1848. Also see the *Waukesha Democrat,* Sept. 26, 1848.

32. *Assembly Journal, 1848,* 49, 91–93; *Senate Journal, 1848,* 37, 48, 53; *Southport Telegraph,* June 16, 23, 1848. Some were squeamish about the resolutions, and in fact the resolutions

were watered down to include only a petition that favored free territory; nonetheless they illustrate the minimum sentiment held by nearly all Wisconsinites and were deliberately weak so as to offend no one.

33. *Potosi Republican,* Oct. 19, 1848; see too the *Wisconsin Democrat,* Oct. 28, 1848.

34. *Weekly Wisconsin,* Dec. 1, 1847, July 5, 1848; *Potosi Republican,* Sept. 14, Oct. 19, 1848; *Green Bay Advocate,* Aug. 24, 1848; *Wisconsin Argus,* Aug. 20, 1848; *Waukesha Democrat,* Aug. 29, Oct. 10, 1848; *Wisconsin Democrat,* Aug. 26, Oct. 28, 1848; *Fond du Lac Journal,* Oct. 6, Nov. 3, 1848.

35. Marshall M. Strong to Horace Tenney, Sept. 11, 1848, Horace Tenney Papers.

36. *Southport Telegraph,* Feb. 21, June 23, 1848; *Racine Advocate,* Feb. 10, 1847, Feb. 2, May 31, 1848; *Fond du Lac Journal,* Oct. 13, 1847, for Chase's views; Alexander Randall to Moses M. Strong, Aug. 20, 1848, Strong Papers; *Rock County Democrat,* in the *Janesville Gazette,* Aug. 24, 31, 1848, and in the *Milwaukee Sentinel,* July 4, 1849. For the attitudes of Free Soilers toward blacks, see Richard H. Sewell, "Slavery, Race, and the Free Soil Party, 1848–1854," 101–24; Eric Foner, "Politics and Prejudice: The Free Soil Party and the Negro, 1849–1852," and "Racial Attitudes of the New York Free Soilers," 311–29; Berwanger, *The Frontier Against Slavery.* The extreme racist element in Wisconsin's Free Soil party was small. In fact, Free Soil attitudes resembled those of the Liberty organization to a striking degree.

37. The Janesville meeting had been called by James Bunner in his *Racine Advocate,* July 12, 1848; also see the *American Freeman,* Aug. 9, 1848, for the proceedings of the meeting. Wisconsin's Buffalo delegation included five Liberty men, two Whigs, and eighteen Democrats.

38. *American Freeman,* Aug. 23, 1848; *Evening Wisconsin,* Mar. 12, 1897, contains some reminiscences of Booth the senior citizen; Blue, *The Free Soilers,* 70–80, 293–96; Theodore Clark Smith, *The Liberty and Free Soil Parties,* 136–43.

39. *American Freeman,* Oct. 1, 3, 1848; *Southport Telegraph,* Oct. 6, 1848; Sewell, *Ballots For Freedom,* 96, 170–89, and Foner, "Politics and Prejudice," give sensitive evaluations of Free Soil attitudes toward blacks. Free Soilers claimed Van Buren favored striking the proposed whites-only clause, but eventually supported a $250 property qualification placed on blacks since it had boiled down to a question of that or total exclusion.

40. Thomas Ogden to John Tweedy, Aug. 27, 1848, Tweedy Papers.

41. *Milwaukee Sentinel,* Aug. 19, Oct. 2, 12, 26, 1848; *Beloit Journal,* Sept. 14, 1848; *Wisconsin Express,* Oct. 12, 1848; *Wisconsin Democrat,* Oct. 14, Nov. 11, 1848; *Wisconsin Argus,* Sept. 26, 1848; Theodore Clark Smith, "Free Soil Party in Wisconsin," 114–18.

42. Walworth, Waukesha, Racine, and Milwaukee; Kenosha County later was carved out of Racine to complete the district. It should also be noted that Walworth, Waukesha, and Racine cast slightly more than forty-four hundred or 88 percent of the district's Free Soil vote, while immigrant Milwaukee remained hostile to so-called abolitionist candidates.

43. Manitowoc, Milwaukee, and Washington Counties all contained foreign-born majorities and were overwhelmingly Democratic; the three-county total gave Cass 4,031 votes, Taylor 1,602, and Van Buren 1,021. Most of the latter two totals were from Milwaukee, a fact that still gave the Democrats in that county a two-to-one preponderance. Grant, Iowa, Lafayette, St. Croix, and Crawford Counties in the west were closely divided between the major parties, with 3,608 votes for the Democracy, 3,383 to the Whigs, and a pitiful 306 for the Free Soilers.

44. *Wisconsin Express,* Feb. 6, 1849. Also see the *Fond du Lac Journal,* Nov. 3, 1848, for a typical statement respecting the statewide free soil consensus.

45. *Racine Advocate*, June 12, July 12, 1848. Sholes is quoted in the *Southport Telegraph*, June 2, Oct. 20, 1848. Also see the *American Freeman*, Aug. 9, 1848; Marshall M. Strong to Horace Tenney, Sept. 11, 1848, Tenney Papers.

46. *Racine Advocate*, June 14, July 5, 12, 1848; *Southport Telegraph*, Apr. 7, 28, June 2, Oct. 27, 1848, provide good summaries of Free Soil attitudes. Also see Sewell, *Ballots for Freedom*, 170–201.

47. *Racine Advocate*, June 14, July 12, 1848; *Southport Telegraph*, Apr. 7, 28, June 2, Oct. 27, 1848.

48. *Southport Telegraph*, June 2, Oct. 27, 1848.

49. *American Freeman*, Oct. 25, 1848; *Southport Telegraph*, Sept. 8, 15, Oct. 6, 13, 20, 1848; *Racine Advocate*, Feb. 2, June 7, 14, 1848.

50. Moses M. Strong to Horace Tenney, Sept. 11, 1848, Alexander Randall to Moses M. Strong, Aug. 20, 1848, Strong Papers; *Southport Telegraph*, June 23, Oct. 27, 1848; *Racine Advocate*, June 28, July 5, 1848, Feb. 10, 1847.

51. *Racine Advocate*, June 28, 1848; *Southport Telegraph*, Apr. 7, 21, 28, June 2, 14, Dec. 1, 1848; Sewell, "Slavery, Race, and the Free Soil Party," 101–19. Curbs on press and speech freedoms and censorship of mails most frequently were pointed to by Free Soilers to illustrate Southern "tyranny."

52. *Southport Telegraph*, June 21, 1850; also see Dec. 8, 1848, June 20, 1849, Jan. 4, 7, 1850; *Racine Advocate*, Feb. 2, June 28, 1848; *Wisconsin Free Democrat* (formerly the *American Freeman*), Jan. 2, Feb. 20, 1850.

53. The 68 percent figure was derived by dividing the Free Soil party's prosuffrage entry (11.1) by its presidential total (16.4), and the other percentages in the same way.

FOUR *A Party Separate and Distinct*

1. Sixteen assembly seats, three senate seats; Blue, *Free Soilers*, 142.

2. *Wisconsin Free Democrat*, Jan. 17, 24, 1849; *Milwaukee Sentinel*, Jan. 15, 16, 17, 1849.

3. *Wisconsin Express*, Jan. 16, 1849; *Milwaukee Sentinel*, Jan. 17, 1849; *Wisconsin Free Democrat*, Feb. 24, 1849.

4. *Milwaukee Sentinel*, Jan. 17, 1849; *Wisconsin Express*, Jan. 16, 1849; Rufus King to John Tweedy, March 5, 1848, Tweedy Papers.

5. *Weekly Wisconsin*, Dec. 6, 1848; *Wisconsin Argus*, Nov. 14, 1848; *Fond du Lac Journal*, Nov. 24, 1848; Moses M. Strong to Byron Kilbourn, Nov. 24, 1848, Byron Kilbourn Papers; Byron Kilbourn to Moses M. Strong, Dec. 12, 1848, Moses M. Strong Papers; C. L. Sholes to Morgan L. Martin, Dec. 15, 1848, Morgan L. Martin Papers. The old negrophobe Strong had addressed the January 11 Free Soil convention in favor of a coalition.

6. *Wisconsin Democrat*, Nov. 19, Dec. 10, 1848.

7. *Wisconsin Democrat*, Jan. 20, 1849.

8. Ibid.; *Wisconsin Argus*, Jan. 16, 29, 1849.

9. *Assembly Journal, 1849*, 40–41; *Wisconsin Argus*, Jan. 30, 1849; *Wisconsin Free Democrat*, Feb. 14, 1849.

10. The Democrats voted twenty-seven to three to strike the resolve, three Democrats abstained; the Whigs split, six to strike, eight to retain the measure; thirteen Free Soilers voted to retain, two to strike.

11. *Assembly Journal, 1849*, 79–81. The Democrats favored the proposal twenty-three to six, the Whigs split seven to seven, and the Free Soilers opposed the measure thirteen to two.

12. *Assembly Journal, 1849*, 111–12.

13. Ibid., 177–79; *Senate Journal, 1849*, 117, 119, 136, 146–51, provides the full range of the debates. The Whig Assemblymen voted eleven to four and the Free Soilers fourteen to zero in favor of the senate version; only nine Democrats voted for it, twenty against.

14. *Assembly Journal, 1849*, 539–40, 567–72. At the outset of the debate, the Democrats voted twelve to eleven in favor of the Walker bill, with ten abstentions; final passage came with Democrats still split, fifteen in favor, nine against, and nine abstaining. Free Soilers gave all fifteen of their votes in favor, the Whigs twelve, with only two against.

15. *Senate Journal, 1849*, 567–72, 633, 655. Democrats voted four in favor, five against the resolution, with one abstention; Whigs four-one-one; Free Soilers, two-zero-one.

16. *Assembly Journal, 1849*, 333, 386–88; *Senate Journal, 1849*, 418, 430, 440, 497. Also see the *Southport Telegraph*, Mar. 16, 1849; *Wisconsin Argus*, Mar. 20, 1849. John Reymert, a Norwegian-born Free Soiler, introduced the suffrage measure. The combined Democratic vote was fifteen for the referendum, nineteen against, and nine abstaining; Whigs favored the measure twelve to eight, Free Soilers nineteen to zero.

17. *Southport Telegraph*, Feb. 2, 9, 1849; *Wisconsin Free Democrat*, Feb. 7, 14, 21, 28, 1849.

18. For Booth's continued optimism, see his letter to Salmon P. Chase, Apr. 5, 1849, in the Booth Papers. The *Waukesha Democrat*, Feb. 6, 13, 20, 27, Mar. 6, 13, 1849; *Fond du Lac Journal*, Apr. 6, 1849; *Oshkosh True Democrat*, Apr. 13, 1849; and the *Milwaukee Sentinel*, Feb. 26, Mar. 8, 1849, cover the joint meetings.

19. *Shullsburg Telegraph*, July 26, 1849. Booth was well aware of the disinclination of the conservatives to work with "old abolitionists" like himself; see the *Wisconsin Free Democrat*, Feb. 21, 28, 1849, and the *Waukesha Democrat*, Feb. 6, 27, 1849.

20. *Wisconsin Free Democrat*, Feb. 21, 1849; *Southport Telegraph*, Feb. 18, 1849; and the *Weekly Wisconsin*, Feb. 7, 1849.

21. *Wisconsin Free Democrat*, Mar. 28, Apr. 4, 1849; *Southport Telegraph*, Apr. 6, 1849.

22. Theodore Clark Smith, "The Free Soil Party in Wisconsin," 125.

23. See the *Wisconsin Democrat*, Aug. 25, 1849, for a public letter from John Delaney to Beriah Brown designed to clear up misconceptions about the purpose and accomplishments of the March 30 meeting. Delaney was a Democratic assemblyman from Portage.

24. *Wisconsin Argus*, June 5, 1849; *Wisconsin Democrat*, June 2, 1849; *Weekly Wisconsin*, June 27, 1849; *Wisconsin Free Democrat*, June 20, 1849.

25. The *Milwaukee Sentinel*, July 7, 1849 contains the committee's call.

26. *Southport Telegraph*, June 29, 1849; *Wisconsin Free Democrat*, July 4, 1849.

27. *Waukesha Democrat*, July 10, 17, 24, 1849; *Wisconsin Free Democrat*, July 18, 1849; *Southport Telegraph*, July 20, 27, 1849.

28. *Waukesha Democrat*, July 31, 1849; *Fond du Lac Journal*, July 20, Aug. 10, 17, 1849; *Wisconsin Free Democrat*, July 25, 1849.

29. *Oshkosh True Democrat*, July 25, 1849; Theodore Clark Smith, "Free Soil Party in Wisconsin," 126–27.

30. *Milwaukee Daily Free Democrat*, Mar. 16, 1857, gives a retrospective view of the problems confronting the Free Soilers in 1849; also see James Simmons to Jairus Fairchild, May 28, 1849, in the Fairchild Papers; *Wisconsin Free Democrat*, May 2, 1849; *Milwaukee Sentinel*, June 30, 1849.

31. *Wisconsin Free Democrat*, Aug. 8, 1849.

32. *Milwaukee Sentinel*, Sept. 8, 1849; *Wisconsin Free Democrat*, Sept. 12, 1849. The proviso vote was twenty-three to fifteen with twenty-three abstentions.

33. Ibid.

34. *Wisconsin Democrat,* Sept. 8, 15, 1849; the *Wisconsin Express,* Sept. 11, 1849, reported the "deal"; *Green Bay Advocate,* Sept. 13, 1849; *Oshkosh True Democrat,* Sept. 28, 1849; *Milwaukee Sentinel,* Sept. 29, 1849.

35. *Wisconsin Free Democrat,* Sept. 12, 1849; *Wisconsin Democrat,* Sept. 8, 15, 1849; *Milwaukee Sentinel,* Sept. 10, 11, 1849; Theodore Clark Smith, "Free Soil Party in Wisconsin," 126–28.

36. *Wisconsin Free Democrat,* Sept. 12, Oct. 3, 1849.

37. *Oshkosh True Democrat,* Oct. 5, 12, 1849; *Wisconsin Democrat,* Sept. 29, 1849; *Wisconsin Free Democrat,* Oct. 3, 1849; *Elkhorn Independent,* Feb. 5, 1856, with Densmore as editor, provides further details as to the motivations of the Free Soil delegates in their 1849 convention.

38. The quotation comes from the *Port Washington Advocate* and was reprinted in the *Southport Telegraph,* Aug. 17, 1849.

39. *Wisconsin Free Democrat,* Oct. 17, 1849.

40. A. E. Elmore, Sat Clark, George Clark to Jairus Fairchild, Sept. 27, 1849, Elmore to Fairchild, Sept. 28, 1849, Fairchild Papers. The *Wisconsin Democrat,* Oct. 27, 1849, contain the candidates' statements.

41. Alexander Randall to Jairus Fairchild, Oct. 16, 1849, Fairchild Papers; Michael Frank, Diary, Oct. 23, 1849, Michael Frank Papers, discusses one such meeting at which Randall spoke. Randall, claiming poverty, also demanded and apparently received financial compensation for his efforts. Also see Theodore Clark Smith, "Free Soil Party in Wisconsin," for commentary concerning the health of the Free Soil organization as the campaign wound down.

42. *Milwaukee Sentinel,* Sept. 17, 1849.

43. Dewey won 18,274 votes; Collins, the Whig, 12,039; and Chase, 3,765.

44. *Janesville Gazette,* Oct. 25, 1849, for Alden's comments; *Milwaukee Sentinel,* Nov. 5, 1849, for King's. Also see the *Beloit Journal,* Oct. 4, 1849; *Southport American,* Oct. 10, 1849; *Wisconsin Express,* Dec. 25, 1849; *Wisconsin Free Democrat,* Oct. 24, 1849; *Oshkosh True Democrat,* Aug. 10, Sept. 14, 1849.

45. *Wisconsin Free Democrat,* Nov. 21, 1849.

46. Fewer than seven hundred blacks were in Wisconsin in 1850, Alice Smith, *History of Wisconsin,* 475.

47. Christopher Sholes said as much in the *Southport Telegraph,* Nov. 30, 1849.

FIVE *The Principles of the Free Soil and Whig Parties Are Identical*

1. *Wisconsin Free Democrat,* Nov. 14, 1849; *Southport Telegraph,* Nov. 30, 1849.

2. The Whigs received 41.2 percent of the vote cast in the 1848 governor's election, 35.1 percent of the ballots in the 1848 presidential contest, and 35.4 percent in 1849's canvass.

3. Holman Hamilton, *Prologue To Conflict: The Crisis and Compromise of 1850,* 43–62; Mark Stegmaier, *Texas, New Mexico and the Compromise of 1850,* 97–101; Potter, *The Impending Crisis,* 90–120; Michael F. Holt, *The Political Crisis of the 1850s,* 67–99.

4. *Wisconsin Express,* Feb. 11, 1850; also Feb. 19, Mar. 5, Apr. 9, June 11. For a sampling of similar Whig responses to the controversy see the *Milwaukee Sentinel,* Jan. 31, Feb. 14, 28, Mar. 4, 15, Apr. 9, June 5, 27, Aug. 28, 1850; *Beloit Journal,* Apr. 11, Aug. 9, 1850; *Janesville Gazette,* Feb. 7, 21, 28, 1850.

5. Potter, *Impending Crisis,* 94–116.

6. Wisconsin's Whigs were closely allied to New York's William Seward-Thurlow Weed wing of the party. Seward had been a close advisor to Taylor, and the elevation of

Fillmore, Seward's major intraparty rival in New York, put the state's Whigs in an uncomfortable position. If they failed to back down they risked party isolation and the loss of patronage and power in the state.

7. Horace Tenney, once a strong Democratic advocate of the proviso, now disregarded it as "ridiculous." See his *Wisconsin Argus,* July 9, 1850. Beriah Brown, Tenney's crosstown rival and an antiproviso Democrat, came to the same conclusion in the *Wisconsin Democrat,* March 2, 1850. Also see the *Milwaukee Commercial Advertiser,* July 9, 24, 1850.

8. *Wisconsin Free Democrat,* Jan. 2, 1850, Feb. 20, 27, Mar. 6, 20, 1850. Sholes echoed Booth's sentiments in his *Southport Telegraph,* June 7, 21, 1850.

9. *Wisconsin Express,* Dec. 12, 1850.

10. Sewell, *Ballots For Freedom,* 231–53.

11. Morris, *Free Men All,* 130–47.

12. *Wisconsin Argus,* Oct. 29, 1850; Speech of Byron Paine, undated, probably 1851, Byron Paine Papers.

13. *Milwaukee Sentinel,* Oct. 11, 12, 1850. For Booth's comments, see the *Wisconsin Free Democrat,* Mar. 26, 1851, Oct. 16, 1850; William J. Vollmar, "The Negro in a Midwest Frontier City, Milwaukee: 1835–1870: (master's thesis, Marquette University, 1968), 22–33. About one hundred blacks lived in Milwaukee in 1850.

14. See, for example, the speech of Christopher Sholes to the state legislature in the *Assembly Journal, 1853,* 719–32. The *Wisconsin Free Democrat,* Jan. 22, 1851, contains Booth's statement.

15. *Wisconsin Democrat,* Oct. 26, 1850.

16. *Weekly Wisconsin,* Sept. 18, Oct. 16, 23, 1850; *Milwaukee Commercial Advertiser,* Nov. 8, 1850; *Grant County Herald,* June 26, 1854, provide a retrospective view of why this Whig editor from the lead district favored the compromise; *Milwaukee Sentinel,* Sept. 26, 1850, discusses the frustration and fatigue felt by many over the continuing controversy; Cyrus Woodman to William J. Russell, Sept. 26, 1851, Cyrus Woodman Papers, is the Democrat cited.

17. *Oshkosh True Democrat,* Nov. 18, 1850, Jan. 10, 1851; *Wisconsin Free Democrat,* Oct. 23, 1850; Current, *History of Wisconsin,* 209.

18. *Weekly Wisconsin,* Aug. 27, 1851; *Milwaukee Sentinel,* May 29, July 14, 1851; *Wisconsin Argus,* May 28, 1851; *Green Bay Advocate,* July 17, 1851; Potter, *Impending Crisis,* 121–22, 130–40; Holt, *Political Crisis of the 1850s,* 95–99.

19. On fugitive slave cases, see the *Milwaukee Sentinel,* Mar. 10, Apr. 11, 1851; *Wisconsin Express,* Aug. 28, 1851; *Wisconsin Free Democrat,* Apr. 10, 23, June 11, 1851. For the response to *Uncle Tom's Cabin,* see, for example, Dustin Grow Cheever, Diary, Dec. 28, 1853, Dustin Grow Cheever Papers; and Potter, *Impending Crisis,* 140. On itinerant black speakers, again see Cheever, Diary, Mar. 28, Oct. 8, 1853, and Willet S. Main, Diary, Oct. 30, 1851, Willet S. Main Papers. For a sober analysis of northern accommodation to the law, see Stanley W. Campbell, *The Slave Catchers: Enforcement of the Fugitive Slave Law, 1850–1860.*

20. *Senate Journal, Appendix, 1851,* 39–49; *Senate Journal, 1851,* 17, 35, 51, 94, 134, 184–85; *Assembly Journal, 1851,* 252, 263, 429, 653.

21. The debates and votes can be followed in the senate and assembly journals in the previous citation.

22. *Senate Journal, 1852,* 273, 690.

23. Ibid.

24. *Oshkosh Democrat,* May 31, 1850.

25. Booth to Chase, Feb. 2, 1850, Booth Papers.

26. *Southport Telegraph,* Mar. 22, 1850; Durkee to John Fox Potter, Aug. 26, 1850, John Fox Potter Papers.

27. *Wisconsin Free Democrat,* Aug. 7, 14, 21, 1850.

28. Ibid., Sept. 25, Oct. 30, 1850; Sewell, *Ballots for Freedom,* 202–30; Theodore Clark Smith, *The Free Soil Party in the Northwest,* 199–225.

29. *Wisconsin Free Democrat,* Sept. 25, Oct. 16, 1850.

30. *Milwaukee Sentinel,* Oct. 15–30, 1850; *Wisconsin Free Democrat,* Oct. 16, 30, 1850; *Weekly Wisconsin,* Oct. 16, 23, 1850.

31. *Wisconsin Free Democrat,* Oct. 30, 1850; Orsamus Cole to George Lakin, Sept. 16, 1850, George Lakin Papers; Cyrus Woodman to Ben Eastman, Nov. 30, 1850, Woodman Papers; Robert R. Flately, "The Wisconsin Congressional Delegation From Statehood to Secession, 1848–1861," 26–27.

32. Ibid.; *Milwaukee Sentinel,* Oct. 24, 25, 28, 29, 1850; *Wisconsin Free Democrat,* Sept. 8, Oct. 30, 1850.

33. *Milwaukee Sentinel,* Oct. 24, 1851; *Wisconsin Free Democrat,* Oct. 15, 1851.

34. *Milwaukee Sentinel,* May 12, 1847, and Aug. 21, 1852, for the number of papers; *Waukesha Democrat,* Sept. 18, 1850, for efforts to set up new papers; *Green Bay Advocate,* Aug. 22, 1851, for one editor who resigned his post in favor of party unity; *Wisconsin Argus,* June 9, 1852, on the termination of the Brown-Tenney feud; J. C. Sneeden to Jairus Fairchild, July 27, 1852, Fairchild Papers, on the Democratic reaction to its termination and the merger of the two papers.

35. *Assembly Journal, 1851,* 62–67; *Senate Journal, 1851,* 40–41. See the *Wisconsin Free Democrat,* July 8, 26, 1851, for rumors that the national party organization had ordered Wisconsin's Democracy "to reverse its position on the slave question . . . and resolve in favor of the Compromise, or its delegates cannot be received into the National Convention."

36. *Wisconsin Free Democrat,* Apr. 30, 1851.

37. *Wisconsin Argus,* Sept. 12, 24, 1851; *Kenosha Telegraph,* Oct. 31, 1851; *Oshkosh Democrat,* Sept. 19, 1851.

38. *Kenosha Democrat,* Sept. 20, 1851.

39. *Milwaukee Sentinel,* Dec. 16, 1850, Apr. 15, Aug. 21, Sept. 3, 1851; *Wisconsin Express,* Dec. 11, 18, 1851.

40. *Wisconsin Free Democrat,* Aug. 13, Sept. 10, 1851; *Kenosha Telegraph,* Aug. 1, 1851, *Racine Advocate,* July 30, 1851.

41. *Evening Wisconsin,* Mar. 12, 1897, for a retrospective view of the proceedings; Theodore Clark Smith, "The Free Soil Party in Wisconsin," 134–35; Theodore Clark Smith, *Liberty and Free Soil Parties in the Northwest,* 234–35.

42. *Wisconsin Free Democrat,* Sept. 24, 1851; *Kenosha Telegraph,* Sept. 26, 1851.

43. *Evening Wisconsin,* Mar. 12, 1897; *Wisconsin Argus,* Oct. 22, 1851.

44. *Green Bay Advocate,* Oct. 16, 1851, and the *Wisconsin Argus,* Oct. 22, 1851, on King's role and advice.

45. *Milwaukee Sentinel,* Sept. 29, 1851; A. M. Thompson, *Political History of Wisconsin,* 76–79.

46. *Milwaukee Sentinel,* Sept. 29, 1851.

47. *Sheboygan Lake Journal,* in the *Racine Advocate,* Oct. 8, 1851.

48. *Milwaukee Sentinel,* Oct. 30, 1851.

49. *Wisconsin Free Democrat,* Oct. 22, 29, 1851; *Janesville Standard,* July 12, 26, Sept. 6, 1854, has J. C. Bunner's recounting of the story behind the letter and Farwell's explanation.

50. Thompson, *Political History of Wisconsin,* 76–77; Ken Winkle, "Voters, Issues, and Parties: Partisan Realignment in Southeastern Wisconsin, 1850–1854" (master's thesis, University of Wisconsin, 1977), 27–28, 97–100. Turnout for the governor's contest was 47 percent; for the bank question, it was 43 percent.

51. *Milwaukee Journal,* in the *Wisconsin Free Democrat,* Nov. 26, 1851.

52. *Milwaukee Sentinel,* Dec. 18, 1851.

53. Ibid., Apr. 30, 1852; *Wisconsin Free Democrat,* Dec. 30, 1851, Jan. 14, 1852.

54. Ibid., Jan. 14, 21, 1852.

55. *Milwaukee Sentinel,* July 3, 15, 21, Sept. 14, 1852, for a sampling of state Democratic attitudes; Potter, *The Impending Crisis,* 141–44, 228–38.

56. *Milwaukee Sentinel,* June 22, July 25, 1852; *Janesville Gazette,* July 3, 1852, Aug. 14, 1852. The *Green Bay Advocate,* July 15, 1852, and the *Weekly Wisconsin,* July 14, 1852, give Democratic comments on the dispirited Whigs.

57. *Milwaukee Daily Free Democrat,* July 1, Nov. 3, 5, 8, 15, 1852; *Kenosha Telegraph,* Nov. 5, 26, 1852; *Milwaukee Sentinel,* Oct. 25, Nov. 1, 5, 8, 1852; Flately, "Wisconsin Congressional Delegation," 48–49; Sewell, *Ballots for Freedom,* 244–45, on the 1852 Free Soil platform.

58. *Milwaukee Daily Free Democrat,* Nov. 3, 1852; George Hyer to Elisha Keyes, Nov. 21, 1852, Keyes Papers.

59. *Milwaukee Daily Free Democrat,* Nov. 27, 1852.

60. Ibid., Jan. 29, 1853.

61. *Washington County Blade,* Mar. ?, 1853, in Theodore Clark Smith, "Free Soil Party in Wisconsin," 139; *Wisconsin State Journal,* May 30, 1853; *Milwaukee Sentinel,* June 1, 1853.

62. *Oshkosh Democrat,* June 6, 1853; see also Dec. 26, 1851.

63. *Wisconsin Free Democrat,* May 11, 19, 26, 1853.

64. *Kenosha Telegraph,* Apr. 8, 22, 1853.

65. *Wisconsin Free Democrat,* Apr. 9, 1853; *Milwaukee Sentinel,* June 1, 1853; *Wisconsin State Journal,* May 30, 1853; *Kenosha Telegraph,* Apr. 8, 1853; *Racine Advocate,* Apr. 20, 1853.

66. *Wisconsin Free Democrat,* May 25, Oct. 26, 1853.

67. *Wisconsin State Journal,* June 7, 8, 1853; *Milwaukee Sentinel,* June 9, 10, 1853; *Wisconsin Free Democrat,* June 9, 10, 1853; *Argus and Democrat,* June 8, 1853; Theodore Clark Smith, "Free Soil Party in the Northwest," 278–84. Farwell had a letter of absolute declination read to the delegates.

68. *Wisconsin Free Democrat,* June 9, 10, 1853; *Janesville Gazette,* Oct. 23, 1853.

69. Greeley's comment is found in Richard W. Hantke, "The Life of Elisha William Keyes," 47; Farwell's thoughts were published in the *National Era,* July 7, 1853, quoted in Theodore Clark Smith, *Liberty and Free Soil Parties in the Northwest,* 280. Also see the *Milwaukee Sentinel,* June 21, July 7, 8, 9, Aug. 6, 15, 24, 1853, and the *Wisconsin State Journal,* Aug. 2, 11, 1853.

70. *Janesville Gazette,* June 18, 25, July 9, Aug. 6, 1853.

71. *Watertown Weekly Register,* Oct. 8, 15, 22, 29, 1853, for Barstow's alleged offenses. Also see Legler, "Josiah Noonan: A Story of Promotion and Excoriation in the Old Northwest," 186–96; Beitzinger, *Edward G. Ryan: Lion of the Law,* 27–42; Current, *History of Wisconsin,* 215.

72. *Wisconsin State Journal,* Sept. 9, 10, 1853; *Argus and Democrat,* Sept. 10, 1853; Legler, "Josiah Noonan," 195–96.

73. Noonan to Fairchild, Sept. 27, 1853, Stephen Carpenter to Fairchild, Oct. 10, 1853, Fairchild Papers; Carpenter to Horace Tenney, Oct. 13, 1853, Tenney Papers; J. R. Sharpstein to George Paul, Nov. 3, 1853, Paul Papers; *Milwaukee Sentinel,* Oct. 12, 14, 1853.

74. *Milwaukee Sentinel*, Oct. 12, 1853.

75. *Wisconsin State Journal*, Sept. 15, 1853; *Milwaukee Sentinel*, Sept. 17, 18, 19, 1853; *Mineral Point Tribune*, Sept. 12, 1853.

76. *Waukesha Independent Press*, Nov. 2, 1853; *Wisconsin Free Democrat*, Oct. 29, 1853.

77. George B. Smith to William Barstow, Sept. 15, 1853, Smith Papers. Baird stayed in the race, although it is not known if Barstow directly attempted to influence him.

78. Josiah Noonan to J. C. Fairchild, Sept. 27, 1853, Fairchild Papers; J. R. Doolittle to George Paul, Sept. 15, 1853, Paul Papers; *Janesville Gazette*, Oct. 15, 1853; *Weekly Wisconsin*, Oct. 14, 19, 26, 1853; *Wisconsin Free Democrat*, Sept. 26, 1853.

79. *Milwaukee Sentinel*, Sept. 28, 1853.

80. *Daily Wisconsin*, Oct. 8, 1853; *Kenosha Democrat*, Oct. 14, 1853; *Wisconsin Free Democrat*, Oct. 12, 1853.

81. *Argus and Democrat*, Oct. 10, 1853; *Daily Wisconsin*, Oct. 11, 1853; *Milwaukee Sentinel*, Oct. 8, 1853; *Janesville Gazette*, Oct. 15, 1853; *Watertown Chronicle*, Oct. 12, 19, 1853; *Wisconsin Free Democrat*, Oct. 8, 12, 1853. Democrats packed the evening meeting as well and easily were able to block coalition efforts.

82. The Democratic supporter was the *Watertown Register;* the one remaining loyal Whig paper was the *Janesville Gazette.* For Holton's western support see the *Mineral Point Tribune*, Nov. 3, 10, 17, 1853, and the *Grant County Herald*, Nov. 2, 9, 1853; Theodore Clark Smith, "Free Soil Party in Wisconsin," 138–49.

83. *Milwaukee Sentinel*, Oct. 24, 1853; *Fond du Lac Herald*, Oct. 21, 1853.

84. *Milwaukee Sentinel*, Nov. 5, 1853; Winkle, "Voters, Issues, and Parties," 64–87; Theodore Clark Smith, "Free Soil Party in Wisconsin," 145–46.

85. See the *Milwaukee Sentinel*, Nov. 5, 1853, for King's belief that there was little interest in the election.

86. Recent political histories of this period emphasize the absolute importance of local issues and ethnicity in helping form party loyalties and shape the changes that occurred. Using turnout in Wisconsin as a variable, it is clear that turnout stagnated and sometimes dropped between 1848 and 1855 and did not pick up again until 1856. The highest turnout for state or local elections during the decade occurred after 1856, and those elections, which will be discussed later, had definite reference to national issues, especially slavery. William E. Gienapp, in *The Origins of the Republican Party, 1852–1856*, emphasizes the importance of the ethnocultural issues, although not to the exclusion of national concerns. Yet Gienapp's statistics suggest that the slumping turnout was not uncommon in the North, especially on those supposedly all-important local questions.

87. *Kenosha Telegraph*, Nov. 25, 1853; *Janesville Gazette*, Oct. 15, 1853. The *Wisconsin State Journal*, Nov. 29, 1853, contains Atwood's remarks.

SIX *We Must Unite or Be Enslaved*

1. Potter, *Impending Crisis*, 145–76.

2. Cheever, Diary, Mar. 11, 1854, Cheever Papers.

3. *Grant County Herald*, Feb. 27, 1854.

4. U.S. Congress, House of Representatives Papers, 1800–1860, 33d Congress, Petitions, contains many petitions from the state. Also see the *Milwaukee Sentinel*, Feb. 28, Mar. 4, 1854. One of these meetings took place in Ripon, the supposed birthplace of the Republican party. It is true that the Ripon gathering did call for a new "Northern party" to work

for repeal of the Kansas-Nebraska Act, if it passed, but so did other anti-Nebraska meetings held throughout the North; while the meeting's organizer, Alvin Bovay, who later claimed to have proposed the name Republican for the new party and to have been its founder, was in New York on July 13 when the Madison meeting, which did give birth to Wisconsin's Republican party, was held. If any one person deserves to be known as the founder of the Republican party, at least in Wisconsin, it is Sherman Booth, who organized the first anti-Nebraska meeting held in the state, in Milwaukee on February 13, but who also worked patiently to forge the antislavery coalition that emerged out of the July meeting. For background on the Ripon meeting, see A. M. Thompson, *Political History of Wisconsin*, 110–11; Current, *History of Wisconsin*, 218–19; for Booth's role in the Milwaukee meeting, see the *Milwaukee Daily Free Democrat*, Feb. 4, 6, 8, 9, 10, 11, 1854, and George C. Brown, "The Genesis of the Wisconsin Republican Party, 1854."

5. *Milwaukee Daily Free Democrat*, Jan. 30, 1854.

6. *Kenosha Democrat*, Feb. 3, 10, 1854; *Green Bay Advocate*, Mar. 2, 1854; *Ozaukee Times*, Feb. 11, 1854; *Milwaukee News*, most issues in February 1854 have comments bearing on the matter. The *News* was Noonan's organ. Also see Richard L. Hanneman, "The First Republican Campaign in Wisconsin, 1854" (master's thesis, University of Wisconsin, 1966), 21–54.

7. *Monroe Sentinel*, May 31, 1854, and *Walworth County Reporter*, June 14, 1854, are examples of Democratic papers that refused to be silenced. The *Watertown Chronicle*, May 31, June 7, 1854, is an anti-Nebraska Democratic paper that stood by the party, supposedly to reform it from within. Also see Beriah Brown's *Argus and Democrat*, Feb. 20, 25, 1854. Brown was a supporter of Governor Barstow, Noonan's chief rival for power and patronage within the state organization. Barstow, who had failed to oust Noonan as the Administration favorite, nonetheless used his considerable influence with Democratic legislators to crush an anti-Nebraska resolution; see, *Assembly Journal, 1854*, 159, 194, 231, 286–88, 368–72, *Senate Journal, 1854*, 303, 372, 377–79.

8. *Milwaukee Sentinel*, Jan. 31, Feb. 6, 14, Mar. 6, 1854; *Beloit Journal*, May 4, 1854; *Wisconsin State Journal*, Mar. 8, 1854; Alexander Mitchell to King, Mar. 8, 1854, Josiah Noonan Papers; Hanneman, "The First Republican Campaign," 46–48.

9. *The Jeffersonian*, in the *Milwaukee Sentinel*, June 12, 1854; Hanneman, "The First Republican Campaign," 32–38.

10. Stone, *Racine and Racine County*, 429–36; John B. Winslow, *The Story of a Great Court*, 67–95; Michael J. McManus, "'Freedom and Liberty First, and the Union Afterwards': State Rights and the Wisconsin Republican Party, 1854–1861," 29–56, recounts the Glover episode and its effect on Wisconsin's Republican party.

11. The *Argus and Democrat*, Sept. 15, 1860, provides a level-headed retrospective of the event; the *Evening Wisconsin*, Mar. 12, 1897, printed a Milwaukee speech the senior Booth gave commemorating the event. See also A. M. Thompson, *A Political History of Wisconsin*, 96–108.

12. *Milwaukee Sentinel*, Mar. 13, 1854; Gregory, *History of Milwaukee, Wisconsin*, 746.

13. *Milwaukee Daily Free Democrat*, Mar. 13, 1854; *Milwaukee Sentinel*, Mar. 13, 15, 17, 1854.

14. *Milwaukee Sentinel*, Mar. 13, 22, 23, 24, 1854; Gregory, *History of Milwaukee, Wisconsin;* Joseph Schafer, "Stormy Days in Court: The Booth Case."

15. The *Milwaukee Sentinel*, Mar. 14, 16, 18, 1854, carried extended treatments of the threats to freedom and states' rights raised by the issue.

16. *Milwaukee Sentinel,* Apr. 10, 14, 1854. Booth had called the meeting, which was attended by more than three hundred delegates.

17. *Kenosha Democrat,* Mar. 31, 1854.

18. *Janesville Gazette,* Mar. 18, 1854; *Watertown Weekly Register,* Mar. 25, 1854; *Milwaukee Sentinel,* Mar. 18, 20, 1854.

19. *Milwaukee Daily Free Democrat,* Apr. 17, 28, 29, May 2, 1854; *Grant County Herald,* Apr. 24, 1854; *Wisconsin State Journal,* Apr. 26, 1854.

20. *Grant County Herald,* May 22, 1854; *Wisconsin Daily Free Democrat,* May 5, 1854; *Wisconsin State Journal,* May 8, 11, 12, 1854; *Beloit Journal,* May 12, 1854.

21. *Wisconsin State Journal,* May 18, 1854; also see May 19, 24.

22. *Milwaukee Daily Free Democrat,* May 26, 27, 1854; *Wisconsin State Journal,* May 26, 1854; *Milwaukee Sentinel,* May 30, 1854. King had stayed out of the debate until now, probably not wishing to alienate party conservatives by once again encouraging a coalition.

23. Ibid., June 7, 1854.

24. *Milwaukee Daily Free Democrat,* June 9, 1854; *Kenosha Telegraph,* June 2, 1854; *Watertown Weekly Register,* June 3, 1854; *Monroe Sentinel,* May 31, 1854; *Burr Oak,* June 5, 1854.

25. *Milwaukee Sentinel,* June 10, 1854; *Wisconsin State Journal,* June 12, 1854.

26. *Mineral Point Tribune,* June 22, July 6, 1854; *Grant County Herald,* June 26, 1854; Joseph Cover to Horace Tenney, Dec. 4, 1854, Tenney Papers, gives a retrospective view of western Wisconsin's opposition to the convention.

27. *Wisconsin State Journal,* May 3, 1854; *Daily Argus,* June 15, 21, 28, 1854; *Wisconsin Patriot,* June 8, 22, 1854. The *Patriot* was the paper set up by Noonan and Tenney. See S. D. Carpenter to Horace Tenney, Oct. 13, 1854, Levi Hubbell to Tenney, Mar. 17, 1854, H. Robbins to J. T. Marston, Apr. 18, 1854, Jerome Brigham to Tenney, Aug. 24, 1853, all in the Horace Tenney Papers for some of the details surrounding the establishment of the paper.

28. *Milwaukee Daily Free Democrat,* June 12, 19, 1854; *Wisconsin State Journal,* June 24, 1854.

29. *Argus and Democrat,* July 13, 1854; *Milwaukee Daily Free Democrat,* July 14, 1854.

30. This estimate from the diary of Willet S. Main, Dane County's Democratic sheriff, on July 13, 1854, is probably as unbiased a projection as we have.

31. The *Daily Argus,* July 14, 1854, gives a good, if somewhat biased, account of the meeting. Also see Brown, "The Genesis of the Wisconsin Republican Party, 1854," for an analysis of the delegates in attendance, esp. ch. 3.

32. *Daily Argus,* July 14, 1854; *Wisconsin State Journal,* July 14, 1854; *Milwaukee Daily Free Democrat,* July 14, 1854; *Milwaukee Sentinel,* July 15, 1854. Sewell, *Ballots for Freedom,* 164, Current, *History of Wisconsin,* 218–19.

33. *Wisconsin State Journal,* July 14, 1854. Blue, *The Free Soilers,* 293–301, contains the 1848 and 1852 Free Soil platforms, for comparison's sake. The founding fathers' quotation is from the 1848 platform.

34. Walworth county Whigs had a history of opposing fusion that dated back to at least 1851. See for example, the *Milwaukee Sentinel,* Sept. 29, 1851, and Oct. 30, 1854. The county was expected to be overwhelmingly Republican in any event. Also see Kenneth Winkle, "Voters, Issues and Parties," 48–80. Brown, "The Genesis of the Republican Party," ch. 3, discusses in detail the organizational continuity and leadership transition. Michael M. Frank, Diary, Sept. 2, 1854, Frank Papers, gives a brief discussion of the effort to organize in his county; *Mineral Point Tribune,* July 22, 1854; *Grant County Herald,* July 31, Aug. 21, 1854,

and Jan. 27, 1898, for an aged Cover's retrospective view of the birth of the party in the southwestern part of the state; *Milwaukee Daily Free Democrat*, Nov. 8, 1854.

35. *Milwaukee Sentinel*, Sept. 7, 8, 11, 1854; *Kenosha Telegraph*, Sept. 7, 1854; *Milwaukee Daily Free Democrat*, Sept. 7, 1854; *Wisconsin State Journal*, Sept. 8, 1854.

36. *Wisconsin State Journal*, Sept. 19, 21, 1854; *Potosi Republican*, Sept. 16, 1854; *Janesville Gazette*, Sept. 29, 1854; *Mineral Point Tribune*, Sept. 20, 1854.

37. *Milwaukee Sentinel*, Sept. 26, 1854; *Argus and Democrat*, Sept. 30, 1854.

38. Daniel Wells to George Paul, May 5 and May 11, 1854, Paul Papers; Gerald W. Wolff, *The Kansas-Nebraska Bill: Party, Section, and the Coming of the Civil War*, 64–69, 267–68, for a good summary of the problems confronting Democrats like Wells.

39. Wells to Paul, Sept. 23, Oct. 17, 19, 27, 1854; Noonan to Paul, Sept. 24, 1854; J. R. Sharpstein to Paul, Aug. 7, Sept. 13, 1854; Daniel Shaw to Paul, Sept. 10, 1854, all in the George Paul Papers; *Milwaukee Daily Free Democrat*, Oct. 5, Nov. 1, 1854; *Milwaukee Sentinel*, Oct. 23, Nov. 1, 1854.

40. *Waukesha Plain Dealer*, Sept. 20, Oct. 4, 11, 24, 1854; Marvin Bovee to Paul, Sept. 18, 1854, Paul Papers.

41. Ben Eastman to Cyrus Woodman, Mar. 21, 1854, and Cyrus Woodman to Henry Hubbard, Sept. 23, 1854, in the Cyrus Woodman Papers; C. C. Remington to Moses M. Strong, Aug. 11, 1854, Sam Crawford to Strong, Aug. 5, 1854, Strong Papers.

42. *Mineral Point Tribune*, Sept. 13, 20, 1854; *Grant County Herald*, Sept. 25, 1854; *Wisconsin State Journal*, Sept. 8, 1854; *Daily Argus and Democrat*, Sept. 13, 1854; *Potosi Republican*, Sept. 9, 1854; *Janesville Gazette*, Sept. 16, 23, 1854.

43. David Noggle to Horace Tenney, Sept. 8, 1854, Tenney Papers; *Potosi Republican*, Sept. 30, 1854; *Janesville Standard*, Sept. 13, 1854; *Daily Argus and Democrat*, Oct. 2, Nov. 14, 1854.

44. *Grant County Herald*, Aug. 4, 1854

45. Barstow's *Janesville Standard*, Sept. 13, 1854, for example, predicted that Hoyt would lose by a significant margin.

46. *Green Bay Advocate*, Oct. 5, 1854; *Milwaukee Sentinel*, Oct. 2, 5, 1854; undated letter from William Barstow to Morgan L. Martin, in the *Green Bay and Prairie du Chien Papers*, vol. 96, details Barstow's efforts on Macy's behalf.

47. *Green Bay Advocate*, Oct. 12, 19, 26, 1854; *Milwaukee Sentinel*, Oct. 13, 23, 1854; Hanneman, "First Republican Campaign," 128–29, 138; Flately, "The Wisconsin Congressional Delegation from Statehood to Secession, 1848–1861," 64–65.

48. Billinghurst received 13,663 votes to 8,683 for Macy and an even 2,000 for H. G. Turner, the administration candidate.

49. Flately, "Wisconsin Congressional Delegation," 68–70. Durkee's election will be discussed in greater detail in ch. 9.

50. William E. Gienapp, *Origins of the Republican Party, 1852–1856*, 475–551, suggests that in several other northern states at certain times, large numbers of prior nonvoters turned out to cast ballots.

51. Joel Silbey, "'There Are Other Questions Beside That Of Slavery Merely': The Democratic Party and Antislavery Politics," 143–75, esp. 144–52. I arrived at this estimate by adding the 15 percent to the 7 percent already mentioned.

52. Comparing the raw returns in 1853 with 1854 suggests that the largest portion of Democratic defectors came from the northern district, while most of the new voters came from the western counties.

53. The *Milwaukee News*, in the *Milwaukee Sentinel*, June 5, 1854.

54. *Potosi Republican*, July 15, 22, 1854; *Milwaukee Sentinel*, July 20, 1854, for examples of this attitude.

55. Main, Diary, Oct. 31, Nov. 7, 1854, Main Papers. Also see Michael F. Holt, *The Political Crisis of the 1850s*, 17–39, 101–38 for an excellent analysis of the increasing irrelevance of the old issues and the growing voter dissatisfaction with politicians.

56. Main, Diary, Dec. 31, 1854, Main Papers. Also see Jairus Fairchild to Lucius Fairchild, Feb. 7, 1855, Fairchild Papers.

57. C.C. Washburne to Cyrus Woodman, Oct. 23, 1857, Woodman Papers.

SEVEN *This Thing Called Know Nothingism*

1. Annual Report of the Secretary of State of the State of Wisconsin for the Year 1855, *Wisconsin Governor's Messages and Accompanying Documents, 1855*, contains the 1855 State census returns. Also see Current, *History of Wisconsin*, 76–82.

2. Ray Allen Billington, *The Protestant Crusade, 1800–1860: A Study of the Origins of American Nativism*, 238–61; Tyler Anbinder, *Nativism and Slavery: The Northern Know Nothings and the Politics of the 1850s*, 2–19; Potter, *Impending Crisis, 1848–1861*, 241–42.

3. Billington, *The Protestant Crusade*, 1–230.

4. Ibid., 263–322; Current, *History of Wisconsin*, 140–45; *Milwaukee Daily American*, Oct. 3, 19, 1855.

5. Gienapp, *Origins of the Republican Party*, 20–31; Holt, *Political Crisis of the 1850s*, 122–31.

6. Billington, *The Protestant Crusade*, 292–95; Gienapp, *Origins of the Republican Party*, 60–65.

7. *Milwaukee Sentinel*, Jan. 14, 1854, for an example of local coverage of Bedini's journey. Billington, *Protestant Crusade*, 300–304; Anbinder, *Nativism and Slavery*, 27–31.

8. Gienapp, *Origins of the Republican Party*, 44–47.

9. Billington, *Protestant Crusade*, 322–38; Holt, *Political Crisis of the 1850s*, 159–65; Anbinder, *Nativism and Slavery*, 32–40; Potter, *Impending Crisis*, 241–46.

10. Billington, *Protestant Crusade*, 380–436; Holt, *Political Crisis of the 1850s*, 162–75, 198–99 and "The Politics of Impatience: The Origins of Know Nothingism," 309–31; Gienapp, *Origins of the Republican Party*, 87–102; Anbinder, *Nativism and Slavery*, 103–26.

11. *Milwaukee Daily American*, Sept. 27, Oct. 3, 27, 29, 1855; Holt, *Political Crisis of the 1850s*, 162–69 and "Politics of Impatience," 311–20. Gienapp, in *The Origins of the Republican Party*, 37–67, traces the "decomposition" of the second party system and the Whigs in the North, and he rightly credits the role ethnocultural issues played in this process. Indeed, Gienapp argues that those issues "more than any other factor . . . destroyed the second party system." Yet, in spite of the monumental research he brings to bear, he remains unconvincing. Without question, ethnocultural conflict did help bring down the Jacksonian system, but the parties had been in a state of decomposition since at least 1849, and the Whigs, especially in Wisconsin, were near death well before 1854. The Whig party disappeared on the heels of the breakdown in sectional harmony between its northern and southern wings and its resulting irrelevance as a national organization. Party loyalty seemed pointless without a national bond and purpose. The Whig inability to capitalize on the outstanding state and local issues of the early 1850s emphasizes the profound alienation many Americans felt with the political system and their desire to vent their frustrations with its unresponsiveness. The Know Nothing party filled this void temporarily, but as Eric Foner, convincingly I think,

points out, a distinction between nativism as a "cultural impulse" and as "a force in politics" must be made. Many Republicans found at least a part of the nativist message appealing, but it is not likely that the weighty decision to join and remain with the new party, with the ominous significance it had for national unity, resulted from hatred of foreigners and Catholics. Also see Anbinder, *Nativism and Slavery*, 52–102; Stephen E. Maizlish, *The Triumph of Sectionalism: The Transformation of Ohio Politics, 1844–1856*.

12. Current, *History of Wisconsin*, 117–96; Conzen, *Immigrant Milwaukee*; Schafer, *Four Wisconsin Counties*, esp. 171–93; also see Schafer's, "Yankee and the Teuton in Wisconsin" and "Know Nothingism in Wisconsin."

13. Joseph Schafer, "Prohibition in Early Wisconsin," recounts early attempts to curb the liquor trade in Wisconsin; Frank L. Byrne, "Maine Law Versus Lager Beer: A Dilemma of Wisconsin's Young Republican Party," 115–20; Current, *History of Wisconsin*, 142–43.

14. Winkle, "Voters, Issues and Parties, 48–64.

15. Schafer, "Prohibition in Early Wisconsin," 297–99.

16. Gienapp, *Origins of the Republican Party*, 103–66, for fusion efforts in the 1854 elections. Myron Clark, the victorious New York Whig, was himself a Know Nothing. Also see Anbinder, *Nativism and Slavery*, 94–102, for the importance of the slavery issue to many Northerners who were attracted to the Know Nothings.

17. William H. Seward, the favorite among Wisconsin's Whigs, had a long history of opposition to nativism. Rufus King, for example, had worked on Seward's New York paper, the *Albany Journal*, before moving to Wisconsin. See Foner, *Free Soil, Free Labor, Free Men*, 234–36.

18. Schafer, "Know Nothingism in Wisconsin," 7–12; Sewell, *Ballots For Freedom*, 272; Foner, *Free Soil, Free Labor, Free Men*, 246; Current, *History of Wisconsin*, 117–96. The foreign-born in Wisconsin represented at least one-third of the potential electorate. The rupture of the Know Nothing party over slavery in June, 1855, also effectively doomed any attempt to set up a separate organization in the state.

19. Atwood was coeditor of the *Wisconsin State Journal*.

20. It should be noted that few public figures escaped the Know Nothing charge in the heated political atmosphere of 1855.

21. *Daily Wisconsin Free Democrat*, June 10, 1854, has a discussion of Know Nothingism by Booth wherein he suggests that the organization was more an outlet for men to demonstrate their Americanism than to express opposition to the foreign-born. Foreigners, it should be added, formed their own organizations, such as the Irish, who put together a militia company in the Milwaukee area, as did native-born citizens. Also see the *Milwaukee Sentinel*, May 29, 1854; James S. Buck, *Pioneer History of Milwaukee* 4:30–31; Charles King, "The Wisconsin National Guard," 346–48. If one defines hard-core Know Nothing membership as the difference between the vote received by the Republican gubernatorial and state treasurer candidates, native and foreign-born men respectively, in the 1855 state elections, we come up with a number of about thirty-three hundred, a small number given the time and space devoted to them.

22. *Milwaukee Daily American*, Oct. 4, 1855; Billington, *The Protestant Crusade*, 380–97; Gienapp, *Origins of the Republican Party*, 92–100. See note 21 for a definition of "hard-core" Know Nothingism.

23. *Wisconsin Daily Free Democrat*, June 10, 13, 1854; *Milwaukee Sentinel*, Oct. 19, 1854; *Racine Advocate*, Oct. 23, 1854; *Kenosha Telegraph*, Nov. 2, 1854; Gienapp, *Origins of the Republican Party*, 106. In some locales, the Know Nothing issue apparently did burn bright. In the town of Bristol, where residents were overwhelmingly from the northeast, the diarist

Michael Frank wrote, "All political issues entirely lost sight of. The only issue Know Nothing and anti-Know Nothing." Frank, Diary, Nov. 7, 1854, Frank Papers. Bristol's demographic characteristic are contained in Winkle, "Voters, Issues and Parties," 104.

24. Byrne, "Maine Law Versus Lager Beer," 117–20; Schafer, "Prohibition in Early Wisconsin," 296–99; Gienapp, *Origins of the Republican Party*, 206–7.

25. *Wisconsin Daily Free Democrat*, June 13, 1855. The Know Nothings were also rumored to be trying to work their way into the Democratic organization, but the threat was perceived, rightly, as far greater to the Republicans.

26. Ibid., June 29, July 2, 10, 1855.

27. Ibid., June 13, 1855. The September 3, 1855 edition contains a copy of Lockwood's circular. Also see the Aug. 21, 1855, *Wisconsin State Journal* and *Milwaukee Sentinel*, for further discussion of the Lockwood circular and the designs of the Know Nothings.

28. *Wisconsin Daily Free Democrat*, Aug. 25, 31, 1855; *Milwaukee Sentinel*, Aug. 25, 1855; *Weekly Argus and Democrat*, Sept. 4, 1855; Samuel Bean to Elisha Keyes, Aug. 27, 1855, Keyes Papers. Keyes had been a Know Nothing delegate from Wisconsin to the party's recent national convention in Philadelphia.

29. *Wisconsin Daily Free Democrat*, July 24, 1855.

30. *Chicago Tribune*, in the *Baraboo Republic*, Aug. 4, 1855; D. C. Roundy to Samuel Hastings, July 5, 1855, Samuel D. Hastings Papers, and the *Weekly Argus and Democrat*, Aug. 22, 1855.

31. *Elkhorn Independent*, in the *Daily Argus and Democrat*, Aug. 28, 1855.

32. *Wisconsin State Journal*, July 27, 1855; *Janesville Gazette*, July 28, Aug. 4, 1855; *Mineral Point Tribune*, Aug. 1, 1855. Willet S. Main, Diary entry, July 25, 1855, Willet S. Main Papers, states that Booth's nomination would also run afoul of "the *[Milwaukee] Sentinel* influence," which opposed him.

33. *Grant County Herald*, Aug. 18, 1855.

34. *Milwaukee Daily American*, Sept. 27, Oct. 27, 1855. The *American*, established in July, claimed that the Know Nothings had hundreds of fully operational lodges in Wisconsin and at least twenty thousand members. Also see the *Baraboo Republic*, June 23, 1855; *Wisconsin Daily Free Democrat*, Sept. 3, 1855.

35. Fourth of July Oration, delivered at Dover, Iowa County, Wisconsin, July 4, 1855, by Dr. William H. Brisbane, William Henry Brisbane Papers; *Milwaukee Sentinel*, Aug. 13, 15, 1855; *Wisconsin State Journal*, Aug. 21, 1855; *Baraboo Republic*, June 23, 1855.

36. *Wisconsin Daily Free Democrat*, Sept. 3, 1855.

37. Ibid., Aug. 31, 1855.

38. Ibid., Aug. 31, Sept. 6. Also see Dec. 1, 1855, where Booth recounts the order's effort to elect its members as delegates to the Republican convention and warns that if the party "is owned by the Know Nothings . . . they can take it and run it. We will be neither leader, wheel, horse, or passenger."

39. Ibid., Sept. 6, 1855.

40. Ibid., Aug. 31, Sept. 3, 1855; *Weekly Argus and Democrat*, Sept. 11, 1885; Elisha Keyes, *History of Dane County* (Madison, 1906), 216. Keyes, himself a Know Nothing delegate to the state convention, later wrote, "The convention was largely controlled by a secret political organization, known as the Know Nothings, although masquerading under the name of Republican in the convention." At the convention, Coles Bashford, the Republican nominee for governor, claimed only 70 of the 214 delegates were Know Nothings; see the *Daily Wisconsin Free Democrat*, Sept. 6, 1855.

41. *Wisconsin Daily Free Democrat*, Sept. 6, 7, 1855; *Milwaukee Sentinel*, Sept. 7, 1855.

42. *Monroe Sentinel*, Sept. 12, 1855; *Wisconsin Daily Free Democrat*, Sept. 6, 1855.

43. *Wisconsin Daily Free Democrat*, Sept. 6, 1855. Coles Bashford to Samuel Hastings, Oct. 22, 1855, Hastings Papers. In this letter Bashford declared, *"I am not a member of the Order of Know Nothings and Never have been!!"*

44. See ibid., Sept. 7, 1855, for the candidates and Keyes, *History of Dane County*, 216, for the retrospective.

45. *Milwaukee Sentinel*, Sept. 10, 1855.

46. *Monroe Sentinel*, Sept. 12, 1855; *Wisconsin Daily Free Democrat*, Sept. 7, 11, 1855; *Weekly Argus and Democrat*, Feb. 26, 1856; ? (probably John Lockwood) to Elisha Keyes, Jan. 28, 1856, Keyes Papers. The Know Nothings were Elisha Keyes, S. S. Daggett, H. D. Holt, and D. E. Wood. David Atwood, one of the *Wisconsin State Journal*'s editors was also reputedly a lodge member, something the paper's editorials would seem to belie, as was William C. Rogers. The Americans were offset by antislavery radicals John Fox Potter, William A. White, and Lysander Frisby.

47. *Mineral Point Tribune*, Sept. 11, 1855. Also see the *Milwaukee Sentinel*, Sept. 8, 10, 1855; *Daily Wisconsin Free Democrat*, Sept. 7, 1855; Main, Diary, Sept. 5, 6, 1855, Main Papers.

48. Unlike the Republican antiproscription resolution, cited above.

49. *Milwaukee Sentinel*, Sept. 4, 5, 1855.

50. Schafer, "Know Nothingism in Wisconsin," 15–17.

51. *Wisconsin Daily Free Democrat*, Sept. 21, 1855.

52. R. C. Chandler to Elisha Keyes, Sept. 24, 1855; Keyes to John Lockwood, Sept. 12, 1855; John Lockwood to Keyes, Oct. 30, 1855, all in the Keyes Papers; *Milwaukee Daily American*, Nov. 10, 1855.

53. Current, *History of Wisconsin*, 227–30, gives a good, brief account of the election controversy. Turnout in 1855 climbed to 52 percent from the prior year's 48 percent. A good deal of the increase came from the state's foreign-born, who rallied to the antiprohibitionist governor's support and against Know Nothingism.

54. Charles Roeser, the German-born Republican running for state treasurer, ran furthest of all the party's candidates behind Bashford, but even with him, only 9 percent of the total number of Republican voters felt strongly enough in their nativist sentiments to scratch his name from the ballot. That hardly suggests that Know Nothing principles deeply affected large numbers of men or significantly influenced their political actions.

55. In the five counties with populations 50 percent or more foreign-born, Bashford ran 642 votes behind 1854's total. In all counties containing at least one-third foreigners, he trailed by 558 votes. The other Republican candidates did worse.

56. From 32,614 in 1854 to 36,074 in 1855, an increase of 3,460.

57. *Milwaukee Sentinel*, Apr. 4, 22, 1856. With the exception of Dane, those seven counties had a foreign-born population that constituted less than one-third of the whole. Dane's foreign born made up 37 percent of the population.

58. The statistical analysis suggests that over 50 percent of the 1854 Democratic loyalists stayed home on election day in 1855.

59. Democratic candidates in 1854 received 27,157 votes, Barstow 35,750, an increase of 8,593. A majority of the residents of Manitowoc, Milwaukee, Ozaukee, Sheboygan, and Washington counties were foreign-born. Those five counties gave Barstow 3,526 more votes than they gave to the 1854 Democrats and represented 41 percent of the increase in 1855.

60. Overall, the Democrats seem to have suffered greater upheavals than the Republicans as a result of the corruption, Know Nothing, and prohibition issues. The Republican coalition in 1855 was shaken but remained largely intact.

61. On the eve of the election, King published, in the *Milwaukee Sentinel,* a letter from the candidate in which he denied being a member of the Order. Schafer, "Know Nothingism in Wisconsin," 19.

62. Know Nothings claimed to have polled more than twenty thousand votes for Bashford; that total was surely exaggerated. The bulk of the Republican support came from men who had supported the party in 1854, when slavery was the dominant issue. See note 21 for my estimate and analysis and compare to the *Milwaukee Daily American,* Nov. 10, 1855, for the twenty-thousand-vote claim.

63. *Wisconsin State Journal,* Nov. 21, 23, 27, 28, 1855; *Milwaukee Sentinel,* Nov. 14, 15, 17, 21, 1855; *Janesville Gazette,* Nov. 15, 1855; *Grant County Herald,* Nov. 14, 1855; *Kenosha Telegraph,* Nov. 21, 1855; *Wisconsin Daily Free Democrat,* Nov. 14, 15, 16, 21, 26, 1855; P. Gilder to Samuel Hastings, Nov. 27, 1855, Hastings Papers.

64. *Milwaukee Sentinel,* Dec. 5, 1855; *Wisconsin State Journal,* Nov. 28, Dec. 4, 10, 1855; *Daily Wisconsin Free Democrat,* Nov. 15, 21, Dec. 3, 4, 1855; *Milwaukee Daily American,* Nov. 7, 1855, Feb. 2, 1856; John Lockwood to Elisha Keyes, Oct. 30, 1855, Keyes Papers.

65. William A. White to Elisha Keyes, Jan. 24, 1856, Keyes Papers; *Wisconsin State Journal,* Jan. 25, 1856.

66. ? (probably John Lockwood) posted from Milwaukee to Elisha Keyes, Jan. 28, 1856, Keyes Papers.

67. *Milwaukee Sentinel,* Feb. 11, 12, 13, 1856; *Wisconsin State Journal,* Feb. 9, 1856; *Kenosha Tribune,* Jan. 31, 1856.

68. *Wisconsin State Journal,* Dec. 27, 1855, Jan. 7, 16, 1856; *Daily Wisconsin Free Democrat,* Jan. 18, 1856. Booth's battle with the *State Journal* was particularly embittered, although other "old line" Whigs joined in "from time to time."

69. *Daily Wisconsin Free Democrat,* Feb. 8, 11, 13, 1856.

70. *Milwaukee Sentinel,* Apr. 4, 16, 22, 1856.

71. *Daily Wisconsin Free Democrat,* Apr. 15, 18, 1856.

72. Sherman Booth to John Fox Potter, Apr. 19, 1856, John Fox Potter Papers.

73. *Kenosha Tribune and Telegraph,* Apr. 24, May 1, 3, 8, 1856; *Janesville Gazette,* Apr. 19, 26, 1856; *Milwaukee Sentinel,* Apr. 16, 25, 1856; *Wisconsin State Journal,* Apr. 17, 23, 1856; Moses M. Davis to John Fox Potter, Apr. 24, 1856, John Fox Potter Papers.

74. *Daily Wisconsin Free Democrat,* May 4, 1856; *Wisconsin State Journal,* May 5, 6, 1856.

75. Moses M. Davis to John Fox Potter, Apr. 24, 1854, Potter Papers; also see Main, Diary, May 24, 1856, Main Papers.

EIGHT *Freedom and Liberty First, and the Union Afterwards*

1. Gienapp, *Origins of the Republican Party,* 297–99; Potter, *Impending Crisis,* 207–9; Nevins, *Ordeal of the Union* 2:434–37; James A. Rawley, *Race and Politics: "Bleeding Kansas" and the Coming of the Civil War,* 129–34.

2. Potter, *Impending Crisis,* 217–24; Gienapp, *Origins of the Republican Party,* 298–99.

3. *Wisconsin State Journal,* May 27, 29, 1856; *Milwaukee Sentinel,* May 24, 30, 31, 1856; *Monroe Sentinel,* May 24, 28, 1856. These papers provide representative Republican responses to the sack of Lawrence.

4. Michael Fellman, "Rehearsal for the Civil War: Antislavery and Proslavery at the Fighting Point in Kansas, 1854–1856," 287–307; Potter, *Impending Crisis,* 199–201. Kansas

settlers, employing the doctrine of popular sovereignty, as mandated by the Kansas-Nebraska Act, would decide if slavery would be permitted.

5. *Milwaukee Sentinel,* June 17, 19, 1854, published reports on the Kansas situation and the threats from Missourians; also see Nevins, *Ordeal of the Union* 2:300–306.

6. *Milwaukee Sentinel,* Dec. 23, 1854; also see Dec. 7, 8, 9, 29; *Monroe Sentinel,* Dec. 20, 1854; Nevins, *Ordeal of the Union* 2:312–14; Rawley, *Race and Politics,* 87–92.

7. *Wisconsin State Journal,* May 10, 12, 1855; *Milwaukee Sentinel,* July 24, 1855; *Monroe Sentinel,* Aug. 29, 1855; Gienapp, *Origins of the Republican Party,* 169–71.

8. Potter, *Impending Crisis,* 203–8; Rawley, *Race and Politics,* 93–99.

9. Potter, in his superb work, *Impending Crisis,* 217–24, focuses on the propaganda campaign waged by the Republicans, thereby underestimating both the importance of disturbing events that were undeniably true and the genuine concern they gave rise to among many fairly sophisticated observers at the time. Gienapp, *Origins of the Republican Party,* uncritically endorses Potter's viewpoint. Gene Wise, *American Historical Explanations: A Strategy for Grounded Inquiry,* 32–41, argues that people's perceptions about what is going on in their world may not be "objectively correct," but the manner in which they interpret events as they are received is what matters. Kansas provides an excellent example of a historical drama being reported in a way that was out of proportion to what was really happening. But enough crucial truth did exist, such as the ballot box frauds and passage of the slave codes, that other events are viewed in light of those facts that helped shape people's perception of and response to the controversy as a whole.

10. *Wisconsin State Journal,* Apr. 21, 27, May 3, June 7, 20, 1854, May 10, July 5, 1855, Jan. 10, Apr. 29, 1856; *Milwaukee Sentinel,* June 14, 16, 1854, Dec. 30, 1855; *Monroe Sentinel,* May 24, 1855; *Kenosha Tribune and Telegraph,* May 8, 1856. President Pierce, under pressure from southern supporters, dismissed the territorial governor, Andrew Reeder, for opposing the proslavery legislature. Reeder, however, was also involved in questionable land deals, which by themselves were sufficient justification for his removal. Republicans, of course, ignored the land issue and castigated the president as a tool of the "Slave Oligarchy." See the *Milwaukee Sentinel,* for example, July 31, 1855; Main, Diary, Dec. 31, 1855, Main Papers. Main wrote, "Kansas is the battleground. Pierce performed the mean act of removing Gov. Reeder who is for a Free State and appointing that doughface Shannon. Civil War almost rages in Kansas now. Shame that this great nation . . . should still support the . . . extension of the abominable institution." Nevins, *Ordeal of the Union* 2:383–88, 416–19.

11. *Wisconsin State Journal,* May 10, 1855, Feb. 23, Apr. 29, May 28, June 2, Aug. 20, 1856; *Monroe Sentinel,* May 24, 1855; *Kenosha Telegraph,* May 8, 1856; *Milwaukee Sentinel,* Dec. 29, 1854, Sept. 17, Dec. 21, 1855, Mar. 7, 1856; *Wisconsin Daily Free Democrat,* Aug. 6, Sept. 18, Dec. 14, 1855, provide a sample of the endless Republican editorials on Kansas matters and their meaning to the future of the nation. One can pick up almost any Republican paper after mid-1855 and find some mention of Kansas. On proceedings of some of the "Freedom for Kansas" meetings, see the *Milwaukee Sentinel,* Feb. 26, Mar. 7, June 13, 18, 19, July 7, 9, 1856, and the *Janesville Gazette,* Mar. 8, 15, 22, 1856. On occasion, those meetings stimulated the formation of local Republican clubs in preparation for the upcoming presidential campaign.

12. M. Gill to Coles Bashford, Apr. 13, 1856, Papers of the Executive Department of the State of Wisconsin, Routine and General Correspondence.

13. *Milwaukee Sentinel,* Apr. 23, 1856, recounts the Milwaukee meeting. Also see Feb. 4, June 18, 19, 20, 21, July 7, 9, 13, 1856, for the proceedings and resolves of other meetings held in the state, as well as the efforts of Daniels; and the *Wisconsin Daily Free Democrat,* May 17, Dec. 14, 17, 1855; *Kenosha Tribune and Telegraph,* Aug. 30, 1855, May 8, 1856; *Baraboo Republic,*

Sept. 13, Oct. 20, 1856; *Wisconsin State Journal,* Dec. 5, 1855, for Republican editorials on violence.

14. Cyrus Woodman to Almira Foss, Apr. 20, 1856, Woodman Papers. Also see the *Wisconsin State Journal,* Feb. 5, 1855, May 28, June 2, 1856, and the *Milwaukee Sentinel,* Mar. 7, Apr. 11, 1856, for other Republican expressions of the need to stand up to the South in Kansas.

15. David Donald, *Charles Sumner and the Coming of the Civil War,* 278–348, is the best analysis of the details and aftermath of the attack. See also, William Gienapp, "The Crime Against Sumner: The Caning of Charles Sumner and the Rise of the Republican Party," 218–45.

16. *Wisconsin State Journal,* May 28, June 2, 1856; *Milwaukee Sentinel,* May 24, 30, June 7, 1856; *Portage Independent,* June 5, 12, September 15, 1856; *Daily Milwaukee News,* Nov. 2, 1856.

17. *Portage Independent,* June 5, 12, 1856; *Milwaukee Sentinel,* May 24, 31, 1856; *Milwaukee Daily Free Democrat,* May 26, 28, 1856; provide a sample of the Republican reaction in Wisconsin to the assault. Also see Gienapp, *Origins of the Republican Party,* 299–303.

18. James Kendall to John Fox Potter, July 8, 1856, Potter Papers. Also see Main, Diary entries, May 22, 23, 24, 26, 30, 1856, Main Papers.

19. *Milwaukee Sentinel,* May 30, 31, July 3, Sept. 23, 1856; *Monroe Sentinel,* July 26, 1856; *Baraboo Republic,* July 26, 1856; *Wisconsin State Journal,* May 28, 1856. Gienapp, *Origins of the Republican Party,* 301–2, rightly notes the overall significance of the Sumner assault on Republican political fortunes in 1856 and the credence the attack gave to the party's "mainstay" issue, Kansas.

20. Gienapp, *Origins of the Republican Party,* 301–3, 440–43, Anbinder, *Nativism and Slavery,* 163–219. The Know Nothings already were running aground due to divisions over slavery; Kansas and Sumner created additional insuperable problems.

21. *Wisconsin State Journal,* Apr. 10, 1856; *Milwaukee Sentinel,* Apr. 10, 1856; *Milwaukee Daily American,* July 28, Sept. 8, 12, 1856; David Atwood to John Fox Potter, Nov. 8, 1856, Potter Papers; Current, *History of Wisconsin,* 232–33; Gienapp, *Origins of the Republican Party,* 425–27; Sewell, *Ballots For Freedom,* 272–73.

22. *Milwaukee Sentinel,* Mar. 10, 1856. Also see David Atwood to John Fox Potter, Nov. 8, 1856, Christopher Sholes to Potter, July 19, 24, 1856, all in the Potter Papers, for expressions of Republican willingness to accept Know Nothing support only if nativism was subordinated to the slavery question. James Miller to Elisha Keyes, July 17, 1856, Keyes Papers, indicates that Know Nothing leaders took up the Republican offer.

23. *Milwaukee Daily American,* June 28, 1856.

24. Ibid., Aug. 18, Sept. 8, 11, 12, 24, on Know Nothing support for the Republicans. It should be borne in mind that hard-core Know Nothings probably never numbered more than a few thousand in Wisconsin. It should likewise be remembered that Republicans never made any secret of their desire to court Know Nothing support. But they always had insisted that Americans subordinate their nativist attitudes to the Republicans' antislavery platform. It is hard to imagine how, under those circumstances, Know Nothings could have found the Republican party, at least in Wisconsin, a satisfactory outlet for their nativist leanings, and some may have dropped out of politics or, instead, embraced the Democrats and their absolute Unionism. Gienapp, *Origins of the Republican Party,* 167–303, details the formation of the party in other states and the difficulties encountered in some, owing to Know Nothing strength.

25. *Kenosha Tribune and Telegraph,* May 28, 1856; *Wisconsin State Journal,* May 28, 1856.

26. *Wisconsin Daily Free Democrat,* June 5, 1856; *Wisconsin State Journal,* June 5, 6, 1856; *Milwaukee Sentinel,* June 6, 1856; *Janesville Gazette,* June 14, 1856.

27. *Milwaukee Sentinel,* June 9, 1856, contains the platform.

28. Main, Diary, Sept. 18, 1856, Main Papers.

29. Nevins, *Ordeal of the Union* 2:452–60.

30. *Milwaukee Sentinel,* Aug. 1, 8, 16, Sept. 11, 1856; *Wisconsin State Journal,* Aug. 18, Sept. 9, 1856.

31. *Weekly Wisconsin Argus,* Aug. 19, 1856. Also see the *Daily Milwaukee News,* Nov. 2, 1856.

32. George B. Smith to Dock ? (illegible), July 11, 1856, Smith Papers; *Daily Milwaukee News,* Sept. 27, Oct. 29, 1856; *Janesville Gazette,* Oct. 27, 1856.

33. Lyman Draper to Moses Strong, Oct. 31, 1856, Strong Papers; J. A. Bryan to George Paul, Oct. 20, 1856, Paul Papers; George B. Smith to Elyra Miller, July 5, 1856, Smith Papers; *Beaver Dam Sentinel and Republican,* Aug. 5, 12, Sept. 23, 1856; *Janesville Standard,* Sept. 5, 1855.

34. George B. Smith to J. W. Horney, July 25, 1856, Smith Papers; *Beaver Dam Sentinel and Republican,* Sept. 23, 1856; *Weekly Wisconsin Argus and Democrat,* Aug. 19, 26, Sept. 2, 1856.

35. Samuel Crawford, the Democratic congressional candidate from the western district and former associate justice of the state supreme court, who in 1854 upheld the right of Congress to legislate on the rendition of fugitive slaves, championed popular sovereignty whatever the outcome. His position is found in the *Wisconsin State Journal,* Sept. 18, 1856, and the *Janesville Gazette,* Oct. 27, 1856.

36. *Daily Milwaukee News,* Sept. 27, Oct. 29, 1856, Jan. 9, 1857; *Weekly Argus and Democrat,* July 15, 1856.

37. Gienapp, *Origins of the Republican Party,* 413–14.

38. Ibid., 375–414; Nevins, *Ordeal of the Union* 2:487–514.

39. The Republican vote surged from 36,074 for Bashford in 1855 to 66,108 for Fremont. The Democrats went from 35,750 to 52,875.

40. Gienapp, *Origins of the Republican Party,* 519–37; Ray M. Shortridge, "The Voter Realignment in the Midwest during the 1850s," *American Politics Quarterly* (Apr. 1976): 193–215.

41. Gienapp, *Origins of the Republican Party,* 446–47; Silbey, "'There Are Other Questions Beside That of Slavery Merely,'" 147–52; Shortridge, "Voter Realignment in the Midwest During the 1850s," 193–215.

42. J. R. Doolittle to F. S. Lovell, Sept. 5, 1856, in the *Milwaukee Sentinel,* Sept. 9, 1856; William Dutcher to Horace Tenney, July 31, 1856, Horace Tenney Papers; Gienapp, *Origins of the Republican Party,* 418, 423; Shortridge, "Voter Realignment in the Midwest During the 1850s," 208–9.

43. Sheboygan County was equally divided between foreign- and native-born, and contained a large number of German Protestants. Buchanan squeezed out a narrow victory in the county that, unlike other immigrant counties, leaned heavily toward the Democrats. See Gienapp, *Origins of the Republican Party,* 423–31, for voting patterns among the foreign- and native-born in 1856, and Current, *History of Wisconsin,* 233–34, 287–88.

44. Foner, *Free Soil, Free Labor, Free Men,* 103–48, 186–225.

45. *Milwaukee Sentinel,* July 11, 1855.

46. *Menasha Conservator,* Apr. 30, 1856, voiced the common Republican position that Northern Democrats, in return for a share in the spoils of office, worked with slaveowners to "perpetuate their tyranny over 20 millions of freemen."

47. *Milwaukee Sentinel,* Oct. 8, 16, 27, 1856, Oct. 6, 7, 1858; *Monroe Sentinel,* Sept. 5, 29, 1855, Nov. 5, 1856; *Wisconsin Daily Free Democrat,* Aug. 6, 1855, illustrate the basic Republican theories regarding the slave power. Also see, David Brian Davis, *The Slave Power Conspiracy*

and the Paranoid Style, esp. 51–61; Nye, *Fettered Freedom,* 282–315; Foner, *Free Soil, Free Labor, Free Men,* 73–102, and "Politics, Ideology, and the Origins of the American Civil War," 15–34; and Gienapp, *Origins of the Republican Party,* 357–65.

48. *Racine Advocate,* July 18, 1856; *Milwaukee Sentinel,* Mar. 10, 1857, and the *Menasha Conservator,* Apr. 30, 1859.

49. *Kenosha Tribune and Telegraph,* May 28, 1856; *Wisconsin State Journal,* Oct. 15, 1858, and the *Wisconsin Daily Free Democrat,* Aug. 6, 1855, for similar expressions.

50. *Milwaukee Sentinel,* Oct. 16, 1856, Aug. 3, 1857.

51. *Milwaukee Sentinel,* Aug. 3, 1857, Oct. 7, 1858; *Portage Independent,* Mar. 3, 1856; *Wisconsin State Journal,* May 26, July 25, Aug. 4, 18, 1856; *Monroe Sentinel,* July 21, 1856.

52. *Milwaukee Sentinel,* Sept. 22, 1856.

53. Ibid. Also see Oct. 3, 16, 27, 1856, Oct. 16, 1859; *Wisconsin State Journal,* July 25, Aug. 18, 1856, Oct. 15, 1858; *Monroe Sentinel,* Nov. 5, 1856; *Daily Wisconsin Free Democrat,* Aug. 5, 1855; Moses M. Davis to John Fox Potter, Oct. 27, 1857, Potter Papers.

54. The quotes come from resolves adopted by Green County Republicans and printed in the *Monroe Sentinel,* Sept. 5, 1855.

55. *Portage Independent,* June 12, 1856.

56. *Kenosha Tribune and Telegraph,* Jan. 10, 1856; *Wisconsin Daily Free Democrat,* May 17, 1854, Nov. 4, 1856, Aug. 21, 1857; *Portage Independent,* Feb. 7, Mar. 6, 1856; *Baraboo Republic,* Aug. 23, Sept. 6, 1856; *Portage City Record,* Oct. 10, 1858, provide some examples of this aspect of Republicanism.

57. *Monroe Sentinel,* May 17, June 14, 1854; *Baraboo Republic,* Mar. 8, 22, 1860; *Milwaukee Sentinel,* Jan. 23, 1861; *Portage Independent,* Feb. 3, 8, 1855. Sewell, *Ballots For Freedom,* argues that "hostility toward slavery lay at the very core of Republican ideology" and that historians have exaggerated the dilution of the party's moral appeal vis-à-vis their Liberty and Free Soil forebears, 7, 34, 38, 292; Holt, *Political Crisis of the 1850s,* 134–35, maintains that the Republican opposition to slavery had a meaning quite apart from that relating to black servitude—it was more deeply rooted in the republican ideology inherited from the revolutionary generation and had greater concern with the threat to white freedom posed by the slave power. Both Sewell and Holt, I believe, are correct, and their views are more complementary than contradictory.

58. The *Milwaukee Sentinel,* Sept. 3, 1856, reprints Barstow's message; also see the *Monroe Sentinel,* Nov. 26, 1856, for an excellent editorial implicating slavery as the source of all the nation's difficulties.

59. *Wisconsin State Journal,* July 4, 1855; also see the *Monroe Sentinel,* Nov. 26, 1856; *Portage Independent,* Feb. 8, 1855; Message of the Governor of Wisconsin to the Special Session of the Legislature, Sept. 3, 1856, printed in the *Milwaukee Sentinel,* Sept. 4, 1856, and the *Menasha Conservator,* July 17, 1857, for a nice summary of the reordering of political values occasioned by the events of 1854–1856 and Stampp, "Race, Slavery and the Republican Party of the 1850s," 105–35, esp. 122–23.

60. *Racine Advocate,* Jan. 1, 1855; Sewell, *Ballots for Freedom,* 304–12; Foner, *Free Soil, Free Labor, Free Men,* 115–16, 311–12.

61. *Menasha Conservator,* June 26, July 17, 1856, Aug. 7, 1857; *Grant County Herald,* Sept. 11, 25, 1858; *Wisconsin State Journal,* May 12, 1855; *Racine Advocate,* Jan. 31, May 22, 29, 1854; Jan. 1, 1855, Nov. 23, 1859; *Monroe Sentinel,* Feb. 2, May 17, Oct. 11, 1854, Nov. 26, 1856, Jan. 7, 1857; *Janesville Gazette,* Aug. 23, 1856; *Milwaukee Sentinel,* May 29, Aug. 5, 1854, Oct. 22, 1855, Jan. 3, 5, Aug. 7, 1857, Oct. 6, 1858, Jan. 23, 1861; *Baraboo Republic,* Apr. 23, 1857, Mar. 22, 1860; *Racine Weekly Journal,* Oct. 6, 1858; *Wisconsin Daily Free Democrat,* Dec. 10, 1856, Sept. 22,

1858; *Portage City Record,* Nov. 11, 25, 1857, Jan. 27, 1858, Sept. 26, 1860; *Portage Independent,* Feb. 8, 1858; *Mineral Point Tribune,* July 1, 1856, Dec. 8, 1859. These Republican sources contain but a few references to the notion that restricting slavery would gradually kill it.

62. *Baraboo Republic,* Mar. 22, 1860; also James Sutherland to the *Janesville Gazette,* June 26, 1859, manuscript copy in the James Sutherland Papers; *Wisconsin Daily Free Democrat,* Sept. 22, 1858; *Milwaukee Sentinel,* Jan. 23, 1861.

63. Speech of Carl Schurz to the Republican Party Meeting in Chicago, Sept. 28, 1858, printed in the *Milwaukee Sentinel,* Oct. 7, 1858, in which he highlights this axiom.

64. *Wisconsin State Journal,* May 26, 1856, May 23, 1860; *Milwaukee Sentinel,* Oct. 6, 8, 1858, Dec. 3, 1859; *Kenosha Tribune and Telegraph,* July 22, 1858; *Monroe Sentinel,* Feb. 2, 1859; *Wisconsin Daily Free Democrat,* Dec. 15, 1856, Aug. 21, 1857. Foner gives the fullest treatment of the Free Labor ideology in his *Free Soil, Free Labor, Free Men,* while Gienapp, *Origins of the Republican Party,* 355–57, rightly points out that the free labor values were shared by nearly all Northerners.

65. *Wisconsin State Journal,* May 2, 1856; *Milwaukee Sentinel,* Oct. 16, 1856; Foner, *Free Soil, Free Labor, Free Men,* 44–51.

66. *Wisconsin State Journal,* May 23, 1860; *Milwaukee Sentinel,* Oct. 7, 1858, for the Schurz quotation; also see Dec. 3, 1859; *Kenosha Tribune and Telegraph,* July 22, 1858; *Monroe Sentinel,* Feb. 2, 1859; *Wisconsin Daily Free Democrat,* Dec. 15, 1856, Aug. 21, 1857.

67. As the Liberty and Free Soil parties did before them.

68. *Milwaukee Sentinel,* Oct. 17, 1855, Mar. 21, 1856, Sept. 4, 1857, Oct. 7, 1858; *Wisconsin Daily Free Democrat,* July 16, 1856; *Mineral Point Tribune,* July 14, Aug. 11, 1857; *Monroe Sentinel,* Jan. 16, 1856; *Kenosha Telegraph,* Aug. 26, Oct. 28, 1858; Wisconsin Governor's Message, Jan. 12, 1860, *Annual Messages of the Governors of Wisconsin, 1841–1875;* Freehling, "The Founding Fathers and Slavery," 82–86.

69. *Milwaukee Sentinel,* Apr. 26, Dec. 4, 1856; *Mineral Point Tribune,* Aug. 11, 1857; *Monroe Sentinel,* Aug. 13, 1856; Speech of William H. Brisbane, n.d., in the William H. Brisbane Papers; Wisconsin Governor's Message, Jan. 15, 1858, in the *Wisconsin State Journal,* Jan. 16, 1858; Freehling, "The Founding Fathers and Slavery," 86; Donald Robinson, *Slavery in the Structure of American Politics, 1765–1820,* provides a substantive analysis of the problems confronting the founders in dealing with the slavery issue and republican idealism.

70. *Milwaukee Sentinel,* Oct. 17, 1855, Oct. 7, 1858; *Kenosha Telegraph,* Aug. 26, Oct. 21, 1858; A. H. Cerajin to Moses Davis, Nov. 18, 1856, Davis Papers; H. Crocker to John Fox Potter, Nov. 5, 1856, Potter Papers.

71. *Neenah-Menasha Conservator,* Nov. 21, 1859.

72. *Kenosha Tribune and Telegraph,* Jan. 20, 27, Mar. 24, 1854, Aug. 2, Oct. 2, 1855; *Milwaukee Sentinel,* Apr. 8, May 17, 29, 1854; *Wisconsin Daily Free Democrat,* July 18, 1854, July 12, 1855; *Wisconsin State Journal,* July, 8, 1854.

73. M. M. Holmes to the *Watertown Chronicle,* July 12, 1854. Paul C. Nagel chronicles the American attitudes toward the Union in *One Nation Indivisible.*

74. *Milwaukee Sentinel,* Apr. 8, 1854; *Wisconsin Daily Free Democrat,* July 18, 1855; *Wisconsin State Journal,* June 1, 20, 1855; *Baraboo Republic,* July 28, Aug. 16, 1855; *Monroe Sentinel,* July 16, 1856.

75. *Wisconsin State Journal,* May 8, 1854.

76. Ibid.; *Racine Advocate,* June 12, 1854; *Monroe Sentinel,* Feb. 21, 1855, July 8, 1857; *Wisconsin Daily Free Democrat,* July 18, 1855, Apr. 10, 1855; *Milwaukee Sentinel,* Feb. 1, 1855, June 3, 1856; *Kenosha Tribune and Telegraph,* Oct. 2, 1856; *Baraboo Republic,* Jan. 15, 1856; *Menasha Conservator,* Dec. 15, 1859; D. K. Noyes to John Fox Potter, Nov. 23, 1856, and C. L. Sholes to

Potter, Nov. 11, 1856, both in the Potter Papers. Also see the Majority Report of the Wisconsin Senate Committee on State Affairs, printed in the *Milwaukee Sentinel*, Feb. 2, 1858.

77. Perhaps some long-time Garrisonian "non-resistors" could no longer justify sitting out elections and were moved to support the Republican cause owing to the increased threat of the slave power. Sewell, *Ballots For Freedom*, 285–88, suggests as much.

78. Earlier chapters of this work point to the growing disillusionment of Whigs. Welter, *The Mind of America, 1882–1860*, 351–64, also picks up on this. Conservative Whigs saw preservation of the Union as an end in itself, but Conscience Whigs dominated in Wisconsin, and they were most disheartened by the growing dominance of the South over the previous decade. It also is open to question whether conservatives even joined the Republican cause. See the letter of the Wisconsin Silver Grey, Henry Baird, to Joshua Hathaway, August 13, 1856, Henry S. Baird Papers, where he expresses his opposition to both nativism and Republicanism. Baird was a former Whig candidate for governor of Wisconsin. Gienapp, *Origins of the Republican Party*, 416, blames "the party's failure to win greater support from conservative Whigs and Know Nothings" for the Republican defeat in 1856. And it was the fear of disunion that a Republican triumph would likely precipitate that held them back.

79. Foner, *Free Soil, Free Labor, Free Men*, 178–81, points this out, but Gienapp, *Origins of the Republican Party*, 446–47, correctly I think, notes that Democratic defections to the Republican party were, on the whole, quite small. I also question the influence of Democrats in the Republican coalition, especially in Wisconsin. For the different positions of former Democrats on the Union, compare Alexander Randall and James Doolittle with John Walworth, editor of the *Monroe Sentinel*. Walworth, on more than one occasion clamored, *"Without Liberty the Union is a curse." Monroe Sentinel*, Feb. 21, 1855, July 9, 1856. For reference to the absolute unionism of Randall and Doolittle, see note 83.

80. *Milwaukee Sentinel*, Aug. 19, Sept. 23, Oct. 3, 1856, Oct. 6, 1858, May 23, July 20, 1859; *Monroe Sentinel*, July 9, 1856; *Portage Independent*, Aug. 14, 1856; *Wisconsin Daily Free Democrat*, July 18, 1855; Cyrus Woodman to Jacob Merrick, May 21, 1856, and to C. C. Washburne, May 27, 1856, Woodman Papers.

81. *Wisconsin State Journal*, May 8, 1854; *Janesville Gazette*, June 3, 1854; *Kenosha Tribune and Telegraph*, Jan. 14, Feb. 11, 1858.

82. John Fox Potter to Edward Potter, Dec. 20, 1857, Potter Papers; *Wisconsin State Journal*, July 8, 1854; *Kenosha Tribune and Telegraph*, Aug. 2, 1855, Oct. 2, 1856.

83. James Doolittle to E. L. Runals, Dec. 25, 1856, James Doolittle Papers; Message of Governor Alexander Randall to the Citizens of Wisconsin, in the *Milwaukee Sentinel*, Jan. 16, 1858.

84. Liberty men focused on the evil of slavery itself, Free Soilers on the territorial question. Sewell, *Ballots For Freedom*, correctly emphasizes the links between the three parties and the changing focus of each.

NINE *The Dangerous Doctrine of Nullification*

1. "In Re Sherman Booth," *Wisconsin Reports (1854)*, 20. Other essays on the Glover Affair include, McManus, "'Freedom and Liberty First, and the Union Afterwards'"; Schafer, "Stormy Days in Court: The Booth Case," 89–110; Vroman Mason, "The Fugitive Slave Law in Wisconsin; with Reference to Nullification Sentiment"; Joseph A. Ranney, "'Suffering the Agonies of Their Righteousness': The Rise and Fall of the States Rights Movement in Wisconsin, 1854–1861."

2. "The Argument of Byron Paine, Esquire: Regarding the Unconstitutionality of the Fugitive Slave Act," *Wisconsin Miscellaneous Pamphlets, 27,* 1–23.

3. "In Re Sherman Booth," *Wisconsin Reports (1854),* 13–54, esp. 32–46.

4. *Milwaukee Sentinel,* July 20–25, 1854. A federal grand jury had issued a warrant for Booth's arrest on July 11 for violating the Fugitive Slave Law. The federal district court judge, Andrew G. Miller, waited until the state court decision to act on the warrant.

5. "Ex Parte Sherman Booth," *Wisconsin Reports (1854),* 134–44.

6. Ranney, "'Suffering the Agonies of Their Righteousness,'" 92–96, gives a good account of the trial and the actions of Judge Miller in the case.

7. *Milwaukee Sentinel,* Jan. 15, Feb. 6, 1855.

8. Morris, *Free Men All,* 167–85.

9. The opinions of Wisconsin's three supreme court justices can be followed in *Wisconsin Reports (1854),* "In Re Sherman Booth," 13–54, for Smith's original decree, "In Re Sherman Booth," 54–134, for the decision of the full court in June 1854, and "In Re Booth and Rycraft," 144–97, for the February 1855 reaffirmation of the June ruling and the reversal of the federal court decision.

10. "In Re Sherman Booth," 72–86, "In Re Booth and Rycraft," 170–72. Don E. Fehrenbacher, *The Dred Scott Case: Its Significance in American Law and Politics,* 43–47; and Paul Finkelman, "*Prigg v. Pennsylvania* and Northern State Courts: Antislavery use of a Proslavery Decision," 5–35.

11. "In Re Sherman Booth," 54–71; "In Re Booth and Rycraft," 160–61.

12. Smith designed his opinion around Paine's defense, sustaining every one of his main positions, which embraced the Virginia and Kentucky Resolutions and quoted liberally from them. Paine, "Argument of Byron Paine," 2–3. Also see Paine to Charles Sumner, Jan. 12, 1856, Byron Paine Papers, where he admits the influence of John C. Calhoun on his thinking; Foner, *Free Soil, Free Labor, Free Men,* 135; and William W. Freehling, *Prelude to Civil War: The Nullification Controversy in South Carolina, 1816–1836,* 134–76, for the South Carolinian's theory.

13. "In Re Sherman Booth," 39–40; "In Re Booth and Rycraft," 177–79; Schafer, "Stormy Days in Court," 91–101.

14. "In Re Sherman Booth," 49–54, 97–134; Fehrenbacher, *The Dred Scott Case;* Finkelman, "*Prigg v. Pennsylvania* and Northern State Courts," 5–14; Schafer, "Stormy Days in Court," 102–3.

15. "In Re Sherman Booth," 32–38, 90–91; "In Re Booth and Rycraft," 181–85. Also see the *Walworth County Independent,* in the *Wisconsin Daily Free Democrat,* June 19, 1854, for an elaboration of the theory of state judicial nullification; Herman Belz, *A New Birth of Freedom: The Republican Party and Freedmen's Rights, 1861–1866,* ix–xiv.

16. "In Re Sherman Booth," 86–92; "In Re Booth and Rycraft," 182–89.

17. *Walworth County Independent,* in the *Wisconsin Daily Free Democrat,* June 19, 1854; Potter, *The Impending Crisis,* 294–95; Morris, *Free Men All,* 174–75; Freehling, *Prelude to Civil War,* 159–73.

18. Bestor, "State Sovereignty and Slavery," 140–80; Freehling, *Prelude to Civil War,* 219–301.

19. Paine, "Argument of Byron Paine," 1–3; "In Re Booth and Rycraft," 188–89; A. D. Smith to William Cullen Bryant, Horace Greeley, et al., published in the *Milwaukee Sentinel,* Mar. 27, 1857; Morris, *Free Men All,* 156–85.

20. "In Re Booth and Rycraft," 172–76; Adrienne Koch and Harry Ammon, "The Virginia and Kentucky Resolutions: An Episode in Jefferson and Madison's Defense of Civil

Liberties"; Arthur Bestor, "State Sovereignty and Slavery: A Reinterpretation of Pro-Slavery Constitutional Doctrine, 1846–1860," 136–37; Potter, *The Impending Crisis*, 294–95.

21. Charles Sumner to Byron Paine, Aug. 8 and Dec. 28, 1854, Jan. 18, 1856, and Wendell Phillips to Paine, Nov. 24, 1854, all in the Byron Paine Papers; Greeley's editorial was reprinted in the *Milwaukee Sentinel*, July 17, 1854; letter of Judge A. D. Smith to William Cullen Bryant, Horace Greeley, et al., printed in the *Milwaukee Sentinel*, Apr. 16, 1857; Schafer, "Stormy Days in Court," 92; Mason, "The Fugitive Slave Law in Wisconsin," 133.

22. Rufus King to William H. Seward, Feb. 11, 1855, William H. Seward Papers; *Janesville Gazette*, Feb. 3, 1855; *Milwaukee Sentinel*, Feb. 6, 1855; *Wisconsin State Journal*, Feb. 5, 1855; *Kenosha Tribune and Telegraph*, Feb. 8, 1855; *Portage Independent*, Mar. 4, 1855; *Walworth County Independent*, June 19, 1854; *Potosi Republican*, Feb. 17, 1855; *Monroe Sentinel*, Mar. 7, 14, 1855. These contain a sampling of Republican opinion. The *Milwaukee Morning News*, July 22, 1854, contains a representative Democratic response, which labeled the decision a threat to republicanism and the Union.

23. The Senate race can be followed in the *Wisconsin Daily Free Democrat*, Dec. 22, 27, 1854, Jan. 11, 17, 22, 1855; the *Wisconsin State Journal*, Jan. 11, 30, 31, 1855; and the *Weekly Argus and Democrat*, Jan. 30, 1855. Also see Aaron M. Boom, "The Development of Sectional Attitudes in Wisconsin, 1848–1861," 110–14; Flately, "The Wisconsin Congressional Delegation from Statehood to Secession," 61–70. Byron Kilbourn was president of the LaCrosse and Milwaukee Railroad and a former Free Soil Democrat.

24. Booth, recently discharged from jail, led the Free Soil faction and reportedly vowed that "no one but Durkee shall be elected" by the Republican coalition. The Free Soilers looked to avenge Durkee's 1852 defeat for reelection to Congress, when a number of Whigs allegedly crossed party lines and helped to elect Durkee's Democratic opponent. For Booth's "dictation," see the *Weekly Argus and Democrat*, Jan. 30, 1855, and the *Wisconsin Daily Free Democrat*, Jan. 22, 1855. Byron Kilbourn to Horace Tenney, Dec. 15, 1854, Horace Tenney Papers, gives details on the efforts of Kilbourn to court his former Free Soil allies; and Rufus King to William H. Seward, Feb. 11, 1855, William H. Seward Papers, for King's report on the difficulty of reconciling the Free Soilers, Whigs and anti-Nebraska Democrats in the Republican coalition.

25. *Wisconsin State Journal*, Feb. 15, 1855; *Janesville Gazette*, Mar. 3, 1855.

26. *Wisconsin Daily Free Democrat*, Jan. 5, 15, 1857. On these dates Booth published a retrospective on the 1855 caucus meetings. Also see the Feb. 26, Mar. 2 and 16, 1855, editions; the *Janesville Gazette*, Mar. 10 and 14, 1855; and the *Mineral Point Tribune*, Mar. 14, 1855. For Cole's early support of the states' rights position, see the *Milwaukee Sentinel*, July 22, 1854.

27. *Milwaukee Sentinel*, Apr. 21, 1855; *Janesville Gazette*, Apr. 14, 1855. More than 80 percent of the 1854 Democratic voters cast a ballot for Crawford; nearly 90 percent of the 1854 Republican electorate voted for Cole.

28. The Republicans dominated the senate, nineteen to eleven, and the assembly, sixty-five to thirty-one.

29. Rublee and King remained publicly uncommitted to any candidate; probably they were confident about Howe's prospects and did not want to stir up any intraparty feuds. The *Menasha Conservator*, Jan. 15, 29, 1857, carried information on the maneuvering by the candidates and their backers, as did the *Grant County Herald*, Jan. 24, 31, 1857, the *Daily Milwaukee News*, Jan. 24, Feb. 13, 1857, the *Wisconsin Daily Free Democrat*, Jan. 24, 1857, and the *Wisconsin Argus and Democrat*, Jan. 10, 1857. John Lockwood, the Know Nothing chieftain,

supposedly was working diligently for Howe, but, according to Harrison Reed, editor of the *Menasha Conservator* and a keen observer of goings-on in Madison, he commanded a paltry four Republican votes in the caucus.

30. Sherman Booth to Samuel D. Hastings, Dec. 15, 1856, Samuel D. Hastings Papers; George B. Smith, Diary, Jan. 19, 1857, George B. Smith Papers; *Wisconsin Daily Free Democrat,* Dec. 22, 1856, Jan. 24, 1857.

31. Doolittle had been elected to a judgeship on the state circuit court in 1854 but had resigned the position in 1856. He joined the Republican party in 1856 after being bypassed for the Democratic nomination to Congress from his district, and he worked actively for Frémont during the presidential campaign. The state constitution barred state judges from holding any other public office, except another judgeship, "during the term for which they are . . . elected." Even though he had resigned, his term ran to 1860, and so, his opponents charged, he was not eligible to stand for the United States Senate. Only Doolittle's hometown newspaper, the *Racine Advocate,* endorsed him, although he expected to pick up some support from former Democrats in the legislature.

32. *Menasha Conservator,* Jan. 29, 1857; *Daily Argus and Democrat,* Jan. 10, 1857.

33. Sherman Booth to Samuel D. Hastings, Dec. 15, 1856, Samuel D. Hastings Papers; *Wisconsin Daily Free Democrat,* Dec. 22, 29, 1856, Jan. 24, 26, 1857.

34. *Wisconsin Daily Free Democrat,* Jan. 5, 1857, for Booth's report of the conversation with Howe, and Mar. 23, 1857. Before publishing the substance of the discussion, Booth read it back to Howe and obtained his agreement that it fairly represented his views. James L. Sellers, "Republicanism and State Rights in Wisconsin," 213–29, recounts the episode and contains the Democratic quotation; Ranney, "Suffering the Agonies of Their Righteousness," 98–102.

35. *Menasha Conservator,* Jan. 8, 15, 1857; *Grant County Herald,* Jan. 24, 1857; *Racine Advocate,* Jan. 24, 1857; *Wisconsin Daily Free Democrat,* Jan. 14, 1857. The Democratic *Daily Milwaukee News,* Jan. 17, 1857, reported that Booth's manifesto against Howe gave the Republican legislators fits and effectively blew apart his coalition. George B. Smith, Diary entry, Jan. 16, 1857, George B. Smith Papers. Smith, a Democrat, closely followed the controversy among Republicans in choosing a senator.

36. *Wisconsin State Journal,* Jan. 16, 1857; *Milwaukee Sentinel,* Jan. 19, 1857; *Wisconsin Daily Free Democrat,* Jan. 17, 1857.

37. Booth's *Wisconsin Daily Free Democrat,* Jan. 20, 1857, claims that the caucus passed the resolutions by a five-to-one margin.

38. *Wisconsin State Journal,* Jan. 19, 1857.

39. This was a direct reference to South Carolina's controversial application of states' rights and nullification doctrine in 1832–1833.

40. *Wisconsin State Journal,* Jan. 20, 21, 1857, for the letter of Howe and the other candidates. The caucus had by this time declared Doolittle eligible for the seat.

41. Ibid., Jan. 22, 1857.

42. Ibid.

43. Moses M. Davis to John Fox Potter, Jan. 28, Feb. 22, 1857, John Fox Potter Papers; *Wisconsin Daily Free Democrat,* Jan. 24, 26, 1857; *Wisconsin State Journal,* Jan. 23, 24, 1857.

44. *Wisconsin State Journal,* Jan. 17, 19, 20, 21, Feb. 2, 5, 1857; *Milwaukee Sentinel,* Jan. 20, 21, 1857; *Wisconsin Daily Free Democrat,* Jan. 24, 1857. The accusations that the Know Nothings actively worked for Howe's election and indeed that he was himself a Know Nothing comprised the "trumped up and false issue" referred to by his supporters.

45. Moses M. Davis to John Fox Potter, Jan. 28, 1857, Potter Papers; *Grant County Herald,* Jan. 24, 1857; *Wisconsin Daily Free Democrat,* Jan. 24, 26, 1857; *Kenosha Tribune and Telegraph,* Jan. 22, 29, 1857; *Wisconsin State Journal,* Feb. 2, 5, 1857.

46. Moses M. Davis to John Fox Potter, Feb. 22, 1857, Potter Papers; *Menasha Conservator,* Jan. 22, 1857. George B. Smith noted in his diary, Jan. 19, 1857, that outside of the "old" abolitionists, Booth was hated within the party. Undoubtedly he made many enemies with his overbearing, abrasive, self-righteous personality, but he also was accorded a good deal of respect for standing firm on principle.

47. *Wisconsin State Journal,* Jan. 24, 1857; *Menasha Conservator,* Jan. 22, 1857.

48. *Assembly Journal, 1853,* 97, 719–31, *1855,* 48–50, 752–55, *1856,* 228, 497; *Senate Journal, 1853,* 23, 76, 83, 213–16, *1855,* 603, 749; *Weekly Wisconsin,* Jan. 26, Feb. 2, 16, 1853; *Wisconsin Free Democrat,* Apr. 2, 1853; *Milwaukee Sentinel,* Feb. 9, 1856; Morris, *Free Men All,* 163–64. On the one vote taken on a personal liberty proposal, in 1856, Republicans supported the measure by a seven-to-one margin, while three Democrats opposed it to every one in favor.

49. *Senate Journal, 1857,* 166.

50. Ibid., 241–42.

51. *Assembly Journal, 1857,* 431–32, 439–40, 456–62, 486–87; George B. Smith, Diary, Feb. 17, 18, 19, 1857, Smith Papers; *Milwaukee Sentinel,* Feb. 21, 1857. Booth was actively lobbying the assembly for the relief clause because the federal district court, in January 1857, had ordered his printing press and steam engine, valued at $3,000, to be sold at public auction in order to defray the expenses that Garland, Glover's alleged owner, had suffered for the loss of his slave. The property was purchased for $175, after which Booth sued for and received a writ of replevin and had it returned pending the outcome of further court action. For Booth's travails, see his *Wisconsin Daily Free Democrat,* Feb. 23, 24, Apr. 6, 1857, June 28, 1858.

52. *Senate Journal, 1857,* 287, 290; *Assembly Journal, 1857,* 1183. Forty-six Assembly Republicans voted for the final bill and five opposed it. In the Senate, only three Republicans favored the relief provision.

53. *Milwaukee Sentinel,* Feb. 21, 1857; *Mineral Point Tribune,* Mar. 17, 1857; *Janesville Gazette,* Feb. 28, 1957; Timothy Howe to Horace Rublee, Apr. 5, 1857, Timothy Howe Papers. For the Democratic perspective, see the *Weekly Argus and Democrat,* Mar. 31, 1857 and the *Daily Milwaukee News,* Mar. 26, 1857.

54. The decision was handed down on Mar. 6, 1857, two days after the inauguration of the new president of the United States, James Buchanan.

55. Fehrenbacher, *The Dred Scott Case;* Potter, *The Impending Crisis,* 267–96. Congress had repealed the Missouri Compromise three years earlier in the Kansas-Nebraska Act.

56. *Milwaukee Sentinel,* Mar. 14, 1857; *Wisconsin State Journal,* June 4, 1857; *Portage City Record,* Oct. 27, 1858; *Wisconsin Daily Free Democrat,* Mar. 7, 1857; *Grant County Herald,* Mar. 24, 1857; Willet S. Main, Diary, Mar. 13, 17, 1857, Willet S. Main Papers. The Buchanan administration took the proslavery implications of the Dred Scott decision to the limit when it claimed in the pages of the *Washington Union,* the mouthpiece of the national Democratic party, that it validated the right of slaveowners to settle in the territories with their bondsmen and declared unconstitutional state laws banning slavery. The *Milwaukee Sentinel,* Sept. 15, 21, 25, Dec. 2, 4, 1857, carried articles arguing these points from the *Union.* Also see Fehrenbacher, *The Dred Scott Case,* 453, 467.

57. *Mineral Point Tribune,* Mar. 31, 1857; *Grant County Herald,* Mar. 28, 1857; *Wisconsin State Journal,* Mar. 28, 1857; *Menasha Conservator,* Mar. 26, 1857; *Milwaukee Sentinel,* Mar. 24, 25, 1857; *Wisconsin Daily Free Democrat,* Mar. 23, 1857.

58. *Daily Milwaukee News,* Mar. 18, 26, 1857; *Weekly Argus and Democrat,* Mar. 10, 31, 1857.

59. Using 1857 population estimates, about 54 percent of the estimated eligible voters turned out for the election. Presidential races drew by far the largest turnout from statehood in 1848 through 1860. The 1855 governor's contest had attracted about 52 percent of the eligible electorate—the highest turnout for a state contest before the 1857 judicial election.

60. *Wisconsin State Journal,* Apr. 8, 1857.

61. Timothy Howe to Horace Rublee, Apr. 5, May 17, 1857, Timothy Howe Papers; *Wisconsin State Journal,* Mar. 13, 1857.

62. Moses M. Davis to "My Dear Sir" (probably Byron Paine), Mar. [?] 1857, Moses M. Davis Papers; Timothy Howe to Horace Rublee, Apr. 3, 1857, Timothy Howe Papers; *Menasha Conservator,* Apr. 2, 23, May 2, 1857; *Wisconsin Daily Free Democrat,* Mar. 23, 27, 30, 1857.

63. *Wisconsin Daily Free Democrat,* Apr. 6, May 5, 11, 1857; *Kenosha Tribune and Telegraph,* May 14, 21, 1857; *Monroe Sentinel,* May 27, 1857.

64. *Wisconsin Daily Free Democrat,* June 17, 18, 1857; *Menasha Conservator,* June 25, July 7, 1857; *Wisconsin State Journal,* June 18, 1857; *Milwaukee Sentinel,* June 18, 1857.

65. *Milwaukee Sentinel,* June 18, 1857.

66. *Menasha Conservator,* June 25, 1857; *Wisconsin State Journal,* June 19, 1857; Moses M. Davis to John Fox Potter, July 3, 1857, John Fox Potter Papers; Timothy Howe to Horace Rublee, Aug. 14, 1857, Timothy Howe Papers.

67. Timothy Howe to Horace Rublee, Aug. 14, 1857, Timothy Howe Papers.

68. *Wisconsin Daily Free Democrat,* Aug. 27, 1857; *Wisconsin State Journal,* Sept. 2, 1857; *Milwaukee Sentinel,* Sept. 4, 5, 1857; *Baraboo Republic,* Sept. 10, 1857; *Monroe Sentinel,* Sept. 9, 1857; *Portage City Record,* Sept. 9, 1857; *Grant County Herald,* Sept. 12, 1857.

69. *Weekly Argus and Democrat,* Sept. 8, 1857. Howe was joined on the committee by two other Republicans known to be cool towards the states' rights position and the Booth faction.

70. Timothy Howe to Horace Tenney, Mar. 27, 1859, Timothy Howe Papers; William Brisbane, Diary, Sept. 3, 1857, William Brisbane Papers; *Daily Argus and Democrat,* Sept. 3, 4, 1857; *Daily Wisconsin Patriot,* Sept. 5, 1857; *Wisconsin Daily Free Democrat,* Sept. 7, 10, 1857; *Wisconsin State Journal,* Sept. 4, 1857.

71. See, for example, William Brisbane's comments in his Sept. 3, 1857, diary entry, in the Brisbane Papers.

TEN *A Little Matter of Justice*

1. *Milwaukee Daily Free Democrat,* May 17, 1854, Aug. 21, 1857; *Portage City Record,* Oct. 20, 1858.

2. Newspaper debate, newspaper unnamed, between A.W. Arrington and William H. Brisbane, regarding the Dred Scott decision, June, 1857, in the Brisbane Papers; *Portage City Record,* Oct. 20, 1858.

3. *Milwaukee Sentinel,* May 29, 1854; also see the *Monroe Sentinel,* Jan. 7, 14, 1857; *Wisconsin Daily Free Democrat,* May 17, 1854, Aug. 6, 1855. The following suffrage discussion is a modified version of my article, "Wisconsin Republicans and Negro Suffrage: Attitudes and Behavior, 1857."

4. See the *Assembly Journal, 1850*, 160, 199–200, 232, 239–41, 285–86, 362; *1851*, 205, 367, 481; *1852*, 588, 866; *Senate Journal, 1852*, 690. In 1850, approximately 635 blacks made their homes in Wisconsin; in 1855 their number climbed to 788, and in 1860 it neared twelve hundred. The 1850 and 1855 numbers come from census data published in the *Senate Journal, 1856, Appendix 1*, 65–78. The 1860 enumeration was derived from the *Eighth Census of the United States, 1860*.

5. *Wisconsin State Journal*, Sept. 8, 1855.

6. *Wisconsin Daily Free Democrat*, Nov. 10, 1855, for the legislative proceedings; Robert N. Kroncke, "Race and Politics in Wisconsin, 1854–1865," 19; Leslie H. Fishel, "Wisconsin and Negro Suffrage," 185.

7. Two of the petitions submitted to the legislature in 1857 survive in the files of the Secretary of State, *Petitions, Remonstrances, and Resolutions Presented to the Senate and/or Assembly, 1857;* also see the *Senate Journal, 1857*, 59, 117, 197; *Assembly Journal, 1857*, 301, 318, 386–87, 591, 711. For a retrospective view of the Republican party's birth in the lead district and the hesitation its founders had in bringing the "ultra abolition" Mills into its councils, see the *Grant County Herald*, Jan. 27, 1898. Mills was a long-time resident of the lead district and a well-known and seemingly popular radical. The *Grant County Herald*, May 18, 1844, contains a Mills lecture on the beauties of human "diversity."

8. *Assembly Journal, 1857, Appendix 2*, 3–12, contains the full text of the Mills report.

9. Ibid.

10. *Assembly Journal, 1857*, 712–13, 751, 757, 759; *Senate Journal, 1857*, 429–32, 456, 466, 529. Republicans in the assembly voted thirty to thirteen in favor of the Mills report, while the Democrats were twenty to seven against. The same majority prevailed in the final vote on the senate version. In the senate, Republicans came down thirteen to four in favor of their bill, while the Democrats were against it by an eight to one margin.

11. *Daily Milwaukee News*, Aug. 12; *Daily Argus and Democrat*, Aug. 13; *Appleton Crescent*, June 27; *Waukesha County Democrat*, Aug. 19; *Lafayette County Herald*, July 31; *Superior Chronicle*, Mar. 10; *Horicon Argus*, July, 24. Unless otherwise noted, all of the remaining newspaper citations in this chapter are from 1857.

12. *Daily Argus and Democrat*, Aug. 29.

13. *Prescott Transcript*, Aug. 15; *Delavan Messenger*, May 6; *Fond Du Lac Commonwealth*, June 10, July 1; *Columbus Republican Journal*, Aug. 18; *Milwaukee Daily Free Democrat*, Aug. 7.

14. *Wisconsin State Journal*, Aug. 1; *Waukesha Republican*, Apr. 14.

15. *Daily Argus and Democrat*, Sept. 3, 4, 7; *Daily Wisconsin Patriot*, Sept. 5; *Wisconsin State Journal*, Sept. 3, 4, 5.

16. *Daily Argus and Democrat*, Sept. 7; *Weekly Wisconsin Patriot*, Sept. 12.

17. *Daily Argus and Democrat*, Sept. 11; *Milwaukee Daily News*, Aug. 27, Oct. 22; *Kenosha Times*, Sept. 10; *Appleton Crescent*, Sept. 26, Oct. 24; *Superior Chronicle*, Sept. 29; *Racine Democrat*, Aug. 31; *Fond Du Lac Union*, Oct. 29; *Weekly Wisconsin Patriot*, Sept. 26.

18. *Appleton Crescent*, Sept. 26; *Racine Democrat*, Aug. 31; *Superior Chronicle*, Sept. 29; *Wisconsin Pinery*, Oct. 8; *Reedsburg Herald*, Oct. 31; *Manitowoc Herald*, Sept. 19.

19. *Fond Du Lac Union*, Oct. 29; *Lafayette County Herald*, Oct. 16. The fear of "amalgamation" was played on regularly by the Democrats.

20. The *Prairie Du Chien Courier*, Sept. 24 and the *Wisconsin Pinery* offer good examples of this appeal to the foreign-born.

21. The *Elkhorn Independent*, Nov. 13, claims that expediency was precisely the motive of the candidates in their campaign of silence. Also see the *Daily Argus and Democrat*, Sept. 12;

Horace Tenney and David Atwood, *Memorial Record of the Fathers of Wisconsin*, 133–41, and Moses M. Strong, *History of the Wisconsin Territory*, 521–22.

22. The first quote comes from the *Appleton Crescent*, Sept. 26, the second from the *Daily Argus and Democrat*, Sept. 19. The widespread support does not sustain Eugene Berwanger's contention in his *Frontier Against Slavery*, 43, that "Republican editors [in Wisconsin] remained strangely silent about Negro suffrage" in 1857.

23. *Neenah-Menasha Conservator*, Aug. 6, Oct. 29; also see the *Prescott Transcript*, Aug. 15; *Prairie Du Chien Leader*, Oct. 24, 31; *Janesville Gazette*, Oct. 24; *Whitewater Register*, Oct. 24; *Wisconsin State Journal*, Sept. 4, 8, 21, Oct. 28; *Mineral Point Tribune*, Aug. 25.

24. *Milwaukee Sentinel*, Sept. 19. Echoing King's view were the *Baraboo Republic*, Oct. 8; *Racine Advocate*, Sept. 2; *Richland County Observer*, Sept. 29; *Dodge County Citizen*, Oct. 20; *Milwaukee Daily Free Democrat*, Sept. 10.

25. *Wisconsin Mirror*, Sept. 29, Oct. 27; *Elkhorn Independent*, Oct. 23; *Richland County Herald*, Aug. 25; *Monroe Sentinel*, Oct. 7; *Fond Du Lac Commonwealth*, Aug. 26.

26. *Mineral Point Tribune*, Aug. 25; also see the *Whitewater Register*, Oct. 24; *Racine Advocate*, Sept. 2; *Prescott Transcript*, Sept. 19; *Elkhorn Independent*, Oct. 24; *Waukesha Republican*, Oct. 27.

27. *Milwaukee Sentinel*, Aug. 20; *Monroe Sentinel*, Oct. 28.

28. *Portage City Record*, Sept. 30; *Racine Advocate*, Sept. 2; *Wisconsin State Journal*, Aug. 1.

29. *Elkhorn Independent*, Oct. 23; *Prescott Transcript*, Aug. 15; *Racine Advocate*, Sept. 2; *Monroe Sentinel*, Oct. 7.

30. *Hudson Chronicle*, quoted in the *Milwaukee Sentinel*, Aug. 22; *Fond Du Lac Commonwealth*, Oct. 28. These sentiments were given similar expression in many Republican papers, e.g., the *Dodge County Citizen*, Oct. 20, 27; *Baraboo Republic*, Oct. 24; *Janesville Gazette*, Oct. 24; *Prairie Du Chien Leader*, Oct. 24, 31; *Neenah-Menasha Conservator*, Oct. 29; *Columbus Republican Journal*, Sept. 8; *Richland County Observer*, Sept. 29; *Waukesha Republican*, Oct. 27; *Milwaukee Sentinel*, Sept. 24; *Monroe Sentinel*, Sept. 24; *Berlin Courant*, quoted in *Argus and Democrat*, Sept. 7.

31. *Columbus Republican Journal*, Sept. 8; *Monroe Sentinel*, Oct. 8; *Baraboo Republic*, Oct. 28; *Racine Advocate*, Sept. 2; *Milwaukee Daily Free Democrat*, Aug. 7.

32. *Janesville Gazette*, Sept. 17; *Dodge County Citizen*, Oct. 27.

33. *Janesville Gazette*, Oct. 17.

34. Cover and other Whigs had for years carefully cultivated the region's strong anti-bank, prointernal improvement sentiments and won many converts to the party who later shifted to the Republicans.

35. *Grant County Herald*, Oct. 24.

36. Ibid.; also see the *LaCrosse Independent*, Oct. 31, another western antisuffrage Republican paper. The *Milwaukee Daily News*, Sept. 25, discusses the petition containing Cross's signature.

37. *Daily Argus and Democrat*, Sept. 15.

38. *Columbus Republican Journal*, Oct. 20. See the *Daily Argus and Democrat*, Apr. 27, Sept. 19, for a typical Democratic response to the black spokesmen.

39. William Brisbane Diary, Oct. 31, 1857, Brisbane Papers.

40. The Bad Ax, Ozaukee, and Rock County suffrage returns were not contained in the records of the secretary of state, but were found in local papers. For Bad Ax, see the *Western Times*, Nov. 18; for Rock, the *Janesville Gazette*, Nov. 16; for Ozaukee, the *Milwaukee Sentinel*, Nov. 17.

41. *Wisconsin State Journal,* Dec. 19; *Wisconsin Patriot,* Nov. 5; *Prairie Du Chien Courier,* Nov. 20.

42. Current, *History of Wisconsin,* 262–67; Kroncke, "Race and Politics in Wisconsin, 1854–1865," 23–34.

43. For a description of cross-pressure voting, see Lane, *Political Life,* 199–201.

44. *Weekly Wisconsin Patriot,* Sept. 16, Oct. 17; *Milwaukee Sentinel,* Sept. 8, 9, 17.

45. *Milwaukee Sentinel,* Sept. 17; *Weekly Wisconsin Patriot,* Sept. 16, 26.

46. *Weekly Wisconsin Patriot,* Sept. 16, 26.

47. Ibid., Oct. 24, 31; *Milwaukee Sentinel,* Oct. 21, 22. The reform ticket received a scattering of votes, suggesting that Democrats choosing to oppose Cross more likely did so by sitting out the election, although they may have shown up and registered an opinion on the suffrage question.

48. *Milwaukee American,* Sept. 23, 24, Oct. 5, 1857; *Daily Wisconsin Patriot,* Sept. 26. Two German Democratic papers, the *Milwaukee Grad Aus* and the *Watertown Anzeiger,* bolted the Cross ticket in favor of the "reformers." It was rumored that Noonan had purchased the *American* and was actively doing everything he could to bring about Cross's defeat. It was even hinted that, as a friend of Randall's, Noonan had helped engineer Randall's nomination and was working behind the scenes to secure his election. See the *Weekly Argus and Democrat,* Apr. 14, May 19, 1857; *Daily Milwaukee News,* Feb. 13, 1857; *Milwaukee Daily Free Democrat,* Nov. 18, 1857.

49. Sewell, *Ballots for Freedom,* 20–42, provides a description of the nonresistors and their opponents who wanted to take a more active part in politics.

50. To compare election returns, refer to James R. Donoghue, *How Wisconsin Voted* and *The Wisconsin Blue Book,* 1862 and 1874.

51. Frank, Diary, Oct. 27, 1857, Frank Papers; also Current, *History of Wisconsin,* 237–59, for details on the impact of the financial panic of 1857 in Wisconsin.

52. Current, *History of Wisconsin,* Oct. 26, 31, Nov. 10, 1857. The *Wisconsin State Journal,* Nov. 5, 12, 1857, also contains typical Republican postelection commentaries on voters' overconfidence and economic concerns, which brought about their apathy in the 1857 election.

53. The blacks in those twenty-four counties represented 65 percent of the total in the state. Three went Republican and antisuffrage, one Democratic and prosuffrage. It should be borne in mind that in all counties, blacks constituted less than 1 percent of the population, so they did not have great visibility, except perhaps in Milwaukee.

54. *Elkhorn Independent,* Nov. 13; *Milwaukee Sentinel,* Nov. 20.

55. *Milwaukee Sentinel,* Nov. 20.

56. Evidence of this "liberality" among Republicans can be found in Phyllis F. Field, "Republicans and Black Suffrage in New York State: The Grass Roots Response"; Robert R. Dykstra and Harlan Hahn, "Northern Voters and Negro Suffrage: The Case of Iowa, 1868"; Robert R. Dykstra, *Bright Radical Star: Black Freedom and White Supremacy on the Hawkeye Frontier;* LaWanda Cox and John Cox, "Negro Suffrage and Republican Politics: The Problem of Motivation in Reconstruction Historiography"; Glenn M. Linden, "A Note on Negro Suffrage and Republican Politics"; John M. Rozett, "Racism and Republican Emergence in Illinois, 1848–1860: A Re-evaluation of Republican Negrophobia." For the argument that the Republican party basically embraced the racist assumptions of the day, see Berwanger, *The Frontier Against Slavery;* James Rawley, *Race and Politics: Bleeding Kansas and the Coming of the Civil War;* Litwack, *North of Slavery.* Sewell, *Ballots for Freedom,* and Foner, *Free Soil, Free Labor, Free Men,* argue for the complexity and diversity of Republican

attitudes toward blacks, but they still see fundamental party ideology as supportive of basic natural and civil rights for blacks.

57. The following comments regarding Iowa are from Dykstra's *Bright Radical Star,* esp. 172–91, 282.

58. Alice Smith, *History of Wisconsin,* 464–73; Current, *History of Wisconsin,* 76–82; Dykstra, *Bright Radical Star,* 282.

59. Sewell, *Ballots for Freedom,* 99, 185–87.

60. James Doolittle to John Fox Potter, July 25, 1859, Potter Papers; the *Wisconsin State Journal,* Sept. 2, 8, 1859, contains a speech on colonization presented by Doolittle to the Republican state convention; the *Racine Advocate,* Doolittle's home organ, also gave considerable space to his views and the colonization issue in general; see, for example, August 24, 1859. On the ideology of Southern expansion into the Caribbean and Central America, see Urban, "The Ideology of Southern Imperialism, 48–73.

61. James Doolittle to John Fox Potter, Nov. 7, 1860, Potter Papers; Blair's strategy was printed in the *Milwaukee Sentinel,* Feb. 2, 1859; Foner, *Free Soil, Free Labor, Free Men,* 267–95, gives a detailed summary of the Republican position on colonization.

62. Annual Message of Governor Alexander Randall to the Citizens of Wisconsin, Jan. 12, 1860, *Wisconsin Governors Messages; Racine Advocate,* Oct. 24, 1860; *Grant County Herald,* Sept. 8, 1860.

63. The Blair quotation is from a Boston speech reprinted in the *Milwaukee Sentinel,* Feb. 11, 1859; also see the *Wisconsin State Journal,* Sept. 8, 1859; *Oconto Pioneer,* May 12, 1860; *Grant County Herald,* Jan. 5, Feb. 21, 1861; James Doolittle to John Fox Potter, Nov. 7, 1860, Potter Papers.

64. *Wisconsin State Journal,* Sept. 3, 8, 1859, May 8, 1860; *Racine Advocate,* Aug. 3, 24, 1859.

65. C. C. Sholes to James Doolitle, May 21, 1860, Doolittle Papers; *Racine Advocate,* Aug. 17, 1859; *Kenosha Telegraph,* Sept. 1, 1859; *Wisconsin State Journal,* Sept. 3, 1859.

66. *Milwaukee Daily Free Democrat,* June 14, 1858; *Daily Life,* Dec. 21, 1861; Kroncke, "Race and Politics in Wisconsin, 1854–1865," 61–64, discusses the seeming lack of interest displayed in colonization; Foner, *Free Soil, Free Labor, Free Men,* 274–76, discusses support among the free black leadership for colonization, although there is little evidence that this support was widespread among rank-and-file blacks.

67. *Grant County Herald,* Feb. 14, 21, 1861.

ELEVEN *It Looks Like Civil War Is Inevitable*

1. *Wisconsin State Journal,* July 8, 1854.

2. Allan Nevins, *The Emergence of Lincoln* 1:60–89; Potter, *Impending Crisis,* 297–98; Roy F. Nichols, *The Disruption of American Democracy.*

3. See chapter 9 for a discussion of the Dred Scott decision. Also Potter, *Impending Crisis,* 279–92.

4. The *Milwaukee Sentinel* and the *Wisconsin State Journal,* May 8 through 22, 1857, address Republican concerns with popular sovereignty. Also see Potter, *Impending Crisis,* 297–327; Fehrenbacher, *The Dred Scott Case,* 449–83; Nevins, *Emergence of Lincoln* 1:60–89; 148–75; Sewell, *Ballots For Freedom,* 299–300.

5. *Milwaukee Sentinel,* May 8, 12, Dec. 11, 1857; Nevins, *Emergence of Lincoln* 1:229–49; Rawley, *Race and Politics,* 202–22.

6. Nevins, *Emergence of Lincoln* 1:64–67.

7. Nevins, *Emergence of Lincoln* 1:229–304, gives a dramatic rendering of events. The constitution with slavery had been overwhelmingly endorsed in another election, boycotted by free-state men, on December 21, 1857. In an election the following month, called by the territorial legislature, slave staters abstained, and the whole Lecompton charter was rejected. Buchanan backed the December results. Potter, *Impending Crisis,* 318.

8. Potter, *Impending Crisis,* 308–27; Nevins, *Emergence of Lincoln* 1:250–304. Kansas finally achieved statehood in 1861.

9. J. R. Sharpstein to George H. Paul, Mar. 3, 1858, Paul Papers. Sharpstein was editor of the *Milwaukee Daily News* and postmaster of that city. Paul edited the *Kenosha Democrat* and occupied the postmastership there. Sharpstein advised Paul that the president had received reassurances that Paul stood behind him on the Lecompton question, and thus he would be retained in his position. The *Milwaukee Sentinel,* Feb. 8, 9, 10, 11, July 2, 10, 12, 14, 16, 18, 22, 1858, recounts some of the pressure the administration was putting on state officeholders.

10. Sylvanus Cadwallader to George H. Paul, Mar. 8, 15, 1858, Paul Papers, provide examples of a local leader under pressure to reject Lecompton and the administration position. The *Milwaukee Sentinel,* Dec. 19, 22, 25, 1857, highlighted cracks in Democratic support of the administration that were coming to the surface. The state's Democrats constantly fought each other, of course, but they usually could be counted on to back their national leaders.

11. *Kenosha Tribune and Telegraph,* Jan. 7, 1858; *Milwaukee Sentinel,* Jan. 4, 1858.

12. *Wisconsin State Journal,* Jan. 14, 1858; *Milwaukee Sentinel,* Jan. 15, Mar. 6, 8, 1858; *Milwaukee Daily News,* Mar. 8, 1858; *Wisconsin Daily Free Democrat,* Mar. 8, 1858.

13. Boom, "The Development of Sectional Attitudes in Wisconsin," 166–72.

14. *Milwaukee Sentinel,* Dec. 19, 1857; *Wisconsin Daily Free Democrat,* Dec. 19, 21, 1857; Sewell, *Ballots For Freedom,* 343–48; Potter, *Impending Crisis,* 320–22; Nevins, *Emergence of Lincoln* 1:261–64.

15. See chapter 8 for a discussion of Democratic attitudes; *Milwaukee Sentinel,* Aug. 9, 14, 1858.

16. *Milwaukee Sentinel,* Mar. 8, 1858, reprints the resolutions of the Milwaukee Democratic meeting in which this distinction is made clear. Also see the *Sheboygan Journal,* Mar. 10, 1858; *Milwaukee Daily News,* Mar. 8, 1858; *Wisconsin Daily Free Democrat,* Dec. 12, 1857; Potter, *Impending Crisis,* 172–74, 320–21, 329–30.

17. Moses M. Davis to John Fox Potter, Oct. 25, 1857, Potter Papers; *Kenosha Tribune and Telegraph,* Aug. 5, 1858; *Milwaukee Sentinel,* Nov. 18, 1857. Lecompton resolutions were debated in the Wisconsin assembly and senate in 1858. Those debates clearly illustrate the differences between Republicans and Democrats, with Republicans focusing on the slavery question, Democrats on popular sovereignty. See the *Senate Journal, 1858,* 251, 266–67, 314–18, 326–27, 380–82 and the *Assembly Journal, 1858,* 217–18, 239–41, 1107–13, 1130–31, 1162–64; Bestor, "State Sovereignty and Slavery," 122–27. Many Northern Democrats expressed that same desire, but they relied instead on "geographical conditions," such as soil and climate, to keep slavery penned up, not on positive action. Thus, while one does not have to question the sincerity of their antislavery professions, it seems reasonable to suggest that they may have been halfhearted, more concerned with ending slavery agitation than slavery itself.

18. *Milwaukee Sentinel,* Mar. 14, Dec. 19, 1857; *Kenosha Tribune and Telegraph,* Aug. 5, Sept. 23, 1858; Moses M. Davis to John Fox Potter, July 31, 1857, V. H. Hewes to John Fox Potter, Mar. 6, 1858, Potter Papers; Fehrenbacher, *The Dred Scott Case,* 451–55; Potter, *Impending Crisis,* 287–89, 308–9; Foner, *Free Soil, Free Labor, Free Men,* 100.

19. Moses M. Davis to John Fox Potter, Dec. 24, 1857, Davis to Potter, July 31, Oct. 25, 1857, A. A. Huntington to Potter, Mar. 27, 1857, all in the Potter Papers; *Milwaukee Sentinel,* Sept. 10, 1857, Feb. 27, Mar. 4, 15, 27, 30, 1858; *Monroe Sentinel,* Jan. 6, Feb. 13, 1858; *Wisconsin Daily Free Democrat,* Feb. 8, Mar. 15, 1858; *Portage City Record,* Dec. 23, 1857; *Kenosha Tribune and Telegraph,* Feb. 25, 1858.

20. Moses M. Davis to John Fox Potter, Apr. 5, 1858, John Jenkins to Nathaniel P. Banks, Feb. 9, 1858, both in the Potter Papers.

21. "Badger" to the *Monroe Sentinel,* Feb. 10, 1858.

22. Frank was now editing the *Kenosha Tribune and Telegraph,* see Jan. 14, 1858, as well as Feb. 11, 1858; *Milwaukee Sentinel,* Nov. 18, 1857, Jan. 28, 1858; E. G. Dyer to John Fox Potter, Feb. 17, 1858, Potter Papers; *Wisconsin Daily Free Democrat,* Apr. 10, 1858.

23. *Baraboo Republic,* Apr. 23, 1857; *Janesville Gazette,* Mar. 27, 1857; *Fond Du Lac Commonwealth,* Mar. 20, 1857; *Wisconsin Daily Free Democrat,* Mar. 20, 1857.

24. *Portage City Record,* Oct. 27, 1858; *Wisconsin State Journal,* June 4, 1857. Also see Potter's conclusion in *The Impending Crisis,* 291–96, Fehrenbacher's in *The Dred Scott Case,* 453, and Sewell's in *Ballots For Freedom,* 299–303.

25. S. S. Bradford to John Fox Potter, May 14, 1858, Potter Papers. Historians have correctly pointed out Republican attempts to tone down their antislavery appeal in order to woo conservatives in the presidential campaign of 1860, but they fail to credit the determination of the radicals and most moderates to stand fast in their antislavery position, no matter the consequences. And if Wisconsin is at all representative, radicals and moderates made up a huge majority of the party faithful. Potter, *The Impending Crisis,* 419–28, discusses the pressures on Republicans to moderate their antislavery stance.

26. James Doolittle to Horace Tenney, Sept. 27, 1858, Tenney Papers, and Nevins, *Emergence of Lincoln* 1:254, on Republican electoral disappointments in 1857.

27. *Annual Messages of the Governors of Wisconsin, 1848–1875,* 34–42, contains Randall's address of January 15, 1858. See Josiah Noonan to Horace Tenney, Feb. 18, 1856, and Feb. 23, 1857, Dec. 14, 1857, Tenney Papers, for Noonan's early petitions to inquire into the allegations of widespread fraud in the 1855 legislature and his frustration with the Republican's failure to inquire into the matter. It was later revealed that Republican governor Bashford had accepted a fifty thousand dollar bribe for signing the measure, thus helping account for his reluctance to investigate. For Noonan's support of Randall, see Noonan to Tenney, Sept. 2, 1857, also in the Tenney Papers. He hoped by helping the Republicans to "break them [the Barstowites] . . . to pieces." Noonan's assistance to the Republicans also was prompted by the favoritism shown by Buchanan for Barstow men in dispensing the patronage. Noonan himself had been removed from his position as Milwaukee's postmaster. He offered to help the Republican in the investigation so long as it was conducted in a nonpartisan fashion. Noonan, it should be added, was cosigning notes for Randall, who as usual was broke. For other sources on the Noonan-Republican connection, see Noonan's correspondence from John Fox Potter, Jan. 14, Mar. 8, 20, Apr. 2, 5, 19, 25, 29, May 5, 1858, Alexander Randall to Noonan, Jan. 5, Feb. 1, 3, 15, 25, Mar. 23, 1858, all in the Noonan Papers; Josiah Noonan to Horace Tenney, Feb. 9, Mar. 1, 1858, in the Tenney Papers, and the *Weekly Wisconsin Patriot,* July 7, Aug. 7, 21, Sept. 4, 26, Oct. 2, 1858, which ran an expose of Noonan's alleged influence in obtaining backing for Randall in the 1857 Republican convention. The allegations were put together by E. B. Quiner, a Republican opponent of Randall. Booth, in the *Wisconsin Daily Free Democrat,* Nov. 18, 1857, also claimed that Noonan, an "ingrained proslavery man," had helped the governor. Current, *History of Wisconsin,* 242–48, 267–68, gives details on the investigation.

28. *Wisconsin Daily Free Democrat,* Feb. 18, 27, June 7, July 24, 27, Aug. 2, 1858; *Monroe Sentinel,* Aug. 26, 1858; *Menasha Conservator,* Aug. 5, 1858; *Mineral Point Tribune,* July 27, 1858; *Portage City Record,* Aug. 14, 1858; *Wisconsin State Journal,* June 5, Aug. 4, Sept. 2, 1858. The Address of the German Republicans is in the *Free Democrat,* Aug. 28, 1858, and the *Milwaukee Sentinel,* Aug. 30, 1858. The *Milwaukee Sentinel,* whose editor, Rufus King, had been named the recipient of railroad promoter largesse during the 1858 investigation, kept largely silent during this controversy, perhaps not wishing to incur the wrath of Randall, who, to popular acclaim, conducted the investigation in an even-handed manner.

29. *Wisconsin Daily Free Democrat,* June 9, 10, 1858; *Wisconsin State Journal,* Aug. 4, 5, 1858.

30. *Wisconsin State Journal,* July 12, Sept. 27, 1857. Booth and Rublee traded increasingly bitter words and accused each other of trying to rule the party, but instead divided it. See the *Journal,* Aug. 24, 25, 1858, and Josiah Noonan to Horace Tenney, Aug. 26, 1857, Tenney Papers, for the attitude of Randall's men toward "Booth, the mercenary curse," and the *Free Democrat,* Sept. 27, 1858, for Booth's side.

31. Timothy Howe to Horace Rublee, Aug. 23, 1858, Howe Papers.

32. William Rogers to Horace Tenney, July 13, 1858, E. L. Phillips to Tenney, July 14, 1858, George Garry to Tenney, July 26, 1858, Gregor Menzel to Tenney, July 14, 1858, G. S. Graves to Tenney, July 26, 1858, William P. Lyons to Tenney, July 13, 1858, all in the Tenney Papers. Randall, Rufus King, John Fox Potter, James Doolittle, and Josiah Noonan were reportedly the prime movers behind the suggestion for the call. See John Fox Potter to Horace Tenney, Oct. 1, 1858, and James Doolittle to Tenney, Sept. 27, 1858, in the Tenney Papers, the *Milwaukee Sentinel,* Aug. 6, 1858, and the *Baraboo Republic,* Aug. 19, 1858. Tenney's recent appointment as state comptroller also brought down the wrath of Booth, with whom he had been quarreling for years. He was also a close ally of Randall and Noonan, and once had been accused of attempting to rig the bidding for state printing jobs while Barstow was governor.

33. *Wisconsin Daily Free Democrat,* Aug. 4, 5, 6, 1858.

34. *Wisconsin State Journal,* July 30, Aug. 5, 24, 25, 27, Sept. 14, 1858; *Weekly Wisconsin Patriot,* Aug. 7, 1858. The *Patriot* noted that the *Journal*'s offensive against Booth had been devised by Noonan. That may have been true since Noonan had advised Tenney that Randall and the Republican party needed a stronger, bolder, more assertive paper than the *State Journal.* Rublee seems to have gotten the word and immediately gone on the offensive. See Noonan to Horace Tenney, July 27, Aug. 26, 1858, Tenney Papers.

35. *Wisconsin Daily Free Democrat,* Aug. 17, Sept. 13, 1858. Booth was referring to Tenney's alleged attempt to win state printing contracts while still a Democratic editor by bribing Barstow and other influential Democrats in his administration who made up "the Balance."

36. Ibid., Aug. 4, 17, 20, Sept. 25, 27, 28, 1858.

37. Ibid., Sept. 27, 28, 1858; *Wisconsin State Journal,* Sept. 18, 25, 1858. Booth and Harrison Reed had consulted about the necessity of another Madison paper, and Reed had agreed "to assume charge" of one if the need arose.

38. *Wisconsin Daily Free Democrat,* Oct. 6, 7, 1858.

39. *Milwaukee Sentinel,* Oct. 7, 8, 1858; *Monroe Sentinel,* Oct. 13, 20, 1858; *Portage City Record,* Oct. 13, 1858. Current, *History of Wisconsin,* 268, notes that the Republican resolution called for opposition to the "further extension of the African race upon this continent," in a "cynical appeal to [party] racists." In fact, the resolution called for opposition to the extension of the "slavery of the African Race upon this continent." The *Sentinel,* on October 8, had incorrectly printed the resolve as picked up by Current and other historians. Others appointed to compose the address included Moses Davis, Carl Schurz, Harrison Reed, and Edward Daniels, all well-known states' righters and party radicals.

40. The *Milwaukee Sentinel,* Oct. 14, 1858, contains the "Address of the Republican State Convention to the People Of the State of Wisconsin," which was signed by Booth, Rublee, and King, presumably as a show of party unity.

41. The *Wisconsin State Journal,* Oct. 9, 18, 30, 1858, printed the campaign schedules of the Democratic speakers and warned Republicans not to be complacent.

42. Potter and Washburne won reelection; Billinghurst lost in a close contest to Charles Larrabee, a good friend of Douglas.

43. The party regularity from 1856 to 1858 assumes those same people were in the state in 1856 or that, if they were Democrats or Republicans in 1856, they remained the same two years later.

44. *Grant County Herald,* Nov. 13, 27, Dec. 11, 25, 1858. Joseph Cover especially was critical of the "fearful, let-alone and cowardly" *State Journal,* and he hoped it would cease to do business in favor of a stronger, more reliable Republican paper. Although Washburn gained reelection, his total vote in 1858 was ten thousand less than in 1856, which lent some credence to the charge. However, most of the falloff was probably a result of lower turnout. Still, the Democratic total in Dane County did increase dramatically over 1857's total, while the Republican tally declined, suggesting that at least a few Republicans voted for the Democratic challenger.

45. Carl Schurz to Moses M. Davis, Aug. 24, 1858, Davis Papers, for one Republican's dissatisfaction with Billinghurst. Also see Flately, "The Wisconsin Congressional Delegation from Statehood to Secession, 1848–1861," 87–91. It is more likely that Billinghurst lost more due to Douglas's popularity in the traditionally heavily Democratic northern district than to stay-at-home states' righters. In addition, Larrabee was a well-known Democrat and judge from the area and was himself popular with the region's voters.

46. Taney's decision is in the *Records of Cases Argued and Adjudged in the Supreme Court of the United States: In the Matter of the United States v. Sherman M. Booth; and Stephen V. R. Ableman, Plaintiff in Error, v. Sherman M. Booth, Dec. Term, 1858, Vol. XXI, 1859, 21 Howard,* 506–26 (hereafter referred to as *Ableman v. Booth*). Also see Morris, *Free Men All,* 175–76; Bestor, "State Sovereignty and Slavery," 136–42; Mason, "The Fugitive Slave Law in Wisconsin With Reference To Nullification Sentiment," 138–40, for other perspectives on the decision.

47. *Ableman v. Booth,* 517–21.

48. Ibid., 525–26; Morris, *Free Men All,* 178–80.

49. *Ableman v. Booth,* 526.

50. The *Laws of Wisconsin, 1859,* 247–48, contains the Joint Resolution. For the legislative proceedings, see the *Assembly Journal, 1859,* 777–79, 863–65, and the *Senate Journal, 1859,* 749–50. This resolution echoed one Thomas Jefferson wrote and the Kentucky legislature adopted on November 10, 1798.

51. *Laws of Wisconsin, 1859,* 248. The lawmakers substituted "positive defiance" for "nullification."

52. The assembly vote was forty-seven to thirty-six, with the Republicans providing all of the votes in favor and only three against the resolves; four abstained. In the senate, the tally was thirteen to twelve. No Republican senator voted against the resolves; one abstained.

53. The quote is from the *Kenosha Tribune and Telegraph,* Mar. 24, 1859; *Wisconsin Daily Free Democrat,* Mar. 21, 1859; *Milwaukee Sentinel,* Mar. 15, 1859; *Wisconsin State Journal,* Mar. 11, 1859. Timothy Howe, unsurprisingly, did not support the resolves, and he mistakenly asserted that "they are copied mainly from Mr. Calhoun." Timothy Howe to Horace Rublee, Mar. 24, 1859, Howe Papers.

54. Byron Kilbourn to Rufus King, in the *Mineral Point Tribune,* June 8, 1858; *Menasha Conservator,* Feb. 19, 1859. Kilbourn claimed that Barstow's charges were "untrue, unsound and dangerous . . . sacrificing truth to his desire for revenge."

55. *Wisconsin State Journal,* Feb. 10, Mar. 4, 1859; *Menasha Conservator,* Feb. 19, 26, 1859; *Wisconsin Daily Free Democrat,* Feb. 7, Mar. 28, 1859.

56. *Wisconsin State Journal,* Feb. 17, 1859; *Wisconsin Daily Free Democrat,* Feb. 14, 21, 1859; Timothy Howe to Horace Rublee, Aug. 23, 1859, Howe Papers. Current, *History of Wisconsin,* 268–70, recounts the Republican desire to maintain a clean political image. Remarkably, the Democrats in 1858 ran five candidates who had received a total of $305,000 in railroad bonds.

57. The *Wisconsin State Journal,* Jan. 12, 22, Feb. 10, 22, 1859, and the *Mineral Point Tribune,* Jan. 25, Feb. 22, 1859, seemed to think backing Smith as an independent solved the problem of having to keep or set aside the judge. The Democratic course changed all that.

58. *Wisconsin State Journal,* Feb. 17, 1859; *Milwaukee Sentinel,* Feb. 18, 1859; *Wisconsin Daily Free Democrat,* Feb. 21, 1859; *Menasha Conservator,* Feb. 19, 26, 1859. Thirty-six of the fifty Republican legislators present at the meeting reportedly voted for Paine.

59. *Milwaukee Sentinel,* Feb. 28, 1859; *Wisconsin State Journal,* February 21, 1859.

60. *Wisconsin Daily Free Democrat,* Feb. 22, 26, 28, 1859.

61. *Wisconsin State Journal,* Mar. 4, 1859; *Menasha Conservator,* Mar. 5, 12, 1859; *Milwaukee Sentinel,* Mar. 7, 1859; *Wisconsin Daily Free Democrat,* Mar. 5, 1859. Smith formally withdrew from the race on March 15, lest his independent candidacy split the Republican vote. The *Milwaukee Sentinel,* Mar. 17, 1859, carried Smith's statement.

62. The *Milwaukee Sentinel,* Mar. 9, 1859, contains the "Address."

63. Ibid.

64. Ibid., Mar. 24, 1859, contains Schurz's speech in full; also see Apr. 4, 1859, for a similar public address Schurz gave in Kenosha on March 31. He eulogized Jefferson and the Kentucky Resolutions and denounced the Democratic party for its continuous "submission" to every enactment of the slave power. He called on Wisconsinites to stand firm on "the question of State Rights. . . . Here is the battlefield, every man to his gun." Schurz later claimed that his Milwaukee speech was the most well received of any he ever gave, but after the war he did not include it among his published addresses because his views had changed. Sellers, "Republicanism and State Rights in Wisconsin," 227.

65. *Milwaukee Sentinel,* Mar. 28, 1859; *Wisconsin State Journal,* Mar. 25, 26, 1859; *Kenosha Telegraph,* Mar. 24, 1859; *Wisconsin Daily Free Democrat,* Mar. 25, 28, 1859; *Mineral Point Tribune,* Apr. 5, 1859; *Grant County Herald,* Mar. 25, 1859; *Menasha Conservator,* Mar. 26, 1859; *Monroe Sentinel,* Mar. 30, 1859; William H. Brisbane to Carl Schurz, Apr. 4, 1859, Schurz Papers, for examples of Republican support for Paine on the basis of states' rights.

66. About one thousand more votes were recorded in that election than in the prior year's record-setting congressional contest, representing about 65 percent of the eligible electors; it was the largest turnout for a state elective office to date.

67. Table 16, which looks at the 1859 judicial and 1858 congressional elections shows no evidence of crossover. Table 17, an analysis of the 1859 judicial and gubernatorial contests, suggests that some crossover occurred. Estimated relationships between the 1860 state supreme court election with the 1859 judicial and governor's races, show a significantly less pronounced tendency of Republicans to cross over and vote for their opponents. My overall impression is that the estimate of seventy-five hundred crossover Republican votes from Paine to Lynde is probably too high, especially given Lynde's well-known conservatism on slavery issues.

68. Rublee, in the *Wisconsin State Journal,* Apr. 14, 1859, acknowledged that "the great mass of Republicans in this state differ with Judge Howe and agree with Judge Paine," but he insisted, inaccurately I think, that they did not necessarily "endorse the doctrine of nullification." Also see McManus, "'Freedom and Liberty First, and the Union Afterwards,'" 51–52.

69. *Portage City Record,* Apr. 20, 1859. Also see the *Kenosha Telegraph,* Apr. 14, 1859, and the *Wisconsin Daily Free Democrat,* Apr. 13, 1859, now under the editorship of Christopher Sholes, for similar sentiments, and the *Menasha Conservator,* Aug. 5, 1858, for an expression of the centrality of the principle of "state sovereignty" to the Republican creed. Compare these expressions to Rublee's in the prior note.

70. Timothy Howe to Horace Rublee, Mar. 24, 25, Apr. 3, 1859, and Aug. 14, 1857; Howe to John Tweedy, Apr. 11, 17, 1859, all in the Howe Papers. Also see the *Wisconsin State Journal,* Apr. 14, 1859.

71. Timothy Howe to Horace Rublee, Apr. 3, 1859, Howe Papers; *Wisconsin State Journal,* Apr. 11, 22, 1859; *Wisconsin Daily Free Democrat,* Apr. 7, 14, 22, 1859.

72. Howe apparently chose the Oshkosh paper, which was one of the few Republican organs friendly to his views, instead of the *Journal,* perhaps fearing that his friend Rublee would be hurt if he was viewed as siding with Howe.

73. *Portage City Record,* Apr. 20, 1859; *Racine Advocate,* June 22, 1859; *Wisconsin State Journal,* Apr. 22, 23, May 7, 19, 30, June 25, 1859; *Wisconsin Daily Free Democrat,* Apr. 22, May 17, 1859; Timothy Howe to Horace Rublee, Apr. 11, 14, 1859, Howe Papers.

74. Edward Daniels to Horace Tenney, March 5, 1859, Tenney Papers. Daniels was a Randall appointee to the post of state geologist and an ardent antislavery man who deeply resented Booth's "impolitic" and "contemptible" opposition to the governor's appointment policies. Booth had little use for the state party committee, considering it the tool of wire-pulling politicians. He instead preferred platform and even important policy decisions to be made by the people meeting in mass convention. As a result, he often ignored appointments to the committee, with the result that some of his greatest enemies, the Know Nothings in 1855 and Horace Tenney in 1858, succeeded in obtaining important positions on it from which to exert influence.

75. The *Whitewater Register,* in the *Menasha Conservator,* Mar. 19, 1859. Also see the *Conservator,* Mar. 5, 12, 26, for evidence of other disaffection with Booth, as well the *Wisconsin Daily Free Democrat,* Mar. 8, 12, 1859, for Booth's denial of dictating to the party, and the *Wisconsin State Journal,* Mar. 8, 1859, which admits that both the *Free Democrat* and the *Journal* were under attack from some of their editorial brethren, who were demanding that the party's leading papers be placed in the hands of "less dictatorial and less vulnerable men."

76. Horace Tenney to Alexander Randall, Mar. 12, 1859, Tenney Papers; C. C. Washburn to John Fox Potter, July 10, 1859, Potter Papers; *Racine Weekly Journal,* Feb. 11, 23, Mar. 9, June 29, 1859; *Wisconsin Daily Free Democrat,* Feb. 7, 8, 17, 19, 23, 1859. Noonan was reported to be in Madison actively working on Tenney's behalf.

77. Carl Schurz to John Fox Potter, Dec. 24, 1858, Aug. 12, 1859, Potter Papers; D. W. Clark to Horace Tenney, Aug. 22, 1859, Tenney Papers; George W. Tenney to Carl Schurz, Aug. 19, 1859, J. W. Hoyt to Schurz, Aug. 19, 1859, Schurz Papers; Timothy Howe to Horace Rublee, Aug. 21, 1857, Howe Papers; *Wisconsin State Journal,* July 14, 15, Aug. 4, 1859; *Wisconsin Daily Free Democrat,* Aug. 22, 1859; *Racine Weekly Journal,* June 29, Aug. 13, Sept. 7, 14, 1859; *Weekly Wisconsin Patriot,* Dec. 31, 1859. Timothy Howe, to no one's surprise, endorsed the governor over Schurz, the states' rights candidate. A. M. Thompson, *A Political History of Wisconsin,* 142–45; William H. Russell, "Timothy O. Howe, Stalwart Republican," 90–99. In shoring up support among his opponents, Randall, for example, had appointed the editors of

the *Beaver Dam Citizen* and the *Manitowoc Tribune* to minor offices and thereby muted their criticism. David Atwood, former editor of the *State Journal,* was named state librarian; William Watson, King's assistant at the *Sentinel,* was Randall's personal secretary; and Harrison Reed, to the wonder of many, had taken over the editorship of the *State Journal.* After the election, the governor continued to pursue his strategy of consolidating his power and bringing harmony to the party when he appointed Christopher Sholes to the vacant post of secretary of state and Louis P. Harvey to a clerkship within the department.

78. For brief accounts of the trial, see Current, *History of Wisconsin,* 272–73; Beitzinger, *Edward G. Ryan, Lion of the Law,* 63–64, and E. Bruce Thompson, *Matthew Hale Carpenter, Webster of the West,* 61–62.

79. *Weekly Wisconsin Patriot,* Mar. 26, 1859.

80. *Menasha Conservator,* Apr. 9, 16, 1859. In the wake of his indictment, Booth wisely surrendered control of the *Freeman* to his old ally Christopher Sholes. *Wisconsin Daily Free Democrat,* Mar. 26, 1859.

81. The *Mineral Point Tribune,* Feb. 15, 1855, published the address. Also see the *Menasha Conservator,* Apr. 16, 1859, and the *Wisconsin State Journal,* Apr. 19, 1859, on Whiton's death and Dixon's appointment, and the *Racine Advocate,* Apr. 27, 1859, for the rumor that Dixon was cut in the Howe mold. For background on the assurances Randall received from Moses Davis, an ardent states' rights man, on Dixon's soundness, and on Davis's denial of providing those assurances, see the *Racine Advocate,* Mar. 28, 1860, and the *Portage City Record,* Apr. 4, 1860. The *Record* was Davis's home organ. Henry Tenney to Horace Tenney, Apr. 15, 1859, Tenney Papers, states to his brother that this was an "opportune" time to place Dixon on the bench, perhaps alluding to Booth's problems and hoping to slip Dixon in while the Milwaukee editor's political influence was declining.

82. *Wisconsin Daily Free Democrat,* Apr. 22, 29, 1859. Sholes probably received his information from Moses Davis, who may have been misled by Dixon.

83. *Wisconsin Reports, 1860, Ableman v. Booth,* unpaginated; Ranney, "Suffering the Agonies of their Righteousness," 107–8.

84. *Racine Advocate,* Dec. 21, 1859, Jan. 25, 1860; *Portage City Record,* Dec. 28, 1859, Jan. 4, 1860; *Wisconsin Daily Free Democrat,* Dec. 15, 1859; *Kenosha Telegraph,* Feb. 9, 23, 1860.

85. *Portage City Record,* Feb. 1, 8, 1860; *Baraboo Republic,* Jan. 19, 26, 1860; *Kenosha Telegraph,* Feb. 23, 1860; *Racine Advocate,* Jan. 18, 25, 1860; *Wisconsin State Journal,* Jan. 20, 22, 27, 1860. The *Milwaukee Sentinel,* Jan. 14, 19, 20, 30, 31, 1860, ran a series of pieces written by different Republicans arguing the merits and drawbacks of making a nomination and taking a stand on the states' rights question.

86. *Wisconsin State Journal,* Mar. 2, 1860; *Milwaukee Sentinel,* Mar. 2, 1860; *Baraboo Republic,* Mar. 1, 1860; Carl Schurz to John Fox Potter, Apr. 12, 1860, Potter Papers.

87. *Wisconsin State Journal,* Mar. 1, 1860; *Portage City Record,* Mar. 7, 1860; *Milwaukee Sentinel,* Mar. 2, 1860; *Racine Advocate,* Mar. 7, 1860. About 230 delegates attended the convention, so Dixon's support seems to have been negligible.

88. C. L Sholes to John Fox Potter, Mar. 10, 1860, Potter Papers; *Wisconsin State Journal,* Feb. 17, 1860; *Portage City Record,* Mar. 7, 21, 1860; "Republican" to the *Milwaukee Sentinel,* Jan. 19, 1860; *Beloit Courier,* in the *Milwaukee Sentinel,* Mar. 17, 1860; *Oconto Pioneer,* Feb. 4, 1860.

89. Moses M. Davis to John Fox Potter, Apr. 8, 1860, Davis Papers; Mathilde to Fritz Anneke, July 4, 1860, Anneke Papers. The Annekes were a prominent German-born Milwaukee couple and good friends of Booth and his wife. They earlier had noted the inability of the states' rights faction to contend with Randall and his friends without Booth to lead

them. Mathilde stated simply, they did not "know what to do." Mathilde to Fritz Anneke, Sept. 26, 1859, also in the Anneke Papers.

90. C. L. Sholes to John Fox Potter, Mar. 10, 1860, Potter Papers; *Racine Advocate,* Mar. 7, 1860; *Milwaukee Sentinel,* Mar. 12, 1860; *Wisconsin State Journal,* Mar. 8, 1860; *Portage City Record,* Feb. 1, 1860. Horace Tenney, still smarting from the attacks of Booth and the "state rights party," was the most prominent Republican named in the petition to Dixon urging him to run, along with the former Know Nothing Republican and member of the Republican state committee, Elisha Keyes. Keyes actively worked with Democratic leaders to get out the vote for Dixon. See George M. Paul to Elisha Keyes, Mar. 24, 1860, A. L. Hayes to Keyes, Mar. 25, 1860, Moses M. Strong to Keyes, Mar. 26, 1860, Samuel C. Bean to Keyes, Mar. 26, 1860, all in the Keyes Papers; Elisha M. Keyes to George M. Paul, Mar. 25, 1860, Paul Papers.

91. Clement's quotation comes from his *Racine Advocate,* Mar. 14, 1860; *Wisconsin Daily Free Democrat,* Mar. 6, 8, 1860; *Kenosha Telegraph,* Mar. 8, 1860; *Grant County Herald,* Mar. 17, 1860; *Wisconsin State Journal,* Mar. 5, 7, 1860; Henry J. Paine to John Fox Potter, Mar. 12, 1860, Potter Papers. The *State Journal,* unlike most party papers, urged Sloan not to reply to the demands of those seeking a public statement from him.

92. A. Scott Sloan to Elisha Keyes, Mar. 6, 1860, Keyes Papers; C. L. Sholes to John Fox Potter, Mar. 10, 1860, Potter Papers; *Wisconsin State Journal,* Mar. 17, 1860.

93. *Wisconsin State Journal,* Mar. 15, 17, 1860, contains Sloan's Mar. 6 letter to his brother. Also see the *Wisconsin Daily Free Democrat,* Mar. 17, 1860; *Grant County Herald,* Mar. 24, 1860; *Racine Advocate,* Mar. 21, 28, 1860. A number of Republicans, including the *State Journal,* were incensed with those who had coerced Sloan into making known his opinions and seeming once again to be placing the party officially in favor of states' rights. They claimed it would only divide the party. The fact is, Sloan was in a very uncomfortable position. He probably would have lost far more states' rights support had he not gone public, than he lost by doing so. For the attitudes of Republicans upset with the candidate's public avowal, see S. J. Torld to Elisha Keyes, Mar. 22, 1860, J. B. Quimby to Keyes, Mar. 23, 1860, both in the Keyes Papers.

94. Dixon received four thousand more votes than Lynde and Sloan about forty-six hundred less than Paine. Probably four thousand Republican abstainers and crossover voters put Dixon over the top, but it is worth noting that the Republican masses still overwhelmingly backed Sloan and the states' rights position.

95. Reed was accused of abandoning states' rights shortly after he took over the editorial duties of the *State Journal* and, according to Charles Clement, came "under the seductive influence of public patronage." See Clement's *Racine Advocate,* Jan. 18, 25, Apr. 11, 18, 1860. Joseph Cover, in his *Grant County Herald,* Apr. 14, 1860, also vigorously denounced Reed and the *Journal* for allegedly being allied with Madison Republicans who were working against Sloan. Reed denied he had abandoned the states' rights position, but he urged that the looming race for the presidency take precedence over all else. For that reason, he thought it was unwise to push the states' rights position, "Regardless of the consequences to the unity and success of the Republican party." Republicans like Reed and Rufus King seemed to believe it far more likely that Howe and his backers would bolt the party if they continued to suffer "proscription" at the hands of the Republican majority and the states' rights leadership than that the states' righters would abandon the Republican party. *Wisconsin State Journal,* Jan. 27, Feb. 17, Apr. 5, 10, 11, 1860. King too had begun to tone down his position on states' rights. See the *Milwaukee Sentinel,* Mar. 27, 1860. Carl Schurz, who was beginning to moderate his states' rights position, like Reed, blamed the states' righters for Sloan's defeat; see Schurz to

John Fox Potter, Apr. 12, 1860, Potter Papers. For the suggestion that Schurz, who "dabbles in fashionable politics," was beginning to trim on states' rights, on "orders from his chief," William H. Seward, see Mathilde to Fritz Anneke, Mar. 31, July 4, 1860, in the Anneke Papers. Charles Durkee to Moses M. Davis, Apr. 11, 1860, Davis Papers; and Moses M. Davis to John Fox Potter, Apr. 8, 1860, Potter Papers, for the despondency of states' righters.

TWELVE *The End of the Antislavery Question Has Arrived*

1. *Milwaukee Sentinel,* Feb. 3, 1860, for an early statement of support for Seward, and May 22, 1860, for King's postconvention comments; Potter, *Impending Crisis,* 418–30; Current, *History of Wisconsin,* 282–83; Nevins, *Emergence of Lincoln* 2:229–60. Sewell, *Ballots For Freedom,* 358–64, provides a useful and more balanced analysis of the notion that the Republicans took a more distinctly conservative stance on slavery in 1860. Mark W. Summers, *The Plundering Generation: Corruption and the Crisis of the Union, 1849–1861,* 269–80; David A. Meerse, "Buchanan, Corruption and the Election of 1860," *Civil War History,* 116–31.

2. Major Keyes [?—illegible, probably Elisha's brother] to Elisha Keyes, Oct. 14, 1860, Keyes Papers; Frank, Diary, Oct. 24, 1860, Frank Papers; *Milwaukee Sentinel,* July 12, 1860, for some evidence of Republican enthusiasm in Wisconsin. Also see Potter, *Impending Crisis,* 434–36; Nevins, *The Emergence of Lincoln* 2:298–305.

3. Current, *History of Wisconsin,* 281, 285–86; Potter, *Impending Crisis,* 407–16, 440–41; Nevins, *The Emergence of Lincoln* 2:290–98. A fourth candidate, John Bell of Tennessee, was put forward by an "Old Gentlemen's Party," comprised primarily of alarmed conservatives, most of whom had Whig antecedents, in support of the Constitution and the Union. Neither Bell's nor Breckinridge's candidacy was a factor in the Wisconsin race, the latter ultimately picking up 889 votes, the former 151.

4. For analyses of the South on the eve of the war, see J. Mills Thornton III, *Power and Politics in a Slave Society: Alabama, 1800–1860;* Steven A. Channing, *Crisis of Fear; Secession in South Carolina;* William L. Barney, *The Secessionist Impulse: Alabama and Mississippi in 1860;* Potter, *Impending Crisis,* 430–32; Holt, *Political Crisis of the 1850s,* 219–59; Sewell, *Ballots For Freedom,* 343, 364–65.

5. By contrast, Frémont's support from previous nonvoters was probably around 45 percent.

6. See Nevins, *Emergence of Lincoln* 2:298–306, for a critique of Republican complacency on the danger the nation faced.

7. Sewell, *Ballots For Freedom,* 361–64.

8. The *Milwaukee Sentinel,* Jan. 23, 1858, and the *Wisconsin Daily Free Democrat,* Apr. 10, 1858, provide two Republican responses to the disunion cry during the Lecompton crisis. Chapter eight discusses Wisconsin Republican Unionism in greater detail.

9. Main, Diary, Oct. 20, Nov. 2, 4, 24, 25, Dec. 2, 1859, Main Papers; Cheever, Diary, Dec. 3, 1859, Cheever Papers; *Kenosha Telegraph,* Nov. 24, 1859; *Monroe Sentinel,* Oct. 26, Dec. 7, 1859; *Milwaukee Sentinel,* Dec. 1, 1859; *Racine Advocate,* Dec. 7, 1859; *Wisconsin State Journal,* Dec. 2, 1859. The Democrats, of course, were outraged at Brown's raid and called it "the inevitable tendency of Republican teachings." *Weekly Wisconsin Patriot,* Oct. 22, 1859. For the reflections of one prominent Democrat, see Smith, Diary, Oct. 19, Nov. 16, 17, Dec. 2, 1859, Smith Papers.

10. Timothy Howe to Horace Rublee, Oct. 26, Dec. 5, 1859, Howe Papers; *Wisconsin State Journal*, Nov. 31, Dec. 2, 1859; *Wisconsin Daily Free Democrat*, Oct. 20, 1859.

11. These sentiments were adopted at a radical meeting in Milwaukee, attended by the German Republicans Gregor Menzel and Bernard Domschke, as well as Edward Holton, Charles Sholes, and James H. Paine, all prominent party men. The *Milwaukee Sentinel*, Dec. 3, 1859, contains the resolutions adopted at that meeting. Also see the *Kenosha Telegraph*, Nov. 24, 1859, the *Monroe Sentinel*, Dec. 7, 1859, and the *Wisconsin Daily Free Democrat*, Oct. 25, 1859. An alarmed John Tweedy warned radicals not to misrepresent the Republican position on Brown with avowals of support. The *Sentinel* printed Tweedy's concerns on December 7, 1859.

12. *Racine Advocate*, Dec. 7, 1859; *Kenosha Telegraph*, Dec. 1, 1859.

13. *Milwaukee Sentinel*, Nov. 28, Dec. 3, 1859, Feb. 3, 1860; *Wisconsin Daily Free Democrat*, Nov. 10, 14, 1859; *Prescott Transcript*, Jan. 21, 1860.

14. *Wisconsin State Journal*, July 27, 1860; *Milwaukee Sentinel*, Nov. 28, 1859, Aug. 9, Nov. 6, 1860.

15. *Milwaukee Sentinel*, Nov. 20, 1860; *Kenosha Telegraph*, Nov. 22, 1860.

16. Christopher Sholes to John Fox Potter, Nov. 18, Dec. 27, 1860, Feb. 6, 1861, Edwin Palmer to Potter, Feb. 11, 1861, Jared Thompson to Potter, undated, probably late 1860, Potter Papers; Henry to James Doolittle, Nov. 28, 1860, Doolittle Papers; Jerome R. Brigham to John Fox Potter, Dec. 8, 1860, Jerome R. Brigham Papers; Main, Diary, Nov. 9, 1860, Main Papers; *Baraboo Republic*, Nov. 15, 1860; *Portage City Record*, Feb. 13, 1861.

17. Stampp, "Concept of a Perpetual Union," 4–36, rightly notes that the principle of states' rights battled for supremacy with the concept of absolute unionism from the earliest days of the Republic up to the outbreak of the Civil War.

18. Special Message of Governor Alexander Randall, May 15, 1861, *Messages of the Governors of Wisconsin, 1861*, 7–8. For other examples of growing Republican willingness to accept force to preserve the Union, see the *Kenosha Telegraph*, Nov. 22, 1860, Feb. 7, 1861; *Baraboo Republic*, Apr. 11, 1861; *Wisconsin State Journal*, Feb. 5, 6, 1861.

19. Bestor, "State Sovereignty and Slavery," 136–40; Belz, *A New Birth of Freedom*, 113–82.

20. George M. Dennison, *The Dorr War: Republicanism on Trial, 1831–1861* (Lexington, 1976), 6–8, 195–205, takes a similar stand.

21. *Baraboo Republic*, Mar. 8, 22, 1860.

22. *Wisconsin State Journal*, Aug. 20, 1860; *Milwaukee Sentinel*, Aug. 23, 1860.

23. *Racine Weekly Journal*, Oct. 31, 1860. Sewell, *Ballots For Freedom*, most effectively makes the argument for the continuity between Liberty party policies and later political abolitionists.

24. The *Milwaukee Sentinel*, June 15, Nov. 6, 1860, contains excellent editorials on the Republican perception of the degree to which slavery suffused every aspect of American life and threatened its future development.

25. Stampp, "Race, Slavery and the Republican Party," 122–23.

26. Joel Silbey, "The Surge of Republican Power: Partisan Antipathy, American Social Conflict, and the Coming of the Civil War," for a discussion of New England cultural values and politics.

27. Joseph Trotter Mills, Diary, Sept. [?,] 1861, Joseph Trotter Mills Papers.

28. Moses M. Davis to John Fox Potter, Dec. 17, 1860, Davis Papers; E. M. MacGraw to John Fox Potter, May 5, 1861, Potter Papers; *Milwaukee Sentinel*, Jan. 7, Oct. 15, 1861; *Racine Advocate*, July 24, Oct. 23, Nov. 13, 1861; *Racine Daily Journal*, June 5, July 3, 19, 1861; *Kenosha*

Telegraph, Apr. 25, July 18, 1861; Benjamin Piper to the editors of the *Wisconsin State Journal,* Jan. 3, 1862; *Mineral Point Tribune,* May 7, Aug. 2, 1861; *Baraboo Republic,* Feb. 28, Apr. 25, Nov. 13, 1861; *Prescott Transcript,* May 18, 1861; *Grant County Herald,* May 9, June 20, 23, 1861.

29. *Milwaukee Sentinel,* May 27, Oct. 15, Nov. 26, 1861; *Wisconsin State Journal,* May 4, Sept. 2, 1861; *Mineral Point Tribune,* May 21, 1862; *Kenosha Telegraph,* June 20, Aug. 1, 1861; for Republican support of the Lincoln administration. James Prince to John Fox Potter, Jan. 1, 1862, Peter Yates to Potter, Mar. 15, 1862, John Lockwood to Potter, Apr. 17, 1862, Charles Durkee to Potter, Apr. 22, 1862, Marshall M. Strong to Potter, June 10, 1862, all in the Potter Papers, calling for a more aggressive administration position toward slavery. Also see Timothy to Grace Howe, Dec. 13, 1861, for a similar expression. For a Democratic perspective, see George B. Smith, Diary, Oct. 7, 1861, July 25, 1862, Sept. 26, 28, 1862, in the Smith Papers and Donald E. Rasmussen, "Wisconsin Editors and the Civil War: A Study of the Reaction of Wisconsin Editors to the Major Controversial Issues of the Civil War," 52–83.

30. Willet S. Main, Diary, May 19, 1865; also see the entries on Sept. 26, Dec. 31, 1862; Michael Frank, Diary, Dec. 31, 1862, Frank Papers; *Milwaukee Sentinel,* Aug. 2, 8, 1862.

31. See McManus, "Wisconsin Republicans and Negro Suffrage," 36–54, for a more detailed discussion of Republican racial attitudes in Wisconsin.

32. John O. Holzhueter, "Ezekiel Gillespie, Lost and Found," 179–84.

33. Main, Diary, Mar. 31, 1870, Main Papers.

BIBLIOGRAPHY

Manuscript Collections, State Historical Society of Wisconsin

Anneke, Mathilde and Fritz. Papers
Baird, Henry S. Papers
Booth, Sherman M. Papers
Brigham, Jerome R. Papers
Brisbane, William Henry. Papers
Buttles, Anson W. Papers
Cheever, Dustin Grow. Papers
Clark, John G. Papers
Cover, Joseph. Papers
Davis, Moses M. Papers
Dewey, Nelson. Papers
Doolittle, James R. Papers
Fairchild, Lucius. Papers
Frank, Michael. Papers
Hastings, Samuel D. Papers
Holton, Edward D. Papers
Howe, Timothy O. Papers
Jenkins, G. A. Papers
Keyes, Elisha W. Papers

Kilbourn, Byron. Papers
King, Rufus and Charles. Papers
Lakin, George. Papers
Lewis, James T. Papers
Main, Willet S. Papers
Martin, Morgan L. Papers
Mills, Joseph Trotter. Papers
Noonan, Josiah A. Papers
Paine, Byron W. Papers
Paul, George H. Papers
Potter, John Fox. Papers
Schurz, Carl. Papers
Smith, George B. Papers
Strong, Moses M. Papers
Sutherland, James. Papers
Tenney, Horace A. Papers
Tweedy, John H. Papers
Washburn, Cadwallader C. Papers
Woodman, Cyrus. Papers

Wisconsin Newspapers

American Freeman
Appleton Crescent

Baraboo Republic
Beaver Dam Sentinel and Republican

Beloit Journal
Berlin Courant
Chilton Times Journal
Columbus Republican Journal
Daily Argus and Democrat
Daily Milwaukee News
Delavan Messenger
Dodge County Citizen
Elkhorn Independent
Evergreen City Times
Fond du Lac Commonwealth
Fond du Lac Journal
Fond du Lac Union
Fond du Lac Whig
Grant County Herald
Green Bay Advocate
Horicon Argus
Hudson Chronicle
Janesville Gazette
Janesville Standard
Kenosha Democrat
Kenosha Telegraph
Kenosha Times
Kenosha Tribune and Telegraph
La Crosse Democrat
La Crosse Independent Republican
Lafayette City Herald
Manitowoc Herald
Menasha Conservative
Milwaukee Commercial Advertiser
Milwaukee Courier
Milwaukee Daily American
Milwaukee Daily Free Democrat
Milwaukee Democrat
Mineral Point Tribune
Monroe Sentinel
Oconto Pioneer
Omro Republican
Oshkosh Courier

Oshkosh True Democrat
Ozaukee County Advertiser
Platteville Independent American
Portage City Record
Portage Independent
Potosi Republican
Prairie du Chien Courier
Prairie du Chien Leader
Prairie du Chien Patriot
Prescott Transcript
Racine Advocate
Racine Democrat
Racine Weekly Journal
Reedland County Herald
Reedsburg Herald
Sheboygan Journal
Shullsburgh Telegraph
Southport American
Superior Chronicle
Viroqua Herald
Watertown Chronicle
Watertown Democrat
Watertown Weekly Register
Waukesha Democrat
Waukesha Plain Dealer
Waukesha Republican
Weekly Wisconsin
Weekly Wisconsin Patriot
Western Times
Whitewater Register
Wisconsin Argus
Wisconsin Daily Free Democrat
Wisconsin Democrat
Wisconsin Express
Wisconsin Mirror
Wisconsin Pinery
Wisconsin State Journal
Wisconsin Tribune

STATE OF WISCONSIN

Annual Messages of the Governors of the State of Wisconsin, 1848–1875

The Argument of Byron Paine, Esquire: Regarding the Unconstitutionality of the Fugitive Slave Act. Wisconsin Miscellaneous Pamphlets Collection. State Historical Society of Wisconsin.

Executive Department Records: Administration, Routine and Departmental Correspondence, 1836–1871

Green Bay and Prairie Du Chien Papers

Journal of the Convention to Form a Constitution for the State of Wisconsin, Begun and Held at Madison, on the Fifth Day of October, 1846

Journal of the Convention to Form a Constitution for the State of Wisconsin, with a Sketch of the Debates, Begun and Held at Madison, on the Fifteenth Day of December, 1847

Journals of the Assembly of the State of Wisconsin, 1848–1863

Journals of the Council of the Territory of Wisconsin, 1836–1848

Journals of the House of the Territory of Wisconsin, 1836–1848

Journals of the Senate of the State of Wisconsin, 1848–1863

Papers of the Executive Department of the State of Wisconsin: Routine and General Correspondence

Records of Cases Argued and Adjudged in the Supreme Court of the United States: In the Matter of the United States v. Sherman M. Booth; and Stephen V. R. Ableman, Plaintiff in Error, v. Sherman M. Booth, December Term, 1858, Vol. XXI, 1859, 21 Howard

Secretary of State Records: Annual Report of the Secretary of the State of Wisconsin for the Year 1855, Wisconsin Governor's Messages and Accompanying Documents, including the State Census, 1855

Secretary of State Records: Election Certificates from County and State Boards of Canvassers, 1847–1857

Secretary of State Records: Election Certificates of the State Board of Canvassers, 1848–1863

Secretary of State Records: Original Petitions, Remonstrances and Memorials Presented to the Senate and/or Assembly, 1845–1870

Secretary of State Records: Papers of the 1846 Constitutional Convention

Secretary of State Records: Papers of the 1847–1848 Constitutional Convention

Wisconsin Reports: Reports of the Cases Argued and Determined in the Supreme Court of the State of Wisconsin, 1854 and 1855

Eighth Census of the United States: 1850

Seventh Census of the United States: 1850

U.S. Congress, House of Representatives Papers, 1800–1860, Thirty-third Congress, Petitions

Books, Journals, Theses

Adams, James T. "Disfranchisement of Negroes in New England." *American Historical Review* (April 1925): 543–47.

Agnew, Dwight L., et al. *Dictionary of Wisconsin Biography.* Madison: State Historical Society of Wisconsin, 1960.

Alexander, Edward P. "Wisconsin, New York's Daughter State." *Wisconsin Magazine of History* (September 1946): 11–30.

Anbinder, Tyler. *Nativism and Slavery: The Northern Know Nothings and the Politics of the 1850s.* New York: Oxford University Press, 1992.

Baker, Florence E. "A Bibliographical History of the Two Wisconsin Constitutional Conventions, to Which Are Added Annotated Lists of the Delegates." *State Historical Society of Wisconsin Proceedings* (1897): 123–60.

———. "A Brief History of the Elective Franchise in Wisconsin." *State Historical Society of Wisconsin Proceedings* (1893): 113–30.

Barnes, Gilbert H. *The Antislavery Impulse, 1830–1844.* New York: D. Appleton-Century, 1933.

Barney, William L. *The Secessionist Impulse: Alabama and Mississippi in 1860.* Princeton: Princeton University Press, 1974.

Baum, Dale. *The Civil War Party System: The Case of Massachusetts, 1848–1876.* Chapel Hill: University of North Carolina Press, 1984.

———. "Know Nothingism and the Republican Majority in Massachusetts: The Political Realignment of the 1850s." *Journal of American History* (March 1978): 959–86.

Beckwith, Albert C. *History of Walworth County, Wisconsin.* 2 vols. Indianapolis: B. F. Bowen and Co., 1912.

Beitzinger, Alfons J. *Edward G. Ryan: Lion of the Law.* Madison: State Historical Society of Wisconsin, 1960.

Belz, Herman. *A New Birth of Freedom: The Republican Party and Freedmen's Rights, 1861–1866.* Westport, Conn.: Greenwood Press, 1976.

Benson, Lee. *The Concept of Jacksonian Democracy: New York as a Test Case.* Princeton: Princeton University Press, 1961.

Berrier, G. Galin. "The Negro Suffrage Issue in Iowa: 1865–1868." *Annals of Iowa* (Spring 1968): 241–61.

{ Bibliography }

Berwanger, Eugene H. *The Frontier Against Slavery: Western Anti-Negro Prejudice and the Slavery Extension Controversy*. Urbana: University of Illinois Press, 1967.

Bestor, Arthur. "State Sovereignty and Slavery: A Reinterpretation of Pro-Slavery Constitutional Doctrine, 1846–1860." *Illinois State Historical Society Journal* (1961): 117–80.

Billington, Ray Allen. *The Protestant Crusade 1800–1860: A Study of the Origins of American Nativism*. New York: Macmillan, 1938.

Block, Herman D. "The New York Negro's Battle for Political Rights, 1777–1865." *International Review of Social History*, pt. 1 (1964): 65–80.

Blue, Frederick J. "The Free Soil Party and the Election of 1848 in Wisconsin." Master's thesis. University of Wisconsin, 1962.

———. *The Free Soilers: Third Party Politics, 1848–1854*. Urbana: University of Illinois Press, 1973.

Boom, Aaron M. "The Development of Sectional Attitudes in Wisconsin, 1848–1861." Ph.D. dissertation. University of Chicago, 1948.

Brock, William R. *Conflict and Transformation: The United States, 1844–1877*. New York: Harper and Row, 1973.

Brown, George C. "The Genesis of the Wisconsin Republican Party, 1854." Master's thesis. University of Wisconsin, 1978.

Buck, James S. *Pioneer History of Milwaukee*. 4 vols. Milwaukee: Western Historical Company, 1876–86.

Burnham, Walter Dean. "The Changing Shape of the American Political Universe." *American Political Science Review* (March 1965): 7–28.

Butterfield, C.W. *The History of Grant County, Wisconsin*. Chicago: Western Historical Company, 1881.

———. *History of Walworth County, Wisconsin*. Chicago: Western Historical Company, 1882.

———. *History of Waukesha County, Wisconsin*. Chicago: Western Historical Company, 1880.

Byrne, Frank L. "Maine Law Versus Lager Beer: A Dilemma of Wisconsin's Young Republican Party." *Wisconsin Magazine of History* (Winter 1958–59): 115–20.

Campbell, Stanley. *The Slave Catchers: Enforcement of the Fugitive Slave Law, 1850–1860*. Chapel Hill: University of North Carolina Press, 1968.

Carter, George W. "The Booth War in Ripon." *State Historical Society of Wisconsin, Proceedings* (1902): 161–72.

Channing, Steven A. *Crisis of Fear: Secession in South Carolina*. New York: Norton, 1970.

Codding, Hannah M. P. "Ichabod Codding." *State Historical Society of Wisconsin Proceedings* (1897): 169–96.

Conner, James. "The Antislavery Movement in Iowa." *Annals of Iowa* (Summer 1970): 343–76; (Fall 1970): 450–79.

Conzen, Cathleen. *Immigrant Milwaukee, 1836–1860: Accommodation and Community in a Frontier City.* Cambridge: Harvard University Press, 1976.

Cooper, William J., Jr. *The South and the Politics of Slavery, 1828–1856.* Baton Rouge: Louisiana State University Press, 1978.

Cover, Joseph C. "Memories of a Pioneer County Editor." *Wisconsin Magazine of History* (March 1928): 247–68.

Cox, LaWanda, and John Cox. "Negro Suffrage and Republican Politics: The Problem of Motivation in Reconstruction Historiography." *Journal of Southern History* (August 1967): 303–30.

Cross, Whitney R. *The Burned-Over District: The Social and Intellectual History of Enthusiastic Religion in Western New York, 1800–1850.* New York: Harper and Row, 1954.

Current, Richard H. "The First Newspaperman in Oshkosh [James Densmore]." *Wisconsin Magazine of History* (June 1947): 408–22.

Current, Richard N. *The History of Wisconsin.* Vol. 2: *The Civil War Era, 1848–1873.* Madison: University of Wisconsin Press, 1976.

Dalzell, Robert F., Jr. *Daniel Webster and the Trial of American Nationalism, 1843–1852.* New York: Norton, 1972.

Davidson, John Nelson. "Negro Slavery in Wisconsin." *State Historical Society of Wisconsin Proceedings* (1892): 82–86.

Davis, David Brian. "The Emergence of Immediatism in British and American Antislavery Thought." *Mississippi Valley Historical Review* (September 1962): 209–30.

———. *The Slave Power Conspiracy and the Paranoid Style.* Baton Rouge: Louisiana State University Press, 1969.

———. "Some Ideological Functions of Prejudice in Anti-Bellum America." *American Quarterly* (Summer 1963): 115–25.

Dennison, George M. *The Dorr War: Republicanism on Trial, 1831–1861.* Lexington: University of Kentucky Press, 1976.

Donald, David. *Charles Sumner and the Coming of the Civil War.* New York: Alfred A. Knopf, 1967.

Donoghue, James R. *How Wisconsin Voted.* 3d ed. Madison: University of Wisconsin Extension, 1974.

Duckett, Kenneth W. "Politics, Brown Bread, and Bologna." *Wisconsin Magazine of History* (1952–53): 178–81, 202, 215–17.

Dunbar, Willis F., and William G. Shade. "The Black Man Gains the Vote: The Centennial of 'Impartial Suffrage' in Michigan." *Michigan History* (Spring 1972): 42–57.

Dykstra, Robert R. *Bright Radical Star: Black Freedom and White Supremacy on the Hawkeye Frontier.* Cambridge: Harvard University Press, 1993.

Dykstra, Robert R., and Harlan Hahn. "Northern Voters and Negro Suffrage: The Case of Iowa, 1868." *Public Opinion Quarterly* (Summer 1968): 202–15.

Elles, David Maldwyn. "The Yankee Invasion of New York, 1783–1850." *New York History* (January 1951): 1–17.

Ellis, Richard E. *The Union at Risk: Jacksonian Democracy, States' Rights, and the Nullification Crisis.* New York: Oxford University Press, 1987.

Erbe, Carl H. "Constitutional Provisions for Suffrage in Iowa." *Iowa Journal of History and Politics* (April 1924): 163–216.

Erickson, Leonard. "Politics and the Repeal of Ohio's Black Laws, 1837–1849." *Ohio History* 83 (year?): 154–75.

Ershkowitz, Herbert, and William G. Shade. "Consensus or Conflict? Political Behavior in the State Legislatures during the Jacksonian Era." *Journal of American History* (December 1971): 591–621.

Evans, Jonathan Henny. "Some Reminiscences of Early Grant County." *State Historical Society of Wisconsin Proceedings* (1909): 232–45.

Fair, Clinton. "Internal Improvements and the Sectional Controversy." Master's thesis. University of Wisconsin, 1937.

Fehrenbacher, Don E. *The Dred Scott Case: Its Significance in American Law and Politics.* New York: Oxford University Press, 1978.

———. "Only His Stepchildren: Lincoln and the Negro." *Civil War History* (December 1974): 293–310.

Field, Phyllis F. "Republicans and Black Suffrage in New York State: The Grass Roots Response." *Civil War History* (June 1975): 136–47.

———. "The Struggle for Black Suffrage in New York State, 1846–1869." Ph.D. dissertation. Cornell University, 1974.

Fellman, Michael. "Rehearsal for the Civil War: Antislavery and Proslavery at the Fighting Point, 1854–1856." In *Antislavery Reconsidered: New Perspectives on the Abolitionists.* Edited by Lewis Perry and Michael Fellman. Baton Rouge: Louisiana State University Press, 1979. 287–307.

Filler, Louis. *The Crusade Against Slavery: 1830–1860.* New York: Harper and Row, 1960.

Finkelman, Paul. "*Prigg v. Pennsylvania* and Northern State Courts: Antislavery Use of a Pro-Slavery Decision." *Civil War History* (March 1979): 5–35.

Fishel, Leslie H. "Wisconsin and Negro Suffrage." *Wisconsin Magazine of History* (Spring 1963): 180–96.

Flately, Robert R. "The Wisconsin Congressional Delegation from Statehood to Secession, 1848–1861." Bachelor's thesis. University of Wisconsin, 1951.

Foner, Eric. *Free Soil, Free Labor, Free Men: The Ideology of the Republican Party Before the Civil War.* New York: Oxford University Press, 1970.

———. "Politics and Prejudice: The Free Soil Party and the Negro, 1849–1852." *Journal of Negro History* (October 1965): 239–56.

———. "Politics, Ideology, and the Origins of the American Civil War." In *Politics and Ideology in the Age of the Civil War.* New York: Oxford University Press, 1980. 34–53.

———. "Racial Attitudes of the New York Free-Soilers." *New York History* (October 1965): 311–29.

———. "The Wilmot Proviso Controversy Revisited." *Journal of American History* (September 1969): 262–79.

Formisano, Ronald P. *The Birth of Mass Political Parties: Michigan, 1837–1861.* Princeton: Princeton University Press, 1961.

———. "The Edge of Caste: Colored Suffrage in Michigan, 1827–1861." *Michigan History* (Spring 1972): 19–41.

Fox, Dixon Ryan. "The Negro Vote in Old New York." *Political Science Quarterly* 32 (1917): 252–75.

Fredrickson, George M. *The Black Image in the White Mind: The Debate on Afro-American Character and Destiny, 1817–1914.* New York: Harper and Row, 1971.

———. "A Man but Not a Brother: Abraham Lincoln and Racial Equality." *Journal of Southern History* (February 1975): 39–58.

Freehling, William W. "The Founding Fathers and Slavery." *American Historical Review* (February 1972): 81–93.

———. *Prelude to Civil War: The Nullification Controversy in South Carolina, 1816–1836.* New York: Harper and Row, 1965.

Gara, Larry. *Westernized Yankee: The Story of Cyrus Woodman.* Madison: State Historical Society of Wisconsin, 1956.

Genovese, Eugene. *The Political Economy of Slavery: Studies in the Economy and Society of the Slave South.* New York: Vintage, 1967.

Gerteis, Louis S. "An Abolitionist in Territorial Wisconsin: The Journal of Reverend Edward Matthews." *Wisconsin Magazine of History* 52 (Autumn 1968–Summer 1969): 3–18, 117–31, 248–62, 330–43.

———. "Antislavery Agitation in Wisconsin, 1836–1848." Master's thesis. University of Wisconsin, 1966.

Gienapp, William E. "The Crime Against Sumner: The Caning of Charles Sumner and the Rise of the Republican Party." *Civil War History* (September 1979): 218–45.

———. *The Origins of the Republican Party 1852–1856.* New York: Oxford University Press, 1987.

Gillette, William. *The Right to Vote: Politics and the Passing of the Fifteenth Amendment.* Baltimore: The Johns Hopkins Press, 1969.

Goodman, Leo A. "Some Alternatives to Ecological Correlation." *American Journal of Sociology* (May 1959): 610–25.

Gregory, John G. *History of Milwaukee, Wisconsin.* Vol. 2. Milwaukee: Western Historical Company, 1931.

Hagan, Horace H. "Ableman vs. Booth: Effect of Fugitive Slave Law on Opinions as to the Rights of Federal Government and of States in the North and South." *American Bar Association Journal* (1931): 19–24.

Hamilton, Holman. *Prologue to Conflict: The Crisis and Compromise of 1850.* Lexington: University of Kentucky Press, 1964.

Hanneman, Richard L. "The First Republican Campaign in Wisconsin, 1854." Master's thesis. University of Wisconsin, 1966.

Hantke, Richard W. "The Life of Elisha William Keyes." Ph.D. dissertation. University of Wisconsin, 1942.

Haygood, William C., ed. "An Abolitionist in Territorial Wisconsin: The Journal of Rev. Edward Matthews." *Wisconsin Magazine of History* (Autumn 1968–Summer 1969): 3–18, 117–31, 248–62, 330–43; (Spring 1969): 250–53.

Hofstadter, Richard. *The Idea of a Party System: The Rise of Legitimate Opposition in the United States, 1780–1840.* Berkeley: University of California Press, 1969.

———. "The Paranoid Style in American Politics." In *The Paranoid Style in American Politics and Other Essays.* New York: Vintage, 1967. 3–40.

Holmes, Frederick L. "First Constitutional Convention in Wisconsin, 1846." *State Historical Society, Proceedings* (1905): 227–57.

Holt, Michael F. *The Political Crisis of the 1850s.* New York: John Wiley and Son, 1978.

———. "The Politics of Impatience: The Origins of Know Nothingism." *Journal of American History* (September 1963): 309–31.

Holzhueter, John O. "Ezekiel Gillespie, Lost and Found." *Wisconsin Magazine of History* (Spring 1977): 179–84.

Howe, Daniel W. *The Political Culture of the American Whigs.* Chicago: University of Chicago Press, 1979.

Jones, E. Terrence. "Ecological Inference and Electoral Analysis." *Journal of Interdisciplinary History* (Winter 1972): 249–62.

Jordan, Winthrop. *White Over Black: American Attitudes Toward the Negro, 1550–1812.* Chapel Hill: University of North Carolina Press, 1968.

Keyes, Elisha. *History of Dane County.* Madison: Western Historical Company, 1906.

King, Charles. "The Wisconsin National Guard." *Wisconsin Blue Book* (1923): 346–48.

Koch, Adrienne. *Jefferson and Madison: The Great Collaboration.* New York: Oxford University Press, 1950.

Koch, Adrienne, and Harry Ammon. "The Virginia and Kentucky Resolutions: An Episode in Jefferson and Madison's Defense of Civil Liberties." *William and Mary Quarterly* (April 1948): 145–76.

Kousser, J. Morgan. "Ecological Repression and the Analysis of Past Politics." *Journal of Interdisciplinary History* (Autumn 1973): 237–62.

———. *The Shaping of Southern Politics: Suffrage Restriction and the Establishment of the One-Party South, 1880–1910.* New Haven: Yale University Press, 1974.

Kraditor, Aileen S. *Means and Ends in American Abolitionism: Garrison and His Critics on Strategy and Tactics, 1834–1850.* New York: Random House, 1967.

Kroncke, Robert N. "Race and Politics in Wisconsin, 1854–1865." Master's thesis. University of Wisconsin, 1968.

Lane, Robert. *Political Life: Why People Get Involved In Politics.* Glencoe, N.Y.: Glencoe Press, 1959.

Latner, Richard B. "The Nullification Crisis and Republican Subversion." *Journal of Southern History* (February 1977): 19–38.

Legler, P. F. "Josiah Noonan: A Story of Promotion and Excoriation in the Old Northwest." Master's thesis. University of Wisconsin, 1953.

Libman, Gary. "Minnesota and the Struggle for Black Suffrage, 1849–1870: A Study in Party Motivation." Ph.D. dissertation. University of Minnesota, 1972.

Linden, Glenn M. "A Note on Negro Suffrage and Republican Politics." *Journal of Southern History* (August 1970): 411–20.

Litwack, Leon. *North of Slavery: The Negro in the Free States, 1790–1860.* Chicago: University of Chicago Press, 1961.

Lyman, Frank H., ed. *The City of Kenosha and Kenosha County, Wisconsin.* Chicago: S. J. Clarke Publishing Co., 1916.

McCrary, Peyton. *Abraham Lincoln and Reconstruction: The Louisiana Experiment.* Princeton: Princeton University Press, 1978.

McCrary, Peyton, Clark Miller, and Dale Baum, "Class and Party in the Secession Crisis: Voting Behavior in the Deep South, 1856–1861." *Journal of Interdisciplinary History* (Winter 1978): 429–57.

McDonald, Sister M. Justelle. *History of the Irish in Wisconsin in the Nineteenth Century.* Washington D.C.: Catholic University Press, 1954.

McLaughlin, Tom L. "Grass Roots Attitudes Toward Black Rights in Twelve Non-Slaveholding States: 1846–1869." *Mid-America* (July 1974): 175–81.

———. "Popular Reactions to the Idea of Negro Equality in Twelve Nonslaveholding States, 1846–1869. A Quantitative Analysis." Ph.D. dissertation. Washington State University, 1969.

McManus, Michael J. "'Freedom and Liberty First, and the Union Afterwards': State Rights and the Wisconsin Republican Party, 1854–1861." In *Union & Emancipation: Essays on Politics and Race in the Civil War Era.* Ed. David W. Blight and Brooks D. Simpson. Kent, Ohio: Kent State University Press, 1997. 29–56.

———. "Wisconsin Republicans and Negro Suffrage: Attitudes and Behavior, 1857." *Civil War History* (March 1979): 36–54.

Maizlish, Stephen E. *The Triumph of Sectionalism: The Transformation of Ohio Politics 1844–1856*. Kent, Ohio: Kent State University Press, 1983.

Mason, Vroman. "The Fugitive Slave Law in Wisconsin, with Reference to Nullification Sentiment." *State Historical Society of Wisconsin Proceedings* (1895): 117–44.

Mathews, Lois K. *The Expansion of New England: The Spread of New England Settlement and Institutions to the Mississippi River, 1620–1865*. Cambridge: Riverside Press, 1909.

Meerse, David A., "Buchanan, Corruption and the Election of 1860." *Civil War History* (December 1966): 116–31.

Merk, Frederick. *Slavery and the Annexation of Texas*. New York: Alfred A. Knopf, 1972.

Meyers, Marvin. *The Jacksonian Persuasion: Politics and Belief.* Stanford: Stanford University Press, 1957.

Miller, John C. *The Wolf by the Ears: Thomas Jefferson and Slavery*. New York: Free Press, 1977.

Morris, Thomas D. *Free Men All: The Personal Liberty Laws of the North, 1780–1861*. Baltimore: The Johns Hopkins Press, 1974.

Morrison, Chaplain W. *Democratic Politics and Sectionalism: The Wilmot Proviso Controversy*. Chapel Hill: University of North Carolina Press, 1967.

Nagel, Paul C. *One Nation Indivisible: The Union in American Thought, 1776–1861*. New York: Oxford University Press, 1964.

Nevins, Allan. *The Emergence of Lincoln*. 2 vols. New York: Charles Scribner's Sons, 1950.

———. *The Ordeal of the Union*. 2 vols. New York: Charles Scribner's Sons, New York, 1947.

Nichols, Roy F. *The Democratic Machine, 1850–1854*. New York: Columbia University Press, 1923.

———. *The Disruption of American Democracy*. New York: Macmillan, 1948.

———. "The Kansas-Nebraska Act: A Century of Historiography." *Mississippi Valley Historical Review* (1923): 187–212.

Nye, Russell B. *Fettered Freedom: Civil Liberties and the Slavery Controversy, 1830–1860*. Urbana: University of Illinois Press, 1963.

Olbrich, Emil. *The Development of Negro Suffrage to 1860*. Madison: University of Wisconsin Press, 1912.

———. "The Development of Sentiment on Negro Suffrage to 1860." *Bulletin of the University of Wisconsin* (1912): 1–135.

Olin, C. C. *A Complete Record of the John Olin Family*. Indianapolis: Baker, Randolph Co., 1893.

Paxson, Frederic. "Wisconsin: A Constitution of Democracy." In *The Movement for Statehood*. Ed. Milo M. Quaife. Madison: State Historical Society of Wisconsin, 1918. 30–52.

Pease, William H., and Jane H. Pease. "Antislavery Ambivalence: Immediatism, Expediency, Race." *American Quarterly* (Winter 1965): 682–95.

———. "Ends, Means and Attitudes: Black-White Conflict in the Antislavery Movement." *Civil War History* (June 1972): 117–28.

Phelan, Raymond V. "Slavery in the Old Northwest." *State Historical Society of Wisconsin Proceedings* (1905): 252–64.

Potter, David. *The Impending Crisis, 1848–1861.* New York: Harper and Row, 1976.

Quaife, Milo M., ed. *The Attainment of Statehood.* Madison: State Historical Society of Wisconsin, 1928.

———. *The Convention of 1846.* Madison: State Historical Society of Wisconsin, 1919.

———. *The Movement for Statehood, 1845–1846.* Madison: State Historical Society of Wisconsin, 1918.

———. *The Struggle Over Ratification, 1846–1847.* Madison: State Historical Society of Wisconsin, 1920.

Ramsdell, Charles W. "The Natural Limits of Slavery Expansion." *Mississippi Valley Historical Review* (September 1929): 151–71.

Ranney, Joseph A. "'Suffering the Agonies of Their Righteousness': The Rise and Fall of the States Rights Movement in Wisconsin." *Wisconsin Magazine of History* (Winter 1991–92): 83–116.

Rasmussen, Donald E. "Wisconsin Editors and the Civil War: A Study of the Reaction of Wisconsin Editors to the Major Controversial Issues of the Civil War." Master's thesis. University of Wisconsin, 1952.

Rawley, James A. *Race and Politics: "Bleeding Kansas" and the Coming of the Civil War.* New York: J. P Lippincott Co., 1969.

Rayback, Joseph G. *Free Soil: The Election of 1848.* Lexington: University of Kentucky Press, 1970.

Reed, Parker M. *Bench and Bar of Wisconsin.* Milwaukee: P. M. Reed, 1882.

Richards, Leonard L. *'Gentlemen of Property and Standing': Anti-Abolition Mobs in Jacksonian America.* New York: Oxford University Press, 1970.

———. "The Jacksonians and Slavery." In *Antislavery Reconsidered: New Perspectives on the Abolitionists.* Ed. Lewis Perry and Michael Fellman. Baton Rouge: Louisiana State University Press, 1979. 99–118.

Robinson, Donald. *Slavery in the Structure of American Politics, 1765–1820.* New York: Norton, 1971.

Robinson, W. S. "Ecological Correlations and the Behavior of Individuals." *American Sociological Review* (June 1950): 351–57.

Ross, Sam. *The Empty Sleeve: A Biography of Lucius Fairchild.* Madison: State Historical Society of Wisconsin, 1964.

Rozett, John M. "Racism and Republican Emergence in Illinois, 1848–1860: A Re-Evaluation of Republican Negrophobia." *Civil War History* (June 1976): 101–15.

Russel, Robert R. "The Issues in the Congressional Struggle Over the Kansas-Nebraska Bill, 1854." *Journal of Southern History* (May 1963): 187–210.

Russell, William H. "Timothy O. Howe, Stalwart Republican." *Wisconsin Magazine of History* (Winter 1951): 90–99.

Rutland, Robert A. *James Madison: The Founding Father.* New York: Macmillan, 1987.

Schafer, Joseph. *Four Wisconsin Counties, Prairie and Forest.* Madison: State Historical Society of Wisconsin, 1927.

———. "Know-Nothingism in Wisconsin." *Wisconsin Magazine of History* (September 1924): 3–21.

———. "Prohibition in Early Wisconsin." *Wisconsin Magazine of History* (March 1925): 280–99.

———. "Stormy Days in Court: The Booth Case." *Wisconsin Magazine of History* (September 1936): 89–110.

———. *The Winnebago-Horicon Basin—A Type Study in Western History.* Madison: State Historical Society of Wisconsin, 1937.

———. *The Wisconsin Lead Region.* Madison: State Historical Society of Wisconsin, 1932.

———. "The Yankee and the Teuton in Wisconsin." *Wisconsin Magazine of History* 6 (1922–23): 125–44, 261–79, 386–402; 7 (1923–24): 3–19, 148–71.

Sellers, James L. "James R. Doolittle." *Wisconsin Magazine of History* (December 1933; March, June, September 1934): 17, 168–78, 277–306, 393–401; 18, 20–41, 178–87.

———. "Republicanism and State Rights in Wisconsin." *Mississippi Valley Historical Review* (September 1930): 213–29.

Sewell, Richard H. *Ballots for Freedom: AntiSlavery Politics in the United States, 1837–1860.* New York: Oxford University Press, 1976.

———. *John P. Hale and the Politics of Abolition.* Cambridge: Harvard University Press, 1965.

———. "Slavery, Race, and the Free Soil Party, 1848–1854." In *Crusaders and Compromisers: Essays on the Relationship of the Antislavery Struggle to the Antebellum Party System.* Ed. Alan M. Kraut. Westport, Conn.: Greenwood Press, 1983. 101–24.

Shortridge, Ray M. "The Voter Realignment in the Midwest during the 1850s." *American Politics Quarterly* (April 1976).

Shively, W. Phillip. "Ecological Inference: The Use of Aggregate Data to Study Individuals." *American Political Science Review* (December 1969): 1183–96.

Silbey, Joel H. *A Respectable Minority: The Democratic Party in the Civil War Era, 1860–1868.* New York: Norton, 1977.

———. "The Surge of Republican Power: Partisan Antipathy, American Social Conflict, and the Coming of the Civil War." In *Essays on American Antebellum*

Politics, 1840–1860. Ed. Stephen E. Maizlish and John J. Kushma. College Station, Tex.: N.p., 1982. 199–229.

———. "'There are Other Questions Beside That of Slavery Merely': The Democratic Party and Antislavery Politics." In *Crusaders and Compromisers: Essays on the Relationship of the Antislavery Struggle to the Antebellum Party System.* Ed. Alan M. Kraut. Westport, Conn.: Greenwood Press, 1983. 143–75.

Smith, Alice E. *The History of Wisconsin.* Vol. 1: *From Exploration to Statehood.* Madison: University of Wisconsin Press, 1973.

Smith, Theodore Clark. "The Free Soil Party in Wisconsin." *State Historical Society of Wisconsin Proceedings* (1894): 97–162.

———. *The Liberty and Free Soil Parties in the Northwest.* Cambridge: Harvard University Press, 1897.

Sorin, Gerald. *Abolitionism: A New Perspective.* New York: Praeger, 1972.

———. *The New York Abolitionists: A Case Study of Political Radicalism.* Westport, Conn.: Greenwood Press, 1971.

Stampp, Kenneth M. "The Concept of a Perpetual Union." *Journal of American History* (June 1978): 5–34.

———. *The Imperiled Union: Essays on the Background of the Civil War.* New York: Oxford University Press, 1980.

———. "The Irrepressible Conflict." In *The Imperiled Union.* 191–245.

———. "Race, Slavery, and the Republican Party of the 1850s." In *The Imperiled Union.* 105–35.

Stanley, John L. "Majority Tyranny in Tocqueville's America: The Failure of Negro Suffrage, 1846." *Political Science Quarterly* (September 1969): 412–35.

———. "Majority Tyranny in Tocqueville's America: The Failure of Negro Suffrage in New York State in 1846." Ph.D. dissertation. Cornell University, 1966.

Stanton, William R. *The Leopard's Spots: Scientific Attitudes Toward Race in America, 1815–59.* Chicago: University of Chicago Press, 1960.

Stegmaier, Mark. *Texas, New Mexico and the Compromise of 1850.* Kent, Ohio: Kent State University Press, 1996.

Stewart, James Brewer. "Abolitionists, Insurgents, and Third Parties: Sectionalism and Partisan Politics in Northern Whiggery, 1836–1844." In *Crusaders and Compromisers: Essays on the Relationship of the Antislavery Struggle to the Antebellum Party System.* Ed. Alan M. Kraut. Westport, Conn.: Greenwood Press, 1983. 25–43.

———. *Holy Warriors: The Abolitionists and American Slavery.* New York: Hill and Wang, 1976.

Stone, Fanny S., ed. *Racine and Racine County Wisconsin.* Vol. 1. Chicago: S. J. Clarke Publishing Co., 1916.

Strong, Moses M. *History of the Wisconsin Territory, from 1836–1848.* Madison: Democrat Printing Company, 1885.

Summers, Mark W. *The Plundering Generation: Corruption and the Crisis of the Union, 1849–1861*. New York: Oxford University Press, 1987.

Sweeney, Kevin. "Rum, Romanism, Representation and Reform: Coalitional Politics in Massachusetts, 1847–1853." *Civil War History* (June 1976): 116–37.

Tenney, Horace A., and David Atwood. *Memorial Record of the Fathers of Wisconsin, Containing Sketches of the Lives and Careers of the Members of the Constitutional Conventions of 1846 and 1847–1848, with a History of Early Settlement in Wisconsin*. Madison: Tenney and Atwood, 1880.

Thompson, A. M. *A Political History of Wisconsin*. 2d ed. Milwaukee: C. N. Caspar Co., 1902.

Thompson, E. Bruce. *Matthew Hale Carpenter, Webster of the West*. Madison: University of Wisconsin Press, 1954.

Thornton, J. Mills, III. *Power and Politics in a Slave Society: Alabama, 1800–1860*. Baton Rouge: Louisiana State University Press, 1978.

Tomlinson, Kenneth Larry. "Indiana Republicans and the Negro Suffrage Issue, 1865–1867." Ph.D. dissertation. Ball State University, 1971.

Urban, C. Stanley. "The Ideology of Southern Imperialism: New Orleans and the Caribbean, 1845–1860." *Louisiana Historical Quarterly* (January 1956): 48–73.

Van Deusen, Glyndon. *The Jacksonian Era: 1828–1848*. New York: Harper and Row, 1959.

Virginia Commission on Constitutional Government. *We the People: An Anthology of Historic Documents and Commentaries Thereon, Expounding the State and Federal Relationship*. Richmond, Va.: William Byrd Press, 1964.

Voegeli, V. Jacques. *Free but Not Equal: The Midwest and the Negro During the Civil War*. Chicago: University of Chicago Press, 1967.

———. "The Northwest and the Race Issue, 1861–1862." *Mississippi Valley Historical Review* (September 1963): 235–51.

Vollmar, William J. "The Negro in a Midwest Frontier City, Milwaukee, 1835–1870." Master's thesis. Marquette University, 1968.

Volpe, Vernon. *Forlorn Hope of Freedom: The Liberty Party in the Old Northwest, 1838–1848*. Kent, Ohio: Kent State University Press, 1990.

Welter, Rush. *The Mind of America, 1820–1860*. New York: Columbia University Press, 1975.

Wilson, Major L. "'Liberty and Union': An Analysis of Three Concepts Involved in the Nullification Controversy." In *Essays on Jacksonian America*. Ed. Frank Otto Gatell. New York: Holt, Rhinehart, Winston, 1970. 133–47.

———. *Space, Time and Freedom: The Quest for Nationality and the Irrepressible Conlict, 1815–1861*. Westport, Conn.: Greenwood Press, 1974.

Winkle, Ken. "Voters, Issues, and Parties: Partisan Realignment in Southeastern Wisconsin, 1850–1854." Master's thesis. University of Wisconsin, 1977.

Winslow, John Bradley. *The Story of a Great Court*. Chicago: T. H. Flood and Co., 1912.

Wise, Gene. *American Historical Explanations: A Strategy for Grounded Inquiry*. Homewood: The Dorsey Press, 1973.

Wise, Karen. "Wisconsin and the Fourteenth Amendment, 1865–1867." Master's thesis. University of Wisconsin, 1966.

Wolff, Gerald W. *The Kansas-Nebraska Bill: Party, Section, and the Coming of the Civil War*. New York: Revisionist Press, 1977.

INDEX

Booth, Sherman M.: abolitionist views of, 39; background of, 39–40; and black suffrage, 193; candidacy of, 93, 106–7, 108; decline of influence, 179–81; and factionalism, 121, 171–72, 179–81; and Farwell's candidacy, 75, 76–77; and Free Soil coalitions, 40, 41, 47, 58, 60, 62, 73, 77–78, 79; on Fugitive Slave Law, 70; in fugitive slave rescue, 88, 133; and Howe's candidacy, 140, 145, 146–47; imprisonment of, 182, 183; in judicial election, 175–77; and Know Nothing threat, 104, 105, 108, 109, 110, 113–14; and nativism, 107; in Nebraska bill resistance, 86, 87, 89, 90; and People's coalition, 82; seduction charge against, 180–81; states' rights challenge to fugitive slave law, 133–38, 173–74, 181–82

Border ruffians, 115

Breckinridge, John C., 186

Brisbane, William H., 154, 156

Brooks, Preston S., 118–19

Brown, Beriah, 31, 44, 56, 62, 74, 80, 90; on Fugitive Slave Law, 70–71

Brown, John, 145, 187–88

Buchanan, James, 121, 123, 165; and Lecompton constitution, 166, 167, 168

Buffalo Free Soil convention, 38–39, 40, 41, 47

Bugh, Samuel, 170

Bunner, James C., 29, 46

Burchard, Charles, black suffrage proposal of, 26–28

Burlington (Wisconsin), 1, 2, 4

"Burnt-Over District," 4

Burr Oak, 93

Butler, Andrew P., 118

Calhoun, John C., 135

California statehood, 67–68

Campbell, James, 100

Carpenter, Samuel, 158, 181

Carpenter, Stephen D., 74, 81

Cass, Lewis, 38, 44, 45, 46, 48

Catholicism: nativist fear of, 99–101; and party affiliation, 100; and public schools, 100, 101

Chase, Enoch, 57

Chase, Salmon P., 73

Chase, Warren, 27, 46, 56, 62, 63

Chicago Tribune, 106

Clay, Henry, 68, 91

Clement, Charles, 91, 93, 183, 191

Codding, Ichabod, 3, 5, 6, 40, 58

Cole, Orsamus, 73–74, 93, 138, 139

Collins, A. L., 76

Colonization, 162–64

Compromise of 1850, 69, 81

Congressional elections: 1847, 31–32; 1848, 48–49, 55; 1850, 73–74; 1854, 93, 96–98, 138, 201; 1858, 172–73, 204, 205

Constitutional convention: black suffrage proposal in, 23–29, 32–34; fugitive slave proposal in, 34; Liberty party influence in, 22–23; opposition to ratification, 29; second, 32–35

Constitution, Wisconsin: black rights in, 34–35; ratification of, 34; suffrage for foreign-born in, 103–4

Cover, Joseph C., 86, 95; antisuffrage views of, 155–56; on Booth's candidacy, 106–7; formation of Republican party, 92–93, 89

Crabb, George W., 46

Cramer, William, 44

Crawford, Samuel, 135, 138, 139

Creed Resolution, 147

Cross, James, 158

Dane County, 24, 30, 95

Daniels, Edward, 118

Davis, Moses M., 114, 168, 170

Delavan (Wisconsin), 2, 4

Democratic party, 5, 32; and black suffrage, 24–25, 26, 28, 29, 30, 32–34, 33, 64, 151–52, 159; antislavery views in, 15, 20–21, 74–75; and Catholic vote, 100; defectors from, 46–47, 64, 111, 123; election returns for, 63, 64, 65, 77, 83–84, 110, 111, 172, 178, 199; factionalism in, 80–81, 85, 90–91, 93–94, 110, 111, 157–58, 159; foreign-born vote for, 123; and Free Soil coalition, 55–63, 73; and Fugitive Slave Law resistance, 88–89; Know

Nothing influence in, 110; minimal government ideology of, 15–16; and nativism, 121–22; and Nebraska bill, 86, 90–91, 94–96; newspapers of, 74; popular sovereignty doctrine of, 166, 168; in presidential elections, 38, 44, 78, 121–23, 186; and slavery extension, 6, 16, 43–47, 48, 69; slavery supporters in, 14–15; split over Lecompton constitution, 166–67; in territorial government, 216n.24; Unionism of, 16–17, 46, 49, 52, 122; Whig dissidents in, 94

Densmore, James, 62, 73, 91

Dewey, Nelson, 61, 62, 63, 80

Dixon, Luther S., 181–82, 183, 184

Dodge, Henry, 2, 31

Dodge County, 30, 49, 58, 59

Doolittle, James R., 140, 141–42, 143, 162, 163

Doty, James Duane, 20, 74

Douglas, Stephen A., 69, 84, 85, 166–67, 186

Dow, Neal, 105

Dred Scott v. John F. A. Sanford, 144, 165

Dunn County, 157

Durkee, Charles, 39, 48–49, 55, 58, 73, 78, 96, 138, 140

Dyer, E. G., Independence Day speech of, 1–2

Eastman, Ben, 94, 95

Eau Claire County, 157

Elections: black suffrage referendums, 29–30, 53, 198, 156–57, 199, 200, 203, 209; immigrant vote in, 49, 83, 111, 123, 157; judicial, 138–39, 144–45, 175–78, 203, 182–84, 201, 203, 205–8; voter turnout in, 65, 83, 97, 123, 159, 172, 183, 210, 229n.86; *See also* Congressional elections; Gubernatorial elections; Legislative elections

Elkhorn Independent, 106

Emancipation, 192–93

Estabrook, Experience, 32–33

Fairchild, Jairus C., 81

Farwell, Leonard J., 75, 76–77, 79, 80, 81

Fillmore, Millard, 69

Fond du Lac County, 30, 49, 58

Foreign-born residents: and black suffrage, 27, 29–30, 152, 157; and Democratic party, 158–59, 152; and Free Soil party, 49; and fugitive slave resolution, 72; nativist resentment of, 99–101, 102; population growth of, 99; and Republican party, 120, 104–5; settlement patterns of, 3–4; suffrage for, 20, 21, 103–4; and temperance issue, 83, 101, 102–3, 105; voter turnout of, 83, 111

Frank, Michael, 20–21, 159, 169

Free Democrats. *See* Free Soil party

Free Soil party, 37; antislavery views of, 50, 53; anti-Southernism of, 51; and black suffrage, 53, 65; and Democratic coalition, 56–63, 73; Democratic converts to, 46–47, 64; election returns for, 48–49, 55, 64, 67, 78; fusion with Whigs, 91–92; homestead policy of, 51–52; and Nebraska bill resistance, 89–90, 91; platform of, 47–48, 49–50, 55–56; in presidential elections, 47, 48, 78; and slavery extension, 50–51; and Unionism, 52; and Whig coalition efforts, 55–56, 73–74, 75–77, 79–80, 84

Frémont, John C., 121, 122–23

Fugitive Slave Law: legislative resolutions on, 71–72, 143; and personal liberty law, 143–44; popular rejection of, 70–71, 139; provisions of, 69–70; and Republican party platform, 92; resistance to, 87–89; states' rights challenge to, 70, 88, 133–38, 173–74

Fugitive slaves: publicizing plight of, 71; rescue of, 87–89, 133

Gale, George, 33

Garland, Bennami, 87, 134

Gibson, Moses, 27

Gillespie, Ezekiel, 193

Gillies, David, 110

Glover, Joshua, 87, 88, 133, 134

Grant, Ulysses S., 193

Grant County, 25, 29, 157

Grant County Herald, 89, 155

Greeley, Horace, 80, 137

Green Bay Advocate, 95

Green County, 8, 30

Gubernatorial elections: 1849, 62, 63–65, 198, 199, 200; 1851, 75–77, 200; 1853, 200, 201; 1855, 96, 106–7, 110–11, 202; 1857, 156–59, 204; 1859, 205, 206, 207, 208; 1865, 209

Hale, John P., 38, 39, 78, 84

Hamilton, William S., 3

Harpers Ferry raid, 187–88

Harvey, Louis P., 33–34

Hastings, Samuel D., 56–57, 152

Heath, B. S., 180

Heubschmann, Francis, 159

Holt, Charles, 89, 90, 91

Holton, Edward D., 4, 39, 63, 75, 80, 82, 83, 106; Senate candidacy of, 140, 141, 142–43

Homestead policy, of Free Soil party, 51–52

Howe, Timothy: Creed Resolution of, 146–47; and Dixon's candidacy, 182; election to Senate, 190; failed candidacy of, 138–41, 142; on John Brown, 187; opposition to states' rights faction, 145, 146, 147, 170, 178–79

Hoyt, Otis, 94–95

Hubbell, Levi, 80

Hunkins, Benjamin, 62, 63

Hyer, George, 59, 60, 78

Immigrants. *See* Foreign-born residents

Iowa, black suffrage referendum in, 161

Iowa County, 29

Jackson (Michigan), 92

Jackson County, 157

Janesville (Wisconsin), 47, 167

Janesville Gazette, 84, 89, 155

Jefferson, Thomas, 88

Jefferson County, 22, 30, 49

Jones, Samuel, 115

Judicial elections, 138–39, 144–45, 175–78, 203, 182–84, 201, 203, 205–8

Kansas: antislavery-proslavery conflict in, 116–18, 119–20; Lawrence raid in, 115–16; and Lecompton constitution, 166–68

Kansas Emigrant Aid Society, 117–18

Kansas-Nebraska Act, 85–86, 89–90

Kenosha (Wisconsin), 5

Keyes, Elisha, 106, 109

Kilbourn, Byron, 138, 170

King, Rufus, 24, 28, 61, 73, 77, 80, 87, 104, 119, 120, 139, 186; and black suffrage, 23, 29, 33, 64, 153; fugitive slave proposal of, 34; and Nebraska bill resistance, 89, 90; and People's coalition, 81–82; racial attitude of, 149; on secession, 188; and Spooner nomination, 93

Kinnie, Augustus C., 33

Know Nothing party: in election of 1855, 110–11; electoral success in states, 103; growth of, 101; influence in Democratic party, 110, 158; influence in Republican party, 105–6, 107–9, 111–14; reformist program of, 102; sectional divisions in, 120; weakness in Wisconsin, 104, 120; *See also* Nativism

Kuehn, Charles, 111

Ladd, Erastus D., 116

Lafayette County, 29

Lawrence (Kansas), raid on, 115–16

Lead region: antiabolitionist feeling in, 3; slaveholders in, 2; suffrage question in, 20

Lecompton constitution, 166–68

Legislative elections: 1848, 49, 55; 1851, 77; 1853, 83–84; 1854, 96–98; 1856, 139

Legislature: antislavery resolutions in, 56–58; balloting for U.S. senator, 138, 139–40, 141–43; black suffrage resolution in, 150–51, 156; Democratic-Free Soil coalition in, 55–63, 73; fugitive slave resolutions in, 71–72, 143; personal liberty law in, 143–44; Republican coalition in, 138; states' rights resolution of, 174–75; and suffrage question, 20–22; temperance issue in, 82–83

Lewis, James T., 33
Liberty Association, 22
Liberty party, 3, 4; arguments against racial prejudice, 9–10; and black equality, 10–11; and black suffrage, 19, 24, 25, 26, 29, 30, 34; and Booth, 39–40; in coalition, 38–39, 41, 52; at constitutional convention, 22–23; formation of, 5; and Free Soil program, 47; and Hale's nomination, 38; newspaper of, 5–6, 39–40; political opposition to, 11–17, 22; political program of, 6–8, 40–41; Unionism of, 8–9; and Wilmot Proviso, 38–39
Lincoln, Abraham, 186–87, 189, 192
Lockwood, John, 105–6
Lynde, William Pitt, 175, 176, 177

McKee, Hiram, 91
McMynn, James, 152
Macy, John, 95
Madison, James, 88
Madison (Wisconsin): 74, 75, 79–80, 90, 91–92, 113, 173
Main, Willet S., 97, 121, 192–93
Maine, prohibition in, 101, 105
Manitowoc County, 4, 29, 83, 159
Marquette County, 60, 157
Massachusetts, Know Nothing party in, 103
Mathews, Edward, 1, 2, 11
Menasha Conservator, 180
Methodists, 3
Mexican War, 31, 37, 41
Mills, Joseph Trotter, on black suffrage, 150–51
Milwaukee (Wisconsin), 25, 30, 74, 167, 170; antislavery societies in, 5; free blacks in, 70, 150, 156; fugitive slave rescue in, 87–88; nativism in, 102; newspapers in, 6, 23, 39–40, 77; temperance opponents in, 83
Milwaukee County, 3, 4, 29, 83, 159, 160
Milwaukee Daily American, 110, 120
Milwaukee Democrat, 6
Milwaukee Sentinel, 23, 77, 116, 182
Mineral Point (Wisconsin), 3

Mineral Point Tribune, 92–93
Missouri Compromise, 85, 86, 144
Mitchell, James, 3
Monroe Sentinel, 91, 230n.7

Nativism: and anti-Catholicism, 99–101; opposition to, 103–4; and temperence issue, 101, 102–3. *See also* Know Nothing party
Nevins, Allan, 186–87
New England, residents from, 2, 3, 30
New Mexico, statehood for, 67–68
Newspapers: foreign-language, 92; fugitive slave coverage of, 71; party, 5, 6, 39–40, 74, 77, 152–53. *See also specific names*
New York State: and black suffrage, 23; Buffalo Free Soil convention, 38–39, 40, 41, 47; election of 1848, 38; Know Nothing party in, 103; Wisconsin residents from, 2, 3, 4, 30
New York Tribune, 80, 137
Noonan, Josiah, 29, 74, 80, 86, 90, 94, 95, 158, 170, 171
Northwest Ordinance, 2
Nullification. *See* States' rights and nullification

Olin, John C., 20
Ordinance of 1787, 63
Orton, Harlow, 91
Orton, Myron, 91
Oshkosh Democrat, 179
Ozaukee County, 159

Paine, Byron, 70, 75, 121, 174; Fugitive Slave law challenge of, 133–34; in judicial election, 176, 177, 178; on Republican principles, 108–9
Parker, Byrd, 156
Paul, George, 94
People's coalition: creation of, 81–82; election of 1853, 84; local issues of, 82; and temperance issue, 82–83
Phillips, Wendell, 137

Pierce, Franklin, 78, 90, 100
Pierce County, 157
Polk, James K., 31, 34, 37, 41
Popular sovereignty doctrine, 127,
166, 168
Portage City Record, 178
Portage County, 83, 157
Potosi (Wisconsin), 3
Potter, John Fox, 108, 113–14, 121, 131
Prairieville (Wisconsin), 6
Presidential elections: 1848, 38, 44, 47,
48–49, 55, 64, 198, 199; 1852, 78, 200;
1856, 113, 121–23, 139, 202, 203; 1860,
185–87, 188, 207, 208
Prigg v. Pennsylvania, 34, 134, 135, 136
Prohibition, 101, 103
Proslavery: in Kansas, 116–18, 119–20; and
Sumner assault, 118–19

Quiner, E. B., 90

Racial attitudes: in Democratic party, 14,
15, 71, 151–52; Liberty party arguments
against, 9–10; in Republican party, 149,
153, 154–56, 161–64; in Whig party, 13
Racine (Wisconsin), 5, 87, 159
Racine Advocate, 29
Racine County, 3, 22, 24–25, 30, 160
Racine Weekly Journal, 191
Randall, Alexander, 46, 63, 81, 94, 169;
antislavery views of, 28; disputes with
Booth, 180; and Dixon appointment, 181; and Free Soil party, 61; in
gubernatorial election, 146, 152, 156; and
railroad land-grant investigation, 170
Reed, Harrison, 146, 184, 190–91
Reeder, Andrew, 238n.10
Religion: and anti-Catholicism, 99–101;
and antislavery views, 1, 4
Republican party: antiextension agenda
of, 126–28, 92; antislavery ideology
of, 123–28, 149, 190–91, 241n.57; anti-
Southernism in, 189; and black suffrage,
149–56, 160, 193; and Booth's candidacy,
106–7; colonization advocates in, 161–64;
congressional nominees of, 93–94;

decline of Booth's standing in, 179–81;
disunity of, 170–72, 173; election returns
for, 96–98, 110–11, 123, 139; emancipation
goal of, 192–93; and foreign-born
residents, 104–5, 120; founding of,
91–92, 192, 229–30n.4; and Harpers
Ferry raid, 187–88; Know Nothing
support for, 103, 105–6, 107–9, 111–14,
239n.24; and Lecompton constitution,
167–68; local organization of, 92–93,
169, 172; platform of, 92, 109, 146–47;
in presidential election of 1856, 121–23;
in presidential election of 1860, 185–87,
188, 254n.25; and prohibition, 105;
racial attitudes in, 149, 153, 154–56,
161–63; rejection of popular sovereignty,
168; slave power conspiracy theory
in, 124–25, 144, 145, 168, 191; states'
rights faction in, 140–43, 145–46, 147,
176–77, 178–79, 185, 190, 260n.95; and
Unionism, 128–31, 168–69, 189–90; war
readiness in, 168–69, 188–89
"Resolves of '59," 174–75, 178
Richland County, 83
Ripon (Wisconsin), 92, 229–30n.4
Robinson, Charles D., 45, 95
Rock County, 22, 25, 49, 60
Rock County Democrat, 46
Roeser, Charles, 111, 121
Rublee, Horace, 89, 90, 117, 139, 145,
146, 179
Ryan, Edward G., 26, 158

Schools, and Catholic Church, 100, 102
Schurz, Carl, 159, 175, 177, 180, 182, 185
Scott, Winfield, 78, 100
Settlement patterns, 2–4, 29–30, 49, 72,
123, 157
Seward, William H., 23, 100, 112, 182, 185,
225n.6
Shafter, James, 93
Sheboygan County, 4
Sholes, Charles Clark: on black equality,
10; and black suffrage, 24, 25; in Liberty
party, 5–6, 22
Sholes, Christopher L., 46, 56, 63, 73, 79,
84, 114, 181; on black equality, 15; and

black suffrage, 29; on homesteads, 51–52; on John Brown, 187; on slave power conspiracy, 124; and Spooner nomination, 93; on Texas annexation, 16; on Unionism, 52

Shullsburg (Wisconsin), 3

Slaveholders, 2–3, 57

Slave power conspiracy theory, 124–25, 144, 145

Slavery extension: and colonization, 162; Compromise of 1850, 69; and Democratic party, 6, 16, 43–47, 48, 69; and Dred Scott decision, 144; and Free Soil party, 50–51; Kansas-Nebraska Act, 85–86; and Liberty party, 5–6, 39; Missouri Compromise, 85, 86, 144; and Nebraska bill resistance, 86–87, 89–92; and Republican party, 92, 126–28; and Whig party, 11–12, 41–43, 48, 68–69; Wilmot Proviso, 37–39, 43, 44–45, 47, 48, 51, 60

Sloan, A. Scott, 182–84

Smith, Abram D., 133–38, 175–76, 180, 189

Smith, A. Hyatt, 81

Smith, David, 20

Smith, George B., 81

Smith, Gerrit, 145

South: secession of, 189–90; settlers from, 2–3; states' rights in, 137

Southport (Wisconsin), 5

Spain, A. H., 108

Spooner, Jedudah, 5

Spooner, Wyman, 71, 93

Stampp, Kenneth, 191

Statehood, 1, 20, 21, 34–35

States' rights and nullification: and Republican party faction, 140–43, 145–46, 176–79, 190, 260n.95; in fugitive slave law challenge, 70, 88, 133–38, 173–74; legislative resolution on, 174–75; in North *vs* South, 137

Stowe, Harriet Beecher, 71

Strong, Marshall M., 15, 16, 21, 28, 29, 31, 46

Strong, Moses M., 21, 26, 28, 31, 32, 33, 56

Suffrage: for foreign-born, 20, 21, 103–4; and territorial law, 19–22; for women, 151. *See also* Black suffrage

Sumner, Charles, 118–19, 137

Supreme Court, U.S.: *Dred Scott v. John F. A. Sanford*, 144, 165; *Prigg v. Pennsylvania*, 34, 134, 135, 136; sovereignty assumption of, 173–74

Supreme Court, Wisconsin: Dixon appointment to, 181; elections to, 138–39, 144–45, 175–78, 182–84, 201, 203, 205–8; fugitive slave law challenge of, 133–38, 173–74; reversal of Booth case decision, 181–82

Taney, Roger B., 173

Taylor, Zachary, 38, 43, 48, 56, 67–68

Temperance: nativist-immigrant tension over, 101, 102–3; referendum on, 82–83; and Republican party, 105

Tenney, Horace, 44, 70, 74, 90, 170, 171, 178, 180

Territorial Antislavery Society, 4, 5

Territorial government: congressional representation of, 31–32; suffrage law of, 19–22; *See also* Constitutional convention

Territorial Liberty Association, 6

Texas, annexation of, 5–6, 11–12, 16, 44

Thayer, Eli, 116

Turner, Andrew Jackson, 178

Turner, Nelson, 87

Tweedy, John, 28, 31–32, 73, 82, 178

Tyler, John, 5, 11

Uncle Tom's Cabin (Stowe), 71

Unionism: and Democratic party, 16–17, 46, 49, 122; and Liberty party, 8–9; and Republican party, 128–31, 168–69, 189–90; and Whig party, 42–43, 68–69, 130

Van Buren, Martin, 38, 44, 47, 48, 49

Voter turnout, 65, 83, 97, 111, 123, 159, 172, 183, 210, 229n.86

Walker, Isaac P., 57–58, 74, 96

Walworth, John, 90, 91

Walworth County, 3, 22, 25, 30, 33, 60, 92, 94

Walworth County Reporter, 230n.7

Washburn, Cadwallader C., 93, 95, 98

Washington County, 4, 27, 29, 159

Watertown (Wisconsin), 81–82

Watertown Chronicle, 230n.7

Waukesha (Wisconsin), 6

Waukesha County, 22, 25, 30, 58, 59, 94

Webster, Daniel, 91

Weed, Thurlow, 103

Weekly Wisconsin, 44

Wells, Daniel, 78, 93–94

Wells, John, 57

Whig party, 5, 6; antislavery views of, 12–14, 23, 49; and black suffrage, 23–29, 30, 33, 64; and Catholic vote, 100; demise of, 84, 233–34n.11; election returns for, 31–32, 63–64, 67, 75–77; and Free Soil coalition efforts, 55–56, 73–74, 75–76, 79–80, 84; and Fugitive Slave Law resistance, 89; fusion with Free Soilers, 91–92; Nebraska bill response of, 86–87, 89; organization of, 216n.24; and People's coalition, 81–82; in presidential elections, 47, 48, 78; and

slavery extension issue, 11–12, 41–43, 48, 68–69; Unionism of, 42–43, 52, 68–69, 130

Whitewater Register, 180

White, William Abijah, 91, 112, 114

Whiton, Edward V., 20, 31, 34, 135, 144, 145, 181

Wilmot Proviso, 37–39, 43, 44–45, 47, 48, 51, 60

Winnebago County, 58, 59

Wisconsin Antislavery Society, 22

Wisconsin Argus, 44, 90

Wisconsin Daily Free Democrat, 189

Wisconsin Democrat, 31

Wisconsin Express, 55, 68

Wisconsin Patriot, 95

Wisconsin State Journal, 89, 91, 117, 170, 171, 179, 182, 184, 187

Women's suffrage, 151

Wood, D. E., 108, 112

Woodman, Cyrus, 118

Wood County, 157

Wyman, William, 12

Yankee settlments, 3, 4, 30, 49

Political Abolitionism in Wisconsin, 1840–1861,
was designed by Will Underwood;
composed in 10½/14 Adobe Caslon
on a Macintosh Power PC system using Quark XPress
by The Book Page, Inc.;
printed by sheet-fed offset lithography
on Lion's Falls 50-pound Turin Book natural stock
(an acid-free, totally chlorine-free paper),
Smyth sewn and bound over binder's boards
in Arrestox B cloth, and wrapped with dust jackets
printed in three colors on 80-pound stock
by Thomson-Shore, Inc.;
and published by
The Kent State University Press
KENT, OHIO 442442